The 12 O'CLOCK HIGH

Logbook

The Unofficial History of the Novel, Motion Picture, and TV Series

ALLAN T. DUFFIN

PAUL MATHEIS

The _12 O'Clock High_ Logbook
The Unofficial History of the Novel, Motion Picture, and TV Series
© 2005 Allan T. Duffin and Paul Matheis

Published in the USA by:

BearManor Media
PO Box 750
Boalsburg, PA 16827
www.BearManorMedia.com

Library of Congress Cataloging-in-Publication Data:
Duffin, Allan T.
The 12 o'clock high logbook : the unofficial history of the novel, motion picture, and TV series / by Allan T. Duffin & Paul Matheis.
     p. cm.
Includes bibliographical references and index.
ISBN 1-59393-033-X
1. Lay, Beirne, 1909- Twelve o'clock high. 2. Lay, Beirne, 1909—Film and video adaptations. 3. World War, 1939-1945—Motion pictures and the war. 4. World War, 1939-1945—Literature and the war. 5. World War, 1939-1945—Television and the war. 6. Twelve o'clock high (Television program) 7. Twelve o'clock high (Motion picture) I. Title: Twelve o'clock high logbook. II. Matheis, Paul. III. Title.

PS3523.A9723T834 2006
813'.54—dc22
                    2005026823
Printed in the United States.

Design and Layout by Roy "Zander" Jaruk and Valerie Thompson.

TABLE OF CONTENTS

To Michele and Melanie,
who help our dreams take flight

ACKNOWLEDGMENTS

This book is a true labor of love, and we're grateful that so many others share our love of *12 O'Clock High*. Our publisher, Ben Ohmart of BearManor Media, has been gracious, helpful, supportive, and enjoyable to work with throughout the entire process. We thank him for being as excited about the topic as we are.

ALLAN'S ACKNOWLEDGMENTS: I'd like to send many, many thanks to our stellar cast of contributors and contributing editors who poured their lifetime experiences into the manuscript and reviewed the draft as it took shape. To keep my notes short and sweet (well, nice try anyway), I've listed my thanks by category and in alphabetical order.

First, I salute the members of the 306th Bombardment Group, veterans of World War II. I had the distinct honor of meeting and working with them on this book: Donald Bevan, George Hood, John McKee, John Lambert, Howard Macreading, Eugene Pollock, Robert "Rip" Riordan, Howard Roth, John Ryan and his daughter Lynne Ryan Gallagher, Dr. Thurman Shuller, Russell Strong, and Andrew Vangalis. Thanks to the 306th Bomb Group Association for providing guidance and photographs.

Additional veterans and leaders who keep the history alive and graciously shared their stories with me: Col. John DeRussy, USAF (Ret.), technical advisor on the film; Dr. Walter Brown, editor of the *Eighth Air Force News;* Chris Christaldi; Jack Craven of the 305th Bomb Group Memorial Association; Beverly Green of the 315th Bomb Wing Association; Neil Halbisen, formerly of the USAF Air Police; Hank Sauer, CMSgt, USAF (Ret.), Newsletter Editor/Publisher for the Airways and Air Communications Service Alumni Association; Arthur Silva of the 487th Bomb Group Association; James Storie, Air Force veteran and an extra in the film; David Tallichet, owner of Specialty Restaurants Corporation and a B-17 veteran of the 100th Bomb Group; and Edward Twohig of the P-51 Mustang Pilots Association.

Ladies and gentlemen involved in the *12 O'Clock High* phenomenon who contributed their experience, advice, and photo collections: Gene Anderson;

Actor Robert Arthaud (Arthur); Bruce Ashcroft of the History Office, Headquarters Air Education & Training Command at Randolph AFB, Texas; David Bartlett, son of writer/producer Sy Bartlett and actress Ellen Drew; John deRussy, Jr., son of Col. John deRussy; Chuck Dunning, writer; Michael Faley, historian for the 100th Bomb Group Foundation and member of the 918th Bomb Group Living Memorial; James H. Farmer, aviation historian, artist, and the authority on the making of the motion picture; aviation artist Keith Ferris; Kevin Gray of the 918th Bomb Group Living Memorial; Steve Jensen, who created the Internet website on actor Robert Arthur; Teresa Lacy, David Menard, and Charles Frey of the U.S. Air Force Museum in Dayton, Ohio; Dr. William McClanahan, nephew of Beirne Lay; Louisa Morton, sister of Beirne Lay; J. Robert Nolley, childhood friend of Frank Armstrong; Bruce Orriss, aviation historian and supplier of military mock-ups and equipment to film studios and museums; Pete Plumb, crafter of replica Toby jugs through his company, Air Corps Classics; Dorothy Walker, secretary to Lt. Gen. Frank Armstrong; and Paul Wurtzel, who worked behind the scenes on both the movie and the television series. Thanks also to Eric Holmes, George Moss, Richard O'Hara, and John Regan.

For making the military a dramatic cornerstone of my life, through active and reserve duty, I'd like to thank Col. Peter Yogis, USAFR, Commander of the 452d Maintenance Group at March Air Reserve Base, California; Col. Robert Miller, USAFR (Ret.), Director of the March Field Museum; Col. Daniel Henderson of the Texas Air National Guard; Lt. Col. Nancy Brooks, USAFR; Maj. Jeffrey Decker, USAF, mentor and friend; Maj. Teri Center, USAF; Maj. Crystal White, USAF; Maj. Jeff Pickard, USAFR; Maj. Cliff Waller, USAFR; Maj. Timothy Lloyd, USAFR; Maj. Donald Traud, USAFR, Chief of Public Affairs at March Air Reserve Base, California; Maj. John Keen of the California Air National Guard; Capt. Kevin Davis, USAFR; Capt. Andrea Granados, USAFR; 1st Lt. John Neubecker, USAFR; CMSgt. David Weber, USAFR; CMSgt. Brian Wels, USAFR; CMSgt. Jeffrey Morris, USAF (Ret.); Brent and Lori Loucks; Mark Bryant; David Hindt; Mark Bryner; William and Ellen Foster; and all of the personnel of the 752d and 452d Aircraft Maintenance Squadrons at March Air Reserve Base, California.

Since this project began as a master's thesis, I owe a debt of gratitude to the people who encouraged my research and writing from the get-go: Prof. William M. Fowler, Jr., Director of the Massachusetts Historical Society and Consulting Editor of The New England Quarterly; Linda Smith Rhoads, Editor of The New England Quarterly; Professors Gerald Herman and Raymond Robinson of the History Department at Northeastern University in Boston, Massachusetts; and Prof. David Ralston of the History Department at the Massachusetts Institute of Technology in Cambridge, Massachusetts.

I salute friends and family who patiently listened to my enthusiastic discussions of all things 12 O'Clock High, and who helped review the manuscript as well. They include my wife Michele; my parents, Lester and Maria Duffin, who generously took time out of their schedule to conduct photo research at the National Archives; my mother-in-law, Suzie Jackson; my brother and sister-in-law, Capt. Nolan Duffin and Maj. Jenifer Petrina, USAF; sister-in-law Lisa Zugschwerdt; and old friends Tom Colones, Christopher Santoro, and Jody Wheeler.

PAUL'S ACKNOWLEDGMENTS: A creative effort the scale of this one involves many people, directly or tangentially. An enormous debt of gratitude is owed to friends, family and professional acquaintances.

For their insight on the production of *12 O'Clock High:* Howard Alston, Robert Blacker, Harold Jack Bloom, George B. Chan, Maurine and William D. Gordon, Constance Harvey, Jack Hawn, Don Ingalls, Sam Korth, Charles Larson, Don Medford, Robert Moreno, Frank Mormillo, Frank V. Phillips, Sutton Roley, William A. Spencer, Greg Thomas, Jack Turley, Al C. Ward and Paul Wurtzel.

For sharing their experiences about performing in *12 O'Clock High:* Frank Aletter, Alan Bergmann, Michael Callan, Paul Carr, Joseph Campanella, Lew Gallo, Peter Graves, Earl Holliman, Marlyn Mason, Lee Meriwether, Lois Nettleton, Tim O'Connor, Chris Robinson and Susan Seaforth Hayes.

FOR SERVICE ABOVE AND BEYOND THE CALL OF DUTY, SPECIAL THANKS GO TO:
- John P. Hermes, for many years of friendship and sharing a mutual passion for classic films and TV programs, among them *12 O'Clock High.*
- Karen Matheis for invaluable production assistance.
- Joseph F. McKenna and Richard Mandel for their inspiration, friendship, humor and dedication to the craft of writing.
- Charlie Reinitz, for his enthusiasm and his encyclopedic knowledge of all things aviation and film related.
- Dik Shepherd, for sharing memories and photos from the set of *12 O'Clock High.*
- Scott A. Thompson for his remarkable accomplishments in documenting the lives and afterlives of vintage warbirds, and his passion for sharing that information.
- Additional thanks to Scott's father, Norman P. Thompson, for providing two of the period photos depicting the 918th HQ compound at Chino.
- Steve and Paula Zorc, Zorc Photo and Design, Cleveland, Ohio, for their exceptional creative support and, most of all, friendship.

INVALUABLE RESEARCH ASSISTANCE WAS PROVIDED BY THE STAFFS OF SEVERAL KEY INSTITUTIONS INCLUDING:
- The staff of The Cleveland Press Collection, Cleveland State University, Cleveland, Ohio.
- The librarians and staff of the microfilm, history and literature departments of the Cleveland Public Library, Main Library, Cleveland, Ohio.

- Barbara Hall and the staff of the Margaret Herrick Library, Department of Special Collections, Academy of Motion Picture Arts & Sciences, Beverly Hills, California.
- The staff of Planes of Fame, Chino Airport, Chino, California.
- The staff of the UCLA Arts Library Special Collections, Los Angeles.
- Ned Comstock of the USC Edward L. Doheny Memorial Library, Los Angeles.

Most importantly, I dedicate this book to my parents, George and Irene Matheis, for triggering my creativity, and my dear, long-suffering wife, Melanie, for showing me how to harness it.

ONE MORE SALUTE: Finally, we'd like to offer a big kiss to our wives, Michele Zugschwerdt and Melanie Matheis, for supporting us through this project and nodding valiantly as we energetically discussed the same plot points over and over again. They understand our need to cram file boxes with research, travel and rack up phone bills in pursuit of the golden interview, and stack memorabilia and collectibles from floor to ceiling in our houses. They support us, sometimes amused, always encouraging, not always understanding our mania for popular culture. And they love us anyway.

FOREWORD

I was introduced to *12 O'Clock High* as a young cadet in the Reserve Officer Training Corps. The film was used as a training aid to develop us as managers by comparing and contrasting the different leadership styles of Col. Keith Davenport and Brig. Gen. Frank Savage. As a college student preoccupied with things other than studying an old war film, I found *12 O'Clock High* interesting but didn't think much else of it at the time.

Fortunately, as I grew older I learned to appreciate the finely detailed story and the complexities of the characters. What caused Savage, a man seemingly made of steel, to lose his ability to function? Why was Ben Gately so scared of flying combat missions? Would Sergeant McIllhenny ever keep his stripes for more than a few days? When I finally thought about it, I realized that these were very interesting people and that I should take a closer look at *12 O'Clock High*.

When I found out that a novel had been written first, and a television series had followed, *12 O'Clock High* began to stand out as something special. I was preparing to enter active duty in the Air Force, and I began to look at how real-life events had inspired the plot points in Beirne Lay and Sy Bartlett's original novel. This wasn't just fiction of a different color; it was fiction based on the blood and sweat of the battleground. Sure, the names had been changed, but these events actually happened during World War II. When it came time to choose a topic for my master's thesis in history, I chose *12 O'Clock High*. This book is an outgrowth of that effort.

Today some of my interests parallel those of Beirne Lay: I'm a writer, producer, and history instructor who serves part-time in the Air Force Reserve. It has been an honor to celebrate *12 O'Clock High* by writing its history, and I sincerely hope that—as I did when I was a cadet—you gain a better appreciation of Beirne Lay and Sy Bartlett's work by reading more about it.

ALLAN T. DUFFIN
LOS ANGELES, CALIFORNIA, JULY 2005

THE NOVEL

On a mission: High-altitude contrails stream from engines of B-17 Flying Fortresses assigned to the 306th Bombardment Group.

"If I had a choice, would I want to relive my wartime experience? Definitely not. I couldn't stand the excitement."
— *Beirne Lay, Jr.*

Published by Harper Brothers in the spring of 1948, *12 O'Clock High* was a very personal project for co-authors Beirne Lay, Jr., and Sy Bartlett. The novel was based primarily on the exploits of the 306th Bombardment Group, one of the first American units exported to England to fight in the air war over Europe during World War II. The popular commander of the 306th was fired after a period of grueling combat losses in late 1942 and early 1943, when the American military was battling critics as well as the enemy to refine and prove its concept of precision bombing by daylight.

A year after the war ended, Hollywood writer-producer Sy Bartlett fought a different battle with his friend and fellow writer Beirne Lay. Bartlett wanted to turn their wartime experiences into a book for posterity, but Lay wouldn't agree to such an emotional project so soon after the last shot had been fired. After some passionate chest-beating, Bartlett convinced his friend that such a novel had merit, and the two men formed a partnership to write what would become *12 O'Clock High*. Blessed with a rich background and superb writing savvy, Lay and Bartlett produced a work that depicted a fictional yet factually accurate account of combat leadership during World War II.

The partnership between Lay and Bartlett was a potent combination of the intense and flamboyant. Lay had joined the Army Air Corps during its formative years. "He was a very interesting man," remembered his friend David Tallichet, a B-17 pilot with the 100th Bomb Group during the war. "He was in the military at a time when the Army Air Corps was very small. He knew the 'who's who' in there, and since he was a writer and a pilot, he did a hell of a job on *12 O'Clock High*." By contrast, Sy Bartlett joined the military when the United States entered World War II. A Hollywood veteran, Bartlett was a passionately creative force, knowledgeable about plotting a strong story and relentless about seeing it through to completion. The pairing of the two equally strong personalities proved ideal for writing a book, and later a movie, about their war experiences.

BEIRNE LAY, JR.: "I WANTED WINGS"

With his two-pronged career as an aviator and author, Beirne Lay balanced a unique mix of military and civilian careers. A gifted writer, Lay often drew from his military service for inspiration. He was born in the tiny mountain retreat of Berkeley Springs, West Virginia, on 1 September 1909. From an early age, Lay demonstrated a knack for taking risks. "He was a daredevil," recalled his sister Louisa Morton. "He was into everything." Upon graduating from St. Paul's School in Concord, New Hampshire, Lay traveled south to Yale College in New Haven, Connecticut, for his undergraduate studies. As a budding scribe, he naturally majored in English. While attending university he also boxed, rowed, and worked part-time as a stenographer and private secretary.

Beirne Lay, Jr., shown here as a Colonel. This photo was taken just prior to the release of Lay's book, *I've Had It: The Survival of a Bomb Group Commander*, on 7 November 1945.

After receiving his B.A. from Yale in the spring of 1931, Lay, inspired by a movie he had seen, decided to become a pilot. The Army Air Corps was a good fit for the patriotic and aggressive Lay. "He was always very self-confident, always sure of his convictions," recounted his nephew, William McClanahan. In July of the following year, he enrolled as a flying cadet at Randolph Field, Texas, one of the Air Corps' primary training bases. The *London Times* noted that Lay left "the shelter of Yale at the height of the American Depression and narrowly escaped complete submergence in it, [and] managed to scramble into what, on his own showing, is probably the world's stiffest school of airmanship." After eight months at Randolph, Lay was transferred to nearby Kelly Field, where he spent four months flying the Keystone B-6 Panther bomber. He was commissioned as a Second Lieutenant in the Army Reserve upon his graduation in June 1933.

The next two years were spent on full-time active duty with the 20th Bombardment Squadron of the 2nd Bombardment Group at Langley Field, Virginia. The 20th Squadron flew the twin-engine B-6 and Curtiss B-2 Condor bombers, along with five Boeing Y1B-9 evaluation aircraft, the first cantilever monoplane bombers in the Army inventory. At various times Lay served as his squadron's engineering (maintenance) officer, armament officer, and communications officer.

During February 1934, the fledgling Army Air Corps temporarily assumed responsibility for delivering air mail across the United States. Responding to years of graft and collusion between the Hoover Administration and the airlines, President Franklin D. Roosevelt signed Executive Order 6591 on 19 February 1934, canceling government contracts to deliver the mail. For the next three months, the Army scrambled to fly the airmail routes using its small fleet of aircraft. Beirne Lay flew the Army's first route southbound from Chicago. Air Corps mail operations proved to be a disaster. Its pilots, unaccustomed to instrument flying or night operations, battled harsh winter weather over unfamiliar terrain. After 12 deaths and 66 crashes, the Air Corps was finished with mail service on 1 June 1934, when the government signed new contracts with the airlines. Upset at the pounding that the Air Corps was taking in the press, Lay wanted to write magazine articles to tell the other side of the story. According to author James Farmer, it was this event that kicked off Lay's prolific writing career.

Lay racked up a rich variety of credentials while serving on active duty. He earned his airplane and engine mechanic's license and qualified as an aerial machine gunner. He instructed aircrews in instrument flying. As his active duty time wound down, Lay cranked up his typewriter. He sold articles to magazines like *Esquire, Harper's, The Sportsman Pilot,* and *Today.* Upon completing his active duty stint in November 1935, Lay reverted to part-time reserve status. Except for periodic training periods, he was a civilian again. Fresh from his success with magazine writing, Lay was hired onto the staff of *The Sportsman Pilot,* a general-interest aviation magazine. He was soon promoted to Managing Editor. On 19 August 1936, Lay received another promotion when the Army Reserve pinned on his First Lieutenant bars.

In August 1936, Lay left *The Sportsman Pilot* to work on his first book. He devoted five months, at 10 to 12 hours a day, transferring his experiences as a flying cadet into the novel *I Wanted Wings*. When it was published by Harper Brothers in 1937, critics were highly complimentary. The *New York Times* called the book "decidedly different" due to its "unfamiliar fact and incident, with adventure, with humor and with human nature. And it is so well written that its interest goes beyond its specific subject to the wider field of a human document." Lay's energetic writing style impressed the English newspaper *The Manchester Guardian* as well: "This book is full of information about the United States Army Air Corps, but its chief recommendation is the gift which the author has of making his readers live with him through all his experiences. It is an intensely living book, and there are few who will not enjoy it."

Hollywood was also interested in *I Wanted Wings*. Arthur Hornblow, Jr., a producer at Paramount Pictures, bought the movie rights. Lay co-wrote the screenplay, his first. Partly filmed at Lay's old haunts, Kelly and Randolph Fields, *I Wanted Wings* was released in March 1941. The film, starring Ray Milland, William Holden, and Veronica Lake, did well at the box office and won the Academy Award for outstanding special effects.

During this period, Lay married Philippa Ludwell Lee and also met Capt. Frank Armstrong, who would later inspire the character of "Frank Savage" in *12 O'Clock High*. Armstrong was serving with the 13th Bombardment Squadron at Barksdale Field, Louisiana.

But even with the success of *I Wanted Wings,* Beirne Lay grew restless. "The itch to fly again, instead of writing about it, got the better of me," he wrote. So 1st Lt. Lay rejoined the Army Air Corps full-time in the fall of 1939 as a flight instructor at Cal-Aero Field in Chino, California. Lay's timing was fortuitous. Germany had triggered a new war in Europe with the invasion of Poland on 1 September 1939; and despite declarations of neutrality, the United States began a military buildup, supplying arms and other equipment to its overseas allies. In little more than a year, Lay would find himself right in the middle of the war.

Meanwhile, Col. Ira Eaker, chief of the Air Corps Information Division in Washington, D.C., had come across some of Lay's work and wanted to meet the young lieutenant. A former Army infantry officer and one of the pioneers of American airpower, Eaker was also a part-time writer with a graduate degree in journalism and three books—*This Flying Game* (1936), *Winged Warfare* (1941), and the upcoming *Army Flyer* (1942)—to his credit. Intrigued with Beirne Lay's talent, Eaker arranged a get-together. According to author DeWitt Copp, Eaker was impressed with Lay's "outgoing manner and quick-witted style." And so, just three months after rejoining the full-time ranks, Beirne Lay moved to the nation's capital to serve as Eaker's intelligence officer. Lay, now a captain, was also tasked with writing speeches for Maj. Gen. Henry "Hap" Arnold, the chief of the Air Corps.

After Germany declared war on the United States on 11 December 1941, Eaker was promoted to Brigadier General and directed to form a new organization called VIII Bomber Command, which would fly combat missions from England over enemy-occupied Europe. Eaker's first step was to assemble a core staff, and

(National Archives)

naturally he relied on men he trusted. Characteristically taciturn, Eaker didn't explain what he was doing when he anointed his new officers. He snagged Beirne Lay in a rush one day. According to DeWitt Copp, Eaker and Lay "passed in a corridor as Eaker was hurrying to a meeting. 'Beirne, do you want to come with me?' he called. 'Yes sir,' was Capt. Lay's immediate reply, although he had no idea where his answer meant he was going." Lay didn't know it at the time, but he was headed to England with five other officers Eaker had selected to staff the new Bomber Command: Lt. Col. Frank Armstrong, operations officer; Maj. Peter Beasley, supply; Capt. Frederick Castle and 1st Lt. Harris Hull, intelligence; and 2nd Lt. William Cowart, junior aide. They traveled by air to England, arriving in London in late February 1942.

Brig. Gen. Ira C. Eaker, commanding general of VIII Bomber Command, with mascot "Winston Churchill," August 1942.

At first, Eaker assigned Lay as his senior aide and historian. While the job utilized Lay's flair for public relations, it wasn't terribly fulfilling. According to DeWitt Copp, Lay "was not content with an Eighth Air Force career that included being a publicist, historian, and aide to Hap Arnold when he came to visit." After a year and a half of recording the war instead of fighting it, Lay was getting antsy. "That's a long time to watch from behind a desk," he thought. So Lay requested, and finally received, an assignment to combat duty.

First, however, he needed to get up to speed. In early August 1943, Lay was assigned to the 100th Bombardment Group at Thorpe Abbotts, 90 miles northeast of London, for orientation on the B-17 bomber. His first 10 days were a blur of activity, "full of the swift action of participating in four combat missions and checking out for the first time as a four-engine pilot," he wrote. Lay's previous experience had been in single-engine fighters and twin-engine bombers, so the B-17 Flying Fortress, with its four roaring Wright Cyclone engines, was a significant change to the menu.

Now a lieutenant colonel, Lay's next combat mission was a memorable one. On 17 August 1943 he accompanied the 100th Bomb Group on the Regensburg-Schweinfurt raid into Germany, flying as an observer in the B-17 *Picadilly Lily*.

Air and ground crews of the B-17 *Picadilly Lily*, assigned to the 100th Bomb Group, in late September 1943.

The double-strike mission sent two separate formations to different locations. One would tackle the ball-bearing factories at Schweinfurt, turn around, and return to England. The other formation would pound the Messerschmitt factory at Regensburg and continue to North Africa. There the crews would refuel and rest, then fly back to England, bombing an airfield at Bordeaux, France, en route. It was an interesting plan that would ultimately result in heavy losses for the Eighth Air Force. Beirne Lay, scheduled to fly on the Regensburg portion of the strike, recounted the group intelligence officer's briefing to the crews: "Your aiming point is the center of the Messerschmitt 109G aircraft and engine assembly shops. If you destroy it, you destroy 30 percent of the Luftwaffe's single-engine fighter production. You fellows know what that means to you personally." It meant fewer fighter attacks on American bombers.

Unbeknownst to Lay, a last-minute switch in aircraft assignments saved his life. Lay was originally placed in the second element of the low squadron, flying right seat in *Alice from Dallas*. Maj. Gale "Bucky" Cleven, commander of the 350th Bomb Squadron, knew that the position of Lay's aircraft at the tail end of the formation would be highly vulnerable to enemy fire. Cleven switched Lay to an aircraft in the high squadron, where he would fly with a very experienced pilot and have the protective cover of the group. So Lay joined the crew of the *Picadilly Lily*.

During the mission to Regensburg, Lay witnessed what could have been his own death. *Alice from Dallas*, in the last element of the low squadron, was hit hard with German flak. "I got a good look at that gap in the low squadron where three B-17s had been," he wrote later. "Suddenly I bit my lip hard. The lead ship of that element had pulled out on fire and exploded before anyone bailed out. It was the ship to which I had been originally assigned." Four of the six B-17s in the low squadron plummeted to earth, victims of enemy fire. Lay didn't fail to recognize the irony: "I know that I had long since mentally accepted the fact of death, and that it was simply a question of the next second or the next minute. I learned first-hand that a man can resign himself to the certainty of death without becoming panicky." Of the 146 aircraft that flew to Regensburg that day, 24 were shot down, and still more were lost on the way back from North Africa. The 100th Bomb Group lost nine of its 21 aircraft.

After viewing the results of the raid, Curtis LeMay, commander of the Third Bombardment Division, asked Lay to prepare a personal briefing on Regensburg. Lay finished his report on 25 August 1943, one week after the mission. He added a list of recommendations, including one that was most likely triggered by the shoot-down of *Alice from Dallas:* "That continued thought be given to further protective measures in the formation for the low squadron, which in our group, at least, was the A.P. [aim point] for frontal attacks."

Lay then folded material from his Regensburg report into an article that he submitted to the *Saturday Evening Post*. Titled "I Saw Regensburg Destroyed," the piece ran in the magazine's 6 November 1943 edition. It featured a large photo of the author, clad in flying gear, oxygen mask and goggles. Lay's detailed, nail-biting prose provided an in-the-cockpit view of the mission, including the devastating losses of crews and aircraft to German flak and fighters.

Following Regensburg, Lay flew another five missions with the 100th Bomb Group for a total of ten. He was well familiar with the B-17 by then, but a new bomber, the B-24 Liberator, had been introduced. Lay was sent back to the United States for orientation on the aircraft. From October through November 1943, Lt. Col. Lay served as commander of the 490th Bombardment Group at Salt Lake City, Utah, where its aircrews and support personnel were trained. However, Lay didn't have the opportunity to oversee his unit's move to England, as he had long since returned to Bomber Command by the time the 490th Bomb Group arrived in the town of Eye, Suffolk County, in April 1944.

Eventually, though, Lay got his wish to fly again. In February 1944, he was given command of another operational unit, the brand-new 487th Bombardment Group. Lay jumped into the assignment with both feet. He supervised the unit's move from its stateside training base at Alamogordo, New Mexico, through Camp Kilmer, New Jersey, to its new home at Lavenham in Suffolk County, England. The 487th BG boasted four squadrons of brand-new B-24 bombers and the forceful motto "The Gentlemen from Hell." After 12 years in the Air Corps, Beirne Lay finally had a flying command. The group flew its first combat mission on 7 May 1944 and would continue launching aircraft until April of 1945.

When Lay arrived at the 487th, he was already known as a writer who mined his military experiences for material. "He had a flair for the dramatic," noted William Colburn in *Aviation History* magazine many years later. "Many of us had read his *I Wanted Wings* or had seen the much different movie version. Some of us were a bit leery that we might become material for future works. It didn't work out that way."

Perhaps Lay had little time to think about writing because his tenure as commander was so short-lived. On a mission to the marshaling yards at Troyes, France, on 11 May 1944, the 487th Bomb Group was ordered to fly at an altitude of 12,000 feet, well within the reach of German anti-aircraft batteries. Lay was flying his fourth combat mission as commanding officer of the 487th. It would be his last. About 120 miles southeast of Paris, heavy winds forced the group to take a shortcut to catch up with the wing formation. The B-24s were over the town of Châteaudun when, as Art Silva recalled, "We strayed over a German night fighter base—in daylight. Three of our B-24s were shot down. There was also a cripple." The cripple was Beirne Lay's airplane. German flak knocked out two of the four engines, quickly followed by a third. Then his controls jammed.

Lay ordered his crew to bail out. All 10 men parachuted safely, landing in German-occupied territory below. *The Washington Post* reported that the rest of the formation "watched the men land and reach cover before they too were attacked by enemy fighters." Lay evaded capture by hiding out in a farmhouse, and with the help of the French underground returned to his base in England three months later. Unfortunately, his love of flying was once again hindered by circumstance. Due to his knowledge of the French resistance movement, the Army couldn't risk his recapture. He was not allowed to return to combat.

Realizing that the story of his escape had all the elements of a good drama, Lay turned his experience into the book *I've Had It: The Survival of a Bomb Group Commander,* published by Harper Brothers in the fall of 1945. *Book Week* was generous in its praise: "Col. Lay's earlier books and magazine pieces disclosed him as a master of the difficult craft of presenting melodramatic personal experiences with objectivity, clarity and directness. *I've Had It* should enhance his standing among the more able writers of our day." The *Weekly Book Review's* Herbert Kupferberg lauded *I've Had It* as "one of the classic escape stories of the war."

Dodd, Mead Publishers re-released the book in 1980 under a new title, *Presumed Dead.* Lay penned a new epilogue in which he recalled a humorous story about his return home. After he was shot down in 1944, and despite his family's assumption that he had perished, his wife Luddy never gave up hope that he was still alive. She was proven right. One day she received the following phone call from the U.S. Army.

"Yes, Colonel," she said, "this is Mrs. Lay . . . he's *what?*" Her shoulders began to shake in uncontrollable laughter. "Thank you very much, Colonel, but you see, Colonel Lay is sitting right beside me on the bed." I could sense the consternation on the other end of the line. The Colonel's great moment had fizzled.

After she hung up, she turned to me and said, "It's official, straight from the Pentagon. You are alive and well and will be home in a few days."

In 1946, Lay left full-time military service with the rank of Colonel and transferred back into the Air Force Reserve. He moved to Los Angeles, where he continued to write aviation-themed articles and books. He sold his work to magazines like *Fortune, Reader's Digest, The Saturday Evening Post,* and *Esquire.* Meanwhile, across town at Twentieth Century-Fox studios, one of Lay's friends was mulling over a concept he had nurtured for several years: why not write a book and film about their experiences in World War II? The idea man was an energetic producer named Sy Bartlett, who had served with Lay in the Eighth Air Force.

SY BARTLETT: "THE BIG BRAIN"

(David Bartlett Collection)

Writer-producer Sy Bartlett, who co-authored *12 O'Clock High.*

Lay's writing partner for *12 O'Clock High* was born Sacha Baraniev on 10 July 1900 in the seaport city of Mykolayiv in the southern Ukraine. When he was four years old, he and his parents moved to the United States, settling in Chicago, Illinois. Known as Sidney ("Sy") Bartlett, he attended the Medill School of Journalism at Northwestern University and went to work as a newspaper correspondent. But Bartlett was more interested in writing fiction, so he traveled to Hollywood, California, to work as a screenwriter. In 1933, he penned the screenplay for the film *The Big Brain,* a quickie from RKO Studios featuring actress Fay Wray. From the 1930s into the early 1940s, Bartlett racked up story and screenplay credits for a rich variety of dramas, musicals, and comedies with titles like *Kansas City Princess, Going Highbrow, Under Your Spell, Danger Patrol,* and *Bullet Scars.* Perhaps his most memorable film of the period was *Road to Zanzibar,* produced at Paramount in 1941. Bartlett co-wrote the story for this second in the series of "Road" pictures starring Bob Hope and Bing Crosby.

"He was a very charming, intelligent man," remembered his son, David, whose mother, actress Ellen Drew, became Bartlett's second wife in 1941. They met while working on the musical comedy *Coconut Grove* (1938). Bartlett co-wrote the screenplay, and Drew, a contract player with Paramount Pictures, played a receptionist in the film. The very social Bartlett often hosted Sunday barbeques for his friends and family. "Dad loved to entertain," recalled David Bartlett. "He loved to have a large group of people around him." Bartlett was an avid horseman who played polo with Twentieth Century-Fox studio chief Darryl Zanuck on a regular basis. A fervent spokesman against the Nazi Party, Bartlett received some interesting press after he punched a German attaché in the jaw during an argument in a Hollywood nightclub in 1940. The recipient of Bartlett's anger, Werner Plack, was an employee of the German consulate. "He used to 'Heil Hitler' all the time," said Bartlett. "I got pretty tired of it."

With America's entry into World War II, Bartlett, a strong proponent of airpower, joined the military and was assigned to the Army Pictorial Service. The Army wanted him to create training films, but Bartlett wanted to be in the middle of the action. According to author Steven Jay Rubin, "A war was coming and the last thing he wanted to do was edit training documentaries." Bartlett was familiar with the movie *I Wanted Wings* and knew that its writer, Beirne Lay, was now on Brig. Gen. Ira Eaker's staff. So Bartlett cleverly consulted with his friend Arthur Hornblow, the producer of *I Wanted Wings,* and asked Hornblow to arrange a meeting with Lay.

As a fellow writer-turned-serviceman, Lay understood Bartlett's situation and brought him into the inner circle of the Eighth Air Force. The two men began a close friendship, which netted Capt. Bartlett a plum assignment as the aide-de-camp to Maj. Gen. Carl "Tooey" Spaatz, commander of the Eighth Air Force. Bartlett joined Spaatz in England on 3 June 1942 as the U.S. Army Air Corps scrambled to build a bomber fleet to use against German-occupied Europe. Bartlett was later part of VIII Bomber Command's intelligence unit, where he learned how the Royal Air Force conducted its nighttime bombing raids. Occasionally he flew on RAF missions as an observer.

With his background in journalism and the Hollywood movie factory, Bartlett easily recognized public relations opportunities when he saw them. On 27 January 1943, Col. Frank Armstrong, newly installed as commander of the 306th Bomb Group, led a formation of 54 B-17 aircraft on a bombing raid to Wilhelmshaven, Germany. It was the first American mission into Germany proper, and Bartlett, who had befriended Armstrong, went along. During the raid, Bartlett had the dubious distinction of toggling the first bomb load. Donald Bevan, a waist gunner in the 306th, recalled that near the target, "the bomb load from a plane to the left of us—from the formation flying in the hole—dropped away prematurely, causing the bombardiers to doubt their own sighting calculations. Confusion reigned over the intercoms." Why had one of the B-17s toggled its bombs early?

B-17s of the 306th Bomb Group at point of bomb release. The small white burst with trailing smoke was the signal for all aircraft to drop their bomb loads. The cloud of trailing black smoke on the right is pouring from a flak-damaged engine.

After the 306th landed safely at its base at Thurleigh, the general comment from the aircrews was, "Who was the son-of-a-bitch who did that?" One aircraft mechanic told Bevan in a huff that Col. Armstrong's "Hollywood VIP friend" had toggled the bomb load early by mistake. Whether this was true or not, Bartlett had inadvertently created a very uncomfortable situation for himself and the crews that flew the mission. "It was the number-one reaction to the historic raid," recalled Bevan, who was unsure whether Bartlett was the culprit until several years later, when he had a revealing conversation with his mother-in-law, film star Nancy Carroll. She had dated Bartlett for awhile and knew him pretty well. "He said that he was the first American to drop bombs over Germany during the war," Carroll recounted.

Bartlett's next adventure occurred in late March 1943, when he arranged to fly on a bombing mission with the Royal Air Force. The target was Berlin. Bartlett convinced the bombardier in his airplane to allow him to toggle the bomb drop, which he did. "Then," according to James Parton, a staff officer with the Eighth Air Force, "Bartlett's show-business instincts toggled *him*. Back in London before breakfast, he called a press conference at Claridge's Hotel that led to large headlines in the afternoon tabloids proclaiming him as the 'First American to Bomb Berlin.'"

Obviously Bartlett hadn't cleared his actions with his superiors at headquarters. Maj. Gen. Eaker, recently promoted to commander of the Eighth Air Force, learned about Bartlett's escapade during the next morning's staff meeting. The briefing officer wryly informed the general that "last night Maj. S.S. Bartlett of the United States Army Air Forces bombed Berlin—escorted by 1000 bombers of the Royal Air Force." Eaker, mindful of how the event could damage American-British relations, quickly slapped Bartlett with a reprimand expressing the need to "acquaint you with the proper channels for releasing publicity in the future and to take the necessary steps to ensure that you follow these channels."

Col. Frank Armstrong, leader of the first American heavy bomber mission into occupied Europe, chats with newspaper correspondents in December 1942.

It was during this time that the seeds for *12 O'Clock High* were planted. Bartlett learned that Col. Frank Armstrong had been sent to take over and shape up the 306th Bombardment Group, whose previous commander had been fired. Bartlett made note of the unit's trials and tribulations, believing that the story would make a fine book or film. More than a year later, in the fall of 1944, Bartlett and his friend Beirne Lay were having a chat with Armstrong. Lay was preparing to return Stateside following his harrowing return to England after being shot down in combat. The three men talked about their wartime experiences—and about writing them down. With Armstrong's story in mind, Bartlett began developing the plot for a novel. He was passionate about recording events that occurred during the war. As related by author Stephen Jay Rubin, Bartlett told Beirne Lay, "You know, when the war ends, people are going to forget what happened here. They won't care anymore. To prevent that from happening, you and I are going to write a novel about the Air Corps. It will take place at a solitary field like this one and we'll have a central character like Frank Armstrong." Ever the astute movie producer, Bartlett also had a film in mind. "When we finish the novel," he continued, "we'll write a screenplay. It will be the best war film ever. With your combat experience and my inside knowledge of the command structure, we can write this thing from a unique point of view."

By 1945, at the end of the war in the Pacific, Frank Armstrong was commander of the 315th Bombardment Wing based on the island of Guam, and Bartlett was serving as his chief intelligence officer. During that time, Bartlett continued to chat up his idea for what would become *12 O'Clock High*. William Leasure, who was Armstrong's staff navigator and plans officer, remembered one such discussion that took place in late 1944 or early 1945. "I overheard conversations between Gen. Armstrong and Sy in which they discussed the 306th experience. Their thoughts and activities were motion-picture-aimed at that time."

After the war ended, Bartlett returned to Hollywood and went to work as a writer and producer at Twentieth Century-Fox Studios.

THE IDEA FOR *12 O'CLOCK HIGH*

According to Frank Armstrong, Sy Bartlett actually began plotting the manuscript that would become *12 O'Clock High* while the 315th Bomb Wing was training in the United States prior to entering combat in the Pacific Theater. When the 315th moved to Guam to begin flying bombing missions, Bartlett had to shelve the story temporarily. Despite the interruption, Bartlett never lost his excitement for writing a story about Frank Armstrong and his time with the 306th Bomb Group, and in the spring of 1946 he convinced a reluctant Beirne Lay to sign on. During a leisurely visit in Santa Barbara, California, Bartlett again pitched his idea to Lay. The latter was reluctant to tackle the project, feeling that it was too soon to write a book and too late to make a film. "The time just isn't right," Lay told his friend. "People are tired of war films." But Bartlett eventually coaxed Lay into agreeing. As Lay remembered later, "It was Sy who kept twisting my arm. Sy literally forced me into joining a venture which I thought was foredoomed so soon after the war. But I finally succumbed to his enthusiasm."

Trying to eke out a living as a screenwriter, Lay and his family were sharing an apartment in Los Angeles with his wife's first cousin. Unable to work in the cramped apartment, he decided to turn the basement of the building into a makeshift office. "Once I had seated myself at the orange crate which served as a desk for my portable [typewriter], illuminated by a naked ceiling bulb and a small cellar window on one wall, I was on my own. There was nothing else to do but write." For the next 15 months, Lay and Bartlett plotted out the story that would become *12 O'Clock High*. Bartlett was still working full-time at Fox studios, so he would get together with Lay during the evenings. Although Lay did most of the writing, he praised Bartlett for being "a natural dramatist" who "contributed a full share of our joint effort." And how did the novel get its title? Credit went to Sy Bartlett's wife at the time, actress Ellen Drew. According to Lay, "She overheard us discussing German fighter tactics, which usually involved head-on attacks from '12 O'Clock High.' 'There's your title!' she cried."

The plot of *12 O'Clock High* was a mix of combat heroics, interpersonal dramas, and romantic affairs. It was a potboiler with a military edge. The story went something like this:

Middle-aged Harvey Stovall finds a Toby mug in a London store, rides a bicycle to his old World War II aerodrome, and reminisces about his days in the 918th Bomb Group, where he served as the ground executive officer . . .

It is 1942, and the Eighth Air Force is slowly assembling a large force of aircraft in England to attack targets in Nazi-held Europe. So far, the planes are few and far between, the combat crews are inexperienced and wary, and military strategy is being developed through trial and error. The Eighth Air Force must prove the effectiveness of daylight precision bombing as a key factor in winning the war. The task is formidable, and the odds are great.

At the 918th Bombardment Group's base in Archbury, England, crews are gathered in the officers' club to relax. Lord Haw Haw, the voice of Nazi radio propaganda, tells the men that their clock is slow. The fact that the enemy knows this is hardly reassuring to the American flyers, whose recent combat record has been miserable.

Dense fog, coupled with a nighttime blackout on the base, brings out the frustration in Col. Keith Davenport, the commander of the 918th. Davenport cares a bit too much about the welfare of his men. This concern makes him a father figure and is causing problems with morale and combat effectiveness.

Davenport drives to Wycombe Abbey, headquarters of Eighth Bomber Command (codename PINETREE) to talk to his friend, Brig Gen. Frank Savage. Savage is assigned as G-2, in charge of intelligence for the Command. He and Davenport discuss strategic bombing and the difficulties involved. They meet RAF Flight Lieutenant Pamela Mallory, who works with "RT-Intercepts," the department responsible for tracking German fighter movement.

Back at the 918th Bomb Group's base at Archbury, traffic from the day's mission is returning to the airstrip. One B-17, its landing gear jammed, belly-lands and screeches to a halt. Part of the pilot's head has been sheared off by enemy gunfire, and the crew is badly shaken.

Col. Davenport is ordered to fly the next mission to the submarine pens at St. Nazaire, France, at a dangerously low altitude of 9000 feet. During the mission, a navigational error results in the 918th being late to rendezvous with the other bomb groups. Maj. Gen. Patrick Pritchard, the wing commander, travels to Archbury with Frank Savage to meet with Davenport about the mission. Realizing that Davenport has become far too attached to his men, Pritchard relieves Davenport of command. Not wanting the 918th's problems to spread to other units, Pritchard assigns Savage to "shape up" the 918th.

When Savage arrives at Archbury the next day to take command, he chastises the MP at the gate for being lax about security. Savage then has the air executive officer, Lt. Col. Benjamin Gately, arrested for dereliction of duty. Gately is demoted to airplane commander of a B-17 named the *Leper Colony*. The crew is comprised of slackers, and it is Gately's responsibility to whip them into shape.

At the Officers' Club, General Savage meets Maj. Joe Cobb, who has had too much to drink. Unaware of Savage's rank, Cobb challenges him to a fight. Savage promptly knocks Cobb to the ground. Impressed with Cobb's vigor, Savage assigns him as the new air executive officer, replacing Ben Gately.

Savage then makes a fiery introductory briefing to his men, telling them to "consider yourselves already dead!" The speech is a harsh slap in the face to an already demoralized group, and the men are angry. Following the briefing, Savage is told that all of the pilots in the group want transfers. Savage needs time to turn the unit around. His ground executive officer, Maj. Harvey Stovall, agrees to delay the paperwork for as long as possible.

After many practice missions, the 918th bombs the submarine pens at La Pallice, France. On the next mission, to Lille, Savage is furious that one B-17 broke formation to fly cover for a friend's crippled plane. Savage puts the pilot into the *Leper Colony* as punishment. He then assigns every man a new roommate so that no one will break formation to protect a friend's aircraft.

Several transfer requests are withdrawn, but the majority of the pilots in the group still want out.

The 918th's next mission is to bomb the railroad marshaling yards at Liege in Belgium. Bad weather over the target triggers a recall for all units to return to base. But Savage ignores the message, making the 918th the only group to bomb the target. The mission is a success, and gives the unit a huge boost in spirits.

Savage is told that he's done a good job with the 918th and will be transferred stateside to train new units there. He argues with his superiors, stating that his men are not quite ready to take over themselves. He is granted additional time at the 918th. Meanwhile, Savage begins a romance with Pamela Mallory, the RAF Flight Lieutenant whom he met earlier.

The 918th is next assigned a bombing mission to Wilhelmshaven—the first mission over Germany proper. Maj. Stovall, Sgt. McIllhenny (Savage's clerk and driver), and the base chaplain all stow away on the mission.

As the days move on, Savage begins to show some psychological strain. He is torn between leading his men and becoming too attached to them. He is developing the same problem that lost Keith Davenport his job as commander of the 918th.

At a meeting of all the group commanders, Savage learns about a new tactic, the "shuttle raid." Half of the groups will bomb the ball-bearing factories at Hambrucken, while the other half will take out the fighter factories at Bonhofen. The strategy should confuse the German fighter units and keep them from attacking the American bombers in force. After bombing Germany, the American B-17s will land in Russia, refuel and reload, and hit Germany again on the way back to England.

The next mission is nicknamed the "Anniversary Mission" because it is scheduled exactly one year to the day of the very first Eighth Air Force bombing run. Savage is ordered to fly the mission because of its propaganda value. During the mission, Joe Cobb's plane is shot down. Savage is forced to ditch his B-17 in the English Channel. McIllhenny dies while firing at an attacking Me 110 fighter.

Without stopping to catch its breath, the Eighth Air Force begins planning for its first mission over Berlin. The strain of command finally becomes too much for Savage, and he suffers a breakdown. He is taken back to his office, where he sits frozen in a state of shock. After he recovers, Savage finally admits that he's ready to leave and asks for a transfer back to the United States. His job at the 918th completed, he jumps in a jeep and drives off to see the woman he loves, Pamela Mallory.

HOT OFF THE PRESSES

Harper Brothers Publishers rolled out the first hardcover edition of *12 O'Clock High* in the spring of 1948, priced at $2.75 per copy. One of the Air Force leaders who had inspired the novel, Lt. Gen. Curtis LeMay, was also one of its biggest fans. While assigned as commander of U.S. Air Forces in Europe (USAFE), LeMay wrote to Sy Bartlett on 10 May 1948:

Dear Sy,

The new book arrived and I read it through in one sitting. As usual you and Beirne have done a good job. To make sure all the boys over here know about it, I have had the PIO [Public Information Office] do a review for *Week-End*, the Sunday supplement to *Stars & Stripes*, *Air Force Times*, *Air Force* magazine, etc. That should help get the news around. I'm sure that everyone who served in the Eighth will want a copy to jog their memory a little when they think things are getting tough.

Keep me posted on how the movie is coming along.
Please give my best to Ellen and the Lays.

Sincerely,
CURTIS E. LEMAY
Lieutenant General, USAF
Commanding

The press release that LeMay promised was highly complimentary, hailing *12 O'Clock High* for its "living, breathing type that rings with the authenticity and GI jargon of the men who flew some of the most trying missions of the war." The novel was an "authentic record of the men and operations of a typical heavy bomber group" and would appeal to war veterans as "a mixture of nostalgia, sorrow and pride." LeMay also looked at things from a leader's perspective: "It was

Lt. Gen. Curtis LeMay, late 1940s. As commander of the 305th Bomb Group in England during World War II, LeMay helped refine the techniques of daylight precision bombing. He later assisted Beirne Lay and Sy Bartlett with publicity for *12 O'Clock High* when it was published in 1948.

the Frank Savages of this war that brought America to final and complete victory through personal disregard of self and other's opinions. Savage's performance throughout the pages of *12 O'Clock High* reflects the necessarily high-handed, impersonal methods of dealing with brave men who, through repeated exposure to wholesale death and destruction, had become imbued with a fear-neurosis and a terror of impending death."

The period in which *12 O'Clock High* was set, late 1942 through early 1943, was a time of trial for the new Eighth Air Force. Strategic bombing was still a relatively new concept, and Bomber Command had to create the rules from scratch. "The Eighth Air Force was determined to start high-altitude bombing during the day, even though the RAF thought we would get all shot up," noted navigator Frank Beadle, who flew 51 combat missions during the war. The trial-and-error process cost the Eighth dearly in men and morale. The steely determination of commanders and crews slowly but surely improved the odds stacked against them. Beirne Lay and Sy Bartlett adapted the stories of those men for *12 O'Clock High,* and the resulting novel had an authentic grittiness and flavor that only true life could inspire.

FACT TO FICTION

Beirne Lay and Sy Bartlett used the story of the real-life 306th Bombardment Group as their framework for *12 O'Clock High.* Other characters and incidents were drawn from the two authors' experiences in various jobs in the military. "Everything Bartlett and Lay ever wrote were facts," noted Col. John deRussy, operations officer for the 305th Bomb Group during the war and later the technical advisor on the 1949 film version of *12 O'Clock High.* "But not all of it happened in the same organization." Donald Bevan, a veteran of the 306th Bomb Group and co-author of the 1951 Broadway play *Stalag 17,* echoed deRussy's thoughts: "Their minor characters and 'in passing' mentions are derived from special, unique, dramatic happenings—from one-of-a-kind events."

American air units were located in rural areas across England. The original caption of this November 1944 photo reads: "Pursuing the peaceful occupation of oat-gathering, pretty Miss Millicent Heyward, English farmerette, is shown on a farm located in the midst of a widely dispersed air service depot where some of the great force of Eighth Air Force B-17 Flying Fortresses are awaiting dispatch for operational use."

THE 306TH BOMBARDMENT GROUP

In addition to fictionalizing real-life names and places for use in *12 O'Clock High's* storyline, Lay multiplied "306" by a factor of three to create the name of Gen. Savage's fictional bomb group, the 918th. Initially, however, the authors of *12 O'Clock High* used a different designation. A synopsis of the novel dated 8 July 1947, when seven of the 12 chapters had been completed, set the story at the "906th Bomb Group" rather than the 918th.

The real-life 306th Bombardment Group, whose B-17s sported a "triangle-H" tail flash, served in combat from October 1942 until April 1945. Nicknamed

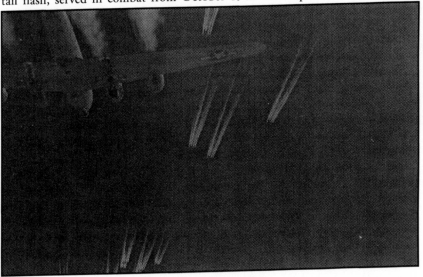

B-17s of the 306th Bomb Group on their way to the target.

"The Reich Wreckers," its four flying squadrons and associated support units were activated at Salt Lake City Air Base, Utah, on 16 March 1942 under the command of Col. Charles B. "Chip" Overacker. "I well remember that momentous morning," noted Overacker, "sitting in a wooden barracks building at the Salt Lake City airport as the procession of fresh, young, eager pilots filed in." Three weeks later, the 306th moved to the open desert of Wendover Air Base, Utah, for flying training. "Busy all day with flying and administrative duties," recalled pilot Bill Lanford, "and in the evenings in the honky-tonk casino or on an occasional cook-out on the salt flats."

First Lieutenant Thurman Shuller, fresh out of the Army's School of Aviation Medicine, joined the group's medical staff as it hurriedly prepared for war. "Four of us graduates were assigned to the 306th. The Captain was assigned as group surgeon and we First Lieutenants were assigned as squadron surgeons. A few weeks into that assignment the group surgeon left the outfit, and I, by virtue of the fact that I had a date of rank about 27 days earlier than the other two, was made group surgeon. So I, a young 27-year-old doctor right out of hospital internship with no unsupervised medical experience, became the chief medical officer of the group."

The doctors weren't the only inexperienced men in the 306th. "No more than a half-dozen of the pilots assigned to the developing group had ever flown in a four-engine aircraft," remembered Shuller. "It was on-the-job training throughout because of the urgent need to rapidly expand the combat units. So nearly all of us were thrown into positions of responsibility we were unprepared for and were literally forced to rise to the occasion." Bill Lanford remembered that his orientation in the B-17 "consisted of two half-hour flights of about six landings and take-offs."

To build such a combat unit, thousands of strangers were brought together for the very first time. "The entire group was made up of young recruits from every facet of life and every state of the union," noted Bill Lanford. "Cooks fresh from civilian life by way of cooks and bakers school, crew chiefs fresh from mechanics school, gunners from gunnery school, clerks straight from boot camp because maybe they had typing in high school. Most of the administrative officers came straight from civilian life where they had received direct commissions due to their educational background. Except for these few, we were all oh so young! Perhaps averaging 20 or 21. I was the old man at 24."

After completing their initial training in July 1942, the men of the 306th prepared for the journey across the Atlantic Ocean to their new airfield in England. Group commander Overacker recalled "the all-too-short training period, the move to Westover, Massachusetts, in preparation for the Atlantic crossing, in new aircraft but minus all qualified co-pilots, who were 'ploughed back' to Second Air Force for further training and subsequent assignment to future groups as aircraft commanders. The balance of the group, less aircrews, made the crossing by sea."

Upon arrival in England on 13 September 1942, the 306th Bombardment Group was based in the village of Thurleigh, 30 miles west of Cambridge. The crews spent the next three weeks in training, sharpening their formation flying, bombing, and gunnery skills. Finally, on 9 October 1942, the group flew its first combat mission, to the steelworks and railroad yards at Lille in northeastern France. It was, according to Overacker, "our introduction to Goering's yellow-nosed Fw 190s [nicknamed "The Abbeville Boys" after the location of their airbase] doing lazy-eights over us at 25,000 feet, and to German flak, and regretfully, our first combat loss."

Ground crews load B-17s with thousand-pound bombs before a mission.

During its first several months in theater, the 306th, as well as the other new American bomb groups in England, suffered heavy losses. "We were averaging 10 percent" on each mission, noted Bill Lanford. "Not a happy thought for those that hoped to complete a 25-raid combat tour." As of 8 January 1943, the 306th had flown 12 missions and, according to Jack Ryan, "by the end of 1942 we had lost 11 aircraft to enemy action and our aircraft inventory had declined seriously. Several others had been damaged beyond field maintenance capability." By April 1943, one of the four flying squadrons had 70 percent of its original personnel listed as killed, missing, or held as prisoners of war.

Bomber Command held the group commander, Col. Chip Overacker, responsible for his unit's weak combat results. Part of the problem was Overacker's growing commitment to his men, which made him more of a protector than a hardnosed combat leader. A social man who cherished close relationships, Overacker enjoyed hitting the Key Club, the local pub in Bedford, with his crews. Up at VIII Bomber Command, Brig. Gen. Ira Eaker was growing

Crewmen of the 423rd Bomb Squadron, 306th Bomb Group, take a break for a cheerful photo. Left to right: Mike Lunburg, bombardier; Harry Quint, pilot; Charles Gibson, pilot. All three men would complete 35 missions each.

more and more concerned with the 306th's performance. According to historian Roger Freeman, "Its losses were high, air discipline was poor and on the last mission most of its aircraft had abandoned the mission before the start point, weakening the force dispatched. [Eaker] found the group had a despondent, defeatist attitude and that the commanding officer was something of a father figure who had become so involved with the misfortunes of his men that he seemed more anxious to defend than improve their poor performance."

To be fair, early tasking orders from VIII Bomber Command were hindered by the staff's lack of experience at planning major bombing operations. No one had used the bomber in such a capacity before. In the rush to build a fleet of aircraft, train crews, and send them into combat against the enemy, not everything went smoothly. A number of staff officers in Bomber Command were unfamiliar with the B-17. Jack Ryan, a pilot in the 306th Bomb Group, pinpointed several problems with early Eighth Air Force bombing missions: "lack of combat experience at all levels of command and lack of a bombardment tactical doctrine"—and a seasoned enemy. "We faced a Luftwaffe blooded in the Spanish Civil War and during three years of combat on two fronts." The American aircrews, by contrast, had to learn by doing. "The lessons from those early missions were learned at the cost of staggering losses," said Ryan.

"Losses are bound to cause morale to deteriorate," noted Delmar Wilson, deputy commander of the group, "and the 306th had the worst record. Some were due to the 306th being selected to lead the Bomber Command stream more than the less-experienced groups. The departure of the 97th and 301st to Africa made the 306th a veteran. New groups arriving such as the 305th, 91st, and 44th were placed in formation behind 'the old veteran.'" Since the enemy pilots usually hit the lead bombers in the formation first, "the 306th was subjected to more concentrated attacks by German fighters than some other newly-arriving groups."

Although the 306th reportedly fell victim to low morale and discipline, members of the unit provided another point of view. Andrew Vangalis, an aircraft mechanic, arrived at the 306th in December 1942. "The first impression I got," he recalled, "was that the group would have liked to have gotten more missions to fly. And the maintenance people were really going all out to get their assigned bombers ready to fly. The morale of the group from my vantage point was where it should be, under the circumstances we had to face." As for Col. Overacker, he "was the type who felt he could get the best out of his people by letting them know he would do all he could for them."

Robert "Rip" Riordan, a pilot with the 369th Squadron, echoed those sentiments. "I was not aware at the time of any serious and general problems with morale. The great majority of us were gung ho. Our performance was somewhat ragged because it was all new. We were the third group in England and were in on the beginning of bombing missions at high altitude and in daylight to targets in France and Germany. There was no real precedent. But the top man in any organization has to take the responsibility for his unit's performance, which, in our case, was evidently below what the higher brass expected. After all, the worth of daylight bombing was on the line and losses were running at an unacceptable level."

Jack Ryan was the commander of the 367th Bomb Squadron, known as the "Clay Pigeon Squadron" due to its heavy losses. Despite the daily strain of combat, Ryan said, "Our morale never diminished. We had no illusions now of making it through 25 missions. I can truthfully say that I never saw a pilot crack up from fear of flying. Perhaps we had become stoics and didn't realize it. So we tried to do our best knowing that eventually the chances were that we would become just another statistic."

"Aircrew morale was never a problem," said John Lambert, a pilot with the 367th Squadron. "Chip Overacker got in trouble because the loss of the aircrews he had nurtured through training simply overwhelmed him emotionally and robbed him of whatever leadership capabilities he had. Without a firm hand at the top, the group soon became a very loose military organization."

Eugene Pollock, a navigator in the 423rd Squadron, recalled that "group morale and performance during Overacker's tenure was good, but we had to do what Bomber Command said. We did sustain very large losses. It got so bad that we didn't know anybody in the club anymore. Also, on any mission when we got near our target, the Germans were always on us, till they ran out of petrol. It happened every time, almost." Fortunately, by 1944 American bombers were receiving fighter escort by P-51 Mustangs from home base to the target and back, which helped alleviate the problem.

On the ground, the 306th lacked the military discipline that Brig. Gen. Eaker, an old friend of Overacker, expected of his combat units. On 13 November 1942, King George VI toured three American bomber bases in England. He was escorted by Lt. Gen. Carl "Tooey" Spaatz and Eaker. Their aides, Sy Bartlett and James Parton, traveled with them. Parton recalled that the first two stations followed protocol, with "MPs who stood smartly to attention as our cavalcade drew up to the headquarters entrance, where the respective commanders and key officers of their staffs awaited. Despite English mud, there was a great deal of spit and polish."

But when the King arrived at Thurleigh to visit the 306th Bomb Group, there were no MPs around. "Rather, we passed two GIs with unbuttoned jackets, cigarettes dangling from their lips, strolling down the driveway. Neither saluted." Parton located Col. Overacker, and the inspection proceeded as planned. On the drive back, Eaker and Spaatz had a brief conversation about what they had just seen. "Tooey," said Eaker, "I think I'd better relieve Overacker." Spaatz replied, "Ira, I don't think you'd be making a mistake."

A month and a half went by. According to James Parton, "During that time the group's record, measured by number of bombs on target and by B-17s lost, became the worst in VIII Bomber Command." On 4 January 1943, Eaker again visited Thurleigh. Accompanying him in his staff car were Lt. Col. Beirne Lay and Col. Frank Armstrong, the operations officer for Bomber Command. Upon reaching the base, Eaker was nonchalantly motioned through the gate by a sentry who didn't bother to check identification or render a salute to the general.

In the film version of *12 O'Clock High*, Brig. Gen. Savage has a stern conversation with a gate sentry who waves him onto the base without checking identification. This scene was based on a real-life incident in the 306th Bomb Group.

In his book *First Over Germany*, Russell Strong, historian for the 306th Bomb Group Association and a member of the 367th Squadron, recorded the events that followed:

Eaker's car proceeded to group headquarters with the general seething over the affront at the gate. There he picked up Col. Overacker and toured base facilities and sites. "As we visited hangars, shops and offices, I found similar attitudes as seen at the front gate," Eaker later recounted. "The men had a close attachment to their commander, and he to them. But there was a lack of military propriety and I could not help but feel that this might be a part of the problem that was being revealed in combat." The 306th had lost nine planes on its last three missions.

When the visitors returned to group headquarters they entered Col. Overacker's office and, after the door was closed, Eaker said: "Chip, you'd better get your things and go back with me." He then turned to Col. Armstrong, and said: "Frank, you're in command. I'll send your clothes down."

Beirne Lay would later recreate this scene in *12 O'Clock High*.

After Armstrong completed his tenure at the 306th and returned to Bomber Command, Col. Claude Putnam took over and continued to refine the group's battle tactics. According to John Lambert, "On one mission he flew as a tail gunner in my lead airplane so as to observe the entire air division action. During his command the group suffered some of its most severe losses and yet, because of his leadership qualities, aircrew morale never suffered." Another contributing factor to the improving mood was the gradual influx of fresh crews and aircraft arriving in England. "The new bomb groups that were coming over contributed to morale quite a lot," noted Andy Vangalis. The replacement crews relieved "some of the pressure of being such a small amount of bombers going on a mission." In addition, "having long overdue fighter protection all the way to the target" increased the likelihood of surviving each harrowing raid on the enemy.

COL. CHARLES B. "CHIP" OVERACKER – "COLONEL KEITH DAVENPORT"

Jack Ryan joined the 306th Bombardment Group in Wendover, Utah, as a temporary instructor pilot and later found himself permanently assigned to the neophyte organization. His first meeting with Chip Overacker was a memorable one: "There he was, dapper as any ace straight out of *The Dawn Patrol*, wiry as a cavalry trooper, neatly mustachioed, soft spoken and undaunted by the challenge of his new command. Only later did I begin to appreciate his fatherly bearing which could put a young officer at ease even in the presence of his Distinguished Flying Cross, Colonel's eagles and command pilot's wings."

(306th Bomb Group Association)

B-17 of the 306th Bomb Group on its hardstand.

Early 306th Bomb Group headquarters staff. Front row, left to right: Maj. John Wright, intelligence; Maj. Douglas Coleman, executive officer; Lt. Col. Delmar Wilson, deputy commander; Col. Charles "Chip" Overacker, group commander; Lt. Col. Docker, British local defense officer; Lt. Col. William Cleveland, operations. Back row: Maj. Harry Holt, commander of the 367th Bomb Squadron; Maj. Ralph Oliver, commander of the 369th Bomb Squadron; Maj William Lanford, commander of the 368th Bomb Squadron.

Born in California on 22 February 1901, Chip Overacker was destined to be a career military man. He earned a bachelor's degree in electrical engineering and joined the Air Corps in the early 1920s. Just prior to America's entry into World War II, Overacker, a seasoned expert in bomber operations, took command of the 39th Bomb Group at Geiger Field in Washington, overseeing patrol missions off the northwest coast of the United States. In March 1942 he was promoted to the rank of Colonel and put in charge of the 306th Bombardment Group. Overacker made it a point to get to know his men. According to Jack Ryan, "Most of the high level of morale and good fellowship which existed at Wendover was in large part due to the Old Man, who made it his business to be everywhere on the field and to know every last man in his command."

While noble, Overacker's socializing could also be a hindrance. Group Surgeon Thurman Shuller noted that the character of Col. Keith Davenport in *12 O'Clock High* closely paralleled the real-life Chip Overacker. "I believe it is true that his failure as a leader was due to the fact that he related too closely personally with the pilots under his command. He was ordered by higher command to quit going on so many missions himself."

During an early scene in *12 O'Clock High*, Col. Davenport is ordered to bomb the submarine pens at St. Nazaire, France, from an altitude of 9000 feet. "They must mean nine*teen* thousand," fumes Davenport. "That's bad enough, but 9000 is what those flak gunners dream about." In reality, Col. Chip Overacker complained about the same thing when ordered to bomb St. Nazaire on 9 November 1942. Previous high-altitude missions to St. Nazaire had failed to penetrate the thick protective concrete of the submarine pens, so Bomber Command decided to fly the next mission closer to the ground. "When the order came for the 9000-foot raid on St. Nazaire," recalled Thurman Shuller, "Overacker protested vigorously to headquarters that it was too dangerous, without effect. He then said that if his crews were going to have to make that flight, he was going to lead them himself, and did." All four squadron commanders also flew with Overacker on the mission. Commented Jack Ryan, "Know-how had to be learned; guts were there in abundance."

According to Russell Strong, some of the mission planners figured that "at 7000 or 8000 feet the bombers would be between the low and high flak. What they may not have realized was how slowly the B-17 moves at those altitudes, at 155 or 160 miles per hour indicated airspeed." Positioned last in a formation of nearly 50 aircraft, the 306th was pummeled by enemy flak which chewed through the thin metal fuselage of the B-17s. Three of the group's 19 aircraft were lost and the remainder limped home, landing at an alternate base just across the English Channel. The results of the St. Nazaire mission were devastating to the men of the 306th. Delmar Wilson remembered seeing crews return from the ill-fated raid: "We had several airplanes crack up landing on a 3500-foot runway. Some without brakes. Some with dead aboard. The crews were highly emotional and under great stress. The RAF Club probably had few glasses left since hundreds were used to toast those left behind in the target area. The fireplace was the target for thrown glasses."

Inspired by real life: Col. Keith Davenport (Gary Merrill) tries to explain his bomb group's poor attitude and combat record in this scene from the film version of *12 O'Clock High*. Gen. Pritchard (Millard Mitchell) hovers over him as Frank Savage (Gregory Peck) looks on. This was a recreation of an actual meeting in Col. Chip Overacker's office at the 306th Bomb Group.

After further combat losses, constant attempts to convince higher headquarters to improve their planning, and with a perceived lack of discipline on his airbase, Col. Overacker's tenure at the 306th Bombardment Group was coming to a close. Eugene Pollock felt that Overacker was fired because "he refused to send his people on a mission without enough replacements. He took care of us from the beginning but became too emotionally involved." According to John McKee, a pilot in the 367th squadron, "Overacker was a grand person, but too, too old to lead a bomb group. *Twelve O'Clock High* gave a very good account on Overacker. I liked him very much! But he could not understand young men being killed." Bill Lanford agreed: "Chip Overacker was a good commander who loved his men. He took our losses, which were many, too much to heart. That, in my opinion, is why he was relieved of his command."

Commanders who were dismissed from combat duty would often move on to desk jobs somewhere else, and Overacker was no exception. According to author DeWitt Copp, Overacker was slated to take over a Combat Crew Replacement Center in England. Unfortunately, Overacker lost this opportunity when he was asked to prepare an analysis of Eighth Air Force resources for the top brass. Overacker nailed Eaker in the report, labeling daylight precision bombing a folly. An annoyed Eaker retracted his plans to put Overacker in command of the replacement center.

His career with the Eighth Air Force at an end, Overacker returned to the United States. He rediscovered his roots as an engineer when he was given command of Field 9, in charge of electronics testing at Eglin Field near Pensacola, Florida. Eglin was home of the Proving Ground Command, a test center for new military equipment. Overacker was later promoted to Deputy Commander of the Command. His friend Jack Ryan joined him as a pilot and later an operations officer. "As an engineer he was in his element as Director of the Proof Division," said Ryan. "Every service test was subjected to his personal scrutiny, and every test program had to carry his approval." Overacker continued his habit of managing by walking around. "It was not at all unusual for the colonel to show up at briefing and then climb aboard on the flight to see for himself how things were progressing."

After assignments at Langley Field, Virginia, and Tokyo, Japan, Overacker moved to Kansas City as the Deputy Chief of Staff for Operations for the Central Air Defense Force, responsible for protecting the continental United States from enemy attack. He completed his active duty career by overseeing training at Randolph Air Force Base in San Antonio, Texas, where he retired as a Colonel on 30 June 1956.

To his credit, Overacker took the ups and downs in his career with class and professionalism. According to Jack Ryan, "In the 41 years I knew Overacker, I never once heard him complain about his departure from the 306th or utter any derogatory remark about any of the actors in the drama. It was a hard pill for him to swallow and outwardly he took it stoically, though down deep it hurt him terribly." Shortly before his death in October 1983, Overacker dictated a farewell letter to the members of his old bomb group who had gathered for a reunion in Omaha, Nebraska. "For those who died, we bow our heads in silent prayer. For those who survived, God bless! Carry on, smartly!"

COL. FRANK A. ARMSTRONG, JR. – "BRIG. GEN. FRANK SAVAGE"

The character of Frank Savage, the tough, charismatic commander who replaced Col. Keith Davenport as commanding officer of the 918th Bombardment Group in *12 O'Clock High*, was based on several leaders whom authors Beirne Lay and Sy Bartlett met during their World War II service. Among them was Col. Curtis LeMay, commander of the 305th Bomb Group and later head of strategic air forces in the Pacific. But since *12 O'Clock High* was primarily based on the tribulations of the 306th Bomb Group during its "shape-up" period in early 1943, Lay and Bartlett logically modeled much of Frank Savage on the man who had been assigned to rework the real-life 306th, Col. Frank Armstrong. According to 306th veteran Don Bevan, "Armstrong was a strong, leading man type, with a Hollywood flair of dress." But it took more than rugged good looks to lead a combat unit. It took experience and leadership, and Frank Armstrong had both.

(National Archives)

Born in Hamilton, North Carolina, on 24 May 1902, Armstrong attended Wake Forest College in Winston-Salem, North Carolina, earning a Bachelor of Laws degree in 1923 and a Bachelor of Science degree in 1925. Before embarking on a military career, he first decided to follow a childhood dream, playing minor league baseball for three years.

In February 1928, Armstrong enlisted as a flying cadet and arrived at Brooks Field, Texas, for training. He received his wings the following March and joined the 2nd Bombardment Group at Langley Field, Virginia. Armstrong married Vernelle Lloyd Hudson of Richmond, Virginia, on 15 March 1929. He called her "Fluffy," a

Frank Armstrong, shown here as a Major General in the 1950s.

nickname that would adorn several of Armstrong's aircraft throughout his career, as well as a fictional B-17 in the film version of *12 O'Clock High*. One year later he became a flight instructor at March Field, California, and then moved to Randolph Field in San Antonio, Texas. By February 1934 Armstrong was a chief pilot at Salt Lake City airport, helping the U.S. Army fly the mail around the western portion of the United States during the airmail crisis of that year. His boss was Capt. Ira Eaker. Impressed with Armstrong's courage and dedication, Eaker nicknamed him "Army."

During the latter half of the 1930s Armstrong logged an interesting series of assignments that included the 78th Pursuit Squadron at Albrook Field in the Panama Canal Zone and the 13th Bombardment Squadron at Barksdale Field, Louisiana, where he served as the unit commander. In 1936 Armstrong was awarded the Distinguished Flying Cross after successfully piloting his way out of a freak accident. While stationed at Albrook Field, he was flying a Douglas OA-4A Dolphin when one of its two engines suddenly exploded. Armstrong was able to land the aircraft safely.

Armstrong's experience in the air would serve him well as America's involvement in the European war deepened. After serving as a combat observer with the Royal Air Force in England from November 1940 to February 1941, where he witnessed the RAF battle the German war machine, Armstrong returned to the United States. On 24 January 1942, Lt. Col. Armstrong was working as the Assistant Chief of Operations (A-3) at Army Air Forces Headquarters in Washington, D.C., when Brig. Gen. Ira Eaker told him that he was joining the newly formed VIII Bomber Command. After packing up and traveling to England, Eaker's staff set up shop at Wycombe Abbey, a former girls' boarding school in High Wycombe, Buckinghamshire. Armstrong served as Bomber Command's first operations officer. He was promoted to full Colonel that same year.

American leaders review mission plans, December 1943. From left to right: Lt. Gen. Ira Eaker, Eighth Air Force commander; Brig. Gen. Frank O. Hunter; Maj. Gen. Carl Spaatz; Gen. Dwight Eisenhower; Brig. Gen. Robert Candee; Maj. Gen. W.H. Frank.

Eaker used Armstrong not only as a headquarters staff member but also as a repairman of sorts, dispatching him to fix combat units that were broken. A strong motivator, Armstrong helped shape up two poorly performing bomb groups during the course of the war. Four months before he took command of the 306th, Armstrong worked with the 97th Bomb Group at Polebrook, Northamptonshire. Ordered by Brig. Gen. Eaker to prepare the 97th for combat operations over Europe, Armstrong replaced Col. Cornelius Cousland on 31 July 1942. James Parton, who served on the staff at Bomber Command, noted that the "restless, pugnacious Armstrong would much rather fly an airplane than a desk, as he had indicated to Eaker more than once. Now Eaker simply said, 'I have asked you to do many things for me. This time I am putting a real load on you. You are going to complete the training of our new heavy bomb group and fight them in 16 days.'" Armstrong, elated, left Eaker's office "whooping and hollering." When asked what was going on, Armstrong replied, "I'm going to combat!"

Overhauling the 97th Bomb Group was a challenging assignment. "Many 97th men had received little training in the duties they would have to perform," related author Roger Freeman. "The basic concepts of high altitude precision bombing had been established back in the U.S. but putting them into practice in Europe involved much trial and error." Historian Martin Bowman outlined the difficulties involved in gearing up for this new kind of combat. "Some air gunners had little or no training in aerial gunnery, some radio operators could not send or receive Morse code and the pilots were not versed in high altitude and formation flying. Many crews, untrained as they were, had only just got to know one another when they were pitched headlong into an air war America thought she could wage in daylight without escort."

After two weeks of training and three postponements, the 97th flew the first American daylight mission over enemy-held territory. On Monday, 17 August 1942, twelve B-17s bombed the railroad marshaling yards at Rouen-Sotteville in northwestern France, while another half dozen bombers flew diversion to St. Omer. Brig. Gen. Eaker flew on the mission as well, aboard the B-17 *Yankee Doodle*. Armstrong, who had not yet been checked out in the B-17, rode as mission commander in the co-pilot's seat of an aircraft politely named *Butcher Shop*. The pilot was Maj. Paul Tibbets, who would later command the B-29 *Enola Gay* as it dropped the first atomic bomb over Hiroshima, Japan.

Protected by four squadrons of Spitfires from the Royal Air Force, Armstrong and his group of B-17s dropped 18 tons of ordnance on their target from an altitude of 23,000 feet. Armstrong's friend Sy Bartlett accompanied him in *Butcher Shop* and was allowed to toggle the first load of bombs. The 97th returned to base with all crews and aircraft intact. Armstrong was thrilled, saying, "We ruined Rouen." Maj. Tibbets elaborated: "A feeling of elation took hold of us as we winged back across the Channel. All the tension was gone. We were no longer novices at this terrible game of war. We had braved the enemy in his own skies and were alive to tell people about it."

Armstrong's work at the 97th Bomb Group foreshadowed his future responsibilities with the 306th. As author Martin Bowman noted, "Col. Armstrong, ably supported by men such as Maj. Paul Tibbets, took the group apart and put it together again in a matter of little more than two weeks." In his 1945 book *I've Had It: The Survival of a Bomb Group Commander*, Beirne Lay praised Armstrong's talents: "As C.O. of the 97th Bomb Group, Col. Armstrong, considered by many to be the most highly skilled natural-born pilot ever to wear Army wings, created a precedent of hard-hitting personal leadership on the ground and in the air that has set the pace for all the heavy bomb group commanders who followed him—a small band of men whose capacity for command under conditions of unparalleled technical complexity, physical strain and mortal hazard has never been equaled."

Five more missions followed the initial one to Rouen, all with Armstrong at the helm. Unfortunately, his tenure at the 97th would be cut short when the group departed to support the invasion of North Africa. Armstrong and his wealth of experience were still needed in Europe. So on 27 September 1942, he left the 97th Bomb Group and returned to the staff of Bomber Command at High Wycombe.

On New Year's Day 1943, Armstrong was 40 years old and again flying a desk at headquarters. He was not happy to be pushing paper when people all around him were going on combat missions. Fortunately, Gen. Eaker had another special assignment for him: overhaul the 306th Bombardment Group at Thurleigh. Eaker asked Armstrong to do it as a favor, and told him that the posting would earn him a promotion to Brigadier General. Armstrong accepted the challenge and spent about six weeks in command of the 306th, from 4 January through 17 February 1943. Despite the 306th Bomb Group's poor reputation with Bomber Command, Armstrong privately thought of the unit as "a sharp outfit with an excellent record." While group discipline improved under his leadership, combat performance wouldn't get better until after Armstrong's departure. As an interim leader, Armstrong was able to bring the group out of the doldrums. "Frank Armstrong was the kind of tough leader that was needed to turn the situation around," remembered John Lambert, "and that is exactly what happened as a natural consequence of his taking command in January of 1943. I do not remember any one thing that he did to get these results. He was just a good combat commander who inspired confidence and, to a man, the group quickly shaped up under his leadership."

Other members of the 306th Bomb Group agreed. "In anticipation of Col. Armstrong's arrival it was felt that he would be much tougher than Col. Overacker," said Eugene Pollock. "But maybe that was needed. Col. Armstrong got us all together and let us know that he expected professional performance from all of us. He showed us rather than telling us, and always seemed interested in why something happened." Andy Vangalis noted that "he did get the group to realize this was going to be a rough war and it was going to be deadly, and that was the only way to see it." John Regan echoed the feeling: "Under Armstrong I think we did better, and if not liked as well as Overacker, at least he was respected."

Casualty totals at the 306th did not change significantly during Armstrong's time at the helm. As Jack Ryan noted, "While Armstrong was the Group C.O., the Group flew seven missions. One was a complete weather abort, one a higher headquarters directed recall, two were flown without any losses, and two were flown with two losses per mission. Our aircraft inventory continued to decline from losses and beyond-repair battle damage."

In August 1942, Armstrong had led a dozen B-17s into Rouen, France, on the Eighth Air Force's first bombing mission over occupied Europe. Five months later, Armstrong spearheaded another historic mission, this time against the U-boat center at Wilhelmshaven. It was the first American heavy bombing raid on Germany, and it took place on 27 January 1943. Sixteen B-17s from the 306th Bombardment Group led the formation. According to 306th veteran Martin Kilcoyne, "The Luftwaffe was bunched in Western France to meet the expected [American] raids. Eaker sent his force around the flank, over the empty North Sea, and into the thinly defended German rear. Armstrong's tactical handling of the raid was ably done as he quickly adjusted to changing conditions over the Weser River, switched from primary Vegesack to secondary Wilhelmshaven, and struck under poor conditions with satisfactory results. The 306th and its men were the weapons with which the colonel achieved this life-saving success."

Despite his tough brand of leadership, Armstrong also had a soft side. Wrote Roger Freeman, "To his compatriots he was a personable, soft-spoken genial man with a sense of humor, enthusiastic and firm in his duties. What many did not sense or see was that he was a very sentimental man, particularly with regard to a longing to be reunited with his wife and son." In fact, Armstrong even carried his son's baby shoes with him on missions.

(National Archives)

Col. Claude Putnam gives the aircrews their early-morning mission brief, March 1944. Putnam took charge of the 306th Bombardment Group after Frank Armstrong's departure.

After several more staff jobs with the Eighth Air Force in England, Armstrong returned to the United States in August 1943 to train airmen for combat overseas. He commanded bomber training wings at Dalhart, Texas; Ardmore, Oklahoma; and Colorado Springs, Colorado. According to John McKee, during that time Armstrong "surrounded himself with as many ex-306th people as he could." In November 1944 Armstrong was given the reins of the new 315th Bomb Wing at Peterson Field, Colorado, a unit that flew the B-29 Superfortress. Six months of preparation and training followed. In May 1945 the unit moved to the island of Guam in the Pacific, where it staged bombing raids over Japanese territory. Armstrong was tasked with destroying 10 different Japanese oil refineries. In August he led a raid on Honshu, Japan, that was another first for the record books: it was the longest bombing mission against the Japanese, flown with very heavy bomb loads and without extra fuel tanks to extend the B-29's range. Armstrong could now claim the distinction of leading the first and last heavy bombing missions of World War II.

In *12 O'Clock High*, authors Beirne Lay and Sy Bartlett named their main character "Frank Savage." The character's first name, of course, was also Armstrong's. J. Robert Nolley, a childhood friend of Armstrong, noted that since Armstrong's heritage included some Native American blood, Lay and Bartlett decided to use "Savage" for their character's last name. Armstrong also served as an unofficial editor for *12 O'Clock High*. The draft manuscript of the novel was reviewed and annotated by Armstrong on 18 October 1947, while he was an instructor at the Armed Forces Staff College in Norfolk, Virginia. Apparently Lay and Bartlett had included a little too much authenticity. When Armstrong returned his notes he had scribbled in the margin, "The book has been revised, eliminating much of the obscene language."

Unlike the character of Frank Savage in *12 O'Clock High*, Armstrong was a man of few words. Said one colleague, "When things get tough I'd rather have Frank Armstrong running the show than any officer I've ever known. Cucumbers could take lessons in coolness from him."

Flight Officer John Morgan – "Lieutenant Jesse Bishop"

At the beginning of *12 O'Clock High*, a B-17 mission is returning from the submarine pens at Lorient, France. One bomber, crippled and unable to lower its landing gear, crash-lands on its belly, skidding to a hard stop on the grassy airfield. As Stovall and Col. Davenport rush to the airplane, its pilot, Lt. McKesson, is brought out on a stretcher through the waist door. His head blasted to shreds by enemy gunfire, McKesson lashes out wildly, resisting the medical corpsmen's efforts to restrain him. As McKesson is placed in an ambulance, Davenport learns that the co-pilot of the bomber, Lt. Jesse Bishop, spent most of the mission fighting the crazed McKesson, who repeatedly tried to wrestle the aircraft controls away from his co-pilot. Bishop, who had to break McKesson's leg to free him from the damaged flight deck, is completely stunned from the experience. He bypasses the post-flight debriefing and heads to the Officers' Club to drown his sorrows. While there, Bishop is accosted by a public relations flack who, oblivious to the young pilot's despair, chirps, "He's due for a Medal of Honor. Boy, what a story!"

The true-life counterpart to that scene in *12 O'Clock High* was just as dramatic. The pilot upon whom the character of Jesse Bishop was based, Flight Officer John Cary Morgan, was indeed awarded the Medal of Honor for his actions. According to author Roger Freeman in his book *The Mighty Eighth* (a term that Freeman coined), the story of Morgan's courage "ranks high in the annals of the Eighth; indeed it has become legend."

When he was rejected by the U.S. Army due to an old injury, six-foot-two Texan John Morgan traveled north to volunteer with the Royal Canadian Air Force. After seven months in the RCAF, he was transferred as a replacement pilot to the

John C. "Red" Morgan, B-17 co-pilot and recipient of the Medal of Honor for a harrowing mission to Hanover, Germany, on 26 July 1943.

Army Air Force's 92nd Bomb Group at Alconbury, England. In late July 1943, Brig. Gen. Ira Eaker ordered a sustained bomber offensive, labeled "Blitz Week," on German positions. On 26 July 1943, the third day of "Blitz Week," 92 B-17s fought poor weather on their way to the Continental Gummi Werke, a rubber and tire factory in Hanover, Germany. Flight Officer John Morgan was flying his first mission as a B-17 co-pilot in *Ruthie II* when fate would make him a hero.

About 15 to 20 minutes from reaching the coast of Germany, a fierce frontal attack by German Fw 190 fighters pummeled the flight deck of the *Ruthie II* with a hail of bullets. According to the official Army account, "the first pass knocked out the oxygen system to the waist, tail, and radio positions. A moment later, a frontal attack from out of the sun at two o'clock put a 20-millimeter and a .30-caliber shell through the windshield on the pilot's side, totally shattering it." First Lieutenant Robert Campbell, the pilot, slumped over the controls as the gunfire sheared off the back of his head. Campbell regained consciousness, but his severe injury made him delirious. He grabbed at the wheel, trying to take back control of the airplane from Morgan, his co-pilot. Morgan forced Campbell away, but it was no easy task. Campbell was a "six foot, 185 pound, heavily-muscled man." For the remainder of the mission, Morgan fought to keep the disoriented Campbell off the controls of the B-17, and brought *Ruthie II* safely home.

Radioman aboard a B-17F switching on a camera intervalometer, which snapped mission photos at regular intervals.

One of *Ruthie's* waist gunners, Eugene Ponte, recalled the details of the mission for National Public Radio in 1991.

"The plane was entering the coast of Germany. Our first attack came around seven o'clock and scattered 20-millimeter shells around the waist compartment, knocking out our oxygen system, and four of the gunners subsequently passed out, including me.

"The second attack came about two o'clock high. One shell, 20-millimeter, came through the co-pilot's window and hit the pilot in the back of the head behind the ear and severed the whole back of his head. He became unconscious for a short time and then recovered himself and continued to try to fly the plane. Morgan took over the controls and flew in formation for approximately two hours, holding the pilot off of his controls and taking severe punishment from the pilot, who was trying to fly the plane and fight John Morgan at the same time.

"[The pilot's behavior] was an automatic reflex, we presume, and he kept trying to grab the controls or else swing at John and hit John in the face and chest and the whole front of his body was black and blue from bruises from the pilot. And we went in, bombed the target and returned."

Unable to see the sky ahead due to the shattered windshield, Morgan realized he needed to move to the pilot's seat in order to land the aircraft. Morgan, navigator 2nd Lt. Keith Koske, and one of the recovered gunners forced Campbell down into the nose section of the B-17, where Koske restrained him. Ninety minutes later, with the help of tail gunner Staff Sgt. John Foley, Morgan was able to bring the crippled aircraft down safely at RAF Foulsham in Norfolk, England. Robert Campbell wasn't so lucky. His injuries finally overcame him, and he died soon after.

Also injured during the mission was the top turret gunner, Staff Sgt. Tyre C. Weaver. As recounted by writer Richard Franks many years later, "His arm was

Scene from the film version of *12 O'Clock High*: "Doc" Kaiser meets the crew of a damaged B-17 that bellied in. The first action sequence in the film adapts the real-life story of John Morgan and the crew of *Ruthie II*.

blown off at the shoulder when a cannon shell smashed through the top gunner's turret, and he started to lose a lot of blood." Weaver also had a wound in his side from a .30-caliber bullet. Lt. Koske tended to Weaver. Realizing that prompt medical attention might save Weaver's life, Koske parachuted him out of the plane at 24,500 feet over enemy territory, approximately 25 miles west of Hanover, Germany. A nine-year-old girl found Weaver lying in a field. He spent a year and a half in a German hospital and was returned to the United States in a casualty exchange. The incident was fictionalized for a brief mention in *12 O'Clock High*: after the B-17 barrels in for a belly landing, Maj. Stovall examines the interior and finds a severed arm inside.

On 6 March 1944, eight months after the Hanover mission that won him the Medal of Honor, Morgan was on a bombing mission over Berlin—ironically, his 25th and final flight before heading back to the United States—when his B-17 was shot down. Remembered Eugene Ponte: "He was blown out of the airplane, and he had the [parachute] chest pack under his arm, and he couldn't get it hooked." Luckily, Morgan was able to connect the pack to his chest harness and pull the ripcord in time. He was captured and spent the remainder of the war as a POW.

Looking back years later, Morgan was modest about his wartime experiences. In his book *First of the Many*, Tex McCrary, a public relations officer with the Eighth Air Force during the war, noted that Morgan "got pretty sore about one hit-and-run correspondent who wrote an article about him for an American magazine, talking about how he was a son of rich parents, a New York playboy brought up in the Stork Club, and a lot of stuff about how he 'faced the supreme test with courage because he was an American boy.' If you talk to him about the trip for which he was awarded the Congressional Medal of Honor, the only story you'll get is the story of his navigator. He doesn't like to talk about himself."

After the war ended, Morgan returned to the Texaco Oil Company, where he had gotten his start as a truck driver prior to the war. He spent the next 42 years there selling aviation fuel. Morgan died on 17 January 1991 at Midlands Hospital in Papillion, Nebraska, of a heart attack. He was 76 years old.

"The boys who will win this war," said Morgan in a wartime interview, "are the ones who make the tough decision quick, and correct." In retrospect, it was quite fitting that Morgan flew with the 92nd Bomb Group. Its motto was "Fame's Favored Few."

Sergeant Donald Bevan – "Sergeant McIllhenny"

Comic relief in *12 O'Clock High* is provided by Gen. Savage's hapless clerk and driver, Sergeant McIllhenny. Always getting caught doing something improper— stowing away on a mission, going shirtless while on duty, "knocking up" his girlfriend—McIllhenny is repeatedly demoted by Savage to buck private, only to be promoted back to his sergeant's rank soon after. Military catch-22s fuel the humor. Savage's driver can't be a private, so McIllhenny gets his sergeant stripes back. After being busted for stowing away on a mission, McIllhenny is reinstated once again when Savage finds out that his clerk's dead-on shooting has made him an ace. At one point, a frustrated Savage tells McIlhenny, "Maybe you'd better get [chevrons] with zippers!"

The character of Sgt. McIllhenny was based on a self-described "artist and sometime driver" in the 306th named Donald Bevan. Although he wasn't a clerk like McIllhenny, Bevan was there to see Frank Armstrong rebuild the group. "I was there when the general arrived," said Bevan. "I sketched his picture for the combat hut wall and got shot down on the raid that climaxes the film."

Bevan was unaware of his personal link to *12 O'Clock High* until he saw the film on late night television years after its original release. He realized that the story was about his old bomb group and recognized a shadow of himself in the character of Sgt. McIllhenny. Noted Bevan, "What identifies the character with me, a non-combatant, is that he rides as stowaway on the first bombing raid over Germany and somehow gets behind a gun to shoot down a couple of enemy fighters. Something like that happened once in the Eighth to me that got quite a bit of press exposure." While Bevan was never a stowaway, he did fly the mission and earned several kills as a waist gunner in the B-17.

An artist for the *New York Daily News* before the war, Bevan had been trained as an armorer and was assigned to the 423rd Squadron of the 306th Bomb Group under the command of Maj. James Wilson. When he learned of Bevan's artistic talent, Wilson lent Bevan his office as a studio and had him sketch squadron personnel to feature on the walls of their combat hut. When Col. Frank

Armstrong arrived to take charge of the 306th in January 1943, Wilson escorted Bevan to the front office to sketch the new group commander. "When I went in," remembered Bevan, "Armstrong was sitting with [actor] Gene Raymond, who was an aircraft recognition officer. They were sitting there in their trench coats with hats on. It was all very Hollywood!"

Bevan also became Wilson's aide of sorts. "Every now and then he'd say, 'C'mon, Bevan, drive me out to wherever." One day Wilson grabbed Bevan to fly in a B-17 during a target practice mission. The squadron's gunners were still new to their jobs and "were firing crazy at the tow target," remembered Bevan. Wilson escorted Bevan to a waist gun position and told him to take a shot. Bevan triggered the .50-caliber machine gun and punched a hole in the target on his first attempt. Wilson quickly anointed Bevan as a B-17 crewmember, and from that day the young Sergeant would fly missions as a waist gunner—17 in all. Bevan's combat indoctrination occurred on a mission to the Luftwaffe base at Romilly-sur-Seine, France, on 12 December 1942. Another crewmember was under the weather, and Bevan volunteered to go in his place. Heavy cloud cover obscured the primary target so the 303rd and 306th Bomb Groups headed for the secondary, the marshaling yards at Rouen. During heavy Luftwaffe fighter attacks, Bevan proved his mettle. His story was reported in the *New York Times:*

> One United States bomber was credited with shooting down four Nazis. This plane

1st Air Hero 'Stowaway' Lost in Raid

By GRAHAM MILLER
London, May 5.—Staff Sergt. Donald Bevan, former New York News artist who put

Sergt. Donald Bevan
Missing in Bremen raid.

aside his brushes to learn aerial machine gunning, has been missing since his Flying Fortress took part in a raid on Bremen on April 17, it was learned today.

His plane was one of the 16 which did not return, and it is not yet known whether he was one of those seen parachuting to ground in enemy territory.

'Luckiest Leave.'

Only two weeks before his last raid Bevan, 22-year-old son of Mr. and Mrs. Walter L. Bevan of Springfield, Mass., sent a message

Newspaper story from 6 May 1943 on Staff Sgt. Donald Bevan, the inspiration for Sgt. McIllhenny in *12 O'Clock High.* Bevan wasn't really a stowaway, but McIllhenny sure was!

was piloted by First Lieutenant Robert Riordan of Houston, Texas, who recently brought a Flying Fortress [*Wahoo*] back from over France so badly shot up that King George, who inspected it, said admiringly that "I don't see how you did it."

> Substituting for a gunner of the plane who had been taken ill, Sgt. Donald Bevan of Springfield, Mass., got his first chance to fire at a real target. He blew up a Focke-Wulf 190 in mid-air as the German menaced the Fortress . . .

Airmen of the 306th Bomb Group enjoy a game of cards, 1944.

Sgt. Bevan's gun jammed and he calmly primed it time and again while the Nazi flier was blazing away at him. When his gun finally started working, Sgt. Bevan got in his aim with deadly accuracy at close range.

Years after the war, while watching *12 O'Clock High* on television, Bevan was intrigued that he might be the inspiration for the character of Sgt. McIllhenny. He wrote to Sy Bartlett, who happened to be a friend of his in-laws. Bartlett had at one time dated actress Nancy Carroll, mother of Patricia Kirkland, who was Bevan's wife. The legal-savvy Bartlett, knowing that it never paid to reveal his sources, didn't answer the question directly but replied that during his time in the Eighth Air Force had had seen "a lot of Maj. James Wilson and Capt. Mack McKay." Now Bevan was positive that he was the model for the Sgt. McIllhenny character. Wilson, McKay, and Bevan had served together in the 423rd Bomb Squadron.

In another interesting coincidence, Bevan was later shot down over Bremen, Germany, and spent two years in Stalag 17B, a German POW camp located alongside the Danube River in Austria. Over 4200 enlisted men were interned in the camp's five compounds. One of Bevan's bunkmates was Staff Sgt. Tyre Weaver, the top-turret gunner who lost his arm and was parachuted out of the *Ruthie II* during the mission for which John Morgan was awarded the Medal of Honor.

During his time at Stalag 17B, Bevan ran a makeshift theatre troupe to entertain his fellow POWs. He wrote, performed, and painted scenery for the productions. Another POW, Edmund Trzcinski, arrived at the camp a year after Bevan. The two men struck up a friendship and formed a comedy team. One night Bevan and Trzcinski stayed up too late and blew the camp curfew. Stuck overnight in the barracks that served as their makeshift theatre, they began writing. "Let's write something for Broadway," said Bevan half-jokingly. That night the two men created characters and a rough plot outline about their experiences in the German prison camp. The project sat on the shelf until after the war, when Bevan and Trczinski spent a week on vacation in Cape Cod, Massachusetts, and cranked out 70 pages of what would become one of the most recognizable WWII productions ever: the stage play *Stalag 17*. *Stalag 17* began its run on Broadway in May 1951 and continued for 472 performances. The film version starred William Holden and was released by Paramount Pictures in July 1953.

THE REGENSBURG-SCHWEINFURT RAID

On 17 August 1942, the embryonic Eighth Air Force carried out its very first bombing mission over Europe. During that mission, the 97th Bomb Group, led by Col. Frank Armstrong, targeted the German marshaling yards at Rouen, France. Exactly one year later, a much stronger Eighth took part in a two-pronged mission to cripple German fighter production. While the 1st Bomb Wing attacked the ball-bearing plants at Schweinfurt, the 4th Bomb Wing simultaneously tackled the Messerschmitt factory at Regensburg. Because it occurred exactly one year after the Eighth's very first mission, the Regensburg-Schweinfurt double-strike was known as "The Anniversary Raid."

That famous mission was a key plot point in *12 O'Clock High*. In fact, Chapter 11 was all about the Regensburg raid. In the novel, Gen. Frank Savage is ordered to fly the mission because of its propaganda value, despite bad weather and countless delays. Co-author Beirne Lay named Savage's airplane the *Picadilly Lily* in honor of the B-17 he had flown in during the Regensburg mission. The aircraft commander was a Captain named Thomas Murphy, whom Lay called "a steady Irishman . . . with whom I had flown before." Lay described the *Lily* as "sinister and complacent, squatting on her fat tires with scarcely a hole in her skin to show for the 12 raids behind her."

Following the Regensburg mission of 17 August 1943, the crew of the *Picadilly Lily* poses for a photograph. Beirne Lay, who rode as an observer, is second from left in the back row.

In reality, the *Picadilly Lily* would survive only another two months after the Regensburg mission. The aircraft met a horrifying end during a mission to Bremen, Germany, on 8 October 1943. On that day, the *Lily* was flying lead in the low squadron of the 100th Bomb Group. Capt. Murphy was on his 24th mission. One more and he would complete his combat tour. John Luckadoo, a 100th Bomb Group veteran, was piloting another aircraft in the formation and recalled what happened next: "On the bomb run, I noticed out of the corner of my eye that a flight of two Fw 190s was attacking us from 11 o'clock and level with our squadron formation. Our gunners were pouring out lead as fast as they could to try and fend them off. Nevertheless, they barreled right through the formation without wavering and the lead pilot, either already dead or grossly miscalculating, collided in mid-air with the *Picadilly Lily* directly in front of me. Others in the formation were also taking devastating fire from flak and fighters and began falling out of formation like flies. I moved up to take over the squadron as Murphy began spiraling down and then exploded shortly after about half the crew bailed out."

The post-mission report stated that the *Lily* had been crippled by enemy flak near the navigator's station and the flight deck. Then the number-three engine suddenly caught fire. "Witnesses indicate the *Lily* entered a near vertical nose-down attitude and exploded." Five crewmembers survived the ordeal; the bodies of the other five were buried in Wesermünde, Germany.

GENERAL SAVAGE'S BREAKDOWN AND THE PSYCHOLOGY OF AIR COMBAT

Despite rumors to the contrary, Gen. Savage's crack-up in *12 O'Clock High* wasn't based on any particular incident that occurred during the war. Author Martin Bowman speculated that Beirne Lay based the incident on the rocky experiences of Brig. Gen. Newton Longfellow, an old friend whom Ira Eaker appointed as commander of the 1st Bomb Wing on 21 August 1942. Three days later, while flying orientation with Maj. Paul Tibbets during a B-17 mission to Le Trait, France, Longfellow panicked when German fighters tore apart the flight deck with 20-millimeter fire. Fighting the General away from the controls, an injured Tibbets finally had to knock Longfellow down to the floor. That December, after Eaker picked Longfellow to replace him at VIII Bomber Command, Longfellow handled the intense stress of the job poorly—"thin-faced, tense and irritable," noted James Parton, who served on the headquarters staff. Longfellow's brusque manner earned him the nickname "Screaming Eagle."

By June of the following year, Longfellow was sent back to the United States to run training at Second Air Force, a job much less taxing than tackling policy and implementation for combat groups. Eaker, who believed that Longfellow had been the best choice available for the jobs he had given him, sent a recommendation letter to the commander of Second Air Force. "I really believe Longfellow will be a great help to you, as he was to me while here," Eaker wrote. "He is a tireless worker, and despite the fact we almost killed him off here working, or carrying the responsibility, for 24 hours a day, seven days a week, I believe he will spring back after a few weeks' rest and do a tremendous job for you and your Air Force."

Generals Ira Eaker and "Tooey" Spaatz in London, early 1944.

In addition to creating a daylight bombing strategy from scratch, the Eighth Air Force also had to map its way through uncharted psychological territory. How would aircrews react to combat, and what was the best way to deal with it? The medical community had to treat not only physical wounds, but also unfamiliar mental conditions that crewmen suffered during the war. These problems ranged from exhaustion to breakdowns like the one Gen. Savage experiences in *12 O'Clock High*.

In his book *The Eighth Air Force Story,* Kenn Rust related the story of a young man in the 306th Bomb Group whose hard-luck experiences were a good example of the combat stresses suffered by B-17 crews. During a mission, the 26-year-old found himself trapped in his gun turret, free-falling from 20,000 feet when his aircraft broke apart. He parachuted and landed safely, rushed over to the wreckage of his aircraft and tried to save one of his fellow crewmen, to no avail. Shaken with nightmares, he flew five more combat missions until the flight surgeon finally grounded him. "He was afraid he would be thought of as a 'quitter' and as 'yellow,'" wrote Rust. "Nothing was farther from the truth—he'd given all he had, taken all he could. He was one of many men, equally heroes, lost in the fight without actually falling to the enemy."

Beirne Lay echoed those thoughts in his *Saturday Evening Post* article about the Regensburg raid. Thirty-five minutes from the target, the 150 Fortresses in Lay's formation had already spent an hour being pounded by enemy flak and fighters. Twenty-four aircraft had been destroyed. "It appeared that our group was faced with extinction. I doubt if a man in the group visualized the possibility of our getting much farther without 100 percent loss. Gunners were becoming exhausted and nerve-tortured from the nagging strain—the strain that sends gunners and pilots to the rest home."

"When a flyer was undone by missions," recalled Harry Crosby of the 100th Bomb Group, "when he saw too many planes blow up in front of him, when his tail gunner was cut in two on a mission, when too many of his friends were killed, he sometimes quit. We did not call them 'cowards,' we called them 'combat failures.'"

In the film version of *12 O'Clock High*, Brig. Gen. Savage (Gregory Peck), wrestling with demons, breaks down on the flightline and is restrained by Col. Davenport (Gary Merrill) and Maj. Stovall (Dean Jagger).

"I still wonder about the residual damage to some of those combat men," said Dr. Thurman Shuller, the 306th's group surgeon. Some of the worst psychiatric problems were suffered by combat crewmen who, while hospitalized for a minor illness or ailment, learned that their crew had been shot down on a mission. The resulting feelings of guilt were only one of a number of unfamiliar combat-related psychiatric issues that Shuller and other doctors dealt with during the war. Air combat had never been experienced on such a huge scale before, and Army Air Force doctors had few precedents to follow. With the lives of the crews at stake, it was an unenviable type of on-the-job training.

The 306th Bomb Group battles enemy flak, c. 1944. This B-17 was positioned to the right of the lead aircraft in the formation. White bursts at upper right are from 105mm anti-aircraft guns, while the black bursts are 88mm "ack-ack."

Compounding the problem were the incredibly high losses suffered by the Eighth Air Force during the early part of the air war. After seven months in combat, the 306th Bomb Group had lost 20 of its original 35 crews, plus several replacement crews. Few of the airmen had even made it to 15 missions before being killed. "This would seem to indicate that the chance of surviving even 20 missions over German territory is very small," wrote Maj. Shuller at the time. The percentage of crewmen missing, killed, or wounded in action in the group's four flying squadrons averaged 61.5 percent.

A table prepared by Shuller on 21 April 1943 further highlighted the problem:

ORIGINAL OFFICERS ASSIGNED TO 306TH BOMB GROUP	SQUADRON			
	367TH	368TH	369TH	423RD
TOTAL FLIERS ENTERING COMBAT	34	41	34	38
TOTAL MIA, KIA, AND WIA	26	25	23	16
PERCENTAGE MIA, KIA, AND WIA	76%	61%	67%	42%
TOTAL FLIERS REMAIN ON COMBAT STATUS	6	9	11	16
PERCENTAGE FLIERS REMAINING	18%	22%	33%	42%
AVG NO. MISSIONS OF REMAINING FLIERS	16.6	15.3	15.8	17.1

Shuller summarized his statistics with a grim prediction: "It should be safe to estimate that no more than 5 to 10 percent of the officers of this Group can ever hope to reach 25 missions."

No one was more aware of the short life expectancy than the air crewmen themselves. "The fliers are now saying among themselves that the only apparent hope of survival in this theatre of war is either to become a prisoner of war or to get 'the jitters' and be removed from combat," wrote Shuller in a report to his group commander, Col. Claude Putnam. "This has brought about a state of morale that can soon become disastrous. One of our officers who has now been on 19 missions has already said that he is turning in his wings, if need be, after completing his 20th mission. And I dare say no board composed of non-combatant officers could have the nerve to suggest this officer is a coward or that he has not already served his country well."

Shuller's blunt report warned that the aircrews in the 306th were "on the verge of a complete psychological breakdown." Although Gen. Eaker had promised in September 1942 to establish a ceiling on the number of missions a crewman had to fly before returning stateside, it was now seven months later and no such directive had been issued. Shuller suggested that Bomber Command set the threshold at 20 missions, but noted that 15 missions "would be nearer the ideal." Just some sort of limit "would be an invaluable morale factor in giving these men at least a small hope for the future and a goal toward which to strive."

Col. Putnam endorsed Shuller's report and forwarded it to Bomber Command, where it caused a huge stir. Said Shuller, "I later learned that when that letter hit the desk of the Chief of Staff at Bomber Command, he was astonished that a lowly Major down in a Group would dare send such a communication to the General." But in the end, Shuller's efforts paid off. With more and more fresh replacement crews arriving in England, Eaker was finally able to establish a mission limit without running out of men to fly the aircraft. After discussing the matter with his staff, Eaker set the limit at 25 missions. This was five more than Shuller and his squadron surgeons had recommended, but finally gave the weary aircrews a goal.

A jubilant crew from the 306th Bomb Group celebrates the completion of 25 missions.

Ironically, when the numbers were calculated, the goal turned out to be impossible to achieve. According to Joseph Landers, a B-24 navigator who arrived in England in December 1943, "They told us we had to do 25 missions, and they said we could count on five percent losses each time. It didn't take a genius to figure out what that meant. Statistically you were dead. The funny part is you accept it. You're too busy to be scared." Landers beat the odds to fly a total of 32 missions.

"In the movie Doc Kaiser sought a meeting with Savage to report that the crews were exceeding their tolerance," recounted Shuller. "I never reported such to Armstrong, but I did discuss this subject with Putnam [his replacement] on several occasions." Shuller noted that "there were no guidelines that would apply to this particular situation because it had never existed before. We learned as we went along, by trial and error. We quickly discovered that the things we had learned in the School of Aviation Medicine did not necessarily apply to our situation in combat."

The connections between the novel 12 O'Clock High and real-life combat experiences strengthened the drama that Beirne Lay and Sy Bartlett packed into the pages of their book. Small wonder that 12 O'Clock High was lauded for its authenticity and grit. At times, truth could indeed be stranger than fiction. In the case of 12 O'Clock High, truth made very good fiction. But would it make a good movie? While they were writing their novel, Lay and Bartlett prepared material for a possible film adaptation. Neither of them was a stranger to motion pictures, having penned screenplays prior to the war. But would audiences buy tickets to see a serious, introspective combat film so soon after the war had ended?

THE MOTION PICTURE

"There wasn't a moment that we weren't determined to make a great movie."
—*Actor Robert Arthur, "Sgt. McIllhenny"*

In 1947, *12 O'Clock High* was a year away from being published as a novel when film producer Louis D. "Bud" Lighton convinced studio chief Darryl F. Zanuck of Twentieth Century-Fox that the story would make a good motion picture. The war years had set off an explosion of military-themed films. Would the public be ready for another one so soon after V-J Day? In addition, Zanuck was well aware that Metro-Goldwyn-Mayer was preparing a film for release the following year titled *Command Decision*. That picture, starring Clark Gable and Walter Pidgeon, was based on the novel and subsequent stage play by William Wister Haines, and dealt with high-level decisions in an Eighth Air Force bombardment group during World War II—a story very similar to *12 O'Clock High*.

So when Bud Lighton brought *12 O'Clock High* to Zanuck, the latter was reluctant to give it the green light. Coincidentally, Sy Bartlett knew both Bud Lighton at Fox and director William Wyler at Paramount. Among many other projects, Wyler had directed the postwar drama *The Best Years of Our Lives*.

Wyler had met Lay and Bartlett while stationed in England during the war. According to David Tallichet, a B-17 pilot with the 100th Bomb Group, "William Wyler was married to my sister. Willie knew Sy in the early part of the war in Hollywood when they were both civilians. Willie volunteered to join the military. He was over age, but they gave him a commission as a Major and sent him to England to do a propaganda movie. He pretty much had his choice as to what he wanted to do, and he wanted to do a movie on World War II bombers. Willie said to Sy Bartlett, 'Where's the most comfortable base?' Sy answered, "Well, Bassingbourn, the 91st Bombardment Group, is a permanent RAF station, and I think you'll like that better than these temporary stations that are springing up everywhere." Facilities at Bassingbourn were so nice that the base was affectionately known as "The Savoy." Wyler hooked up with Col. Stanley Wray, the commander of the 91st BG, who introduced him to pilot Robert Morgan. The resulting documentary film about Morgan's aircraft, *Memphis Belle*, was a wartime classic.

In early 1948, Beirne Lay and Sy Bartlett submitted a story treatment for *12 O'Clock High* to the studios through their agent, Nat Goldstone. Written as a dramatic narrative, the manuscript laid the groundwork for the proposed film project. At the end of the treatment, Bartlett and Lay added a "Production Note" to alleviate the studio's likely concern about the cost of recreating combat on the screen. "No expensive production problem is posed by the final air battle, the famous Schweinfurt-Regensburg mission, since the actual footage of this and other historic air battles is available not only in the Air Force library, but in Army pictures like *The Case of the Tremendous Trifle* and *Operation Titanic*. In addition, hundreds of thousands of feet of film pertinent to the activities of the Eighth Air Force, Ground and Air, are available in the War Department Film Libraries."

The authors also noted that they had taken dramatic license with the real Regensburg-Schweinfurt raid, setting it during early 1942. In real life, the mission was flown more than a year later. "The authors wish to point out that, for story purposes, they have departed from the actual date of the Eighth Air Force's anniversary mission, which was August 17, 1943, and that no delineation of actual commanders at the time of this mission is intended."

Sensing a good deal, Bartlett got both Bud Lighton and William Wyler interested in *12 O'Clock High,* and in no time the Fox and Paramount studios were fighting each other for the story rights. Noticing the heightened interest, Zanuck finally bought Lay and Bartlett's war story for Fox at a price of $100,000, a rather large sum at the time.

With *12 O'Clock High* moving into preproduction, it was time for Darryl Zanuck to select a producer and director for the project. Naturally he chose Bud Lighton as his producer. Lighton's résumé featured a number of war movies including the World War I silent feature *Wings* (1927) and *Test Pilot* (1938). Zanuck then tasked William Wellman with directing duties on *12 O'Clock High*. Like Lighton, Wellman was familiar with war pictures, having directed Lighton's script for *Wings*. Wellman had also helmed *The Public Enemy* (1931), *A Star is Born* (1937), *Thunderbirds* (1942), *The Ox-Bow Incident* (1943), and *The Story of G.I. Joe* (1945).

Next, Zanuck knew that to produce *12 O'Clock High* he would need technical assistance from the Air Force, which would lend its support and loan military equipment to the studio. It was time to phone the Pentagon.

THE AIR FORCE LOOKS AT *12 O'CLOCK HIGH*, SEPTEMBER 1947

At the Pentagon, chief responsibility for overseeing *12 O'Clock High* fell to Col. William P. Nuckols, deputy director of the Air Information Division in the Directorate of Public Relations. In an internal memo dated 29 September 1947, Nuckols' initial reaction to Twentieth Century-Fox's request for help was tepid at best. "*12 O'Clock High* is an interesting piece of fiction," wrote Nuckols. "Throughout *12 O'Clock High* there is a note of authenticity in the details. Likewise there is a note of improbability in the basic facts. Grounds for revocation of the dramatic license are numerous." Nuckols pulled no punches in his opinion of the story: "General Savage, a pugnacious, hard-driving combat pilot, who is impatient if not disdainful of senior staffs in general, takes over a run-down B-17 group. He sneers at his crews, at the wing staff, in fact at anyone or anything that attempts to stand between him and his mission of delivering bombs to the target."

Like Zanuck, Nuckols was concerned about similar films on the market and knew that MGM was readying *Command Decision* for release the following fall. Nuckols continued: "This is a story that has been told before in *Memphis Belle* from a documentary level and apparently will be told in *Command Decision* from a fictional level. It is more kind to the brass than *Command Decision,* if that is a point in its favor. Likewise it is less believable, perhaps for the same reason."

On 3 November, Fox's representative in Washington, D.C., Anthony Muto, submitted a studio synopsis of *12 O'Clock High* to the Pentagon. Muto asked the Air Force to help him obtain "motion picture footage of combat, particularly the Regensburg raid, briefing, maintenance, etc."

Two weeks later, despite his apparent dislike of *12 O'Clock High,* Col. Nuckols told Muto that the Air Force found the movie "of considerable interest." The Air Force would provide assistance to Twentieth Century-Fox, but only if the studio made some changes to the story. In the original treatment, the character of Gen. Ed Henderson, who would later be renamed Pritchard, was torn between his relationship with Col. Davenport and the need to replace Davenport in order to improve the 918th Bomb Group's combat performance. Wrote Col. Nuckols, "We realize that personal enmity existed within the service and will always continue. However, we do not believe that enmity would be carried to the extent of influencing operational policy to the detriment of a war effort."

Nuckols' other concern regarded a plot device that could trigger some bad publicity for the Pentagon. In the story synopsis, Gen. Henderson ordered the Regensburg raid to coincide with the anniversary of the Eighth Air Force's first mission over Germany. Nuckols asked that "official and/or strategic reasons" be used for the scheduling of the raid, rather than as a "grandstand play." According to Nuckols, "We sincerely do not believe that any General would actually order a mission to merely make 'anniversary' headlines. This story 'twist,' we believe, would be detrimental to the relationship between the Air Force and the public." But in real life, selection of the date was most likely a deliberate decision. Beirne Lay had written during the war that regarding the Regensburg mission, "One thing was sure: headquarters had dreamed up the biggest air operation to date to celebrate its birthday in the biggest league of aerial warfare."

The Air Force withheld its official approval of *12 O'Clock High* until a script was submitted and reviewed. But because Fox had cooperated smoothly with the Pentagon on previous films, the Air Force was willing to allow some preliminary assistance. In late November 1947, Fox was cleared to send film editor Robert Miles to the Air Force Central Film Depository at Wright Field, in Dayton, Ohio (now Wright-Patterson Air Force Base). Miles was told to examine whatever combat film footage was available there. After some digging, he selected two Army Air Force films, *Target for Today* and *Operation Titanic,* for possible use in *12 O'Clock High.* At the studio's request, the Air Force would provide two 35-millimeter prints of each film, with reproduction costs paid by Twentieth Century-Fox.

THE PROCESS SLOWS DOWN, DECEMBER 1947 – AUGUST 1948

Meanwhile, Sy Bartlett, Beirne Lay, and producer Bud Lighton labored over the initial draft script of *12 O'Clock High,* a process that would take eight months. While waiting for the script, the Air Force provided Fox with copies of the requested 25,000 feet of film that Robert Miles had chosen at Wright Field.

At Twentieth Century-Fox, the creative staff kicked off preproduction planning. Interiors, including scenes inside the B-17 Flying Fortress, would be shot at the Fox facilities in Hollywood, California. For exteriors, the location department searched for a site that could double as a World War II English airfield. What type of location was needed? According to the studio, "The surrounding terrain should be similar to that of east-central England (flat to rolling, with some forestation and intensive cultivation), and the field itself should be of the combat type with three runways, parallel taxi strips, and well-dispersed hard stands."

At first, Twentieth Century-Fox selected the Santa Maria City Airport to represent the 918th Bomb Group's airbase. The airport was situated halfway between Los Angeles and San Francisco in central California. Built by the Army Corps of Engineers in 1942, Santa Maria Army Air Base had been a training site for ground support personnel and P-38 aircrews during World War II. After the war, the field was turned over to the county of Santa Barbara and became a municipal airport. Fox wanted to launch and land B-17s on the field, and the 5100-foot runway would suit things perfectly. Since only two scheduled flights departed the airport each day, the studio felt that local air traffic wouldn't be inconvenienced during filming.

On 26 July 1948, Lay and Bartlett finished their "first draft continuity" script for Fox. After some revision, the true "first draft" was completed on 17 September. The studio would wait until another version was completed before sending the script to the Air Force for review.

In the meantime, Twentieth Century-Fox asked the Air Force to supply equipment and facilities to help recreate its World War II airbase for *12 O'Clock High*. On 17 September, the same day he received the first draft script for the film, studio chief Darryl Zanuck leapfrogged the entire military chain of command and wrote directly to Gen. Hoyt S. Vandenberg, the Air Force Chief of Staff. In an enthusiastic and name-dropping two-page letter, Zanuck gently prodded Vandenberg for help. "I have just returned from a trip to Europe and I am preparing to select my one personal film production for the year," wrote Zanuck. "My associates have told me of the unsolicited interest that has been shown in the project by General Spaatz, General Eaker and others. I am not certain but I think that indirectly the Secretary for Air has also evidenced interest in the story. Now frankly I do not know whether or not I am a fool to attempt this project at this time. It will call for an investment of approximately $2,000,000 at a time when the national box office has slumped and when most producers are looking for the so-called sure-fire box office entertainment."

Continued Zanuck, "There is no doubt in my mind that unquestionably it can serve as tremendous propaganda to stimulate interest in the Air Force. If I decide to go ahead with the project, I will have to have wholehearted cooperation from the Air Force. I can get by with eight or 12 B-17s. Does the Air Force want this film made and do they share our feeling that it will contribute to the Air Force? Perhaps I am presuming on our friendship to address this letter to you but I feel very deeply about the subject and I really have the desire to make it." Careful about the impression he was giving, Zanuck hastened to add, "If I am out of the channels, please do not hesitate to tell me so."

Fortunately, Gen. Vandenberg was interested. He quickly dispatched a letter to Zanuck via teletypewriter. "Your letter in regard to the production of *12 O'Clock High* is most interesting. I have discussed your problem with Mr. Stephen Leo, our Director of Public Relations. He assures me that he will give the matter his personal attention." However, Vandenberg's help was conditional.

He reminded Zanuck that the Air Force was still waiting on a screenplay to read.

While anticipating the arrival of a script, the Air Force checked on the availability of operational B-17 aircraft and Quonset huts, the workhorse semi-cylindrical buildings that housed everything from supplies to personnel to offices. Although the events in *12 O'Clock High* were set just five years in the past, the Air Force had changed considerably since the end of World War II. The National Security Act of 1947 had reorganized the Army Air Forces into a separate Department of the Air Force, on equal footing with the Army and Navy. Wartime technology was rapidly becoming outdated, and the venerable B-17 was no longer of practical use for aerial bombing. Some of the aircraft had been sold as surplus and were living second lives as transports, target drones, and drone controllers. The remaining B-17s on the military rolls were dwindling, dispersed to 85 different locations. During its initial search for B-17s to use in the *12 O'Clock High* project, the Air Force located several useable B-17s and Quonset huts at MacDill AFB near Tampa, Florida. It was a good start.

Revising the First Draft Script, September 1948

On 23 September 1948, Darryl Zanuck finished reviewing the first draft screenplay of *12 O'Clock High* and sent a memo to producer Bud Lighton and director William Wellman. Zanuck was enthusiastic about the project but noted that a lot of work remained to be done.

Dialogue was a big concern. Zanuck knew that some of the scriptwriters' wordy passages would be trimmed, and he wasn't too worried about that. But he *was* concerned about phony-sounding lines. In one scene, Nazi propagandist Lord Haw Haw teased the 918th Bomb Group during his radio broadcast that its clock was inaccurate. Zanuck felt the scene "smacks of spy drama." He also asked for changes in Gen. Savage's thundering introductory speech to his men ("Consider yourselves already dead!"). Originally the speech was written in a highly patriotic fashion. "We're fighting because we don't want barbed wire," said Savage. Concerned that postwar audiences wouldn't warm to such rhetoric, Zanuck instructed the writers to "take out the pep talk and the patriotic lecture and make it crisp and to the point."

Zanuck's opinions about realism extended to several other scenes as well. When Savage first arrived at the 918th Bomb Group, he stepped into the Operations Room and, finding it disorganized and strewn with garbage, cleaned it up by blasting the floor with a fire hose. Zanuck threw the scene out, saying, "This looked like playing soldier." A later scene had Savage dressing down Ben Gately, the air executive officer, for not helping Col. Davenport run the 918th more effectively. As originally written, the furious Savage said he hated Gately "worse than a Nazi." The dialogue was transferred directly from the novel, but Zanuck wanted it soft-pedaled so that Savage didn't sound too "boy-scoutish." On the other hand, the film couldn't be *too* realistic, and Zanuck was well aware that some of the harsher pictures of war had to be left out. "We must be terrifically careful in showing gruesome details of injuries," he wrote. After all, the film needed to pass the Motion Picture Production Code to be deemed suitable for release.

Beirne Lay and Sy Bartlett worked closely with producer Bud Lighton during the rewriting process, and credited him with helping them reshape and focus the story according to Zanuck's instructions. As Lay recalled later, at one point Lighton asked the two authors to define the central idea of *12 O'Clock High*. "We each gave him our answers," said Lay, "and he said, 'Well, Christ, fellows, you're going all over the place here. Give me something you can put down in a paragraph, or preferably in a line, or even four words.'" At that point, Lay and Bartlett decided to make Savage's breakdown the main point of the story. Lighton agreed, telling them, "I don't want one inch of film that does not contribute to telling that central idea."

Finally, Zanuck ordered that any romantic storylines be deleted. Lay and Bartlett had included Gen. Savage's courtship of RAF Flight Lieutenant Pamela Mallory, a subplot from the original novel. But Zanuck felt that a love interest would detract from the main story. "She belongs in this picture about as much as a Mack Sennett comedy cop belongs in it," he grumbled. With a stroke of the pen, *12 O'Clock High* lost its only female cast member except for a few background extras and a Red Cross nurse.

THE AIR FORCE FINALLY RECEIVES A SCRIPT FOR REVIEW, OCTOBER 1948

Lay and Bartlett's new draft of *12 O'Clock High* landed at Twentieth Century-Fox on 18 October 1948. That same day, the studio rushed a copy to the Air Force via Fox representative Anthony Muto in Washington, D.C. More copies would be forthcoming. "It so happens," wrote Muto to the Air Force, "that the copy of the script which I am giving you is Darryl Zanuck's own personal copy." At the time, actors being considered for the film included Gregory Peck, Dana Andrews, Cornel Wilde, Mark Stevens, and Lee J. Cobb. Peck was the only star on the list who would actually appear in the film.

Fox also sent a copy of the screenplay to the Motion Picture Association of America (MPAA), the industry's self-regulating trade association. MPAA would provide suggestions and ensure that Fox met the requirements set by its Production Code. On 25 October, MPAA asked Fox to make several minor changes. "We have read the script for your proposed production," wrote Joseph Breen, Vice President and Director of the Production Code Administration, "and are happy to tell you that the basic story seems to meet the requirements of the Production Code."

However, MPAA targeted two lines of dialogue that it deemed objectionable. In one scene, a frustrated Col. Davenport exclaimed, "They can take England and ram it"—a line that MPAA asked to be modified. Elsewhere in the script, MPAA asked that a line where a character exclaimed, "son-of-a-. . ." be removed.

MPAA also cautioned that any nose art on the B-17 aircraft featured in the film should be tasteful, and that "while most of the drinking in this picture seems legitimate," several scenes could do without it. "We question the necessity of introducing liquor and respectfully suggest that some other business be provided."

During the next month, the Air Force public relations division reviewed the script while preproduction continued at Twentieth Century-Fox. The U.S. Navy dismantled and transferred 12 Quonset huts from its base at Port Hueneme, California, to the Eighth Air Force, which would loan the equipment to the studio. In Beverly Hills, the Associated Motion Picture Pilots heard about *12 O'Clock High* and offered their services to the production. Chartered in 1931, the organization was comprised of pilots who performed in motion pictures. "There are civilian-owned B-17s available for use in *12 O'Clock High* which would provide employment for members of [our organization]," wrote AMPP President E.H. Robinson. Because the Air Force was slated to provide aircraft and pilots for the film, the studio declined AMPP's offer.

In mid-November 1948, the Air Force sent Fox its notes on the draft screenplay. In a letter to Anthony Muto, Col. William Nuckols stated that "no objections are interposed on the grounds of military security." However, the Air Force did list "several items which we would appreciate having changed." Nuckols' greatest concern was the heavy use of alcohol by the commanding officers in the film. While Nuckols didn't ask that the characters be teetotalers, "the use of liquor in innumerable scenes might create an unfavorable public reaction by fostering a belief that the Air Force drank its way through combat and important decisions were made by officers while under the influence of liquor. Two ounces of liquor were given to combat crewmen after a mission. Otherwise, the use of liquor was not condoned during working hours." Nuckols cited several examples in the script including one in which he noted, "Coffee might serve as a nightcap here."

Also of concern to the Air Force was a scene in which a grounded B-17 was deliberately damaged to provide desperately needed spare parts for other aircraft. Again, Nuckols worried about "unfavorable public reaction" and suggested instead that a battle-damaged, inoperative B-17 be selected for "cannibalization," or stripping the airframe for parts.

For the scene in which Gen. Savage suffers a mental breakdown, the Air Force asked Fox to soften its approach. As originally written, Savage "burst out hysterically." The Air Force didn't want the public to think that real commanding officers would react that way. Wrote Col. Nuckols, "It seems that he would be more likely to break down with physical ailments, nervousness, short temper or just plain fatigue." Nuckols was also concerned about the behavior of the base chaplain. "We would prefer not to show the Chaplain actually playing poker as indicated in Scene #14. We believe that the idea that the Chaplain is one of the boys could be achieved if he is standing watching the game just as well as showing him participating in it."

Finally, Nuckols told Muto that the Air Force would provide a technical advisor if Fox wanted one, and that the studio needed to provide a "detailed list" of the materiel it wanted to borrow for the film. After Fox incorporated the Air Force's notes into the screenplay, Nuckols wanted to review it again. Solid cooperation between the military and the studio, said Nuckols, would result in "an outstanding film that will bring to the American people an accurate picture of our combat Air Force."

Fox's "wish list" of Air Force equipment, January 1949

Meanwhile, Twentieth Century-Fox was granted permission to use Santa Maria Airport for location shooting, with a tentative start date of 4 April 1949 for 12 days. Now the studio needed personnel and equipment to dress the outdoor set.

On 12 January 1949, Fox submitted its "wish list" to the Air Force. Titled *Requests for Air Force Personnel and Materiel*, the tremendously detailed document included specifics on runways and buildings; forms, maps, and photographs; personal flight equipment and uniforms; transport, armament, maintenance, and communications equipment; and B-17 aircraft. The studio had thoroughly considered each and every piece of equipment needed, even specifying numbers of dog tags and clipboards. For example, the following items were needed to outfit aircrews appearing in the film: 20 wristwatches, 150 oxygen masks, 130 Mae Wests (flotation vests), 160 parachutes, 160 parachute harnesses, 60 flak suits, 100 escape kits, 140 flight bags, and 60 pairs of sunglasses.

Because the airbase set would need to be populated with servicemen, costuming the film was a major undertaking. The studio asked the Air Force to provide surplus uniform parts in various sizes. These included khaki flying coveralls (36 total), brown leather zippered jackets (50), leather high-altitude helmets with earphones (50), mechanic's coveralls (50 pair), shoes (25 pair), winter wool undershirts (25), green issue socks (125 pair), and even hospital bathrobes (25).

Additional equipment was needed for set dressing. Fox requested the use of 12 Quonset huts, three ambulances, three staff cars, bomb carts, gasoline trucks, and two cleat-track tractors (tugs for towing aircraft). Dummy bombs were also needed, in 100-, 500-, and 1000-pound varieties. "To dress the field and to give the appearance of normal field activity," the studio asked for mechanics' stands, tool kits, fire extinguishers, and 100 wheel chocks. Under "Miscellaneous Items," the studio requested 30 units of K rations, Army flashlights, 10 slide rules, eight coal stoves, and 100 first aid kits. Another important consideration was the communications equipment, which included receivers and transmitters for the control tower, a loudspeaker system, telephones, microphones (standing, hand, and throat), and headsets.

The most important piece of equipment required for *12 O'Clock High* was the B-17F heavy bomber. Since the script called for several flying sequences, the studio wrote that "the production of *12 O'Clock High* will require both practical operational B-17Fs, and also B-17Fs classified for either survey or salvage. The absolute minimum number of operational aircraft with which it would be possible to make the picture would be eight. However, 12 flyable aircraft is the number desired in order to obtain the best results and to give the impression of a fully operating air base." In addition, Fox asked for two B-17s "in battle-damaged condition or which may be damaged at will" for crash sequences in the film.

Also needed was a mock-up of the B-17 aircraft interior. Because shooting scenes inside a real aircraft would be cramped and difficult, a mock-up or approximation of the interior would be constructed so that those scenes could be photographed on a soundstage. Since it didn't already own a mock-up of the B-17, Fox requested that the Air Force give one of its retired aircraft to the studio, where craftsmen could then modify the fuselage to allow for camera access. In order to preserve authenticity, Fox asked that the aircraft interior be "absolutely complete."

In addition to military equipment, Fox asked to borrow 199 servicemen for the production. The personnel would help populate the airbase and also pilot the operational B-17s on loan from the Air Force. Fox noted that any personnel "loaned" by the Air Force would only be needed for two weeks of shooting at Santa Maria, and not during filming on the studio soundstages. "Therefore, their use for the purposes of the picture would not require an extended absence from their ordinary duties." On the list were 40 flying officers, 36 enlisted crewmen, 24 ground crewmen, and 100 assorted ground personnel (truck drivers, bomb loaders, clerks, and the like). Room and board for the troops would be provided at Camp Cooke, an Army installation near Santa Maria. In the late 1950s Camp Cooke would become Vandenberg Air Force Base, a satellite and missile launch facility named after Hoyt S. Vandenberg, the Air Force Chief of Staff.

In an interesting turn of events, Twentieth Century-Fox received assistance from Metro-Goldwyn-Mayer Studios during the making of *12 O'Clock High*. MGM had released the very similar movie *Command Decision* in 1948. Fox borrowed photographs from MGM's research scrapbook to use in its collection of 10 research volumes for *12 O'Clock High*.

SELECTING A TECHNICAL ADVISOR, FEBRUARY 1949

During the preproduction phase for *12 O'Clock High*, Twentieth Century-Fox asked to borrow 20 Army Air Force war films for study. These included the *Memphis Belle* documentary and various training films. Combined with the 25,000 feet of footage already obtained from Wright Field, the films would provide riveting aerial combat scenes for the Regensburg raid depicted in *12 O'Clock High*.

On 10 February 1949 in Washington, D.C., Fox representative Anthony Muto met with Col. Nuckols and Donald Baruch, the Director of Air Information, about the studio's "wish list" of Air Force equipment and personnel. After a one-hour discussion, the trio determined that the list was not feasible and that Twentieth Century-Fox needed to revise it. This was done during the next week or so. The new version of the list was shorter and much less detailed. Fox still requested a dozen flyable B-17s, plus one that could be used as a studio mock-up. But rather than specifying numbers of equipment and personnel for the film, Fox simply asked the Air Force to provide what it could.

Meanwhile, the Air Force considered its choices for a technical advisor for *12 O'Clock High*. Sy Bartlett asked Col. Nuckols to assign the task to Col. Paul Tibbets, who had been Frank Armstrong's co-pilot on the first Eighth Air Force bombing mission out of England during World War II. Later in the war, Tibbets had commanded the B-29 *Enola Gay*, which dropped the first atomic bomb on Hiroshima, Japan, on 6 August 1945. On top of that, Tibbets had inspired the rough-and-tumble character of Maj. Joe Cobb in *12 O'Clock High*. He was currently working in a staff position at the Pentagon. At first, Bartlett's request to use Tibbets as a film advisor was granted. An Air Force memorandum of 10 February 1949 stated that "Col. Paul Tibbets has been appointed as technical advisor and will report on or about 21 February to Twentieth Century-Fox in Hollywood for a period of approximately 90 days." All that remained was for Tibbets to pack his bags.

But just five days later, the plan changed. The Air Force did issue temporary duty orders for a technical advisor, but not to Tibbets. Their final choice for the job, Col. John H. deRussy, was just as capable. Having served as the operations officer for Curtis LeMay's 305th Bombardment Group in Chelveston, England, during the war, deRussy was well versed in the day-to-day operation of an Eighth Air Force combat unit. "I was in a neighboring group," he said, "but was familiar with the 306th and knew many of the key officers very well."

DeRussy began his 31-year military career in 1934 as an Army private in the 27th Infantry Regiment at Schofield Barracks, Hawaii. He later served as a pilot; a squadron, group, and wing commander; an air division commander; an air attaché; and a program manager in research and development. Fort deRussy, in Honolulu, Hawaii, was named for his great-great grandfather, the distinguished Brigadier General Edward deRussy. Gen. deRussy had served as the adjutant and superintendent at West Point and as the Chief of the Corps of Engineers. In its later years Ft. deRussy was turned into a recreation center for the U.S. armed forces.

John deRussy was teaching at the Air Command and Staff school at Maxwell Air Force Base in Montgomery, Alabama, when he received a phone call from the Pentagon informing him that he would be serving as *12 O'Clock High's* technical advisor. On 15 February 1949, he received his temporary duty orders for a 90-day assignment as "Air Force liaison officer-technical advisor with Twentieth Century-Fox." DeRussy was now in charge of obtaining equipment and personnel for the film. Over the next several months, he would coordinate the bulk of those efforts from his office at Maxwell AFB.

Col. John deRussy, technical advisor for the film version of *12 O'Clock High*.

ZANUCK SWITCHES THE PRODUCER AND DIRECTOR

At Fox, studio chief Darryl Zanuck removed producer Louis Lighton from *12 O'Clock High* and took over the producing chores himself. Lighton had been effective at focusing the theme of the story on Gen. Savage's breakdown, but "he concurrently stretched the remaining scenes with reams of dialogue," according to author Steven Jay Rubin. "Zanuck was furious. In the subdued atmosphere of depressing Archbury, *12 O'Clock High* characters had become nonstop chatterboxes." During the winter of 1948–1949, Bartlett and Lay had produced two more versions of the script for *12 O'Clock High*, the "temporary" on 20 December 1948 and the "revised temporary" on 10 January 1949. The authors were incensed about Lighton's departure, having worked so closely with him during the writing process, but there was little they could do about it.

William Wellman, the original director assigned to *12 O'Clock High*, was the next heavy hitter to depart the production. During the latter half of January 1949, Darryl Zanuck reassigned the job to Henry King. A regular on the Fox lot since 1930, King was known for his authentic, straightforward directing style. Raised on the family plantation in Christiansburg, Virginia, he entered the entertainment industry in the early 1900s, working in the circus, in vaudeville, and as an actor with a traveling theater company. Though King had a brief flirtation with medical studies, his true calling was in the fledgling silent film industry. He began as an actor and writer at Philadelphia's Lubin Company in 1912, and directed his first silent film in 1915. During his half-century as a film director, King would earn a reputation as a strong storyteller and expert at nostalgic period pieces. His films included *Stella Dallas* (1925), *State Fair* (1933), *A Yank in the R.A.F.* (1941), *A Bell for Adano* (1945), and *The Captain from Castile* (1948).

King's flair for authenticity undoubtedly influenced Darryl Zanuck in his choice for a new director for *12 O'Clock High*. The Fox publicity department, celebrating King's 35 years as a director, boasted that he was "the first director to go to the exact locale of the story to do a picture, this being *Tol'able David* with Richard Barthelmess in the early 1920s; the first to take a company to a foreign land, for *The White Sister* (1923), which was made in Italy; and the first to seek locations by plane."

Henry King, director of *12 O'Clock High*. This shot is from a pressbook prepared by the Twentieth Century-Fox publicity department.

Zanuck called King, who had just returned from filming the Tyrone Power swashbuckler *Prince of Foxes* in Europe. Zanuck saw *12 O'Clock High* as an unfinished gem. "Henry, I have a story here that we bought, and we've had three scripts made of it," he told the director. "I've put all three of these scripts into one. I'm so damned tired of it, I feel like I never want to see it again. But I've saved this for you. If you don't want to do it we'll throw it away, but if you want to do it, if you can see the story in it, fine."

King was wise to Zanuck's salesmanship. After investing so much time and money into the project, Zanuck was not about to toss it out. King was interested and agreed to look at the screenplay. After reading it, King got back to Zanuck: "Darryl, there's a very fine picture in this when you can get all the deadwood out of it. There's loads of deadwood in it. There's a great story. It's a story about a man. It takes all this action and all this pressure to break that man." With that, King accepted the job. *Twelve O'Clock High* would be his 24th motion picture for Twentieth Century-Fox.

Henry King does his own location scouting, February 1949

While work on the script continued, a curious King decided to take a look at the location that Twentieth Century-Fox had selected for *12 O'Clock High*. King had obtained a private pilot's license in 1918, rumored to be the second one ever issued in the United States. He hopped in his Beech Bonanza and flew up to Santa Maria Airport. Upon landing, he noticed that the airstrip was surrounded by rolling hills—hardly the flat environment of a World War II English airbase.

An unhappy King spoke to Jason Joy, the director of public relations at Fox. In the course of their conversation, Joy explained that the studio was making arrangements to borrow some Air Force B-17s from the East Coast to use at Santa Maria. Surprised, King asked Joy, "Who's going to pay for bringing these B-17s out here? You know what it costs to fly a B-17 from the East Coast to the West Coast?" Joy answered no, and King gave him an estimate.

"That's ridiculous," answered Joy.

"That's what it's going to cost you," replied King.

Joy suggested that the Air Force would help. King set him straight: "You think the government's going to furnish them? They're going to furnish them if you pay for them. If you pay for all the gas, all the expenses, all the people, all the crews, and all that, then they'll do it." Why not shoot at a military installation, King wondered? Equipment would be more readily available. And after all, the geography at Santa Maria just wouldn't do. King then talked to Col. William Nuckols, the Air Force Chief of Public Information, in Washington, D.C. King said that he wanted to scout for a location on his own. Nuckols approved and sent King to Maxwell AFB in Alabama to meet his technical consultant for *12 O'Clock High*.

Col. John deRussy had never advised a movie director before, but he proved to be an excellent choice for the job. He and King reviewed the list of Air Force bases where *12 O'Clock High* could be filmed. Their discussion produced four possibilities: Clinton County AFB in Wilmington, Ohio, a weather research facility; Eglin AFB in Florida (12 B-17s assigned); Maxwell AFB, where deRussy was stationed; and McGuire AFB in New Jersey (11 B-17s). In the end, Twentieth Century-Fox got its wish: the Air Force lent the studio 12 B-17s, drawing them from Eglin AFB, Brookley AFB near Mobile, Alabama, and other sources. Some of the aircraft had performed as drones and drone controllers; others had flown in the 1946 atomic bomb testing program known as Operation Crossroads. Still slightly radioactive, the aircraft were deemed safe to fly for short durations. A number of the B-17s, missing gun turrets due to their conversion for non-combat purposes, had to be refitted.

DeRussy and King got along well. DeRussy remembered the director as a "wonderful" collaborator. "I'm counting on you," King told deRussy, "to be sure that this is completely authentic. I don't want anybody in the Eighth Air Force saying 'We didn't do that.'"

In February 1949 Twentieth Century-Fox sent a cameraman to Eglin AFB to film location shots for a study of the terrain. But when the cameraman was finished shooting, the base intelligence officer confiscated the film, concerned that it might contain classified information about Air Force operations and testing at the airfield. Back in Washington, D.C., Fox representative Tony Muto phoned the Pentagon to complain. On Valentine's Day, the Air Force released the film "to be forwarded to the studio as expeditiously as possible."

Meanwhile, Henry King continued hunting for a location for his movie. According to King, he would travel "nearly 16,000 miles scouting locations in my usual way, taking my own plane and doing the job personally." King loved the airplane, and he loved the advantages it provided to Hollywood filmmakers. "It enables us to use actual story locales in motion pictures, rather than imitations made at home," he told the *New York Herald Tribune*. "This concept has vastly changed Hollywood's attitude and production methods, for we can now use the most remote region as a location site."

Readying his airplane, King received the Air Force's permission to visit Eglin AFB from 27 to 29 February 1949. His passengers included his assistant, Johnny Johnson; director of photography Leon Shamroy; location manager John Adams; and the son-in-law of Jason Joy, the Fox public relations director. The small group left Los Angeles bound for Florida on the 27th, but never reached their destination. King's little Beech Bonanza developed engine trouble "somewhere in Arizona," and King was forced to land and make repairs. At first he planned to delay his visit to Florida by several days, but in the end he was forced to return to Los Angeles for a scheduled script meeting with Darryl Zanuck. Planning ahead, King asked the Air Force for permission to visit McGuire AFB, New Jersey, on 7 March, then fly to Eglin AFB, Florida, the next day.

STORY CONFERENCE, MARCH 1949

At Twentieth Century-Fox studios in Hollywood, Darryl Zanuck continued mulling over the script for *12 O'Clock High*. He suggested a new ending to the film: since the story opened with Harvey Stovall's present-day trip to England and then transitioned to a flashback, Zanuck wanted the film book-ended at its conclusion by returning to Stovall "as he was at the beginning of the picture. He looks out over the field—a last long look—then turns back to his bicycle, mounts and slowly pedals away."

Zanuck held a script conference with Henry King and Sy Bartlett on 2 March 1949. The meeting went smoothly. The three men decided that "all the colorful phrases and expressions" should be uttered by the intense Gen. Savage and not by Col. Davenport or Gen. Pritchard, and that further trims would be made on several key scenes. Also discussed were the rear-projection background "plates" that would be needed for scenes shot in the studio. Scenes set in London would be too expensive to film on location, so Zanuck suggested that King reuse plates from the Fox library. Available footage included scenes of London shot by Otto Preminger for *The Fan* that year, the English countryside from 1947's *The Ghost and Mrs. Muir* (for scenes with Stovall riding his bicycle), and trains arriving at the station from the comedy *Cluny Brown* (1946) and the 1942 drama *This Above All*.

A scene portraying servicemen "sweating out" a mission, waiting for bombers to return from combat, compelled King to scribble a reminder in the script: "Play this for all it is worth." Aware of Zanuck's and the Air Force's concerns about the film being awash in alcohol, King changed a line at the end of the film. Col. Davenport, visiting Savage after the latter's breakdown, asked, "Want to try some brandy, Frank?" King crossed it out and changed the line to "How about a smoke, Frank?"

HENRY KING RESUMES HIS LOCATION SCOUTING

While Sy Bartlett and Beirne Lay revised their script yet again, Henry King hopped back in his plane to continue scouting for an airbase. He landed at McGuire AFB, New Jersey, on 7 March. King and his passengers were met by Col. John deRussy, who had flown in from Maxwell AFB in an Air Force B-26. Though King looked chipper after the long trip, deRussy noticed that King's passengers were pretty tired. "The young guys are ready to drop!" thought deRussy.

Looking around the area, King realized that the surrounding landscape wasn't appropriate for *12 O'Clock High*. "McGuire didn't appeal to me at all for pictures. There wasn't anything there that would give me the impression of England at all," he recalled later.

The next stop was at Eglin AFB in Florida. DeRussy warned King that the scrub oaks in Florida would not look like England either. King wanted to visit Eglin anyway. A weather front had settled in between New Jersey and Florida, making the airplane trip a dangerous one. But having missed his original appointment at Eglin in late February, King refused to delay his visit again. Ignoring deRussy's protests, King "kicked the tires on that old Beech, got in, and took off." DeRussy was unable to follow immediately because he was flying a government-owned B-26 and had some paperwork to do. After filing a flight plan that allowed him to bypass the bad weather, deRussy boarded his airplane and taxied it onto the runway, wondering how King planned to make it through the storm that was brewing.

Several hours later, deRussy landed safely at Eglin AFB and looked around the flightline. There was no sign of Henry King's airplane. But 30 minutes later, King's Beech Bonanza safely touched down on the runway, and he and his companions clambered out. A worried deRussy rushed up to greet them.

"How did you make it through the front?" deRussy asked, assuming that King had flown around the bad weather.

King answered matter-of-factly, "Oh, we went up a few thousand feet and cruised on through!"

Eglin, the proving ground for the Air Force and Navy aviation programs, was a sprawling base of more than 500,000 acres next to Valparaiso and 30 miles east of Pensacola. When it opened in June 1935, the installation was known as the Valparaiso Bombing and Gunnery Base. By World War II, Eglin featured 30 miles of runways and 882 buildings including laboratories and flight test facilities. "Everything is tested here," noted the *New York Herald Tribune.* "Its climatic hangar, for instance, tests the resistance of metals and fabrics in temperatures ranging from 70 degrees below zero to tropical weather." Eglin had 10 satellite airfields. King found the terrain he wanted at Auxiliary Field Number 3, better known

Montage of scenes from the production of *12 O'Clock High,* as presented in the studio pressbook, 1949. At lower left, director Henry King confers with actors Dean Jagger and Gregory Peck.

as Duke Field. Named for 1st Lt. Robert Duke, who worked at the proving ground at Eglin and died in a plane crash in December 1943, the field stood almost 20 miles north of the main base. In later years Duke Field would be used by special operations units of the Air Force Reserve.

King was impressed with Eglin, but he had two more stops to make. He arranged to visit Clinton County AFB in Ohio on the following day, and Maxwell AFB, Alabama, the day after that.

On 10 March 1949, King arrived at Maxwell AFB. Col. John deRussy had already arrived and was waiting for him. The two men checked out Ozark Army Air Field, a quiet, weed-infested airstrip nearby. King figured that he could use the field for some B-17 aerial shots but more specifically for the opening and closing scenes of *12 O'Clock High,* when Harvey Stovall visited his old English airbase, now overgrown and fallen into disuse. "Ozark Field was the ideal answer," said King. "It was more English than any field I have seen in that country. Weeds had grown as high as a man's shoulders in some places, and the adjacent scenery was perfect as an English countryside."

Choosing the Final Location and Obtaining the Last of the Equipment

With his research completed, Henry King needed to make his final choices for location shooting. At a meeting with Sy Bartlett, director of photography Leon Shamroy, and art director Maurice Ransford, King reviewed the data he had collected from his travels. Ozark Field in Alabama would be ideal for shots of Harvey Stovall reminiscing about his World War II service. After filming those scenes, the crew would hire mowing machines from local farmers to trim the grass for some B-17 takeoff and landing scenes, as well as a belly-landing sequence. Meanwhile, a portion of Eglin AFB in Florida would be redressed as an operational WWII airbase. Why were two different airfields needed for *12 O'Clock High*? Eglin's runways were light-colored concrete, while Ozark's were black asphalt. To maintain an authentic look, scenes with flying aircraft were shot at Ozark because British airfields during World War II had dark-colored runways to make them harder for the enemy to see from the air.

Airfield set at Auxiliary Field #3 (also known as Duke Field), Eglin Air Force Base, near Pensacola, Florida. Note camera crew at bottom right.

True to the nature of a bureaucracy, coordination problems developed between the Pentagon and the Air Materiel Command at Wright-Patterson AFB in Ohio, which controlled the Air Force's equipment inventory. To simplify things, the Air Force Chief of Staff's office issued a directive on 18 March 1949 giving Air Materiel Command blanket permission to assist Twentieth Century-Fox with *12 O'Clock High*. This gave Air Materiel Command "a chance to work out cooperation with Fox when they come in for all sorts of little things that are not cleared through the Pentagon."

Meanwhile at Maxwell AFB, technical advisor Col. John deRussy was trying to obtain a surplus B-17 to be modified as a studio mock-up. He found airplanes in storage at Mobile, Alabama, and Peyote, Texas. DeRussy suggested to the Pentagon that Fox pay to have an aircraft restored to working condition and then fly it to Hollywood, where it would be disassembled to construct the mock-up. The public relations office at the Pentagon was unhappy about "cutting up a flyable airplane," and instead decided that a B-17 in mothballs at a storage depot would be pulled apart and shipped in pieces to Hollywood. After completing *12 O'Clock High*, Twentieth Century-Fox was required to transport the aircraft parts to the nearest Air Force base for disposition. Naturally all of this would be done at the studio's expense.

The Air Force picked a B-17 from San Antonio Air Materiel Area in Texas, "with all combat equipment," to provide to Fox. On 28 March 1949, the Air Force sent the following message: "San Antonio AMA, Texas, is being instructed by teletype to release B-17G aircraft serial number 44-83387 and related equipment to Twentieth Century-Fox in accordance with provisions contained in referenced teletype. Signed, Aircraft Distribution Office."

THE SCRIPT IS COMPLETED, MARCH 1949

As March 1949 came to an end, Sy Bartlett and director Henry King prepared the final draft of the screenplay for *12 O'Clock High*. At Zanuck's request, King spirited Bartlett away from the studio to Fort Walton Beach, Florida, where they would complete their revisions to the script. In the sunshine and sea air, the two men stuck to a rigid schedule, writing from 8 A.M. to noon each day, followed by lunch at Bacon's-by-the-Sea, a local hotel. After a good meal, the two men "came out and sat on the beach and chatted about something else for about 30 minutes," remembered King. At 1:30 P.M., King and Bartlett began four and a half additional hours of scriptwriting and wrapped up by 6 P.M. At the end of one week the screenplay was revised to their satisfaction.

Bartlett flew back to Hollywood to have the new script typed and mimeographed, and King joined him shortly thereafter. After another day of revision, King and Bartlett delivered the "2nd revised temporary" script to Darryl Zanuck. As King recalled later, "I sent the script down to Zanuck, and of course Zanuck is one of these people who can't wait. He's read it by the time it's there, almost. He said, 'Go ahead. This is the best script I've ever read.'" Zanuck made that comment about more than one script during his tenure at Fox, but if it boosted morale and got him good scripts, why not? After one more spruce-up, the finished screenplay was delivered on 30 March 1949.

SMOKING A CIGARETTE AT 20,000 FEET

One scene suggested by Zanuck caused major disagreement between King, Bartlett, and John deRussy. When Maj. Joe Cobb's plane exploded during a mission to Hamburg, Gen. Savage, at the controls of his B-17, broke out in a cold sweat. After removing his oxygen mask, Savage tried to light a cigarette. Finding it soaked with perspiration, Savage tossed the cigarette and, pulling out a second one, squeezed the sweat out of it.

When deRussy saw this scene in the script, he was surprised about its lack of authenticity. At such a high altitude, with temperatures hovering around 40 degrees below zero, an airman would be unable to break a good sweat, much less soak a package of cigarettes in his jacket. DeRussy told King about the error. King replied dryly, "Hey, I was waiting for *you* to tell *me*. I knew that!"

In fact, King had already spoken to Sy Bartlett about removing the scene.

Actor Gregory Peck, clad in flying gear, ready for his role as Brig. Gen. Frank Savage, the tough-as-nails commander of the 918th Bomb Group in *12 O'Clock High*.

Bartlett wanted to keep it in the script and stood fast. A frustrated King asked deRussy to solve the problem. Over lunch one day, deRussy tried to convince Bartlett that the scene was ridiculous, but Bartlett wasn't interested. "It's the climax," pleaded Bartlett. "This is where the whole thing peaks out. The scene has to be in there!" When deRussy persisted, Bartlett issued an ultimatum: "If you take it out, I will never speak to you again." DeRussy took his chances and the scene was modified, removing the attempt at cigarette smoking but retaining Savage's cold sweat.

As for Bartlett's threat, "he was true to his word, for about five years," recalled deRussy. In the mid–1950s, Gen. Curtis LeMay, commander-in-chief of the Strategic Air Command (SAC), visited deRussy, who was deployed with the 310th Bombardment Wing in England. Sy Bartlett was the first passenger to step off LeMay's airplane. Bartlett ran over, hugged deRussy and greeted him as an old friend.

DeRussy chuckled at the memory. "By then, of course, the movie had made millions of dollars!"

OZARK FIELD, APRIL 1949

In early April 1949, deRussy contacted Col. Sory Smith, the deputy director of public relations at the Pentagon, about obtaining permission to film at Ozark Field in Alabama. "We've run into one little hitch," deRussy told Smith. Although Ozark was located on the grounds of Maxwell AFB, the field itself was owned by the U.S. Army. "People from the studio went up there and got run off the other day," said deRussy. The Third Army, based at Fort Rucker, was using Ozark as a tactical airstrip. Ozark would later be renamed Cairns Army Air Field and used for aviation training.

Suddenly deRussy had a big coordination problem on his hands. He explained to Col. Smith that "it would probably be best if we could get somebody up there in Washington to go to the Army and get the thing cleared right down through the channels instead of my going to Ozark and fiddling with this, and then to Third Army, and so on." DeRussy paused to catch his breath. "But what [the

Army commander of Ozark Field] tells us is that the field is under command of the Third Army, his headquarters is at Fort MacPherson in Atlanta. I wonder if we could get that handled up there, then?"

Col. Smith wondered if another field could be used instead. Henry King "has definitely selected Ozark. That is where he wants to do it, huh?" said Smith.

"Well, for the flying shots," answered deRussy, annoyed at all of the red tape involved to use the barren airstrip briefly for the film. "There's not a thing on the field, Sory! The Army is just flying stuff in and out, and there's only one building on the whole darn field. But they have the place fenced and locked, and they objected to the studio going in there without clearing through."

"Now is Henry King going to put up anything on this field or what?" asked Col. Smith.

"They're going to build a little fence and a little bit of a roadway. And that's all the building that'll be done over there." The studio wanted to begin construction in several days and shoot for approximately three weeks.

Smith agreed to help clear the project with Third Army. "All right, John. You're getting along all right outside of that little problem, eh?"

Unfortunately, the answer was no. DeRussy had opened a new can of worms when he tried to coordinate the film's belly-landing sequence at Eglin AFB. DeRussy asked to borrow a B-17 that the base was using in weapons testing. Col. Smith had bad news. The Air Force wasn't interested in seeing the studio demolish one of its aircraft. "The idea didn't go very well, John!" he told deRussy.

"It didn't?"

"No, it didn't go at all."

"Well, okay," said deRussy. "What they wanted to do was to show the landing, and then the ambulance and the fire trucks and the crew running out to it." Since Eglin refused to donate one of their aircraft, deRussy figured that Twentieth Century-Fox would have to use stock footage instead.

On 13 April 1949, Col. Smith wrote a last-minute letter to the Army's Public Information Division for permission to use Ozark Field for one month. The studio would arrive "on or about 15 April" to begin construction on their roadway and fence. Smith crossed his fingers. Fortunately, the Army immediately cleared the studio to begin its work.

Back at the Fox studios in Hollywood, Darryl Zanuck considered the Air Force's refusal to supply a B-17 for the belly-landing sequence in *12 O'Clock High*. Zanuck wanted the shot in the movie and once again called upon Gen. Hoyt Vandenberg, the Air Force Chief of Staff, to intercede. Vandenberg replied to Zanuck on 20 April 1949. "Reference your cable of 10 April," wrote Vandenberg. "We are investigating the possibility of making available the B-17 in question. There are numerous technicalities which must be taken into consideration before making such a commitment, however we anticipate no difficulty in providing a salvageable aircraft." Once again, Zanuck had gotten his way by going straight to the top. A week and a half later, the Secretary of the Air

Force wrote to Col. deRussy, informing him that one of the B-17s being used for formation sequences at Eglin would be moved to Maxwell AFB to fly the belly landing: "Subject aircraft will be one of four B-17s from Brookley AFB. Cost of crash landing crew, salvage and return of aircraft to site designated by Brookley will be borne by Twentieth Century-Fox."

Vandenberg's assistance prompted a handwritten thank-you letter from Fox's Frank McCarthy on 22 April 1949. "Dear General, I am sure you will be hearing from Darryl Zanuck, but I want to send you the studio's thanks, along with my own, for the really magnificent cooperation we are receiving all along the line on *12 O'Clock High*, and most especially for your making the B-17 available. This will increase the effectiveness of the film tremendously, and will help us turn out a picture of which I know the Air Force and the company will be very proud. Thanks, best regards, and continued admiration for the job you and your subordinates are doing in providing us with a magnificent Air Force at a time when it is so sorely needed."

COSTUMING

While arranging for airfields and airplanes, Col. deRussy also attempted to gather one million dollars' worth of 1942-era Army Air Force uniforms and equipment for use at Eglin AFB, where Twentieth Century-Fox had already begun construction of the airbase sets. The Air Force couldn't find the requested uniforms at its own depots, so it asked the Third Army quartermaster in Atlanta for help. The Army did its own research and found out that most of the items were already available at Eglin AFB! Since the Air Force had split from the Army to form a separate service barely two years before, Army airfields across the United States were gradually changing into Air Force bases. The transition of personnel and equipment could be confusing to say the least. No wonder the Army found what was needed on an Air Force base.

On 14 April 1949, the Army arranged for a large stock of items to be transferred to the Air Force, which in turn would loan them to Twentieth Century-Fox. The materiel was collected from a number of locations. "Fifty cloth field jackets with wool lining are being shipped air express from the depot in Schenectady, New York. Twelve blouses (Eisenhower jackets substituted); 12 shoulder holsters; 12 hospital corpsmen surgical gowns, are being shipped this date from depots within the Third Army area. It will be noted that the Eisenhower jackets were substituted for wool blouses. This was necessary due to the fact that the issue of wool blouses to enlisted men was discontinued about five years ago and none are available."

As *12 O'Clock High* took shape, Twentieth Century-Fox again consulted the Motion Picture Association about meeting the guidelines of its Production Code. Fox's Jason Joy wrote to the MPAA asking for its comments on a wardrobe production still of four Red Cross nurses who would be featured in the film. The costumes were judged to be tasteful, and Fox received approval the next day.

THE CAST

Since *12 O'Clock High* was primarily a character study, a solid cast was essential to the success of the film. In late February 1949, casting director Jim Ryan compiled lists of possible actors for consideration. For the lead role of "Brig. Gen. Frank Savage," Ryan drafted an interesting list of candidates including James Cagney, Gregory Peck, Dana Andrews, Ralph Bellamy, Van Heflin, Burt Lancaster, Lloyd Nolan, Edmund O'Brien, Robert Preston, Robert Young, and Robert Montgomery. The roles of "Col. Keith Davenport" and "Maj. Gen. Patrick Pritchard" were already slotted for Gary Merrill and Millard Mitchell, respectively. "Maj. Harvey Stovall" was considered for Ralph Bellamy, James Backus, Raymond Burr, Melvyn Douglas, Albert Dekker, Franchot Tone, Gene Raymond, Don Ameche, Tom Ewell, Charles Bickford, Alan Hale, Ward Bond, and Pat O'Brien.

For the secondary cast, Twentieth Century-Fox listed dozens of possibilities. For "Lt. Jesse Bishop": Gig Young, Mark Daniels, Arthur Franz, George Reeves, Harry Carey Jr., or Audie Murphy, among others. For "Maj. Joseph Cobb," the studio short list included Richard Basehart, Barry Nelson, John Ireland, Leif Erickson, Robert Preston, Lloyd Bridges, Mel Ferrer, Howard Duff, Forrest Tucker, Barry Sullivan, John Forsythe, James Whitmore, and Kevin McCarthy. Gen. Savage's driver and clerk, "Sgt. McIllhenny," could have been played by David Wayne, Richard Jaeckel, Eddie Albert, Red Buttons, Dennis Day, or Tom Ewell. The pivotal role of "Lt. Col. Ben Gately," the slacker pilot eventually played by Hugh Marlowe, was considered for William Lundigan, Noah Beery Jr., Gig Young, Craig Stevens, Don Porter, Robert Ryan, and Richard Widmark.

Gregory Peck, as Brig. Gen Frank Savage, addresses the men of the 918th Bombardment Group soon after his arrival.

In the end, Fox assembled a strong mix of actors for *12 O'Clock High*. Headlining the cast was Gregory Peck, who played Brig. Gen. Frank Savage.

Born on 5 April 1916 in La Jolla, California, Peck was classified 4-F during the World War II draft due to an injury and was unable to serve in the military. He eventually relocated to Hollywood and made his film debut in the 1944 war film *Days of Glory*. Peck's handsome looks and authoritative air nabbed him a number of choice roles throughout his career. Prior to *12 O'Clock High*, Peck had appeared in *Spellbound* (1945), *Duel in the Sun* (1946), and *Gentleman's Agreement* (1947). Actress Lauren Bacall once praised him as "the most gorgeous creature I'd ever seen in my life."

Peck was under contract to independent producer David Selznick when *12 O'Clock High* was being cast; Selznick agreed to loan Peck to Twentieth Century-Fox for the film. At first, Peck didn't want to play Frank Savage because *12 O'Clock High* looked too much like *Command Decision*, the 1948 Metro-Goldwyn-Mayer release starring Clark Gable. But an insistent Darryl Zanuck convinced him to change his mind. *Twelve O'Clock High* was the final film in a four-picture deal Peck signed with Twentieth Century-Fox. Although Peck reluctantly accepted the role of Frank Savage, he still had reservations when filming began. During Peck's first meeting with director Henry King, Peck said he liked the part but was wary because he had no military background whatsoever. "It's going to be very easy for you," King reassured him. "You're going to be on a military base where you won't see anything but military training and you'll find out how simple it all is." Perhaps the paycheck helped soothe his concerns as well: according to the *12 O'Clock High* cast sheet dated 5 April 1949, Peck was signed at a salary of $100,000 and was guaranteed 13 weeks of work. If shooting ran longer than that, Peck would receive $4500 per week until the film was completed.

Following his psychological breakdown, Savage sweats out the mission in his office. Looking on are Chaplain Capt. Twombley (Lawrence Dobkin), "Doc" Kaiser (Paul Stewart), Maj. Stovall (Dean Jagger), and Col. Davenport (Gary Merrill).

"I instinctively liked him and respected him as a man and as an actor," remembered Robert Arthur, who played Sgt. McIllhenny, Gen. Savage's clerk. Arthur had worked with Peck the previous year on the western *Yellow Sky* at Twentieth Century-Fox. As *12 O'Clock High* got underway, Arthur wasn't sure what Peck thought of him. "I couldn't tell if he liked me or not. He said almost nothing to me. Peck was a very professional actor and I later realized he was simply in character. After the picture, he asked me to come to his home at the beach—I think it was Pacific Palisades—when he was still married to Greta Peck. He gave me a beautiful white Alsatian police dog as a gift." Typically modest, Peck once said, "I don't look at myself in a mirror. I was not impressed with my appearance. I've never thought about it. I wanted to be a good actor, not a matinee idol."

Dean Jagger (Maj. Harvey Stovall) was born in Lima, Ohio, on 7 November 1903. After performing on the stage and in vaudeville in the 1920s, he moved into motion pictures. By the late 1940s Jagger was in New York performing on radio, television, and the stage. According to the Twentieth Century-Fox publicity department, Jagger was so excited about auditioning for the role in *12 O'Clock High* that he paid his own way from New York to Hollywood. For *12 O'Clock High*, director Henry King wanted Jagger to dispense with his customary toupee. Jagger refused time and again, but King kept upping his salary and Jagger finally relented. He was signed for 10 weeks of shooting at a salary of $20,000. Jagger would later call Maj. Harvey Stovall his favorite role, and no wonder: he would win the Academy Award for Best Supporting Actor for his work in *12 O'Clock High*.

Gary Merrill (Col. Keith Davenport) was born on 2 August 1915 in Hartford, Connecticut. He signed a contract with Twentieth Century-Fox the night before his new stage play, *At War with the Army*, opened on Broadway. Merrill stayed with the production for two weeks before moving to Hollywood. He made his film debut in *Winged Victory* in 1944, playing a Navy commander, and served in the Army during World War II. When he lost a key role in 1947's *Gentleman's Agreement* to John Garfield, Merrill returned to New York and resumed his stage career. But soon Hollywood came calling again. According to the Twentieth Century-Fox casting sheet, Merrill was paid $750 a week for his work on *12 O'Clock High*.

Millard Mitchell (Maj. Gen. Patrick Pritchard) was born in Havana, Cuba, on 14 August 1903. A Broadway star signed to a two-picture-a-year contract with Twentieth Century-Fox, his first film was 1941's *Mr. and Mrs. North*. He went on to appear in *Kiss of Death* (1947) and would follow *12 O'Clock High* with *The Gunfighter*, where he once again co-starred with Gregory Peck. For *12 O'Clock High*, Mitchell was signed for 10 weeks at a salary of $20,000.

Hugh Marlowe (Lt. Col. Benjamin Gately) was born in Philadelphia, Pennsylvania, and moved into acting after working as a radio announcer. Impressed with his work in the motion picture drama *Come to the Stable*, Fox signed Marlowe to a long-term contract. For *12 O'Clock High*, Marlowe received $750 per week. In the April 1949 casting sheet for the film, radio announcer-turned-actor William Lundigan was originally listed in the role.

Rounding out the cast was a varied collection of supporting players. New York native Paul Stewart (Maj. "Doc" Kaiser), a member of Orson Welles' Mercury Theatre troupe, was cast for seven weeks' work at $1000 per week. Robert Arthur (Sgt. McIllhenny), a Fox contract player from Aberdeen, Washington, was a former radio deejay turned actor: "I was cast after one interview with Henry

King, the director. I was under contract to Twentieth Century-Fox so I was assigned to *12 O'Clock High*." Lawrence Dobkin, who played Chaplain Twombley, earned $500 for his one week's work on the film. Bob Patten (Lt. Bishop) was signed to a Fox contract in early 1948, and earned $200 per week on *12 O'Clock High*. Lee MacGregor (Lt. Zimmermann) had worked as studio chief Darryl Zanuck's assistant for a year before moving into acting. His role was originally assigned to Kurt Kreuger. Also appearing in bit parts were Richard Anderson (Lt. McKesson), Don Gordon (patient), and Paul Picerni (bombardier).

ON LOCATION

Once Maxwell and Eglin AFB were selected for location filming, Twentieth Century-Fox began constructing its outdoor sets. At Eglin, Twentieth Century-Fox erected 15 buildings to simulate the Archbury airbase featured in *12 O'Clock High*. "We built technical backgrounds on the field," recalled director Henry King, "and briefing and interrogation rooms. At Eglin we used the experience of men who were members of squadrons actually represented in our story—a story, incidentally, I prefer to think of as one exploring the responsibilities of officers to their men rather than as merely a phase of aerial warfare."

Maj. Gen. William Kepner, the commander of the Air Force Proving Ground at Eglin, was well-versed in the source material for *12 O'Clock High*, having commanded fighter and bomber units in the European Theater during World War II. He had been briefed by the Pentagon and instructed to cooperate with King as much as possible. "I'm now working for you!" Kepner told King with a smile. "You should see the letter that I have from Washington."

King, who found Kepner "a lot of fun" to work with, replied, "No, no. You're a producer of pictures now. You're going to be the producer, and I'm just going to be the director." King and Kepner worked together for eight weeks and became close friends. In an interesting coincidence, they found out that neither of them had finished high school. Yet one was now a successful movie director, and the other was a three-star general. "I never felt as bad about not finishing high school after learning of his career," said King. "He made everything easier. Making *12 O'Clock High* was one of the nicest experiences that I ever had in making a picture."

To move the crew and equipment from Hollywood to Florida, Fox chartered cargo planes that hauled everything cross-country. Although one might assume that the studio would shoot all the necessary scenes at Maxwell and then move everyone to Eglin (or vice versa), the cast and crew of *12 O'Clock High* actually used a DC-4 Skymaster to shuttle between the two bases during the six-week shooting period. Seventy-two members of the production flew from one spot to the other in a short 22 minutes. By car the trip would have taken five hours.

Robert Arthur, who played Sgt. McIllhenny in the film, recalled that the cast got along well. "We were all living at the Valparaiso Inn, an old frame building sinking into a swamp. They had reopened it for our cast and crew. Nearby there was Fort Walton and not too far away, Pensacola. Our restless cast would travel to both places to drink beer."

The star of the picture, Gregory Peck, stayed in Fort Walton at a resort hotel called Bacon's-by-the-Sea. It was the same place where Henry King and Sy Bartlett had spent a week knocking out script revisions several months earlier. The primary set at Eglin AFB was just 20 miles from the hotel. But for scenes shot at Ozark Field, the studio chartered a plane to fly the actor 200 miles round-trip each day to Montgomery, Alabama.

A magazine of the time related an amusing anecdote from one if its readers: "While spending the day shopping in Fort Walton, my sister and I stopped to look at a movie poster advertising a movie with Gregory Peck. My sister exclaimed, 'Isn't he darling?' I laughed, but a young man stepped out of the crowd and said, 'Oh, no, he's actually as ugly as sin.' To everyone's astonishment, it turned out to be Gregory Peck, who was there on location for *12 O'Clock High.*"

During the production of the film, *Modern Screen* magazine sent one of their staff members to visit with Peck on location. The resulting feature revealed many fascinating tidbits about the actor and the film itself. At Ozark Field, the studio's craft services department doled out a lunch of "peanut butter sandwiches, cheese and lemonade." Peck enjoyed canoeing in his free time, a precious hobby given his "rigorous working schedule that called for him to be up at five and on the go till 7:30 P.M." The actor enjoyed a daily breakfast of orange juice, soft-scrambled eggs, toast, two cups of coffee, and grits. "Great stuff, grits," said Peck. "Sticks to your ribs.'"

For the scene in which Gen. Savage discusses how Maj. Cobb died during the bombing raid on Hambrucken, Peck mulled over how to play his character's reaction. "I couldn't figure out how to handle it," he said. "Should I look at the ground, should I turn my back?" Since he was working on an Air Force installation, Peck found his inspiration in the real-life activity all around him. "Some guys at the airbase learned that a friend had been killed in a crack-up. They laughed. They said, 'Well, old Joe finally got it!' To cover their emotions, they treated it almost as if it were a joke. I'll handle the scene pretty much along those lines." And he did.

Cocooned in pounds of flight clothing and equipment, the actors battled the hot, humid Florida environment each day. *Modern Screen* magazine noted that the costumes often consisted of "sheep-lined flying jackets and boots—and a temperature of 90 in the shade! And to make things real dandy, the arc lights were turned on. Arc lights are used to kill shadows—and actors. Now I know how Gregory Peck manages to keep his excellent figure." Technical advisor Col. John deRussy observed the location shooting and came away with a new appreciation of the Hollywood film machine. "I understood why film actors get paid so much. They work hard!" DeRussy recalled that the production crew worked "fantastic hours." Shooting began daily at 8 A.M., and lasted into the evening. Then "dailies," scenes that had recently been filmed, were reviewed until 8 or 9 P.M.

The rigorous daily schedule was necessary to complete the film within a reasonable budget. DeRussy noted that the sets cost $65,000 per day to operate. When the actors arrived on the set, Henry King typically allowed one dry-run rehearsal, and then tried to complete the actual scene in one take. Most of the actors, deRussy recalled, were very young. "Many, by the time they got on the set, hadn't read their lines. It could take all day to do a 15- to 20- second spot!"

Gregory Peck, as Brig. Gen Frank Savage, dresses down the hapless Sergeant McIllhenny, the general's clerk.

Robert Arthur, who played Sgt. McIllhenny, said that "*Twelve O'Clock High* was a serious picture with a serious feeling and attitude all day long." At one point, "rough and tough" Henry King got what he wanted out of Arthur. "Toward the end of the picture he told the cameraman to keep rolling as I stood there in front of everybody. Then he barked to me in his gruff fashion, 'Say something funny, McIllhenny!' I stuttered and stammered and looked bewildered and scared. 'Cut,' he clipped. 'That's the trailer.' And it was!"

"It was a large cast," said Arthur, "and we had been given hundreds of 'dog-faces' for background atmosphere." The "dogfaces" in the movie included John McKee, a pilot who had flown with the 306th Bomb Group during the war. McKee was working as an actor at the time. Sy Bartlett knew him as an original member of the 306th and wanted him in the movie. In fact, in casting director Jim Ryan's notes was a scribbled reminder: "Remind Henry King of John McKee."

In *12 O'Clock High*, McKee appeared as an operations officer, earning $175 for each of his three weeks as an actor on the set. Behind the scenes, McKee also assisted John deRussy as technical advisor throughout the production. "I'm sure I was the only 306th person who worked on the picture," recalled McKee, who, like *12 O'Clock High* co-author Beirne Lay, had survived being shot down in combat. On 20 December 1942, McKee had to bail out of his crippled B-17 over the target, the Luftwaffe air depot at Romilly-sur-Seine, about 70 miles east of Paris. His was one of six B-17s downed by enemy fighters that day. And like Lay, McKee evaded German search teams after he landed. "Thanks to the underground I got to Gibraltar and back to England," he said. During the war McKee served under Col. Chip Overacker and Brig. Gen. Frank Armstrong, so he was a useful consultant for *12 O'Clock High.*

Eglin Air Force Base was a huge facility with a large workforce, so Twentieth Century-Fox was able to use active-duty Air Force personnel as background extras in many scenes. Fresh from basic training, James Storie was at Eglin awaiting an assignment when he volunteered for temporary duty with *12 O'Clock High.* "I was an Airman 3rd Class with spare time on my hands. They asked me if I would be interested in helping out in a movie that was being filmed at Field Number 3. I had no idea at that time what kind of movie it was."

Storie reported to the set five days a week for about three weeks, arriving between seven and eight o'clock each morning. "We then lined up at a building and filed through. There was a counter where some person would judge by sight what size clothes we wore. He put our clothes for that day on the counter and told us to don them." After getting dressed, the airmen were led to a waiting area until the film crew was ready to shoot. As for what rank each background player wore, "It was random selection," remembered Storie. "You might be a captain that day, or a private, or anywhere in between."

Storie enjoyed the atmosphere on the *12 O'Clock High* set, finding it "relaxed and well organized. They brought in good boxed lunches every day." The active-duty airmen even had the opportunity to

(James Storie Collection)

James Storie as an Airman 3rd Class, fresh from basic training, in December 1948. Storie was one of the hundreds of active-duty airmen at Eglin Air Force Base who worked as extras on *12 O'Clock High.*

hang out with some of the cast members. "I met all the stars," said Storie. "We found out quickly that you could not go talk to the stars any time you wanted. But they were nice enough to give us a little time when they could. Gregory Peck did not want to be approached any time he was in his chair studying his lines. Dean Jagger was quiet and didn't mingle too much. Gary Merrill was just one of the guys. We even played poker with him, and he spent a lot of time hanging around with us. He served in the Army during World War II, and that's probably why he was so comfortable with the extras."

As shooting progressed, Storie came to appreciate Gregory Peck's laser-like focus on his craft. Peck always knew his lines and rarely needed to complete more than two takes of each scene. The eager extras, on the other hand, weren't as well trained. In the critical scene where Gen. Savage makes his introductory speech to the 918th Bomb Group, hundreds of airmen playing Savage's crews were crammed into a Quonset hut at Eglin AFB. It took 13 takes to get the scene right. Remembered Storie, "We were dressed in big coats and were given packs of cigarettes to smoke up the room. By the time we finished we were sweating and coughing pretty badly!"

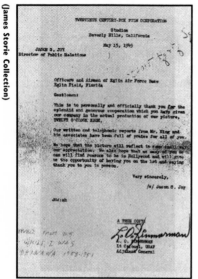

Letter of appreciation mailed to Air Force personnel who assisted in the production of *12 O'Clock High*.

Although the production of *12 O'Clock High* went smoothly, not everything went as planned. Paul Wurtzel, who would later become an assistant director on the *12 O'Clock High* television series, was also on the movie production staff. Wurtzel remembered an incident in which the filming of the B-17 flying sequences almost ended in tragedy. "I remember they had one shot with a B-17 taking off," said Wurtzel. "They had the camera out in the middle of the runway, and the damn plane never got up high enough to clear the camera. One of the wheels was retracting. It hit the top of the camera. There were a couple of cameramen out there that shouldn't have been. They should have just turned it on and run away, you know." But they didn't. "The cameramen waited, and the wheel hit a box of filters that was sitting there, and a lot of red filters went up in the air. And they thought this guy got killed. I remember his name as Red Crawford, the camera assistant. After it was over they went into the NCO Club for a drink or something, and he just fell flat on his face, passed out in a faint. He didn't react 'til a few hours later. He didn't know what had happened to him!"

THE BELLY-LANDING SEQUENCE

After much internal hand-wringing and some nudging from Darryl Zanuck at Twentieth Century-Fox, the Air Force allowed technical advisor John deRussy to select an aircraft to fly the belly-landing scene in *12 O'Clock High*. DeRussy picked a B-17 that had been used for A-bomb testing and was still slightly radioactive, but was safe to fly for short durations. The Air Force cautioned deRussy to be careful about setting up the shot: "In view of possible unfavorable public reaction to belly-landing a B-17 for film sequence, please take such action as you deem advisable to minimize public reaction to the contemplated operation."

Filming of the dangerous sequence took place at Ozark Field, Alabama. There was no room for error. If the scene was unsuccessful, it was doubtful that the Air Force would provide another aircraft for the studio to destroy. Although the Air Force had allowed its personnel to fly B-17s in formation scenes, it refused to lend any of its crews for the stunt crash. John deRussy, who had personally led some of the formation flying, was eager to belly-land a B-17, but as an active duty Air Force officer he was prohibited from doing so. Stunt pilot Paul Mantz—who had already been hired to film the flying sequences from his camera-equipped B-25—volunteered but requested a very high paycheck for the job. When a frustrated King offered to perform the stunt himself, Mantz gave in and settled on a price of $2500.

King set up four cameras to record the shot. According to author Bruce Orriss, Mantz's mechanic loaded the aircraft with minimal fuel and welded a rod across the power switches so that Mantz could cut them as soon as he hit the ground. The scene called for Mantz to barrel the huge ship between two tents and knock down the poles that were holding them up. Behind the controls of the B-17 *Eager Beaver*, Mantz flew at 110 miles per hour and carefully dropped the 38,000-pound aircraft, wheels-up, onto the grass at Ozark Field. It slid almost 1200 feet on its belly and gradually ground to a halt. The nail-biting stunt was quite impressive on screen and would become one of the most memorable scenes in *12 O'Clock High*.

Stunt pilot and aerial cinematographer Paul Mantz shares a canister of film with actress Joyce Mackenzie, who played a Red Cross nurse in *12 O'Clock High*.

The Twentieth Century-Fox publicity department hailed the talented Mantz as "the only man alive who has been insured for nine million dollars. Every time Mantz risks his neck, and he has done so 90 times while cameras recorded the action, he takes out a $100,000 policy with Lloyds of London." Mantz, who had been flying since 1919, had worked on 15 movies at Fox. The studio continued, "He has flown every type of plane, from a Jennie to a Jet, and has the remarkable record of 10,000 hours and 2,000,000 miles." For *12 O'Clock High*, Mantz's special B-25 camera ship featured lenses attached to the tail, nose, and fuselage. "We really got some thrilling shots," he said.

LOCATION FILMING WRAPS, JUNE 1949

Director Henry King and his company of 150 people completed the four-week location shoot in June 1949. It was time to return to the West Coast. As a generous thank-you, King offered technical advisor John deRussy the use of his boat. "John, you can take it easy," said King. "Go fishing." If deRussy was needed during the remainder of production, King would let him know. Unfortunately, the Air Force had other plans. The day after King made his offer, the Pentagon sent orders for deRussy to report back to Maxwell AFB to prepare for his next assignment. DeRussy was surprised, especially since he was supposed to coordinate the safe return of the equipment that the Air Force had lent to the studio. "What do I do with this millions of dollars of property?" he asked the Pentagon. He received a noncommittal answer.

DeRussy soon found out that his next assignment would be overseas and that he was leaving almost immediately. He had no time to take care of the borrowed *12 O'Clock High* materiel. DeRussy was well aware that many actors in the film, enamored of spiffy costume items like the A-2 leather flying jacket, had "lost" the uniforms that were issued to them. How would the studio return the gear if the cast was taking it home? To make matters worse, Twentieth Century-Fox wanted to keep the authentic uniform parts for its wardrobe department. DeRussy was shocked. "Hey! You can't do that!" he told Jason Joy, the Fox public relations director. "I'd get court-martialed!" In jest, deRussy told Joy that if Fox was going to keep the uniforms, the studio should first reimburse deRussy for the salary he would have made had he been able to stay in the Air Force and become a General instead of being court-martialed as a Colonel.

Joy promised deRussy that Fox would return every last piece of borrowed equipment, even if they had to replace the "lost" items. DeRussy suggested that the studio could shop at military surplus stores to find replacements. Satisfied with the arrangement, deRussy returned to Maxwell AFB to prepare for his next Air Force assignment.

Meanwhile, Twentieth Century-Fox continued reviewing stock footage for inclusion in *12 O'Clock High*. On 20 June 1949, Tony Muto phoned the Pentagon to request 297 feet of film that was stored at the U.S. Army Signal Corps Photographic Center in New York. Muto's request included 50 feet of footage of a B-17 falling; 40 feet of "long shot plane streaming smoke, parachute opening"; 120 feet of a German fighter shooting at a B-17, and 87 feet of "plane falling, parachute opening, plane crashing."

WRAPPING IT UP

With location shooting completed, the cast and crew returned to the Fox studios in Hollywood, where craftsmen had built the interior sets for *12 O'Clock High*. The sets included Stovall's and Savage's offices as well as the ornate rooms of Wycombe Abbey, headquarters of Bomber Command. The subsequent five weeks of studio time also involved "process" shooting in the B-17 mock-up. Actors delivered their lines from the mock-up while a rear-projected film of B-17s in formation ran behind them to simulate flight.

Henry King and his company had reached the halfway point in the production of *12 O'Clock High* when Gregory Peck was suddenly hospitalized. An eye infection downed the actor as he traveled from Florida back to Hollywood, delaying his scenes for five days. There was good news to be had, though. Peck's third son, Carey, was born four weeks later. According to a studio publicity release, Peck's telegraph bill went through the ceiling when his son was born. Peck sent telegrams to 23 relatives in Australia, several dozen in the United States, and his wife's 32 relatives in Finland.

Production on *12 O'Clock High* wrapped on 1 July 1949. Jason Joy, the studio's director of public relations, fulfilled his promise to technical advisor John deRussy. He scrounged for any missing items and returned all borrowed equipment to the Air Force. Said deRussy, "They turned in everything except a couple pairs of socks and a couple pairs of underwear! I don't know how they did it, but they did." Next, the film entered the editing room, where a rough cut was created.

THE INITIAL PREVIEW, OCTOBER 1949

The first version of *12 O'Clock High* was two hours and 20 minutes long. On 20 October 1949, the rough cut was screened at a special preview at the Fox Theater in Riverside, California. David Lackie, the theater manager, filed a confidential report to Fox executives. "This is a big picture," he wrote, "big in every way and should be a contender for top honors when the ballots are tallied. The first five names mentioned in the cast [Peck, Marlowe, Merrill, Mitchell, Jagger] really have a field day for acting which held the audience in their seats throughout the picture. The whole film is tense with action, relieved only by the humor of the briefing scenes and the occasionally humorous disciplinary scenes; and the air shots of the planes on bombing runs, battling enemy fighters, are magnificent." Lackie added, "Production values are excellent and the direction is in the usual high Henry King standard." However, he did say that the film "should be cut at least 20 minutes, even at the cost of losing some entertainment value." Daryl Zanuck relayed Lackie's memo to director Henry King on 3 November 1949. Compromising, King trimmed *12 O'Clock High* by eight minutes for its general release.

Due to delays at the studio, Fox was slow in preparing a print for the Air Force. The scheduled mid-November preview for the Air Force brass was delayed until Monday, 21 November. Meanwhile, the Air Force had reassigned technical advisor Col. John deRussy to Hungary, where he was serving as an air attaché officer. The studio sent a print of *12 O'Clock High* to Paris for a special personal screening.

Twentieth Century-Fox wanted to thank deRussy by giving him a few gifts, but deRussy reminded studio executives that Air Force regulations forbade such activity. Jason Joy persisted: "Hey, if you come down one day and a Cadillac is in front of the hotel with a license plate 'JdeR,' what can you do?" DeRussy thanked Joy but still said no. Joy said that when Navy technical advisors worked on Hollywood features, they "bought fur coats for their wives and diamond rings for their girlfriends. You're not living it up!" DeRussy stood firm. In the end the studio sent a modest gift: a personally inscribed watch.

In order to qualify for Oscar consideration among the films released in 1949, Twentieth Century-Fox decided to launch *12 O'Clock High* before the year was over, just in time for Christmas. As the date for the world premiere—21 December 1949—approached, the studio's marketing wizards got cracking on their promotional strategy. Advertising slogans blared, "The world stands still at *12 O'Clock High!*" Another ad rallied the audience with breathless prose: "Out of the sun . . . where danger waited! Out of the thunder and the night . . . that sounded the high fury of battle . . . comes the star-spangled story of the heroic Eighth Air Force!" To grab the female audience, posters proclaimed, "A story of twelve men as their women never knew them."

The Fox publicity department prepared three "teaser trailers" for theaters. "Out of the sun . . . the stars . . . the thunder . . . and the night comes *12 O'Clock High*," announced one of them excitedly. Gregory Peck's narration encouraged audiences to flock to their local theater: "I volunteered to do this because I believe that *12 O'Clock High* is a particularly fine picture, a great and unusual picture. Certainly no other I have ever seen has moved me as much. The role of Savage in *12 O'Clock High,* which I had the good fortune to play, is the most satisfying of my movie career. Savage is an exceptional personality, who dares to be all things to twelve men—a man who crosses wings with destiny. Because of what *12 O'Clock High* will do emotionally for those who see it, I urge you not to miss this magnificent entertainment."

Twentieth Century-Fox provided several promotional ideas to theater owners, trumpeting that *12 O'Clock High* was "worthy of your maximum showmanship effort. Give it the gun and watch your boxoffice soar to new heights!" Marketing-savvy theaters could offer free tickets to the first 50 patrons "who send in tear sheets with the words '12,' 'O'Clock' and 'High' circled with red pencil." The words could be culled from advertisements and news articles. "Your newspaper will be glad to give this stunt a big play because it will insure the reading of every page until the three magic words—*12 O'Clock High*—are found." For aircraft aficionados, Fox recommended a miniature airplane model contest for grade school and high school boys. In coordination with local schools, theater owners could award a $25 savings bond and free tickets to students who built the best miniatures. Another contest option was a high school essay of 300 words: "Today when leadership in politics, civic affairs, good citizenship, inter-racial activities, educational endeavors and even in the defense of the nation is uppermost in the minds of everyone, this high school essay contest can be an important facet of publicity for *12 O'Clock High*." Of course, students were "urged to read the book which is available in a 25-cent edition."

For audience members interested in collectibles, Fox encouraged theater owners to work with local antique dealers and specialty shops to create window displays featuring the Toby mug from the film. Also recommended was an auction of war trophies "volunteered from local members and former members of the armed forces. On opening night stage an auction of the trophies with the proceeds going to a suitable charity or an American Legion fund. The display will have a 'war museum' slant to attract crowds throughout the run."

Less complicated marketing efforts involved a clock, a truck, a jewelry store, and a stack of books. "Set up a large, spectacular electric clock over your box office," crowed Fox. Free tickets would go to customers who arrived at the theater at 12 o'clock sharp. For those theater owners with vehicles handy, "rig up a truck with two huge cutout clocks mounted on each side with the hands pointing to 12 o'clock. Send this truck on a tour of your city in advance of your playdate." Jewelry stores were encouraged to create window displays spotlighting— what else?—clocks and watches set at 12 o'clock. Meanwhile, Bantam Books printed 250,000 fresh copies of the novel, with cover artwork that featured a stern Gregory Peck staring directly at the reader. "Was this soldier too daring?" asked the headline above the title.

Twentieth Century-Fox also provided theater owners with a comprehensive list of military contacts, including members of the local Air Force Association and public information officers at military bases around the world. The exhibitors' handbook noted that "top Air Force officers in the Pentagon building in Washington have put their stamp of approval on *12 O'Clock High* and are making Air Force personnel and equipment available for use by alert showmen through-out the United States." From lobby exhibits of military equipment to marching parades and mayoral proclamations, the studio encouraged maximum use of the military theme.

Radio Marketing

"Pre-sold to 100 million American listeners," the studio proudly proclaimed to the press. Blanketing the airwaves, Fox bought advertising time on radio stations across the nation. "Twentieth Century-Fox took advantage of one of the greatest natural exploitation stunts of the century to advertise *12 O'Clock High* via radio on New Year's Eve. One thousand, two hundred and fifty individual radio stations from coast to coast, covering every section of the United States, played special spot announcements beginning at 11:59, 11:59:30 and 11:59:50." Fox boasted that its advertisements were "the largest single radio plug in the nation," reaching 100 million listeners. Actresses Betty Grable, Jeanne Crain, and Linda Darnell recorded radio spots for the film. Even director Henry King was busy plugging *12 O'Clock High* on the radio. On the Mutual Network, King starred in an eight-minute spot about the film. He also appeared on ABC's *Stop The Music* game show, did an interview for the *Luncheon at Sardi's* program, and was featured on *Hollywood Screen Test, Toast of the Town,* and *This Is New York.*

On 27 January 1950, the day before the New York premiere, the NBC and Mutual networks ran lengthy advertising for *12 O'Clock High*. The NBC interview program *We the People*, the first regular series simulcast on radio and via the fledgling television medium, dedicated its half hour to the film. On the day after the *12 O'Clock High* premiere, Mutual's *Army Air Force Hour* devoted its 30 minutes to "a continuous plug for the picture."

The world premiere – Grauman's Chinese Theatre, Hollywood, 21 December 1949

For premieres across the country, Twentieth Century-Fox planned a number of military extravaganzas. In a letter to the Air Force, Fox executive Frank McCarthy noted that "the care, the skill, and the expense involved in making the picture will have been in vain, from the Air Force point of view as well as our own, unless a high percentage of the American public sees it." Labeling *12 O'Clock High* a "joint venture" between the military and Hollywood, McCarthy asked the Air Force one last time for help to "impress upon the public the value of the film as a document of our times."

To begin, the studio asked for help from the public relations office at March Air Force Base in nearby Riverside, California. For the night of the world premiere in Hollywood, Fox requested that one or two bands perform, "marching from the corner of Hollywood and Vine Streets to the theatre just before the performance begins." A private screening would be held that afternoon for the band members and any other servicemen who participated in the parade. Along the parade route, the studio wanted "any bodies of troops or cadets available in this area" to march with the bands, and that "any airplanes which can be made available" fly overhead. In early January 1950, Fox requested and received from the Air Force a large amount of equipment to be used as display material in theater lobbies. Included in the package were 25 bombsights and two B-17 plexiglas nose assemblies.

Finally, Fox asked the Air Force to provide contacts at local Reserve units and "appropriate officials of West Coast airplane manufacturing plants." By contacting them, Fox could spread the word about *12 O'Clock High*. Mindful of the whole-hearted cooperation the studio received from the Army for the recent film *Battleground*, Fox hoped that the Air Force would provide the same type of assistance, which it did.

After more than two years of hard work, the curtains opened on *12 O'Clock High* at Grauman's Chinese Theatre, the famous movie house on Hollywood Boulevard. Twentieth Century-Fox invited Frank Armstrong, one of the inspirations for *12 O'Clock High*, to attend the premiere. "Dear General Armstrong," read the studio telegram, "We wish to invite you to world premiere of Twentieth Century-Fox film *12 O'Clock High* to be given Wednesday evening December twenty-first at Chinese Theatre Hollywood. Eager to have you as our guest for dinner premiere and reception as well as overnight stay at local hotel. Picture was made with full Air Force cooperation and approval. We are inviting many other wartime Air Force leaders. Hope you will attend."

Lt. Gen. Frank Armstrong during the 1950s. Armstrong retired from the Air Force in July 1961.

Armstrong, at the time the commanding general of Alaskan Air Command, accepted the invitation and flew from Elmendorf AFB, Alaska, to Hollywood. At the premiere he reunited with Ira Eaker, Curtis LeMay, and a host of other Air Force officers. Among the honored guests were three aces: Lt. Col. John Meyer, Lt. Col. Francis Gabreski, and Capt. Dominic Gentile. Arriving at 8 P.M., Armstrong was welcomed by Armed Forces Radio, which was broadcasting the event live, and the 60-piece Air Force band from Lackland AFB in San Antonio, Texas. The movie began at 8:30 P.M. Armstrong felt that the film sometimes stretched the truth but found the aerial combat sequences "frightfully realistic." After the screening, Armstrong attended a party, enjoyed a late dinner, and returned home the next day.

Armstrong later wrote that his only regret about the film was the scene in which Gen. Savage "cracked up" and couldn't climb into his aircraft. Military personnel familiar with *12 O'Clock High* were aware that the character of Savage was based on Armstrong. "At least a hundred times people who did not serve with us in England asked how long it took me to recover from the breakdown," he said, slightly miffed. "Those who were there have never ceased to jokingly tell me, 'It's too bad you never quite got over your mental problem!'"

PREMIERE – ROXY THEATRE, NEW YORK CITY, 28 JANUARY 1950

The East Coast premiere of *12 O'Clock High* was held at the magnificent Roxy Theatre in New York City. The film began regular showings on 28 January 1950, the eighth birthday of the Eighth Air Force and also one day after the seventh anniversary of the Eighth Air Force's first foray into Germany at Wilhelmshaven. The Air Force Association sponsored a special screening at the Roxy, with luminaries like Gen. Carl Spaatz—by then a former Chief of Staff of the Air Force—attending. A newspaper report noted that "75 patrolmen had little difficulty in controlling the crowds, estimated at several thousand by the police. A heavy downpour shortly after 8 P.M. failed to dim the enthusiasm of the onlookers who lined police barricades on Seventh Avenue between 49th and 50th Streets and east on 15th Street." The premiere was announced by a 50-piece Air Force band from nearby Mitchel Field in Hempstead.

Joseph Landers, a navigator with the 392d Bomb Group, remembered a screening at a different New York location—Radio City Music Hall. "The newspapers told us that 12 O'Clock High was opening at Radio City in New York and any and all members of the Eighth Air Force were invited to the initial showing. My wife and I attended, and we were part of a packed house."

PREMIERE - ORPHEUM THEATRE, OMAHA, NEBRASKA

Another big premiere for 12 O'Clock High was held at the Orpheum Theatre in Omaha, Nebraska, the host city for Offutt AFB and the Strategic Air Command. SAC was responsible for overseeing America's nuclear deterrent forces, which included bomber aircraft. The commanding general was none other than cigar-chomping Curtis LeMay, former commander of the 305th Bombardment Group. LeMay originally thought the film would be "a bunch of baloney," recalled technical advisor John deRussy. But the General changed his mind about the film after seeing it, remarking, "I don't believe it. I don't see one technical error in this thing."

Though the 12 O'Clock High celebration in Omaha was on a smaller scale than the Hollywood and New York premieres, it nevertheless had its own special touches. Inside the theater, a group of Air Force military policemen formed a parade of flags of all United Nations members and marched them to the stage. The flags formed a backdrop for the U.S. and Air Force flags, which were positioned front and center. One of the military policemen, then called the Air Police, was Neil Halbisen, who remembered that many movie stars attended the screening. Among them were western actor Rod Cameron and actor-comedian-bandleader Phil Harris with his wife Alice Faye. Halbisen specifically remembered Harris and Faye "because they took the Soviet Union flag from me and hid it backstage—neither they nor I wanted it in the performance." The Cold War years were underway, and anticommunist feelings were running strong.

Before the film rolled, Gen. LeMay said a few words to the audience. He then brought a special guest onstage, a World War II veteran like himself. Recounted Halbisen: "Gen. LeMay introduced this Air Force master sergeant who had picked up a burning phosphorous flare that was burning a hole in the floor of their bomber, carried it to the bomb bay, and threw it out. The sergeant had lost most of his fingers. His face as well as his body was scarred. A real walking hero!"

The flag-waving promotional campaign for *12 O'Clock High* proved very successful, and most of the reviews for the film were highly complimentary. "*12 O'Clock High* is the freshest and most convincing movie of the current cycle about World War II," noted *Time* magazine. "It successfully blends an artistry all too seldom shown by Hollywood and the high technical skill that only Hollywood commands." *Time* complimented the film for having "the uncommon merit of restraint. It avoids such cinemilitary booby traps as self-conscious heroics, overwrought battle scenes and the women left behind or picked up along the way."

Look magazine hailed the "quietly powerful" film as "among the war's top pictures" and billed it as Gregory Peck's best performance to date. *Movie Story* fired a hyperbolic salvo in its description of Peck's role: "Slave-driver, they called him. But he made men of them all!" The *Hollywood Reporter* headline shouted that *12 O'Clock High* "packs tremendous wallop." In an enthusiastic review, the newspaper praised the film for avoiding stereotypes. "Its action matter is thrilling, and its subtle emotional content grips the heart. Its quiet note of patriotism stirs deeply."

The actors received their fair share of kudos as well. "Nothing about the film is better than its performances," remarked *Time*. "Dean Jagger without his toupee seems to have launched an entirely new career." *Look* also praised Jagger, who "with his most important screen role since the memorable *Brigham Young* of 1940, brings a dry humor to the role of a retread still doing his share to help win a war." *Life* praised Jagger as the film's best actor. Gregory Peck garnered acclaim as well: "an extraordinarily able job" (*New York Times*); "a strong, beautifully modulated performance that never lets the role down" and "just about his best work to date" (*Time*). Hugh Marlowe, according to one reviewer, was "extremely satisfactory in what has become a stereotyped war-film character: son of a long line of West Pointers who doesn't like war." The *Philadelphia Inquirer's* Mildred Martin might have said it best: "There is no need for stars in this picture. For every player matters separately."

The authenticity that the production crew worked so hard to achieve did not go unnoticed by the critics. *Cue* noted that "the film has been put together with a remarkable sense of realism." Bosley Crowther of the *New York Times* praised the film's "conspicuous dramatic integrity, genuine emotional appeal and a sense of the moods of an air base that absorb and amuse the mind." *Life* placed Gregory Peck on the cover, clad in flying gear, and noted plainly that "the conventional heroics and the conventional jokes were left out of *12 O'Clock High*. The characters and their problems both look real." Overall praise for Henry King and the movie was summed up in *Life*: "The movie never loses the sense of immediate, undistorted reality that makes it the most honest and powerful of the crop of war pictures currently sprouting in Hollywood."

All of the praise reached its peak at the Academy Awards ceremony on 23 March 1950, where *12 O'Clock High* was nominated four times and captured two honors: Best Supporting Actor (Dean Jagger) and Best Sound Recording. Despite the Academy's plea that winners keep their acceptance speeches short, Dean Jagger took the time to thank all his coworkers. Tom Moulton, W.D. Flick and Roger Heman accepted the Best Sound Recording Oscar. In addition the film scored nominations for Best Picture and Best Actor (Gregory Peck). Although he didn't win the Oscar, Peck would have his day. He was named Best Actor of the Year by the New York Film Critics Circle.

FOR TRAINING PURPOSES

Soon after the film's release, savvy instructors from both military and civilian organizations realized *12 O'Clock High's* potential as a training aid for budding managers. On 25 May 1951, the deputy Adjutant General at Air Training Command, Maj. H.O. Parsons, sent an analysis of both *12 O'Clock High* and *Command Decision* to the Director of Training at the Pentagon. "[*12 O'Clock High*] portrays forcefully the responsibilities of the combat unit commander," Parsons wrote, "as well as those of the individual crew member and the necessity of self-discipline to the welfare of the group." Parsons noted that both films would be useful in training aircrews by providing "a preview" of their responsibilities. "Both seem to be very effective aids to building a common spirit of loyalty and enthusiasm among members of a combat group." To that end, Parsons listed the Air Force courses that would benefit from viewings of *12 O'Clock High*. They included Officers Candidate School, Advanced Pilot Training, Airplane Maintenance Officers Course, Flight Engineer Course, Flexible Gunnery Training, and Radar Observer Training. Parsons recommended that copies of the film be procured for 18 training locations including Lackland, Vance, Reese, Mather, Ellington, Chanute, Lowry, and Keesler Air Force Bases.

In June, the Air Force revised its request, asking for only 10 prints of *12 O'Clock High*. This was reflected in a memo sent by Lt. Col. Rowald Mosher, the deputy in the Training Aids Division at the Pentagon. The request was routed through Air Materiel Command at Wright-Patterson AFB in Dayton, Ohio, the Air Force's main logistics center. On 23 July 1951, Twentieth Century-Fox responded to the Air Force's request with its standard licensing agreement. "Our customary policy in making films available to governmental agencies for orientation and training use is to license these prints for a period of three years at a cost of $600 per print." It would take several weeks to strike the prints.

But by 10 August a problem had developed. After Air Training Command informed the Pentagon that prints of *12 O'Clock High* would cost the government $600 each, Lt. Col. Mosher grumbled that the price was "believed to be excessive for retail on a film which contains questionable parts." Air Training Command asked its subordinate units to provide feedback within four working days. Was *12 O'Clock High* worth the price?

Lackland AFB in San Antonio, Texas—the entry point for basic trainees in the

Air Force—responded with praise for the film. "*12 O'Clock High* is shown following the 12th hour of Leadership Instruction in the Officer Candidate School, and is also included in the Officer Training School course. Student reaction to the leadership problems illustrated in this film has been outstanding, and it is felt that the film has been most successful as a training aid. It is further believed that the leadership phase of the officer training schools would be much less effective if this film were deleted from the curricula." The Adjutant at Lowry AFB in Denver, Colorado, had similar thoughts. "An urgent need exists for some vehicle which is capable of instilling in potential gunnery trainees a strong desire for combat crew training." Concerned that trainees lacked the "warrior attitude," Maj. F.A. Rogers continued: "It is felt that the above-mentioned films will strongly motivate the potential gunner along this line and consequently improve the quality of the finished product." Other training bases responded in similar fashion.

The instructors had spoken. In a letter dated 19 December 1951, Brigadier General Gabriel P. Disosway, the Director of Training for the Air Force, wrote to the Office of the Secretary of Defense, requesting that DoD acquire seven copies of *12 O'Clock High* and four copies of *Command Decision*. It turned out that the Pentagon could compel the studios to provide the films at no cost to the government. On 4 January 1952, Lt. Col. Clair Towne of the DoD Office of Public Information wrote to Anthony Muto, Fox's representative in Washington, D.C., to request copies of *12 O'Clock High*. In his communiqué, Towne referred to the *Guide for Obtaining the Cooperation of the National Military Establishment,* which allowed the military to obtain copies of films that the DoD helped create. "The Directorate of Training of the U.S. Air Force has determined that the picture *12 O'Clock High* is of definite value to the training program of the Air Force. The Office of Public Information, Department of Defense, has considered all of the evidence which supports this determination, and concurs in the requirement for seven 16mm copies of the subject picture for the use of the Training Command of the Air Force."

Civilian companies made use of *12 O'Clock High* as well. In 1980, for example, Intel Corporation, a maker of computer chips, leased six copies of the film for a three-year period. The licensing fee for each copy was $1000. Lynda Shapiro, a program developer in Intel's Corporate Training department, wrote to Twentieth Century-Fox: "We at Intel use the movie for our in-house training of leadership styles. We never charge for our training sessions, and only Intel managers are invited to attend. We would be interested in purchasing six copies of this film so each of our domestic plants could have its own copy."

EDUCATORS OF A DIFFERENT SORT: THE 918TH BOMB GROUP LIVING MEMORIAL

A current organization using *12 O'Clock High* as an educational tool is the 918th Bomb Group Living Memorial. The nonprofit group, founded in 1993, provides costumed interpreters and displays that celebrate the legacy of the

Organizational patch of the 918th Bomb Group Living Memorial, an organization of volunteer historians and collectors who provide educational displays at air shows, veterans' reunions, and other events. Note the inclusion of the Toby jug from *12 O'Clock High* in the design.

B-17 Flying Fortress. "We gratefully acknowledge the service and sacrifices of the brave crews who flew them," says member Kevin Gray, "as well as the tireless ground crews who kept them flying in World War II." The founders of the Living Memorial were inspired by the film *12 O'Clock High* and decided to capture and retell stories about the B-17 bomber. "My love for B-17s started at around age nine," Gray says. "I've always said that, to me, the B-17 is the most beautiful man-made thing with wings."

Many of the members are collectors. "We put together extensive displays of B-17 artifacts, uniforms, and flight gear," notes Gray. Items included in the collection are an aircraft instrument panel, radios, a .50-caliber waist gun, a Norden bombsight, uniforms, mission diaries, flight helmets, goggles, oxygen masks, and even some "Mae West" life preservers. "We even have a few veterans who talk to visitors," Gray says. "They tell their stories, answer questions, and explain the functions of equipment on display."

Members of the 918th Bomb Group Living Memorial, c. 1996. Top row, left to right: Brian Thrailkill, Greg Hatzenbuhler, Ed Gustafson, Roy Test, John Gilbert. Bottom row: Kevin Gray, David Webster, Wilbur Richardson. Not pictured: Charles Workman, Denny Gregory, Mike Faley, David Bybee, Pete Plumb, Mike Yamada, and Vern Grim. Three members are B-17 combat veterans: Grim was a pilot with the 92nd Bomb Group, Test was a co-pilot with the 398th, and Richardson was a ball turret gunner with the 94th.

Over the years the members of the 918th Living Memorial have been invited to install their displays at veterans' reunions and air shows. Michael Faley, a member of the group, says that "the thrill for us is to meet the men who flew the B-17 and hear their stories first hand. When you hear about 'flak so thick you could walk on it' or 'the ship in front of us just blew up, no chutes,' your imagination wanders as the older gentleman in front of you wipes a tear away for a friend who never made it back."

The group also makes research trips to build its artifact collection and learn more about the heritage of the B-17. According to Faley, "One of our most informative trips was when five of us went to England to visit the airfields of the Eighth Air Force B-17 groups. We visited 22 of the airfields in a week's time." While touring the old bases, the group was moved by what it saw—"a hardstand here, a control tower there, Quonset huts ravaged by time," recalls Faley. "Many men took off from each of these bases, never to return."

As costumed interpreters, the members of the 918th Living Memorial consider themselves history teachers. "We field questions from all age groups," states Faley, "but mostly from young children who want to know more about what the artifacts represent. The displays encourage the children to ask their parents, 'What did grandpa do in the war?' If only one child does that, our efforts are a success."

THE MYSTERY OF THE TOBY MUG

Many years after the release of *12 O'Clock High*, a management training company that used the film in its curriculum would be the key to solving a fascinating mystery linked to the film. During the opening scenes of *12 O'Clock High*, a bespectacled Harvey Stovall notices a special goblet in the window of a London curio shop. Called a "Toby," the hand-painted drinking mug turns out to be the same one used by his old bomb group during World War II. Toby jugs have been produced in England since the 18th Century and are traditionally modeled in the shape of a man wearing a hat. In *12 O'Clock High*, the 918th Bomb Group's mug—shaped like Robin Hood, with characteristic mask and hat—resides on the mantelpiece in the Officers' Club. When a mission was scheduled, the mug would be turned to face the room, signaling the crews to prepare themselves without alarming any visitors.

A key scene in the film version of *12 O'Clock High:* In the officers' club, Maj. Stovall (Dean Jagger) rotates the Toby jug forward to signal that a new mission is imminent.

After production wrapped on *12 O'Clock High* in July 1949, the Toby mug used in the film apparently disappeared. But 44 years later an enterprising engineer and pilot named Pete Plumb set out to produce replicas of the classic curio—and find out what had happened to the original.

In 1993 Plumb visited the Planes of Fame museum at Chino, California, where the television version of *12 O'Clock High* had been filmed during the 1960s. Planes of Fame had supplied an operational B-17 for the series, and that aircraft was now on static display outside the museum. As Plumb recalled, "Wilbur Richardson, a ball turret gunner in the 94th Bomb Group during the war, was there that day working on the B-17. We started talking about *12 O'Clock High* and the significance of the Toby jug in the movie. I learned that many people had been looking for the original jug or a replica that might have been produced over the years. Like everyone else, I hunted in every ceramics shop and antique store around town, to no avail."

Undaunted, Plumb hired two sculptors in rapid succession to create a clay and then a plaster model of the Toby mug. Plumb's only reference material was a photo snapped while the movie was running on television. Dissatisfied with the progress and insisting on an accurate reproduction, Plumb taught himself how to carve in plaster. "After a year of trial and error—lots of error—and many, many plaster models, I had a version that looked pretty darn close to the original movie prop." Plumb opened negotiations with Twentieth Century Fox for the right to produce the mug in limited quantities. At first, Fox was a bit confused at his request. "Their response to my statement was, 'You want to do *what* from *what?*'" By August 1993, Plumb had gotten Fox interested and began looking for a manufacturer. Fox provided some studio publicity stills of the mug so that Plumb could finalize his design. To market and sell the product, Plumb created the company Air Corps Classics, based in Shafter, California.

The man with the mug: Pete Plumb sells replicas of the Toby mug featured in *12 O'Clock High*. Here, at a June 2000 air show in Reading, Pennsylvania, he duplicates the movie scene in which Maj. Stovall (Dean Jagger) rotates the jug to face the room, signaling a mission to come.

Plumb's father, who inspired his son's interests in *12 O'Clock High* and flying airplanes, had been a pilot with the 487th Bombardment Group in World War II. Coincidentally, the 487th was also the unit that Lt. Col. Beirne Lay, co-author of *12 O'Clock High,* had commanded from February through May of 1944. Plumb completed the master model of the Toby jug on 17 November 1993, his father's birthday.

Production of the first 1000 mugs kicked off in December. For Plumb, it was a nail-biting experience. "Despite the considerable enthusiasm of friends, I was still not sure how well the jug would sell. The first ads had started to appear in aviation magazines and orders immediately began coming in." Due to growing pains on the production line, Plumb was forced to switch to a larger manufacturer, and as he did his business increased at a brisk pace. By the 1997 holiday season, Plumb had sold more than 2000 copies of the limited edition Toby mug. Ever creative, Plumb then added a new item to his catalog, the "General Savage" jug, which featured a remarkable likeness of actor Gregory Peck. By November 2004 steady interest from the public stimulated a large production run of the item.

Catching a breath from overseeing the production line, Plumb returned to the mystery that had launched his business in the first place. Where was the original Toby mug? "As I developed a customer base," noted Plumb, "I realized that sooner or later someone would call me who knew where the original jug had gone." And indeed someone did. In 1998, Plumb received a phone call from Randy Baker, director of the Center for Leadership Studies, a management training company in Escondido, California. "Randy called to order some jugs because they used *12 O'Clock High* in their curriculum. In the course of our conversation he mentioned that he'd run into a descendant of Gen. Frank Armstrong, and that the original movie jug had been an Armstrong family heirloom since 1949." In fact, Dorothy Walker, the General's secretary, remembered that Armstrong kept a Toby mug in his quarters during the 1950s. Was it the same one from *12 O'Clock High*?

Plumb eventually reached the Armstrong family and was finally able to solve the mystery. "The original movie jug had been presented to Gen. Armstrong as a gift from Henry King at the end of filming," recounted Plumb. "Upon General Armstrong's death, the jug was bequeathed to his sister, who cherished and loved the historic piece." Unfortunately, the story didn't have a happy ending. At some point in the early 1990s, the Toby jug disappeared from the family home. The colorful curio was missing once again.

The Toby mug remains elusive, but there is no mystery about *12 O'Clock High*'s enduring popularity. For military veterans, film buffs, management trainees, and everyone else, *12 O'Clock High* is an excellent example of a detailed historical study of leadership under pressure. For actor Robert Arthur, the quality of the film was evident early on. "I think *12 O'Clock High* has withstood the test of time because it is a very fine example of filmmaking. Frank McCarthy, the producer, was a perfectionist, as were Leon Shamroy, the cinematographer, and of course Henry King, the director. The entire cast and crew was devoted to making a fine example of the spirit of the U.S. Air Force. The sentiments of how servicemen and their officers relate to each other continue to impress us. There wasn't a moment that we weren't determined to make a great movie."

THE TELEVISION SERIES

Nearly 20 years after the end of the war depicted in *12 O'Clock High*, Twentieth Century-Fox was confronted with its own version of D-Day. In 1962, the studio that produced the highly praised war movie was embroiled in a real-life battle for survival. Fox faced crises in leadership, creativity and finances that jeopardized the studio's existence.

The back story of this debacle had its beginnings more than a decade earlier. All of Hollywood's dream factories—Columbia, MGM, Paramount, RKO, Republic, Universal and Warner Brothers, as well as Fox—were backed into a corner. Beginning in the early 1950s, movie ticket sales had been decreasing steadily. The reason: television. In 1951, areas served by TV stations reported mass shuttering of theaters. Fifty-five movie houses closed in New York City, 61 in Massachusetts, 64 in greater Chicago, 70 in Eastern Pennsylvania and 134 in Southern California.

Reacting to decreased demand for their product, studios either cut back production or closed their doors for good. By 1955, the major Hollywood players produced a total of only 215 features, their smallest output to date. In 1957, MGM posted the first loss in its 33-year history. The next year, Columbia, Universal and Warners all experienced declining profits. Republic Pictures stopped producing films in 1956, and RKO followed suit two years later.

GIMMICKS AND GAMBITS

To lure audiences back to the big screen, Fox introduced a new gimmick. CinemaScope changed the look of movies by creating an image 2.55 times wider than its height, which was more rectangular-looking than the the traditional 1.33 to 1 ratio that had been the standard for years. Unveiling such a radical approach to filmmaking was both risky and costly. The studio took a gamble and registered CinemaScope as a trademark of Twentieth Century-Fox Film Corporation. Fox first used the new format on *The Robe*

(1954), which became the studio's biggest money-maker at the time. Subsequent CinemaScope releases also performed very well, proving the investment was well worth the risk.

However creating bigger movies did not result in increased output. With fewer films being made, the layers of infrastructure that supported production and distribution were no longer necessary. Cadres of writers, producers, directors and performers were cut from the studio payrolls.

Hollywood was undergoing a cultural, as well as a technological, revolution. Gone were the halcyon days of yesteryear. Darryl F. Zanuck resigned control of the studio he had ruled since 1935. Zanuck's successors didn't possess his story sense, understanding of audiences or passion for filmmaking. Within two years, mismanagement had burrowed Twentieth Century-Fox into a financial pit. In May 1956 Spyros P. Skouras, then president of Fox, set an unparalleled precedent by leasing 52 vintage Fox films to television for between $2 and $3 million. The move meant that one day soon, *12 O'Clock High* would be seen in living rooms across America.

Skouras also moved to slash studio overhead by selling off the backlot to raise cash. In the glory days of Hollywood, all of the major studios had sprawling acres of exterior sets representing, for example, Europe, the Old West and New York City. These highly-detailed backdrops allowed filmmakers to tell a variety of stories on the assembly line schedule that reigned during the studio system. Divesting its 260 acres filled Fox's war chest with $43 million. Shortly after a scene for the 1961-62 Fox TV series *Bus Stop* was completed, bulldozers began leveling the venerable backlot. Movie legend Henry Fonda, star of many Fox pictures, was on hand for the event. "I made my first picture, *Farmer Takes a Wife*, on one of those sets," said Fonda. "Now they're going. It's kinda sad." The former Fox property became upscale Century City, California.

Much of the money generated from Fox's real estate sale was poured into the studio's 1962 marquee film *Cleopatra*, starring Elizabeth Taylor and Richard Burton. The troubled production dragged on for three years and would eventually run up a tab of $42 million. By comparison, the price tag on Fox's *The Longest Day* was $7.75 million. *Mr. Hobbs Takes a Vacation* cost $4.1 million and *Five Weeks in a Balloon* just $2.34 million. By betting everything on one film, Fox couldn't spare money to finance additional projects. The future of Twentieth Century-Fox was riding on one movie.

A further attempt to generate cash flow was the use of an auxiliary lot called Fox Western Avenue Studios as rental property. Its primary tenant was Four Star Productions, which ground out large quantities of half-hour pulp fiction for TV, mostly westerns and detective shows. *Richard Diamond, The Rifleman, Wanted: Dead or Alive* and more all filmed there until 1962, when Four Star switched its operations to Republic Studios. That left Fox's own *Dobie Gillis* as the only TV series in production there during the 1962-63 season.

THE PRODIGAL RETURNS

Unfortunately, all of these cash-generating schemes weren't saving Twentieth Century-Fox from financial disaster. Deposed studio chief Darryl Zanuck, who had remained the principal stockholder, was understandably concerned about his investment and began a campaign to retake control of Fox. Zanuck was soon back in power. He quickly appointed his son, Richard, as head of production for Fox films and president of Fox television.

Zanuck returned to a desperate situation. In the wake of *Cleopatra*, the studio found itself in serious trouble. But that was only the beginning. Marilyn Monroe, one of Fox's brightest stars of the 1950s, had been cast in a new comedy, *Something's Got to Give*. During production Monroe repeatedly showed up late, didn't know her lines and abruptly bolted for New York City. Fox scrapped the film and took a $2 million write-off. The eternal sex symbol Monroe died a short time later at the age of 36.

Production was subsequently shut down at the studio. A wave of firings took place. Fewer than 200 employees remained on the lot, and the commissary was closed. After *Dobie Gillis* ended its four year network television run, Fox had nothing else to put before the cameras. As a cost-cutting measure, Fox eventually shuttered its Western Avenue facility.

In John Gregory Dunne's *The Studio*, an unvarnished history of Twentieth Century-Fox, Richard Zanuck is quoted as saying, "Things were so tight, we were trying to figure out ways to get another janitor off the payroll."

Fox had to generate money fast. To get there, the studio set its sights on TV.

BIG SCREEN, LITTLE SCREEN

Like most of the major studios, Twentieth Century-Fox at first viewed television as the enemy. As more and more TV antennas went up, movie ticket sales went down. Gradually, as talent, production facilities and—most importantly—audiences slipped away to the enemy camp, the studios finally caved. Columbia Pictures was the first major studio to seize the opportunities afforded by television. To produce material for the new medium, Columbia reactivated a dormant subsidiary, Screen Gems, which originally produced theatrical cartoons.

Despite the curious love-hate relationship between movie studios and the television medium, Hollywood used its backlog of feature films as springboards to create TV fare. *Warner Brothers Presents* was an umbrella series that featured adaptations of the Warner films *Cheyenne*, *King's Row* and *Casablanca*. MGM created stand-alone, weekly series from its movies *National Velvet*, *Northwest Passage* and *The Thin Man*.

The logic was irrefutable. If audiences paid good money to see a film in a theater, they would certainly watch characters and situations they were familiar with week after week in their own home. In marketing terms, the property was "pre-sold" to viewers.

Symbolizing the attitude Hollywood studios had toward television, Fox relegated its small-screen production to its distant Western Avenue studios. *Dobie Gillis* producer Rod Amateau said that working at Fox Western was like being sent to Siberia. Adding insult to injury, Fox also spun off a subsidiary, TCF Television Productions, Inc. as its TV production arm. Naturally TCF stood for "Twentieth Century-Fox."

Fox's early TV efforts were retoolings of its big screen successes. Take, for example, *The Twentieth Century-Fox Hour*, which ran on CBS from 1955 to 1957. Some of the episodes clearly paid homage to their source material, including *Laura, Mr. Belvedere* and *The Miracle on 34th Street*. Other familiar stories simply received new titles: *Red Skies of Montana* (1952) turned into *Smoke Jumpers* and *The Ghost and Mrs. Muir* (1947) became *Strangers in the Night*. These hybrid shows not only slashed the cost of acquiring scripts but also boasted movie-studio production values on TV's shoestring budgets.

Drawing on the success of its small screen adaptations, Fox moved ahead with full-blown weekly series versions of hit films like *Broken Arrow, My Friend Flicka* and *How to Marry a Millionaire*. By the late 1950s, Fox dropped the TCF moniker and began branding its TV product with the powerful Twentieth Century-Fox name, searchlight logo and rousing fanfare.

LAYING THE CORNERSTONE

In October 1962, the new president of Fox Television, Richard Zanuck, took his first step in the rebuilding process. He hired William Self as the new director of all Fox TV activities.

Self once said, "I love the entertainment business," and his résumé showed it. Self knew the industry from the ground up. He spent eight years acting in movies such as *Red River* (1948), *Adam's Rib* (1949) and *The Thing From Another World* (1951). Realizing he was not blessed with star quality, Self moved into production starting in 1952 as assistant producer on the *China Smith* TV series. From there, Self joined *Schlitz Playhouse of Stars*, first as associate producer then working his way up to producer. He was briefly director of entertainment programming for CBS-TV in Hollywood, then joined Fox in 1959 as executive producer of shows such as *Margie, Bus Stop, Hong Kong* and *Dobie Gillis*.

Self understood that the stakes were high. To help reinvigorate the ailing studio, he needed to recruit proven talent. Under Self, Fox TV became a stable for independent producers. He actively recruited seasoned, dependable people and quickly signed contracts with a number of Hollywood's top show runners.

Self dug in and began whipping a dozen properties into pilot form. His counterparts at other production companies were also scouring their vaults for inspiration. *Naked City* and *Dr. Kildare*, both based on feature films, were critical and ratings successes. Eager to capitalize on this new profitable trend, the networks slated *The Virginian, Going My Way* and *Mr. Smith Goes to Washington*—all based on successful movies—for berths in the fall 1962-63 schedule.

Twentieth Century-Fox raided its catalog of classic films and pitched a number of television adaptations including *Peyton Place, Three Coins in the Fountain* and *12 O'Clock High*.

READY FOR TAKEOFF

From the beginning, TV programming experienced cyclical trends: sitcoms, westerns, talk shows, police shows, doctor shows, variety shows, reality shows, and the like.

In the late 1950s, ABC had tremendous success riding the Western genre with a stable of hits from Warner Brothers, including *Maverick, Cheyenne* and *Lawman*. Warners also supplied a steady stream of detective shows to the network, mostly clones of its landmark series *77 Sunset Strip*. All of these shows defined the "alphabet network" during its formative years.

But by 1962 westerns had cooled their heels, and private eyes couldn't buy a clue. ABC was forced to scramble for a new identity. That meant coming up with a fresh programming angle to hook audiences.

At the box office, moviegoers were lining up to see films like *The Guns of Navarone* (1961), *The War Lover* (1962) and Darryl Zanuck's epic *The Longest Day* (1962). As a result, more films with World War II backdrops were either in production or in the planning stages. These films were attracting middle-aged war veterans as well as their baby-boomer children, hungry for action and adventure.

Seizing the opportunity to jump-start a trend, ABC premiered two one-hour World War II dramas, *Combat!* and *The Gallant Men*, within days of each other. The network also launched *McHale's Navy*, a half-hour WWII-themed sitcom. A segment of *The Dick Powell Theatre* titled "Squadron" (airing 30 January 1962) was marketed as a pilot for a proposed series about a World War II Air Corps squadron. While *The Gallant Men* missed the mark, *McHale's Navy* was a ratings winner from the start. *Combat!* single-handedly sent boys and girls pleading with their parents for plastic helmets and toy machine guns to use in their backyard.

With this kind of appeal, the Second World War was officially back in vogue.

ENTER QUINN MARTIN

The elements of *12 O'Clock High* must have felt right to television producer and entrepreneur Quinn Martin, who had enlisted in the Army at age 17 and served in the Signal Corps throughout the European and Pacific theaters from 1940–45. The son of a film editor and producer, Quinn Martin was born Martin Cohn in

New York City on 22 May 1922. After moving his family to California, Martin's father helped his son get a union card and a summer stint as apprentice editor at MGM. After the war, Martin studied English at the University of California at Berkeley. He began his TV career at Ziv Productions during the early 1950s. Ziv was a syndication powerhouse, a small but efficient firm that churned out series such as *Sea Hunt, Highway Patrol, The Cisco Kid* and *Bat Masterson.* Martin spent three years at Ziv, beginning with the 1953–56 espionage series *I Led Three Lives.* He served as an audio supervisor, which was definitely starting out at the bottom. Company president Frederic Ziv called it "about as far down the line as you list on the screen [credits]."

Quinn Martin

Over the next several years, the energetic and ambitious Martin made his way up the Hollywood ladder. Putting his knowledge of English and writing to work, Martin penned scripts for *Four Star Playhouse.* From there, he joined the staff of *Jane Wyman Presents the Fireside Theatre* as a writer and was later promoted to producer. When the series folded in 1958, Martin produced the Westinghouse *Desilu Playhouse* anthology series. One of *Playhouse's* more notable productions during his tenure was the two-part pilot for *The Untouchables,* "The Scarface Mob," which aired on 20 and 27 April 1959. When ABC ordered a weekly series of *The Untouchables* to launch in October of that year, Martin was assigned as its producer.

By 1960, Martin had amassed enough firepower to form his own production company, QM Productions. It would become one of the most successful independent television packagers of the 1960s and 1970s. QM's first series, *The New Breed,* was launched in 1961. Although *The New Breed* lasted only one season, Martin used the experience to begin building the QM brand. That process began by clearly identifying the product. Each episode of a QM series opened with a sight and sound "label": on screen, the series' name appeared accompanied by a voiceover artist, initially Dick Wesson, heralding the title and the fact that the program was "a QM Production." Martin imbued his shows with stature, elevating a TV show to a theatre-like experience by labeling each segment on screen as Act I, II, III, IV and the Epilog. He insisted on fresh faces and quality acting. He spent a substantial amount of money on talent in front of and behind the cameras. Martin's stable of reliable professionals would serve him well during the growth years of his company. They included:

- **DIRECTOR OF PHOTOGRAPHY** MEREDITH M. NICHOLSON
- **COMPOSER AND CONDUCTOR** DOMINIC FRONTIERE

- **PRODUCER-DIRECTOR** JOSEPH PEVNEY
- **PRODUCER-DIRECTOR** WALTER E. GRAUMAN
- **WRITER** DON BRINKLEY
- **PRODUCER** ARTHUR FELLOWS
- **DIRECTOR** JERRY HOPPER
- **EDITOR** JERRY YOUNG
- **EDITOR** CHESTER W. SCHAEFFER

"Quinn compartmentalized his operation," explained Alan A. Armer, producer of the QM shows *The Fugitive, The Invaders* and *Cannon*. "That was different from what most executive producers or company owners did." For example, in the QM organization a producer was in charge of story development, working with writers and editing scripts. Someone else was in charge of postproduction, working with the editors and the music cutters. "Quinn was on top of the whole thing, but under him the facets of production fell into various little compartments. There wasn't a lot of crossover between the various compartments. And that worked very well for Quinn." Armer outlined the primary slots at QM and the key staffers responsible:

HOWARD ALSTON – PRODUCTION MANAGER. "Howard was one of the few creative production managers I've ever known. He rejoiced in giving a show production value. Normally it's a nuts and bolts kind of job. The usual production manager is a tough son of a bitch who sits on the budget and shakes his fist at the director, daring him to spend a dollar more than is allocated. I have more respect for Howard than for almost any other member of QM Productions."

JOHN CONWELL – CASTING. "John knew a tremendous number of actors. He had seen their work, was aware of how they worked and how qualified they were. More specifically, he was sensitive to the chemistry between actors so that when he cast the show he would not be aware of their look or their ability but of that indefinable thing; how they would fit in with the rest of the characters in the show so that the right dramatic value would emerge."

JOHN ELIZALDE – POST-PRODUCTION SUPERVISOR. "John would assign music composers to the shows. He worked with the composers and music cutters and would attend all of the dubbing sessions."

ARTHUR FELLOWS – POST PRODUCTION. Fellows had a rich background in feature motion pictures, including *Gone With the Wind* (1939). "He supervised the editing of the films, the music cutters and the sound effects editors. If there was a problem, he was the guy in charge. Artie would get the kinks out before the films were shown to Quinn."

Following the cancellation of *The New Breed*, QM hit pay dirt with its next show, *The Fugitive* (1963-67). The series, which starred David Janssen as a man wrongly accused of murder, became an international sensation. Much of the show's success was due to the craftsmanship and attention to detail that became a hallmark of QM Productions.

According to Howard Alston, it was Quinn Martin who proposed the *12 O'Clock High* series to Twentieth Century-Fox. Fox had released the 1949 movie and still held the rights to the novel.

"Quinn had the idea that *12 O'Clock High* would make a good series," Alston said. "But the owner of *12 O'Clock High* was Twentieth Century-Fox. So Twentieth Century-Fox and Quinn Martin became partners. Quinn became the creative force. Twentieth Century-Fox had the property and they had the money to make the series." The relationship between Fox and Martin was described by an industry publication as Martin letting Fox "share the driver's seat by taking the financial gamble, but he does the driving."

In the fall of 1963, Paul Monash was assigned to write the *12 O'Clock High* pilot script. Monash had written the two-part *Untouchables* pilot for Quinn Martin back in 1959. Prior to the *12 O'Clock High* assignment, Monash had created and executive produced *Cain's Hundred* (1961–62) at MGM. Earlier in his career, Monash had written for many of television's anthology series, including *Climax; Playhouse 90; Studio One,* also produced by Martin; and *Schlitz Playhouse of Stars,* which netted Monash an Emmy Award in 1958.

At the end of the pilot script, Monash suggested several ideas for future episodes of *12 O'Clock High:* "These are stories of men during a war, not always men at war. We can envision a story taking place entirely in what was called a 'flak house,' a recuperation center. We can play out a romance in war-darkened London. We can follow the fortunes of a crew shot down over Germany. We can tell the story of a man returned to the States. We can go into hospital. We can get behind the scenes at headquarters. We can tell the story of a pilot's wife, or his girl."

Monash's final draft of the pilot episode, titled "Follow the Leader," was credited to both Monash and Beirne Lay, Jr., co-author of the original *12 O'Clock High* novel and screenplay. Despite the shared writing credit, Monash and Lay never met. While the printed script credits both men, the final on-screen credit lists only Lay as screenwriter.

Penning the pilot script for *12 O'Clock High* was Paul Monash's only involvement with the project. In fact, it was the only work he ever did for QM Productions. However, having built the show's format Monash received a royalty check for every subsequent episode of *12 O'Clock High* produced. As an independent producer at Fox, Monash also developed and produced *Peyton Place* (1964–69) and *Judd for the Defense* (1967–69). He made the leap to producing motion pictures with *Butch Cassidy and the Sundance Kid* (1969), also for Fox. The Writer's Guild of America honored Monash with its Lifetime Achievement Award in 2000. He died three years later on 14 January 2003.

Once the script was deemed acceptable, the project was given the green light. *12 O'Clock High* became *12 O'Clock High—The Series* and was officially a co-production of independent Quinn Martin Productions and Twentieth Century-Fox Television.

CASTING CALL

The lead roles for the pilot episode were filled by a group of Broadway-trained veterans:

Robert Lansing

Robert Lansing (Brig. Gen. Frank Savage) was born Robert Howell Brown on 5 June 1928 in San Diego, California. At age nine, he appeared briefly in a tent show production. The experience convinced him to make acting a career. After the death of his mother when he was just 16, Lansing (still Robert Brown) dropped out of school and hitchhiked around the United States "in search of a place and purpose in life." After two years of service with Armed Forces Radio in Osaka, Japan, Lansing became a radio announcer and appeared in productions at the Civic Theater in Fort Wayne, Indiana. He studied acting in New York under the GI Bill.

Just as Lansing was about to hop a bus to his first Actors Equity job, he was told by an Equity rep that there was already a Robert Brown on file. That meant he would have to change his name. The Equity rep asked him, "Where's the bus going?" He said, "Lansing, Michigan." The Equity rep replied, "You're Robert Lansing now." Lansing made his New York stage debut in 1951, replacing another actor in *Stalag 17* and continued with the role when the show went on the road. He then spent some time with the traveling Stanley Woolf Players and, between acting jobs, worked part-time as a check-room clerk, at a plastics factory and as a doorman at the Gilded Cage on Broadway. Jose Ferrer grabbed Lansing for a series of revival plays at New York City Center, including *Cyrano de Bergerac* and *Richard III*. Subsequent performances included *Suddenly, Last Summer* and *Under the Yum Yum Tree*.

Lansing's first appearance on the small screen was on *Kraft Television Theatre* in 1956. He also performed in numerous live TV programs transmitted from New York. He moved to Hollywood in 1961 and accepted his first series role as Detective Steve Carella on *87th Precinct* (1961-62). Following his film debut in the Universal-International B-movie *4-D Man* in 1959, Lansing appeared in *Under the Yum Yum Tree* (1963) and *A Gathering of Eagles* (1963). The latter was a training ground of sorts for Lansing, a loose remake of *12 O'Clock High* updated to the nuclear age and starring Rock Hudson and Rod Taylor as colonels running a Strategic Air Command (SAC) wing. Sy Bartlett penned the script, and Lansing played the maintenance line chief for a fleet of B-52 Stratofortress bombers.

By landing the role of Gen. Savage, Lansing joked that he earned the "biggest promotion in military history." The last time he wore a uniform was while serving in the Army as a private. Lansing's experience gave him a unique perspective on portraying a general. "You don't have to play the authority," he observed. "It's there. Any guy in the service knows that."

John Larkin (Maj. Gen. Wiley Crowe) was born 11 April 1912 in Oakland, California, and served in World War II. Following the war, he was a radio announcer in Kansas City for many years. He made his radio debut in an episode of *Vic and Sade*. The *New York Times* noted that Larkin "appeared in an estimated total of 7,500 radio dramatic shows." His most famous radio role was as Earle Stanley Gardner's indomitable lawyer Perry Mason, which he began in 1948. When *Perry Mason* made the leap to television in 1957, Raymond Burr assumed the role. The cast from the *Perry Mason* radio show, including Larkin, moved to daytime television in 1956 on the new soap opera *The Edge of Night*. Larkin played Detective Mike Karr and stayed with the series until 1962. During that time, *TV Guide* named Larkin as one of daytime TV's matinee idols. From there he co-starred in the short-lived prime time drama *Saints and Sinners* (1962–63) as newspaper editor Mark Grainger.

Larkin had worked on Quinn Martin's *The Fugitive*, *The New Breed* and *The Untouchables*. When he got the call from Martin to do the pilot of *12 O'Clock High*, Larkin was shooting an *Alfred Hitchcock Hour* segment at Revue Studios. "I was a little leery about doing another series because the one I had done before had been a little disastrous," Larkin said. But he steeled his courage and signed on.

Larkin portrayed the 918th Bomb Group's wing commander in *12 O'Clock High*. Gen. Crowe was Savage's boss as well as an old friend and mentor. In real life, John Larkin and Robert Lansing became good friends while working on *12 O'Clock High*.

Frank Overton (Maj. Harvey B. Stovall) was born Frank Emmons Overton in Babylon, Long Island, New York, on 12 March 1918. He acted in high school plays and then served as a shipbuilder's apprentice in Newport News, Virginia, after graduation. While attending Columbia University with the goal of becoming a marine engineer, Overton switched from mathematics, his original major, to drama. He worked at the New York School for Social Research as a set designer and

Frank Overton

actor. Overton made his Broadway debut in 1943, replacing John Ireland in the play *Counterattack*. After more stage appearances, Overton tried film acting in 1950 but decided to go back to the stage. Returning to Hollywood, Overton appeared in movies such as *Desire Under the Elms* (1958), *To Kill a Mockingbird* (1962, with Gregory Peck), and *Fail Safe* (1964). TV appearances included guest roles on *Thriller, Route 66* and *The Twilight Zone*, and a continuing role on the daytime soap *Search for Tomorrow*.

Lew Gallo (Maj. Joe Cobb) was born 12 June 1928 in Mt. Kisco, New York. Gallo began his career in theatre—summer stock, summer tours, Broadway, off-Broadway—and on early live television shows like *Studio One* and *U.S. Steel Hour*. In an episode of *Kraft Television Theatre*, Gallo was directed by William A. Graham, who would later direct the pilot of *12 O'Clock High*. Gallo relocated to Hollywood in 1958, where he did episodic television—including *Lawman, The Detectives* and *The Twilight Zone*—and features, such as *Pork Chop Hill* (1959, with Gregory Peck), *Ocean's Eleven* (1960) and *PT 109* (1963). When the pilot for *12 O'Clock High* was being cast, Gallo called on a friend who happened to be a story editor at Fox. Gallo was called in, renewed his acquaintance with director William Graham and found himself on board the project.

Barney Phillips (Maj. Donald "Doc" Kaiser) played the sardonic flight surgeon of the 918th. Born Bernard Phillips in St. Louis, Missouri on 20 October 1913, Phillips tried his hand at acting as a young student but didn't pursue it seriously until after he graduated from college. Phillips joined the Shakespeare troupe at the Globe Theater in San Diego, California. While there, he appeared with future *12 O'Clock High* guest stars Rhys Williams and Carl Benton Reid. Following service in the Army during World War II, Phillips performed on radio dramas including *Gunsmoke, Wild Bill Hickok, Rocky Fortune, The Six Shooter* and *Fort Laramie*. He then moved on to television, playing Sgt. Ed Jacobs, the second partner of Sgt. Joe Friday on *Dragnet* from 1951 to 1952. His feature films included *Blueprint for Murder* (1953), *I Was a Teenage Werewolf* (1957) and *The True Story of Jesse James* (1957) with Frank Overton. Prior to *12 O'Clock High*, Phillips had guest starring roles in TV series such as *Peter Gunn, Have Gun, Will Travel, The Andy Griffith Show* and *The Fugitive*. He was also a regular in two series, *The Brothers Brannagan* (1960) and *The Brothers* (1956–57). Despite all his credits, Phillips may be best remembered as the three-eyed counter man in the classic 1961 *Twilight Zone* episode "Will the Real Martian Please Stand Up?"

GEARING UP FOR THE SHOOT

Backing up the solid cast was a production staff whose top brass was, ironically, fairly inexperienced. Executive Producer Quinn Martin tapped 42-year-old Frank Glicksman to produce *12 O'Clock High*. A former messenger for MGM's publicity department, Glicksman had been promoted to publicity agent, story analyst and general assistant in the script department. Glicksman sold his first teleplay to the CBS anthology *Climax* and was soon its associate story editor. From there, he became a West Coast story editor for CBS-TV and subsequently a story editor for Twentieth Century-Fox Television. However, Glicksman had never produced a series when Quinn Martin assigned him to the *12 O'Clock High* project. Glicksman quickly hired his friend Charles Larson as associate producer. Earlier in their careers they had worked together in the MGM publicity department. "Frank and I were both absolute babes in the woods so far as producing was concerned," remembered Larson.

Although William Graham helmed the pilot, the trade papers initially reported that Walter Grauman had the job. Grauman had worked successfully with Quinn Martin previously on *The Untouchables*, *The New Breed* and *The Fugitive*. More importantly, he had just finished shooting *633 Squadron*, a slam-bang World War II aviation feature scheduled for release the following year.

Director of photography on the pilot was Meredith Nicholson, who had become part of the QM family by virtue of his work on *The New Breed* and *The Fugitive*. Later, Nicholson worked on QM's pilot for *The Invaders* (1966). He would return to Fox to work on the second season of *Batman* (1966–67) and then *M*A*S*H* (1976–78). Nicholson's other TV work included *Get Smart* (1967–70), *My Three Sons* (1970–71), *Get Christie Love!* (1974) and *Mork and Mindy* (1978–82).

The shooting schedule for "Follow the Leader" was brisk. Lansing was signed for the lead effective 2 December 1963 and the cameras rolled soon after at Fox Hills studios. Hoping to contain production costs while maximizing production values, the production crew simulated the appearance of wartime England by using the Old Writers' Building on the lot. Its Tudor style added period charm to the building's role as The Star and Bottle pub. William Graham kept the cast and crew on a tight schedule, which wrapped one day early on 16 December 1963.

From there, Fox post production coordinator Robert Mintz and QM's post production supervisor John Elizalde turned the footage into an engaging narrative. The real challenge of editing the *12 O'Clock High* pilot was integrating combat footage to make the primary theme of air warfare believable. Having access to footage from the original *12 O'Clock High* movie was a huge benefit to the project.

"I think they used maybe eight or ten shots outside of the aerial scenes of the base," said Lew Gallo. "Obviously, [they used] long shots where you didn't recognize anybody. Things like the tower and the Quonset huts that didn't exist any more." For example, there is a perfect match cut which begins with stock footage of the ground crew playing baseball with the tower in the background. In a long shot from the movie, we see Maj. Cobb (John Kellogg) pick up a set of binoculars and look to the skies. At this point, new footage cuts in with a medium shot of Lansing as Savage looking through binoculars. Perhaps the most spectacular bit of footage reused from the feature film was the B-17 crash landing originally flown by Paul Mantz.

All of the elements worked together perfectly. By early 1964, *TV Guide* reported that *12 O'Clock High* was among ABC's "possibilities" for the upcoming fall season.

MAIDEN VOYAGE

Twentieth Century-Fox Television produced a total of seven pilots for the 1964–65 prime time schedule. Of those, NBC grabbed *Daniel Boone* while ABC picked up four: *Peyton Place, Valentine's Day, Voyage to the Bottom of the Sea* and *12 O'Clock High*.

By spring 1964, the Fox lot was once again humming with activity. Approximately 3,000 employees were on the studio's payroll, marking a strong resurgence in production from the year before, when production at Fox had shut down completely. ABC's and NBC's commitments would pump $18 million in production money into the studio's coffers.

One hurdle to ramping up production to meet the demands of episodic television was the lack of a backlot. As a result, when the Caped Crusaders raced up the stairs of Gotham City Police Headquarters in Fox's smash hit series *Batman*, those stairs were nowhere near Fox property. The production company had to rent the Warner Brothers backlot. *The Green Hornet's* Black Beauty often drove through the shadowy streets of Mayberry because Fox had to rent 40 Acres, the backlot property where *The Andy Griffith Show* also filmed. Likewise, the studio had to lease MGM's backlot to stand in for Frenchman's Bend in its small-screen version of *The Long, Hot Summer*. To bring Prohibition-era Chicago to life for its 1967 feature *The St. Valentine's Day Massacre*, Fox paid a return visit to MGM.

When Fox recycled its hit movie *Peyton Place* as a nighttime soap opera, the studio art department created a small New England town right on the Fox lot by building façades over its existing commissary, soundstages and office buildings. This ingenious tactic for maximizing limited space proved so successful that no corner of the Fox lot was safe from a makeover. Fox's 1965 action hit *Von Ryan's Express* hinged on Allied prisoners escaping from a POW camp in Italy. Although filmed primarily on location in Italy and Spain, the crucial escape sequence was filmed on a set constructed adjacent to the Fox administration building in Los Angeles. Towering sentry posts, barbed wire fences, prisoners' barracks and a stone fortress all conspired to create a perfect illusion, effectively obscuring nearby Beverly Hills. The practice of cosmetic reconstruction was perfected by Fox until, at its zenith, nearly three-fifths of a mile along the studio entryway was transformed into 1890s New York City for *Hello Dolly* (1969). Called Dolly Street, the façade still graces the studio's entrance from Pico Boulevard.

Production begins at Fox Western Avenue

ABC's first draft of its primetime schedule for fall 1964 placed *12 O'Clock High* on Sunday at 9:30 p.m. ET. Network programmers changed their minds, and *12 O'Clock High* was penciled in on Wednesday at 9:30 p.m. ET, and then finally slotted for Friday nights at 9:30 p.m. ET. The series was a logical counter-programming choice for ABC, going up against two comedies, freshman *Gomer Pyle, USMC* on CBS and veteran *The Jack Benny Program* on NBC. The budget was set at $135,000 per episode, the same price tag as another new Fox series, *Voyage to the Bottom of the Sea* and also the dean of TV war shows, *Combat!*

Production schedules demanded an episode every nine days, shooting for seven business days with no work on Saturday or Sunday. Most TV series of the era took five days to shoot an episode. Production manager Howard Alston said that when other producers shot episodes in five or six days, their crews were forced to work as much as 18 hours a day. For *12 O'Clock High*, "We tried to do it in seven days and do it in a reasonable time," Alston said. "Quinn always went a little longer than other people," recalled director Sutton Roley, who met Martin at Ziv Productions in the 1950s. Roley directed three installments of *12 O'Clock High* as well as episodes of QM's *The Fugitive* and *The Invaders*, plus Selmur Productions' *Combat!*

Once ABC gave the nod, preproduction of *12 O'Clock High* began at Fox Western Avenue Studios. The lot, which had been shuttered in 1963 as part of Fox's corporate economy drive, was reopened in May 1964. *12 O'Clock High* alone created at least 45 new jobs by the time filming began on 25 May 1964. Studio space at Western Avenue was shared with another new Fox series, *Daniel Boone*. Located at the junction of Western Avenue and Sunset Boulevard, the street address of Fox Western was 1417 N. Western Avenue Second and third season producer William D. Gordon described the physical layout this way: "The lot was divided by Western Avenue. The administrative side was on the west and production was on the east. Our offices backed on Western on the west side of the boulevard."

The complex was built in 1916 by William Fox. His Fox Film Corporation merged with Twentieth Century Pictures in 1935 to form Twentieth Century-Fox. The legacy of the old Fox studio was alive and well during the production of *12 O'Clock High*. Paul Wurtzel, one of the series' assistant directors, was the son of movie mogul Sol Wurtzel, who worked at the lot from 1917 to 1946. After Fox and Twentieth Century became Twentieth Century-Fox, Sol Wurtzel remained "and produced all the low-budget movies. They used to call them 'B' movies," said Paul. "Darryl Zanuck produced all the high-budget 'A' pictures. And they each made 26 movies a year at the studio. [Sol Wurtzel] stayed at Western Avenue, and Zanuck was at what they call Fox Hills Movietone Studio."

"The stages there weren't among the newest in Hollywood," recalled Lew Gallo, who co-starred as Maj. Joe Cobb during Season One. "But a stage is a stage; it's what goes on it that matters. It was a small studio, where most people knew each other. We were over there, away from the major lot, and it didn't feel as though we were relegated. As a matter of fact, after a while we really got to enjoy it because we went there to work and there was very little else to do. There wasn't any frou-frou. There wasn't any meeting starlets in the commissary, who else was on the lot, who's got the trade papers. We had a job to do and we did it. It was a wonderful place to work."

The *12 O'Clock High* soundstages contained interior sets, used in episode after episode, including:

- SAVAGE'S (AND LATER GALLAGHER'S) OFFICE
- STOVALL'S OFFICE AND ORDERLY ROOM
- BRIEFING SHACK
- OFFICERS CLUB
- WING HEADQUARTERS
- THE STAR AND BOTTLE (THE LOCAL PUB)
- HOSPITAL CORRIDOR, HOSPITAL WARD AND DOC KAISER'S OFFICE
- OFFICERS' QUARTERS
- MOCK-UPS OF THE INTERIOR OF A B-17, AND THE COCKPITS OF A P-51 AND A GERMAN FIGHTER

Across the street from the *12 O'Clock High* stages was the exterior Archbury Street set which stood for London and other European cities. It was also redressed and used as any number of Colonial-era towns during the six-year run of *Daniel Boone*.

Meanwhile, Quinn Martin maintained offices at both Fox Western and the Goldwyn Studios, where *The Fugitive* was filmed. His co-production deal with Fox gave Martin a "four walls" arrangement. The studio provided facilities, stage space and backlot personnel, but Martin hired all his own people to work on the set, including the art director, the cameraman, and the gaffer. Martin explained further: "I pay $15,000 an episode and I have access to everything they [Fox] own, including five stages with 90,000 square feet of floor space and a complete wardrobe of World War II uniforms. But I pick my own people and do my own planning. There are hidden savings when you know where to look for them and where to anticipate the problems that can come up."

Martin wisely chose to pump the savings back into his product—the shows QM made. That allowed Martin to produce what Alan Armer called "the classiest look in town."

CAST AND CREW

The first episode before the cameras was "An Act of War," featuring the core cast from the pilot: Robert Lansing, Frank Overton, John Larkin, Lew Gallo and Bert Remsen.

Also returning from the pilot were Frank Glicksman and Charles Larson. Although credited as producer and associate producer respectively, Larson clarified that they were "in effect, story editors with inflated titles." *12 O'Clock High* provided valuable on-the-job training for them both. Noted Larson, "All [Quinn] wanted us to do was control the story-script side of the series. I think Quinn was probably the first executive

The principal first-season cast (left to right): Frank Overton, Robert Lansing, Lew Gallo and John Larkin.

producer to realize that the best way to ensure a steady stream of scripts was to stroke writers with contracts and pretty titles." Martin made most of the major decisions about the show, which suited Larson just fine. "I was content to write, watch and learn at QM Productions."

As a new producer, Frank Glicksman earned high praise from his staff. "He was a real nice guy, a terrific guy," recalled assistant director Paul Wurtzel. "He was very nervous, producing a show like this, which was rough. Coming from publicity and never having any real experience producing, he was very nervous. He was a very pleasant guy, and he got the job done." Larson praised Glicksman for his "wonderful story mind" and "very sharp casting sense."

KEEPING IT REAL

Executive Producer Quinn Martin was committed to making *12 O'Clock High* an authoritative and comprehensive account of the air war in Europe during World War II. "Whatever we film, we try to make it as real and powerful as we possibly can. We feel that the men of the Eighth Air Force deserve that," Martin said. Reflecting this mandate, actor John Larkin told the press that "we'll be as accurate a show as you'll see on the air this season."

Robert Lansing took flying lessons so that he could bring a sense of realism to the part of Gen. Savage. "I'm finding now that research pays off," Lansing said. He also built up a collection of Air Corps pilot manuals and photographs of an actual B-17 control panel.

When the 1949 feature *12 O'Clock High* was made during the glory days of Hollywood's studio system, Twentieth Century-Fox had a fully staffed research department. Art Director George Chan recounted how the Fox researchers had put together 16 volumes of photos, sketches and stories of the Eighth Air Force in England. "Nothing was left to chance," Chan said. "I would refer to those volumes before starting work on each episode."

To help maintain authenticity, the Air Force provided QM and Fox with a technical advisor. Air Force MSgt. James Doherty was given the job. Producer William D. Gordon recalled that during World War II, Doherty "had flown 50 some missions out of Italy in B-24s as a radio operator. He knew Bomber Command like the back of his hand. He also had the confidence of the Department of Defense." Jack Hawn, third season story consultant, remembered Doherty as a "stubborn Irishman" who was busted several times during his military career. While serving in the Army Air Force, Doherty's bomber was shot down over Yugoslavia, an incident which later inspired episode #76 "Graveyard." His military expertise and contacts made it possible for Doherty to get assignments as technical advisor on films like *Bombers B-52* (1957) and TV series including *Hogan's Heroes* and *I Dream of Jeannie*. During his time in the Air Force, Doherty began writing articles for newspapers and magazines. Once he was assigned to *12 O'Clock High*, Doherty contributed story ideas and eventually began writing scripts. He is credited with two stories and two teleplays for the series. Bill Gordon added, "Based on his knowledge and his experiences, [Doherty] and I cooked up about eight or ten ideas and we fed them to the writers."

Howard Alston said that Doherty "read all the scripts and helped us procure things." Paul Wurtzel remembered that Doherty "wasn't one of those technical guys who would say, 'Oh, you can't do it that way; that's not the way we did it.' He said, 'Who the hell's gonna remember? Go ahead and do it.' We got along great with him."

Air Force cooperation was a win-win deal. *12 O'Clock High* received valuable technical support and in the fall of 1964, ABC and the U.S. Air Force teamed up to use the power of television to launch a recruiting campaign. Posters and advertisements featured *12 O'Clock High* and another new ABC series, *No Time for Sergeants*—also based on a hit movie—to draw potential enlistees in to local Air Force recruiters.

STYLE AND SUBSTANCE

The often brooding nature of *12 O'Clock High* scripts during season one was reflected in the moody black-and-white cinematography.

William W. Spencer, lead director of photography during the first season, crafted a high-contrast look, rich in both detail and dynamics. Episode #10 "Interlude" features examples of his work that range from the intimate—the interior of the Macrae home in Scotland, to the epic—as Robert Lansing and guest star Dana Wynter walk along the coastline and explore the Scottish countryside.

Bill Spencer's overarching style for *12 O'Clock High* was an homage to film noir. He strategically placed shadows in the frame, sometimes obscuring much of a scene in order to highlight the actors. For example, in episode #11 "Here's to Courageous Cowards," guest star Brandon de Wilde's character has a pivotal meeting with Robert Lansing as Gen. Savage. Lansing, in the foreground, is virtually obscured by shadows. At screen right, de Wilde stands in the doorway of Savage's office with backlight framing his body in silhouette. The audience is shown beyond question that the scene will focus on de Wilde's character. A more subtle example is found in episode #16 "In Search of My Enemy," which features a marvelous shot looking forward in the briefing room, where the shadows of window panes cut across the map on the front wall.

Spencer also had an affinity and a genius for creating the chiaroscuro effects of ambient light diffused through rain. Episode #9 "Appointment at Liege," has two such sequences. First, Gary Lockwood barrels along in a jeep with shadows of windshield wipers and rivulets of rain across his face in a close-up. Later, when Lockwood is in Maj. Stovall's office, Lockwood stands at the windows as showers cascade in front of him. In episode #19 "Faith, Hope and Sgt. Aronson," guest stars Sorrell Booke and Antoinette Bower play self-conscious, novice lovers taking shelter from a cloudburst. Their awkwardness is exemplified in a two-shot of them standing at a window streaked by the downpour outside.

Spencer began his 30-year career at MGM when he was 17 years old. He worked his way up through the ranks, beginning as an assistant cameraman. Later, Spencer was involved in many of the studio's extravagant musicals starring the likes of Gene Kelly and Esther Williams. When the MGM lot began producing series for television, Spencer worked on shows such as *The Thin Man* (1957–59), *Peter Gunn* (1960–61) and *Sam Benedict* (1962–63).

"The shooting crew services the director," was Spencer's credo. He had to be ready for any sudden changes that occurred during production of an episode. "You have to sort of wing it all the time."

The 918th operations building at Chino Airport. The Briefing and Interrogation shack.

UPPER LEFT: Quonset huts on the base.

UPPER RIGHT: Archbury tower as seen from the taxiway.

LOWER LEFT: B-17 at hardstand behind the tower.

LOWER RIGHT: Set dressing helped create the illusion of a working air base.

Working with Spencer on the 1963–64 NBC anthology series *The Richard Boone Show* was production manager Howard Alston. After *Richard Boone* shut down, Alston moved to QM Productions. He brought in Bill Spencer to shoot *12 O'Clock High,* and that kicked off Spencer's lengthy stint with QM.

Perhaps the most critical component to bringing the series to life was providing a suitable backdrop.

Quinn Martin was an innovator in many respects but especially in moving television production off the backlots and into real life settings. "Sam Goldwyn's classic comment, 'A bush is a bush, a rock is a rock; shoot it in Griffith Park,' no longer holds," Martin once noted. "The audience probably doesn't know what it is, but they appreciate the feeling of reality that a little more trouble, a little more money contributes. People feel uncomfortable where there's anything phony about a show." With Martin's commitment to realism, the key to successfully producing *12 O'Clock High* would be to find an authentic-looking airfield. Moreover, ingenuity would be essential for convincing the audience that it was seeing sprawling runways, numerous aircraft and hundreds of servicemen—all on a TV budget.

Production manager Howard Alston led missions to scout locations. "We rented an airplane and flew to every little airport around. Every place within a two-hour driving range of Hollywood. Two hours is the absolute maximum you can drive and still do a television show."

"We originally were considering Norton AFB in San Bernadino," revealed Bill Spencer, "but it was too flat and too barren and the jet traffic there would have driven the sound men crazy."

Alston and company settled on the compact Chino Airport in San Bernardino County, California, one hour east of Hollywood. The rural community was nestled in the foothills of the Rocky Mountains and was peppered with stockyards and dairy farms. The airfield began life in 1940 as Cal-Aero Academy, a civilian flight school created to accelerate the training of military pilots. An excellent overview of the facility in near pristine condition can be seen in the 1941 Abbott and Costello comedy *Keep 'Em Flying*. Between 1941 and 1944, Cal-Aero graduated pilots who served with distinction in the European and Pacific Theaters of Operation. Cal-Aero Academy was closed in 1944, converted to a civilian facility and renamed Chino Airport. Over the years, a wide variety of aviation-related businesses occupied the property and kept the facility active and growing.

It took a work crew three weeks to transform portions of Chino Airport into a reasonable facsimile of an American air base in World War II England. Starting with existing buildings from the Cal-Aero days, the art department created the 918th operations building and base hospital. Portions of other Cal-Aero vintage buildings would stand in for structures like the PX in episode #12 "Soldiers Sometimes Kill." Then, on vacant land west of the operations shack, workers built Quonset huts to serve as the briefing shack and officers' club. A guard shack was built on a dirt road parallel to Merrill Avenue, the northern perimeter of the airport; the existing chain link fence facing Merrill helped create the illusion of a military compound. Trees, peaked tents and a bulletin board helped hide the northern mountains, which were not exactly indigenous to the English country-side. A virtual tour of this set appears in episode #7 "Decision." Act I includes a scene where Robert Lansing and Tim O'Connor stroll around the base.

Next, the production crew created the look of a period airstrip. Since Chino Airport was also being used as a firefighting base, the *12 O'Clock High* crew chose a detached strip slightly southeast of the 918th base set to use as a taxiway and hardstand. However, the runway was a light color rather than the painted black of wartime English airfields. Using the airstrip as their canvas, the scenic designers constructed a non-functioning control tower and then placed tents, maintenance equipment and other assorted runway dressing on the outskirts. A tall line of eucalyptus trees near the airstrip blended perfectly with stock footage of WWII English airbases. "We knew we had to get some sort of a match or nobody would believe it," said Alston. The trees would also hide the light air traffic around the airfield. An added plus was a local flock of sheep which would often wander around the airfield and sometimes served as background in certain shots. The sheep made walk-on appearances in episodes #20 "To Heinie, With Love," when Keir Dullea and Jill Haworth meet in the English countryside; and #58 "The Hollow Man," wandering around in the background while Robert Drivas is menaced by a German firing squad.

When it came to transporting cast and crew to Chino, the "30-mile zone" rule applied. The zone stretched outward in a 30-mile radius from the intersection of La Cienega Boulevard and Beverly Boulevard in Los Angeles. If production was located within the zone, then personnel were expected to drive themselves to the shoot location. Outside the zone, the studio or production company had to provide transportation. That meant during one or two days of each shooting week, the *12 O'Clock High* cast and crew piled into buses and cars to drive an hour to the Chino location. The production crew naturally hoped for favorable shooting conditions but the weather didn't always cooperate. Filming went on despite heat, cold, rain or clouds. "This often created matching problems," said Bill Spencer. "We'd shoot part of a sequence in the studio, with an actor entering an office bone dry, and then go to Chino and find it raining." Second season cinematographer Frank Phillips recalled, "I prayed for overcast days so that it would always look like England and not Southern California, with its bright sun." Spencer noted that sometimes the weather was *too* realistic. "Sometimes, when the crew arrived at 6:30 a.m. to film, the field was completely socked in. So the crew had to sit around and wait until [the cloud cover] lifted." Phillips agreed: "Many a day we'd arrive there on a bus and have to walk out to the hardstand to find out where we could work because you couldn't see anything in front of you." Since the crew only traveled to Chino periodically, efficiency was crucial. The days out there were often very long, especially when it was necessary to shoot night-for-night.

Many television series used a technical trick called "day-for-night" shooting. Day-for-night saved time and money. Scenes that occurred at night were shot during the day with special filters and camera settings that darkened the picture to simulate nighttime. *Twelve O'Clock High* avoided the practice. Howard Alston remembered that Quinn Martin was the first producer who was willing to spend the money to shoot night-for-night. It was a trademark of QM shows. "Everyone else tried to avoid it," said Alston, "because it was very expensive and time-consuming."

"Quinn would never shoot day-for-night, never compromised the work," noted Sutton Roley. "If a scene should be at night, he'd shoot it at night, even though it took a little longer." However, Frank Phillips, the director of photography, remembered a few compromises. "I think I talked Quinn into a couple of day-for-night shots. Something that was really difficult to do late at night. It had to be perfect conditions or he wouldn't do it. He was a stickler, no day-for-night."

Late nights were typical. "I remember the long ride home from Chino at midnight or after," added Frank Phillips.

Scenes filmed at Chino were staged creatively to blend with wartime stock footage and shots from the original *12 O'Clock High* feature. Among the scenes recycled from the movie was a sequence showing a jeep driving screen left along the runaway perimeter as B-17s landed, ground personnel and rescue trucks racing toward the runway, and the control tower in the foreground with a

B-17 serial number 44-83684 at Ontario Airport in March 1967.

formation of B-17s flying in the background.

By skillfully combining all the elements, the *12 O'Clock High* production crew successfully transformed its modest outdoor sets into a huge, buzzing airbase.

AN AIR FORCE OF ONE

Now all the airfield needed was an airplane. The novel and feature film versions of *12 O'Clock High* were dependent on the mighty Boeing B-17 Flying Fortress to help tell their stories, and the TV incarnation was no different.

Unfortunately, it was nearly 20 years after World War II, and the supply of operational B-17s around the world was dwindling rapidly.

At the time, aircraft enthusiast Ed Maloney's Air Museum of vintage planes was located at Ontario International Airport, just north of Chino. The collection later developed into the Planes of Fame, which would set up shop at Chino Airport. Through an agreement with the Air Force, Maloney had obtained the last operational B-17 in its inventory. The aircraft, bearing serial number 44-83684, had been retired in 1959 after service as a DB-17 drone controller. The plane had been used recently in the *Dick Powell Theatre* episode "Squadron."

Howard Alston negotiated the lease of the aircraft with Maloney who, as part of the agreement, took care of maintenance. To prepare 44-83684 for the cameras, the Air Museum spiffed up the plane mechanically. Alston explained, "They did have to put in new gas tanks and do different things because it had rotted out while it was sitting."

There was just one catch.

"Our star was grounded," said Bill Spencer, "and while it could taxi, its takeoff would come from stock footage." Howard Alston added, "We taxied it up and down the strip every single week, and it came to the hardstand and stopped."

For *12 O'Clock High*, 44-83684 received a fresh coat of paint. The aircraft's civilian registration number, N3713G, was partially painted out; the remaining 3713 posed as its military serial number. Emblazoned with the triangle-A unit identification marking of the 91st Bomb Group to match footage from the *12 O'Clock High* movie, 44-83684 was given the squadron designation V and aircraft letters HP, painted on both sides of the fuselage. No actual squadron used the V designation. The closest to that coding was HP V, which identified B-24 Liberators of the 567th Squadron, 389th Bomb Group, Second Combat Wing of the Eighth Air Force.

One criticism that aviation enthusiasts had about the plane's color scheme was that its propellers were left with their natural metal finish. Period combat aircraft had black propellers. Other issues with authenticity included the mismatch of a triangle tail emblem with the star-in-circle national insignia; the two never appeared together. Also, beginning in late June 1943 the star-in-circle national logo was set in a white, horizontal bar. That symbol continued until January 1947.

Although 44-83684 proved to be a journeyman actor, it was also Howard Alston's biggest worry. "Because we only had the one, we had no idea what would happen if we lost it," Alston said. "We were always concerned about the maintenance on the B-17. There weren't a lot of spare parts around. It was always a worry that something might happen to the star of our show." Hedging his bets, Alston made several trips around the country to examine privately owned B-17s. Most of them had been converted to firefighters, making them unavailable for *12 O'Clock High*. Moreover, they were unusable because their military hardware had been removed during the conversion process.

"The illusion of a full operating squadron was gained by changing the markings on our 'star' aircraft, augmented with stock shots, process and special effects," said Bill Spencer.

By using 44-83684 and a payload of stock footage, the production team succeeded in creating a full group of B-17 Flying Fortresses. Typically used as Gen. Savage's plane, the *Piccadilly Lily*, its nose art and markings were modified throughout the run of the series so that 44-83684 could pose as any number of the following B-17s. Additional roles that 44-83684 portrayed included:

- Angel Babe
- April Showers
- Four Leaf Clover II
- Girl Friend
- Gus's Revenge
- Hundred Proof
- Leper Colony
- Lorelei
- Lucky Lady
- Nervous Nellie
- Rink's Raidar
- So-Wot
- Terrible Tillie

Illusions

For scenes that took place inside an airplane, the production crew filmed in highly detailed mock-ups of several period aircraft. The mock-ups included a P-51 cockpit—first used by Earl Holliman's character in episode #22 "The Ticket," then used subsequently by Col. Gallagher in the second and third seasons—and a generic German fighter cockpit that served as Fw 190s and Me 109s.

The mock-up that saw the most use by far was the B-17. Just as the B-17 at Chino became a one-plane repertory company, the soundstage-bound mock-up served primarily as the *Piccadilly Lily* but also doubled as a variety of other B-17s as well as an RAF bomber in episode #65 "Fortress Wiesbaden."

Production manager Howard Alston explained that Fox obtained a surplus B-17 fuselage from Norton Air Force Base that was cut apart and transformed into the mock-up. Alston's report of the find was verified by Scott Thompson in his fascinating and well-researched book about the surviving Fortresses, *Final Cut*. However, intrigue went on behind the scenes of the acquisition. Paul Mantz and Frank Tallman, veteran pilots, stunt flyers and partners in Tallmantz Aviation, had been in negotiations with the base commander's office at Norton to obtain the salvaged B-17. They also expressed interest in a P-51 at Norton but were told that Twentieth Century-Fox had first priority. Tallman's work crew arrived at Norton one day only to find that "someone had come in and not only stripped the B-17 but deliberately mutilated the aircraft." Outraged, Tallman fired off a letter of complaint to the Deputy Director of Air Force Information in Washington, D.C. Despite its extensive and positive relationship with the Department of Defense, Tallmantz was unable to take delivery of another B-17 until 1967.

The B-17 mock-up was divided into sections "like giant chunks of bologna," quipped Bill Spencer. George Chan, second and third season art director, identified the segments as "the nose section (pilot compartment and the upper turret), bomb bay section with waist gunner and the tail with the tail gunner." Each section was mounted on high risers and equipped with gimbals so it could be tilted or shaken to simulate the B-17's movements in flight or hits by flak and anti-aircraft fire. Spencer recalled that the camera lens height was approximately 10-12 feet off the studio floor. At times the company wanted to shoot a scene that included, for example, the bomb bay and the flight deck. This was easily done. The art department and special effects craftsmen had rigged the segments so they clamped together "like the snaps on a suitcase," Spencer noted.

To fire at enemy fighters, the B-17 mock-up was outfitted with .50-caliber machine guns in the nose, top turret, and both left and right waist gun positions. In one early episode, more than 12,000 rounds of ammo were fired. Regrettably, the guns had a tendency to jam after several good bursts. Huge exhaust blowers were required to clear the soundstage of gun smoke so that filming could resume. The .50-calibers fired blanks and, according to Alston, only one local gun shop stocked .50-caliber ammunition. The source was Stembridge Gun Rentals, which provided firearms for film productions from 1916 to 1999. Each gun-firing sequence was very expensive; the bullets cost one dollar apiece. But, Alston added, "The Air Force had surplus blank ammunition, so we were able to obtain some of that so we could shoot as much as we wanted to. We had something like 350,000 rounds the first year."

Lew Gallo called the mock-up "very cramped. It was rather difficult at first with all the gear and everything, but after a while we got used to that." Despite the tight quarters, Gallo believed the mock-up was very accurate. "The only unrealistic part was that it didn't get to be 20 or 30 degrees below zero. It was maybe 70 or 80 degrees on the soundstages, which was maybe a little tough on the makeup men who had to come and wipe off perspiration."

Cold sweat was more like what third season associate producer Don Ingalls felt when he sat in the mock-up. "It used to give me the shivers to get in there and sit in the left-hand seat," he said. Ingalls appreciated the mock-up's authenticity because he flew B-17s during the war.

It's all about the process

To provide the illusion of a B-17 in flight, the filmmakers used a tried-and-true technique called "process" or "rear-projection." Film footage of B-17s, clear skies or cloud formations was projected on a screen behind the mock-up. The footage was known collectively as "plates." A movie camera was set up on the soundstage floor to film the combination of live action in the mock-up and movement depicted in the plates. When the background plates were projected, both the projector shutter and the camera shutter were electronically synchronized to open at the same instant to avoid any flutter in the resulting image. Result: the B-17 appeared to be moving forward.

For the most effective footage, the *12 O'Clock High* production staff dug through the Fox collection and found the original background plates used for the 1949 movie. Since the series, like the original film, was shot in black and white and during pre-CinemaScope days, the vintage plates melded perfectly with the new scenes filmed for television.

"The usual length of a photographic background of that type would be around 200 feet," noted second season cinematographer Frank Phillips. "And that was usually more than enough for the scenes you're shooting." Since scenes in the aircraft cockpit were done in "quite a few cuts," the rear-projection film didn't need to be very long. "If you do have a long scene, you'd have to figure a cut in there, and then you'd rewind the projector back there and run it again. It's as simple as that."

Bill Spencer said that when *12 O'Clock High* started production, he did his own process work. But lighting the cast, lighting the mock-up, lining up the camera and setting up the plates became too much of a burden. Fortunately, he was soon able to use the services of Ed Hammeras, a veteran process photographer at Fox.

Producer of seasons two and three, Bill Gordon, revealed another bit of studio magic. "When we were doing flying sequences," Gordon said, "Jim Doherty would crouch under the cockpit and work the controls to match what was on the process screen, so that it would look like the pilot was controlling the airplane properly."

TAKING STOCK

QM Productions had access to more than three million feet of actual War Department and Air Force footage to integrate into the sequences, as well as access to the original Twentieth Century-Fox feature. Among the additional resources QM utilized was the Air Force film library located at the Lookout Mountain Studio near Hollywood. Lookout Mountain's 1352nd Motion Picture Squadron produced classified films and documented nuclear tests for the Department of Defense. Wartime documentaries, such as *Thunderbolt*, *Combat America* and *Fight for the Sky*, as well as training films, provided a rich source of period film clips. In addition to using bits from the feature *12 O'Clock High*, the editors pulled scenes from other vintage Hollywood war films such as *Bombardier* and *Command Decision*.

During production of the first season, cinematographer Bill Spencer admitted, "I never saw a foot of stock prior to shooting, and could only guess how I should integrate to it. Yet we had very many stock long shots of B-17s landing and taking off, which fit right in with our photography at Chino."

On average, each episode had approximately 15,000 feet of combat footage edited in to give the illusion of aerial combat. Attentive viewers noticed that scenes of attacking German fighters seemed to feature animated gunfire flashing from the aircraft wings. "In a lot of the Air Force footage we had, we didn't have people firing," Howard Alston explained. "There were no guns going off." To simulate machine-gun flashes, assistant editor Jim Miller had a brainstorm. Using the head of a pin, he scratched lines directly onto the film itself. The gunshots "were drawn into the film a number of times. That was the only way we could get our enemy airplane shooting back at somebody," Alston said.

When a film editor was putting together a given episode that called for stock footage, he only had the script for guidance. Sometimes the description was highly detailed; more often than not, it was left to the editor's discretion. For example, Jim Doherty's stage directions from episode #77 "A Long Time Dead" were very specific:

EXT. AIR BATTLE – DAY (STOCK) (TO INTERCUT)
A) GERMAN FIGHTERS ATTACK A B-17.
B) B-17 DETAILS AS THE GUNNERS DEFEND.
C) GERMAN FIGHTER DESTROYED BY THE B-17 GUNNERS.
D) KOMANSKY ROTATING THE TURRET, FIRING.

Sometimes, the description was dramatic, such as the following from episode #70 "The Fighter Pilot" by E.B. Anderson:

EXT. SINGLE B-17 – DAY (STOCK) ON ITS WAY DOWN IN A DEATH PLUNGE.

A scriptwriter could be creative with imagery, as Andy White did in episode #46 "Between the Lines":

EXT. – BULLETS HEMSTITCH THE SKIN OF THE WAIST (STOCK)

Or a writer could just state the facts, as Philip Saltzman and Dan Ullman did in episode #44 "We're Not Coming Back":

EXT. B-17 GROUP FORMATION – DAY (STOCK)

From there, the editor went to the stock library and selected footage that best depicted the action as written. The resulting air battles were often a hodgepodge of different markings, such as a square-A or triangle-C on the tail of a B-17 instead of the 918th's triangle-A. In many cases, it was distracting to see an air battle where, for example, a P-51 started as a D model, changed to a B with a birdcage canopy, then turned into a B with a bulged canopy and wound up as a D with markings from a completely different group. But it was necessary to build the action sequences.

GETTING IT RIGHT

QM's top-down management style and commitment to historical accuracy extended to every facet of the production process. It also applied to aspects most viewers took for granted.

"One might say that everything seen on the screen, excluding the cast, is the direct responsibility of the art director and his staff," said George Chan, art director for the second and third seasons. "Our department's responsibility was to be at staff meetings to determine what type of scripts were forthcoming so we were able to build, adapt or revise existing locations or sets on the soundstages."

Chan further explained that because the art director was responsible for sets and set decoration, among other things, he often found himself racing to keep up with the busy production schedule. The position was so demanding that Chan kept active even while the series was on hiatus.

If clothes make the man, the *12 O'Clock High* wardrobe made the aimen. Part of Martin's pact with Twentieth Century-Fox gave him access to the studio's inventory of World War II uniforms. However, most of the wardrobe used in *12 O'Clock High* came from Western Costume Company. Western Costume had served the motion picture industry since 1912 by creating, tailoring, storing and renting costumes to represent any era or genre.

Chris Robinson in flight clothing.

No matter whether an actor was regular cast or a guest star, scenes filmed at Chino and in the mock-ups required flight clothing that included:

- Boots
- Coveralls
- 50 mission crush cap or a leather flight helmet with goggles
- Leather A-2 jacket or shearling jacket
- Mae West-style life preserver vest
- Parachute pack

On the ground, the cast was outfitted in period Army uniforms appropriate for enlisted men or officers, including either a garrison cap or service cap. Shirts and jackets were emblazoned with the Eighth Air Force shoulder patch plus rank insignia, aviator wings and decorations. Both officers and enlisted men were also supplied with a double-breasted greatcoat for those rainy days on Archbury Street.

The official B-17 operating manual instructed the crew to go on oxygen at

10,000 feet. For the pilot episode and a few early shows, the men of the 918th followed the regulations and put on their oxygen masks. But after that, and for the duration of the show's run, the crew went maskless.

"We did take some liberties," said Lew Gallo. "It's hard to read emotion or feelings on a face when it's covered with an oxygen mask. It was dramatic license. If all of us were wearing oxygen masks on film, you wouldn't know who was who."

THE FINISHING TOUCHES

A television series is a product. As such, it is marketed to consumers—in this case, the viewing audience—in much the same way as laundry soap or a loaf of bread at the grocery store. Every television show must have something of substance to offer the audience. Part of the appeal to consumers is in the packaging, also known as the brand identity.

Creating an identity for a TV series is done in a number of ways. The most fundamental component is the title presentation, which includes distinctive visuals and a memorable theme song. Pacific Title and Art Studio was hired to craft the main title for *12 O'Clock High*. Dating back to the silent era, Pacific Title provided credit sequences for movies and, later, TV series including *Checkmate, Maverick, Perry Mason* and *The Twilight Zone*. Starting with a clock face as the design element, Pacific Title created a sequence that used a progression of graphic bars to represent the hours on a clock, concluding with an arrow jutting up to the 12 o'clock position. Superimposed on the clock face was the title of the series, *12 O'Clock High*, rendered in military-style stencil font.

Perfectly accompanying Pacific Title's visual sequence was Dominic Frontiere's dynamic theme music. Since Pacific used the clock as a motif, Frontiere incorporated bells to symbolize the chimes of a clock. In keeping with the QM format, narrator Dick Wesson notified the audience that they were watching "*12 O'Clock High*—A QM Production." The title presentation then cut to images of the lead actors and guest stars. Dick Wesson clearly identified each player and the name of the episode.

Dominic Frontiere was a child prodigy who cut his musical teeth in the burgeoning West Coast jazz scene of the 1950s. In fact, he is known as one the of world's leading jazz accordionists. Frontiere was mentored by film scoring legends Alfred Newman and his brother Lionel Newman. From there, Frontiere set his sights on composing scores for films. He worked for QM from its earliest days, writing the theme and some background cues for *The New Breed*. Frontiere established another solid working relationship with Leslie Stevens' Daystar Productions, initially by writing the theme and score for *Stoney Burke* (1962–63). Arguably Frontiere's finest TV work in the 1960s was for his next project: the theme and scores for Daystar's cult sci-fi series *The Outer Limits* (1963–64).

Dick Wesson began as an announcer in live radio on shows such as *Space*

Patrol. He did voiceovers for numerous movie trailers and began a long relationship with the Walt Disney company in 1954 as the announcer on its various television series. Wesson voiced the title presentation of QM's *The New Breed* and announced each act of *The Fugitive* (1963–67). The "origin story" that opened each *Fugitive* episode was performed by William Conrad, future star of QM's *Cannon* (1971–76). Wesson also did the *Peyton Place* opening narration for Fox TV which, like *12 O'Clock High*, also launched in September 1964. He is often confused with another Dick Wesson, a comedic actor-writer-producer who appeared in movies such as *Destination Moon* and *The Errand Boy*, and on TV in series such as *The People's Choice* and *Love That Bob.* Sadly, that Dick Wesson committed suicide in 1979.

SHOWTIME

As the launch date for *12 O'Clock High* approached, ABC began beating the drums. On-air promos featured air combat between American B-17s and the Luftwaffe. A disquieting voiceover informed viewers that "Their lives were measured in seconds, in minutes. In the beginning, they could tell our airplanes from theirs and they could tell time. Before they were through, they owned the air."

Print ads depicted Robert Lansing sitting in a jeep with co-star Lew Gallo. Behind them stood the *Piccadilly Lily.* The ad copy informed viewers that "the stories will center on the men who flew daylight missions over German-occupied Europe, and on the behind-the-scenes activity on the ground." In its annual fall preview issue, *TV Guide* curiously pictured Lansing not at the controls of a B-17 or giving orders to his staff, but instead hanging from a parachute harness with a smile on his face.

On Friday, 18 September 1964 at 9:30 p.m. ET, *12 O'Clock High* made its debut. However, instead of airing the pilot film, ABC opted to go with the third episode produced, "Golden Boy Had Nine Black Sheep." Don Medford, who directed the episode, recalled that "'Golden Boy' worked out so well that they dumped the pilot and put 'Golden Boy' on first." Scheduling episodes is a network decision. What happened with "Golden Boy" and "Follow the Leader" was not unusual. The pilots for series such as *Combat!, Star Trek, The Monkees* and *I Spy* were also shuffled out of production order.

"Golden Boy" reworked a story arc in the original novel and feature film: Gen. Savage resolved to make Col. Ben Gately, the 918th's self-centered air executive officer, into an effective leader by assigning Gately a hand-picked crew of losers. Savage then ordered Gately to name his ship of misfits the *Leper Colony.* For the TV version of the story, writer Al C. Ward kept the basics but rechristened Col. Gately as Capt. Joe Gallagher.

Judging by the Trendex overnight ratings generated in its first outing, *12 O'Clock High* looked to be a hit:

9:30-10:00

NETWORK	SHOW	RATING	SHARE
ABC	*12 O'Clock High*	23.3	50.9
CBS	*GOP Political Talk*	6.8	14.9
NBC	*On Parade*	9.5	20.7

10:00-10:30

NETWORK	SHOW	RATING	SHARE
ABC	*12 O'Clock High*	24.3	52.1
CBS	*Alfred Hitchcock*	10.0	21.4
NBC	*Smalltown, USA*	5.9	12.6

Going by those numbers, half the audience watching TV that night was enjoying *12 O'Clock High*. However, most of the competition that evening consisted of second-string programming. The national Arbitron numbers for the following week gave a more realistic picture of where *12 O'Clock High* stood in the ratings:

9:30-10:00

NETWORK	SHOW	RATING
ABC	*12 O'Clock High*	11.5
CBS	*Gomer Pyle, USMC*	22.1
NBC	*Jack Benny*	15.8

10:00-10:30

NETWORK	SHOW	RATING
ABC	*12 O'Clock High*	12.0
CBS	*The Reporter*	14.1
NBC	*Jack Paar*	17.8

DEBRIEFING

Most television critics were impressed with "Golden Boy Had Nine Black Sheep," but they were wary of it as well. Jack Gould of the *New York Times* wrote that the episode was "familiar," but was "tautly done under the direction of Don Medford." Like critics of the 1949 film version, Gould was quick to credit the TV series for its authenticity. "The settings of the Air Force base in Britain are of major interest in themselves. A further virtue of *12 O'Clock High* is that it takes time to touch upon the technical aspects of bombing missions." Gould also praised the acting as "consistently first-rate."

Another supporter of the series was *TV Guide*. Its reviewer, curmudgeonly Cleveland Amory, praised *12 O'Clock High* as one of "two fine war shows on the air." The other was *Combat!* Reviewing the first half of the season, Amory noted that "war is bad enough, but bombing war is worse." However, if the audience could stand the bombing missions, then the series was "first-rate TV." Amory was most impressed by the series' star, Robert Lansing. "Make no mistake about it, Robert Lansing is magnificent. He is quite a guy—and, by the time the epilogue rolls around, you love him." A survey of television critics conducted by *TV Guide* gave high marks to *12 O'Clock High*. Comments ranged from "polished and interesting" to "slick, professional" and "a first-class production."

Adding to the praise were *Time* and *Newsweek*. "Robert Lansing is the central figure," noted *Time,* "a flying general named Savage, who can spit 220 nails a minute." According to *Newsweek*, "Unlike most war dramas, the first show was convincing, exciting, beautifully acted and had a fine script by Al C. Ward." ABC took notice of the *Newsweek* review and subsequently used it in print ads for the series.

On the other hand, some critics weren't impressed with *12 O'Clock High*. "It doesn't seem to be worth the effort," wrote Matt Messina in the *New York Daily News*. "Not for viewers who recall the far superior Hollywood version which has been kicking around TV's old movie circuit." Unlike other critics, Messina wasn't happy with the acting, which he felt was "cardboard." Robert Lansing was labeled as "two-dimensional." Messina blamed the script and direction, complaining that "the most exciting scenes were those which the director didn't prepare—combat films showing the B-17s in action."

Echoing Messina's remarks was the *New York Herald Tribune*, which hated the "jiffy-quick character changes and plot solutions." Conflict was solved with "back-slapping camaraderie." Grumbled the *Tribune,* "If you like instant solutions and a group of Air Force officers who look like method actors, this is for you."

Variety also slammed *12 O'Clock High*. Noting that *Combat!* could do many different ground-based infantry stories, *Variety* warned that "there was never much variety to the heroics and histrionics in the air war—not as much, certainly, as the infantry afforded." In addition to an "overly restricted" scenario, *Variety* complained that *12 O'Clock High* would have to be "better and more original than the old wartime pictures which are still in good supply at the TV stations, with bigger star values than Robert Lansing and John Larkin." Although *Variety* called the premiere episode "shopworn" and complained that it exhibited the usual military clichés, it complimented the acting and production values. "Lansing is an appealing star, the production is classy and the story—for all its familiarity—was well told." But overall, *Variety* remained doubtful: "The vehicle has serious engine trouble."

Future scripts, and the longevity of the series, would prove *Variety* wrong. Stories would take place in the base hospital (#19 "Faith, Hope, and Sergeant Aronson"), German-occupied France (#14 "An Act of War") and an air raid shelter (#23 "The Trap"). On the other hand, churning out episodes week after week inevitably led to reliance on Hollywood war movie clichés. For example, episode

#6, "Pressure Point," took its plot from the movie *Command Decision*. The scripts for *12 O'Clock High* would often bear similarity not only to previous war movies and TV shows, but also to each other. James Whitmore guest-starred as an over-the-hill World War I pilot (#32 "The Hero"), a scenario that would be repeated in the second season (#48 "Falling Star").

The fans weren't worried. Noted one viewer: "It is my hope that the 12 million men and women who were in uniform, as I was, will join me in support of *12 O'Clock High*. It has fine drama and acting, and the dress, the language, the songs, the sounds and tensions stir old memories."

MAINTAINING ALTITUDE

As the season progressed, the production crew kept busy creating new segments. Most TV series have a "breaking in" period during the first season. Because of its scale, *12 O'Clock High* had more than its share of challenges.

Paul Monash's original prospectus for *12 O'Clock High* stressed that the series would be about "stories of men *during* a war, not always men *at* war." Lew Gallo believed the series stayed true to that credo. "Our stories were mostly people stories told against a war background," Gallo said. "I don't think the story was up in the air. That's where the danger was, the danger that persisted throughout the show."

"It was, in my memory, a fairly happy series and fairly easy to do," said Charles Larson. The production went smoothly because the cast and crew were capable, efficient and highly skilled. "Making films is one of the most cooperative efforts in the world," noted Howard Alston. "Everybody has to be helpful, or you can't make them. The cameraman plays such a key role, the art director, the editors, the prop man. You have to have a story first. And then you have to have the actors. From then on, it takes teamwork with everybody."

Quinn Martin, Frank Glicksman and Charles Larson were all dedicated to telling realistic and accurate stories about people fighting a war. Scripts had to go through a triumvirate for approval—ABC, Quinn Martin and the Department of Defense. To bring those stories to life, QM brought in some of Hollywood's top writing talent.

Harold Jack Bloom sold his first movie screenplay in 1951 and later worked on the TV series *Richard Diamond*, starring a young David Janssen. After several years at MGM, Bloom moved to Europe where he co-wrote the 1955 feature *Land of the Pharaohs*—Joan Collins' film debut—with William Faulkner, and worked on a television series called *Foreign Intrigue* (1954-55).

When he returned to Hollywood two years later, Bloom found that "the crossover between features and television was becoming very, very much the fashion." So Bloom wrote for some of the leading TV anthology dramas including *Studio One*, *Philco Playhouse* and *Playhouse 90*. He met Quinn Martin socially, but at the time Martin was still several years away from opening his own shop. Then in 1964, when Martin was executive producing *12 O'Clock High*, he called on Bloom for help in improving the series' middling ratings. "I had been in World War II, in photoreconnaissance," said Bloom. "I read all the intelligence briefs from the pilots who came back. So I knew all the language." Bloom signed on to *12 O'Clock High*, contributing four scripts during the first season. One early episode, #3 "The Men and the Boys," worked so well that Bloom was asked to write a sequel for the characters played by Glenn Corbett and Sally Kellerman (#15 "Those Who Are About to Die").

Bloom did his best to keep the *12 O'Clock High* scripts realistic. "The most important thing I did for the show was give it a kind of authenticity, which was natural for me because I didn't have to think about it. It was just something I knew. I'd been in the Air Corps for two and a half years, so all the language and the manners and the customs, everything like that, were second nature to me."

The writer of the premiere episode, Al Ward, served as a Navy officer during World War II. After mustering out, he worked for producer Hal Wallis at Warner Brothers and later at Paramount Studios, where Wallis had his own production company. "I was his executive secretary," remembered Ward. "There was only one hitch: I didn't know how to type or take shorthand. But he didn't know that for a while." Ward did eventually learn how to type. His first scriptwriting assignment was for a Dean Martin film called *Summer Camp*, which was never produced. Later, while writing episodes of *Playhouse 90* and *Climax* at CBS during the 1950s, Ward became friends with Frank Glicksman. When Glicksman was assigned as producer of *12 O'Clock High*, he asked Ward to pen some scripts.

Ward wrote a total of six shows for *12 O'Clock High's* first season, including #30 and #31 "POW," the series' only two-part story. "Frank wanted me to write as many as I could," said Ward. "The most I could write was about one out of every four shows. In fact, I took my family over to Hawaii, and I would sit in the living room of a friend's house. He was an Air Force pilot. And while they were doing whatever they were doing, I'd sit there with a little portable typewriter and knock out a *12 O'Clock High* and mail it back."

Ward noted that his military experience in World War II was a great help in writing for *12 O'Clock High*. "I was in the command office, an aide to a naval captain. So I knew how staff operations went along, and it was quite helpful in some of the nomenclature and certainly in terms of attitudes of characters."

Though Frank Glicksman wanted more scripts from Ward, time constraints prohibited him from writing more. "One, you've got to come up with the idea. And that'll take you a week. And then you have to block it out." After successfully selling the story idea to the network and the producer, Ward took two to three weeks to complete each script.

Ward said he enjoyed the work immensely. "I liked *12 O'Clock High* because I like to write this type of hard, gut-level dialogue, which you can get in military shows. I loved the give-and-take of the characters. I love to write rascals, and in the military you'll find them!"

Rascals were to be found on the set as well. The pilot episode and nearly half of the first season shows were directed by William A. Graham. Paul Wurtzel described Graham as "one of the greatest characters in Hollywood that I ever met. And a very good director." The youngest member of the production staff, Graham would often make the most of his time on the set. "He was teaching himself navigation because he wanted to sail to Hawaii," said Wurtzel. "He used to be reading while they were acting, and I remember a lot of times we'd come to the end of the scene, I'd be standing next to him, and he wouldn't say 'cut' because he's reading the navigation book.

"Finally, Bob Lansing would look up. They'd wait because they ran out of dialogue, and they'd look around. The camera's still running, and Billy hasn't said anything. I remember one day Lansing says, 'Anybody out there listening?' So I nudged Billy and he says, 'What, what, what?' And I say, 'Well, say 'cut'!' But he was fantastic, a hell of a director."

THE BATTLE OF MIDWAY

12 O'Clock High maintained its course and survived the first 13 episodes. On Christmas Day 1964 the series received a present: a new time slot, bumped back a half hour to 10:00 p.m.

It looked as if 12 O'Clock High would have a fresh start for the new year. But just over a month later, supporting cast member John Larkin died of a heart attack. Earlier in the season, Larkin had given the press his take on Wiley Crowe: "He's a command officer, major general, with all of the command responsibilities and tensions and anxieties that go along with that kind of responsible job. He's complex; he's not a simple man. I mean, he has his ups, his downs, his faults as we all do, of course. But generally speaking, he's what you would call a good man and a good general and tries to be both as much as he can."

Six episodes featuring Larkin had yet to be aired. QM Productions had to move ahead to keep the show on schedule and complete its commitment to ABC. In episode #26 "Mutiny at Ten Thousand Feet," Larkin's character, Gen. Crowe, was abruptly transferred to Washington, D.C. John Zaremba, who had portrayed Gen. Stoneman earlier in #8 "The Hours Before Dawn," was brought in to help fill the void.

Soon after the loss of John Larkin, Quinn Martin drafted Charles Larson to produce QM's next major project, The FBI. After much prodding, frequent script contributor Al Ward joined the 12 O'Clock High staff effective 17 February 1965 as the new associate producer. At first, Ward wasn't thrilled. "I just didn't want to do that. I liked being a freelance writer. But eventually I did go on staff." As associate producer, Ward's main responsibility was to ensure that the shooting script was ready when required. "I would work with the writers and with the network, and see what the network's problems were, and either rewrite it myself or have the original writer do it." Ward also participated in post-production, which included cutting and dubbing each episode.

A new time slot, the loss of a key ensemble member and the defection of a lead member of the production staff were tough blows to *12 O'Clock High*, especially since the show was up for renewal. Worst of all, the show's ratings weren't terribly impressive.

ABC was not happy. That meant something had to change. But the wholesale renovation that was being plotted in the executive suites was something no one in the media or the audience could have predicted.

COLLISION COURSE

In early March 1965, ABC renewed *12 O'Clock High* for a second season but the decision came with a couple of caveats: The series would move to Monday at 7:30 p.m. ET and would feature more action-oriented storylines. That was just for starters. Before the dust settled, the show's audience and several of the actors would suffer through an avalanche of controversy.

ABC was not seeing a return on its investment. With middling ratings, *12 O'Clock High* could not pay its way. The reason for switching *12 O'Clock High* to an earlier time slot was purely a matter of economics. The 7:30 p.m. berth would provide an opportunity for younger audience members to watch—young people with disposable income. If *12 O'Clock High* attracted more viewers in that highly coveted demographic, then ABC could charge more for advertising time and the network's revenue stream would receive a solid boost.

That rationale might have made sense from the network's point of view, but the show's core audience was furious. "I have finally realized that ABC is serious about moving *12 O'Clock High* to catch the 'young' audience," wrote an upset viewer to *TV Guide* in May 1965. "I am impelled to ask, What ever happened to adults? Don't they count any more?" Grumbled another writer, "Why not make it an animated cartoon and show it on Saturday mornings along with Bugs Bunny?" The fans seemed to be concerned that *12 O'Clock High* would suddenly go downhill in quality. But ABC's highly successful series *Combat!* had been running in the 7:30 p.m. time period on Tuesdays for three seasons and had been able to retain its trademark gritty, uncompromising—and frequently downbeat—realism. If *Combat!* could stay tough in an early time slot, why not *12 O'Clock High*?

Unfortunately, a new time slot and thematic approach weren't the only modifications intended for the series. The biggest change to *12 O'Clock High* proved to be a lot worse: Robert Lansing was out of the show. He would be replaced in the lead by Paul Burke, returning to the role of Joe Gallagher.

THE AXE FALLS

Screenwriter Harold Jack Bloom remembered ABC saying, "We'll keep the show on the air, but we want a different lead." The network thought that the character of Gen. Savage was not sympathetic to the audience. "He could be seen as a kind of brooding villain," said Bloom. The network wanted less drama and more action, and suggested that the younger audience would identify better with a lower-ranking military character in the starring role. "Supposedly," noted columnist Hal Humphrey in the *Los Angeles Times*, "everyone knows a general is not in such constant jeopardy."

Assistant director Paul Wurtzel recalled the day that Lansing was told he was no longer the star of *12 O'Clock High*. "We had two or three episodes left to do and [several executives] called him aside, right in the middle of the day, and said, 'You know, we're not going to have you back next year. We're replacing you. The network wants a younger guy,' or some goddamn excuse." Sitting in a chair, a dejected Lansing took his "General Savage" nameplate from the desk and held it on his head in defeat.

"Poor Bob. You know, that's a hell of a message to get," said Wurtzel. "And you still have to go ahead and do some work to finish two or three episodes, knowing you're not coming back. He was really crushed. I mean, you can imagine!"

Lansing's co-stars were also shocked by the announcement. "Bob Lansing was absolutely perfect for the role," remarked Lew Gallo. "He lived, breathed and thought of nothing but that part. I can think of many nights where he spent the evening in his dressing room and ordered in dinner so he'd be prepared for the next day. He worked very, very hard."

ON THE WAY OUT

Although the network's announcement came as a surprise, problems had been brewing throughout the first season. For starters, Quinn Martin was no fan of Robert Lansing. "For some reason," remembered associate producer Charles Larson, "Quinn Martin always objected to him. Almost from the first day's rushes, Quinn was always saying that Lansing would have to go. Our ratings during that first season were adequate, but not that spectacular. Before long, Quinn was claiming that it was Lansing's fault."

Chris Robinson, who guest-starred in one first season episode and would become a regular in the second and third seasons, recalled one of his first meetings with Quinn Martin. "There was a brief mention to the fact that Bob Lansing was just too difficult to work with and the network wanted a change," Robinson said. "And because Bob was so difficult, Quinn went along with the network."

Over the ensuing years, Robinson heard variations on the story. "After the show was cancelled," he said, "I remember talking to Quinn and the story changed about 50 percent. Not so much that he was telling me a lie, but that it was what was allowed to be released by the network. It suddenly was not the same story." Later, when Robinson was working on another QM show, he had a heart to heart talk with Martin. According to Robinson, Martin then said it was the biggest mistake they ever made. "They should have never done it, it was a wrong decision but they couldn't go back on it once they had done it. It was probably the biggest factor in why the show never made it longer than it did."

Robinson could never understand why Lansing was dismissed. "I'd worked with Bob in other shows," Robinson said, "I'd done personal appearances with Bob. I never saw Bob Lansing as difficult to work with. He was one of the strongest, neatest actors going. And he was perfect as Gen. Savage. He was sensational."

Despite his dislike of Lansing's acting style, Martin hoped to ease the transition by proposing that the actor continue on the show in a reduced role. In that scenario, Gen. Savage would be promoted to wing commander and relinquish command of the 918th Bombardment Group to Col. Gallagher. Savage would then appear in a recurring role as Gallagher's boss.

"When I realized what changes would be made in the show for that younger audience," Lansing recalled later, "I knew *12 O'Clock High* couldn't be the same quality show next year. And 12 hours a day is too long to work at something you don't like."

Still wanting to bridge the transition, Quinn Martin asked Lansing to guest-star in the second season premiere episode, "The Loneliest Place in the World." But after reading the original draft, Lansing declined. "The part didn't appeal to me," he told columnist Hal Humphrey at the time. In a last-ditch effort to retain Lansing's presence for the second-season premiere, Martin asked him if they could use his photo in the episode.

"By that time I was a little angry," Lansing remembered. "I said, 'No, you can't use a picture of me. To hell with you guys! What are you going to pay me, 18 dollars?'" With that, Lansing was done with *12 O'Clock High*.

A SERIES WITHOUT SAVAGE

Robert Lansing's departure forced for the *12 O'Clock High* staff to create a plausible exit for his character. "How do you write an Air Corps general out of a TV series?" wondered *TV Guide*. "Do you kill him off? Do you transfer him? Or do you just let him fade away and hope viewers won't notice?" The network chose to kill off the character.

Lansing was concerned that after Gen. Savage was killed, people might think that Lansing had died. His concern stemmed from confusion over the death of co-star John Larkin. "I've already received several letters from people who thought that the late John Larkin was me," worried Lansing. "I didn't want to do anything to add to this confusion." Lansing also received a bit of advice on the subject from co-star Barney Phillips. Years earlier, Phillips had appeared as Jack Webb's partner on *Dragnet*. Phillips was written out of the series and then had trouble getting acting work. One day he walked into a producer's office and the producer screamed, "My God! I thought you were dead!"

Stuck in an awkward position, Lansing put things in perspective. He reflected on his experience in *12 O'Clock High* as "more rewarding to me than anything

I've ever done." He added, "I was very satisfied with the show this year. I felt I gained a lot of personal success from my role." Lansing maintained that he held no grudges against ABC, Fox or Quinn Martin. According to an interview he gave at the time, Lansing didn't want to be typecast anyway, and was anxious to try other types of roles. "It's the ideal career-maker to be in a show for a year and be a success in it," he said. "Hating a network would be like hating Dodger Stadium. Maybe I could be sore at the individual executive, but I have no idea who he is. I can't be mad at Quinn, either. He says it was the network's decision, and I have no evidence to make me doubt him."

Not wanting to lose a popular star, ABC asked Quinn Martin to develop a new series for Lansing. Lansing weighed his career options very carefully. "'I was offered five series by ABC, but I want to make motion pictures,'" Lansing said. In fact, for a complete career change the actor told his agents, Kumin-Olenick, to seek out only scripts in which he could play "dirty heavy" roles.

Within the next year, Lansing starred in two feature films (*Namu, the Killer Whale* and *An Eye for An Eye*), a pilot called *The Long Hunt of April Savage* (in which, ironically, Lansing essayed another character named Savage) and went back to work for Twentieth Century-Fox starring in his third TV series, *The Man Who Never Was*. Filmed on location in Europe, the show co-starred Dana Wynter, who had sparred with Lansing in two guest appearances on *12 O'Clock High*. Unfortunately, *The Man Who Never Was* lasted only half a season. During the next decade, Lansing returned to the stage with great success, appeared in guest roles on many television series and made a number of feature films of varying quality—*Scalpel* and *Acapulco Gold*, for example. In the 1980s and 1990s, Lansing played continuing roles on *Automan*, *The Equalizer* and *Kung Fu: The Legend Continues*. He would never attain the stardom he enjoyed as the star of *12 O'Clock High*, but continued to stamp every one of his projects with that distinctive Lansing style. Fans mourned his death when Lansing died of cancer on 23 October 1994.

MAIL CALL

Despite barely adequate ratings on Friday nights, *12 O'Clock High* had a loyal fan following. Disenchanted viewers wrote an avalanche of letters to QM Productions. "Lansing was very, very popular with the public, and they had thousands and thousands of letters," remembered Frank Phillips, second season director of photography.

Shortly after Phillips joined the production staff, he was pulled aside by producer Bill Gordon, also a newcomer to the series. Phillips related how Gordon "took me into a room where they had boxes and boxes of mail about the removal of Robert Lansing. One letter was in the form of a petition. They were going to boycott all of the sponsors' products. It must have had 150 names on it." Nearly a year after Lansing left the role of Gen. Savage, he told reporter

Harriet Peters that he still received letters about his dismissal. "At one point I was getting as many as 400 letters a day. I was amazed how much reaction the show got."

TV Guide told Lansing that his departure from the series generated more viewer mail than any topic since the assassination of John F. Kennedy two years earlier. "*12 O'Clock High* will become 'Six O'Clock Low,'" complained one fan. So much mail arrived at QM Productions that "Quinn got extremely defensive," remembered Lansing. "He started sending me his own personal mail—unopened."

Chris Robinson, another new face on the series, said that during season two "I did public appearance tours for *12 O'Clock High* all over the country. Ninety percent of everyone who came up to me said, 'Why did they change Bob Lansing? Paul Burke is too weak. Bob Lansing was so much better.' I conducted my own survey. Nine out of 10 said they preferred Bob Lansing."

MORE RESTRUCTURING

Along with Lansing, Lew Gallo was also shown the door. "I was pissed at the time," Gallo recalled. "But in retrospect, those are the things that happen. You live with them. It's part of the business."

Gallo maintained ties with Fox, acting in several of the studio's TV series including *Time Tunnel, Felony Squad* and *Lost in Space*. Then he discovered a career behind the cameras. Walter Grauman, who produced *Felony Squad*, agreed to let Gallo observe the production process, from film editing to dubbing sessions. That gave Gallo the expertise and hands-on experience to work as associate producer on the pilot and first season of Fox's *The Ghost and Mrs. Muir* (1968–69). From there he served as associate producer on *That Girl* (1969–71), then produced *Love, American Style; Mary Hartman, Mary Hartman; Lucan* and *The New Mike Hammer*. Gallo died on 11 June 2000 in Los Angeles.

John Zaremba, who joined the cast after John Larkin's death, also did not make the second season cut. The veteran character actor went on to co-star in two additional series, Fox's *Time Tunnel* (1966–67) and *Dallas* (1978–86). He also had the recurring role of Judge Adams in *Little House on the Prairie*. For 15 years, Zaremba played the "very fussy" bean buyer in Hills Bros. coffee commercials until his death on 15 December 1986.

Producer Frank Glicksman, already unhappy with not being allowed to make major decisions for the series due to tight control at QM Productions, was even more frustrated when the word came down about Lansing's removal. "Frank just hit the ceiling," said Charles Larson. "He liked Burke's work, but he fought as hard as he could to retain Lansing."

Quinn Martin would not budge. At that point, Glicksman decided to leave *12 O'Clock High* to produce his own shows. Glicksman neatly segued to the new Fox series *The Long, Hot Summer,* based on the studio's 1958 feature film. Al Ward joined Glicksman as associate producer. When the troubled production was cancelled, Glicksman and Ward remained with Fox Television, but on different projects. Ward produced *The Monroes* (1966-67) and Glicksman produced the short-lived *The Legend of Custer* (1967). Glicksman and Ward later formed their own company, Alpha Productions. At MGM, they co-created and produced the long-running hit *Medical Center* (1969-76), starring Chad Everett. Everett also starred in *Hagen*, co-created by Glicksman and another former *12 O'Clock High* staffer, Charles Larson. Larson executive produced *Nakia* (1974), a show that some references erroneously cite as a QM Production. Glicksman returned to the Fox lot in 1979 as co-creator and producer of *Trapper John, M.D.* Pulling double duty on *Trapper John* as associate producer and production manager was long-time Fox fixture Jack Sonntag.

In addition to Charles Larson, other members of the *12 O'Clock High* production staff moved over to QM's new series, *The FBI*. Directors Bill Graham, Don Medford and Ralph Senesky; director of photography Bill Spencer; art director Richard Haman; assistant director Paul Wurtzel; and film editors Marston Fay and Jerry Young also made the transition.

For his efforts on *12 O'Clock High*, William W. Spencer was awarded the 1965 Emmy for Outstanding Individual Achievement in Cinematography for Entertainment. Spencer returned to *12 O'Clock High*-esque territory when he worked on the 1969 war film *The Thousand Plane Raid*. He reunited with Frank Glicksman on *The Legend of Custer*, and then returned to *The FBI* for the balance of its network run. Following eight years on QM's *Barnaby Jones*, Spencer's final job brought him back to where he began, working at MGM on the first two seasons of *Fame*. After completing some 800 television segments, Spencer retired.

In addition to Spencer's Emmy, the overall quality of season one was recognized by The Hollywood Foreign Press Association. *12 O'Clock High* was nominated for a Golden Globe award for best television series.

THE SECOND WAVE

By mid-1965, Twentieth Century-Fox Television was the industry's Cinderella story.

Just two years earlier, Fox had reported an overall corporate loss of $39 million. But the 1965 financial reports showed Fox Television had more than tripled its income from film series made for TV, from $3.815 million in 1963 to $13.077 million in 1964. Even better news lay ahead for the coming fall. Fox rocketed from having zero network programs during the 1963-64 season to supplying nine hours of network fare each week for 1965-66.

Fox's comeback was generally attributed to two factors. The first was the appointment of Bill Self as the studio's executive vice president. Self was described as "imaginative, dedicated and highly competent." The second reason validated the studio's decision to "invest a lot of money to develop its TV properties and they have now hit the jackpot." Fox's corporate earnings for third quarter 1965 were up 58 percent over the comparable period the year before. The overall corporate financials would look even better with the release of Fox's block-buster *The Sound of Music*. Fox executives fondly dubbed the wildly successful film "The Sound of Money."

In addition to being renewed for a sophomore year, *12 O'Clock High* was also adding to studio coffers through sales of merchandise. A natural tie-in was Ballantine Books' reissue of the novel that started it all. Aurora Plastics created a line of scale model kits of famous World War II aircraft such as the Spitfire, P-51 Mustang and a diorama of three B-17 Flying Fortresses dropping their bomb loads. Two issues of a *12 O'Clock High* comic book series were published by Dell, a leader in TV-based comics. Milton Bradley issued a card game and jigsaw puzzles depicting scenes of aerial combat. Ideal sold a board game, at first with Robert Lansing's image on the box lid. Without so much as a ceremonial salute, store shelves were cleared and the identical game was reissued with Paul Burke's picture instead. Similarly, sheet music for the show's theme was issued in two versions, with Lansing and then Burke on the cover.

THE OFFENSIVE FOR HIGHER RATINGS

Twelve O'Clock High was now more than a link to the studio's past. It was clearly part of Fox's renaissance. But as *12 O'Clock High* entered its second season, the series would encounter heavy flak from all sides.

For the time being, World War II was still in vogue. ABC programmers had renewed *Combat!*, *McHale's Navy* and *12 O'Clock High*. CBS and NBC added four new series set in that era: *Convoy, Hogan's Heroes, Mr. Roberts* and *The Wackiest Ship in the Army*. Midseason would see the debut of Fox's half-hour drama for ABC called *Blue Light*, starring Robert Goulet. Theaters offered moviegoers such big-screen epics as *36 Hours, Battle of the Bulge, In Harm's Way* and Fox's *Von Ryan's Express*. Just in time for holiday gift giving, the National Association of Broadcasters Code Authority reported that upcoming TV commercials showed a "'discernible'" trend toward an "'increase in the number of toy weapons and related war toys.'"

Preparations for the sophomore year of *12 O'Clock High* began before its first season wrapped production. With a commitment from ABC in hand and a time slot on the network's schedule, *12 O'Clock High* had to rebuild itself in order to stay in the game. Quinn Martin started the process by retooling the public image of his show. He needed a new star and his choice was Paul Burke. Already familiar to audiences, Burke had appeared in two first-season episodes as Captain (later Major) Joe Gallagher.

PAUL BURKE ENLISTS

Born on 21 July 1926 in New Orleans, Paul Burke grew up around entertainers.

Paul Burke

His family operated several nightclubs in the city. Burke's apprenticeship with the New Orleans Civic Theater was sidetracked when he was drafted for service in World War II. After he completed his military obligation, talent scouts noticed Burke at the Pasadena Playhouse in California, and he moved into feature films. His earliest appearances in movies such as *Call Me Mister* (1951) and *Fearless Fagan* (1952), were unbilled. *Dragnet* creator and star Jack Webb was impressed with Burke's work on the television anthology *Playhouse 90* and signed the young actor as a TV veterinarian in the series *Noah's Ark* (1956–57). Two other short-lived series followed. In *Harbourmaster* (1957-58), he co-starred with Barry Sullivan, who would later portray Joe Gallagher's father in *12 O'Clock High* episode #42, "Grant Me No Favor." Burke next co-starred in the series *Five Fingers* (1959-60), based on yet another vintage Fox film.

From there, Burke joined the revamped version of Screen Gems' *Naked City*. He took over the young-cop type previously played by James Franciscus. During Burke's three seasons with *Naked City*, he garnered two Emmy nominations for outstanding continued performance by a lead actor in a drama series. Following the cancellation of *Naked City* in 1963, Burke claimed he wanted "six to eight months to rest before making any commitments." However, Jack Webb—during his stormy tenure as head of Warners' TV production arm—quickly approached Burke with a new pilot project. Four Star Productions also talked with Burke about *Royal Bay*, a pilot for the 1964-65 season. Burke's first post-*Naked City* appearances were seen within days of each other on NBC in the fall of 1963, first on *The Lieutenant* ("Captain Thompson") and then *The Eleventh Hour* ("What Did She Mean by Good Luck?").

In early 1965, Quinn Martin had lunch with Burke and asked if he was interested in replacing Robert Lansing as the star of *12 O'Clock High*. Martin had previously offered Burke the lead in QM's *The FBI*, but Burke turned him down. Burke wasn't interested in replacing another actor. He had already done it once, stepping in for James Franciscus in *Naked City*. Undeterred, Martin sweetened the deal, offering Burke part ownership of *12 O'Clock High*. Burke still said no. Before the final episode of season one was filmed, Martin again contacted Burke about the lead role in *12 O'Clock High*. Burke said he would consider the offer on two conditions. First, he wanted the story of Robert Lansing's departure to be properly explained to the public. Second, Burke wanted the scripts to be less military and include more romantic storylines. Martin agreed to both demands, and Paul Burke signed on as the new star and part owner of *12 O'Clock High*.

With Burke aboard, the show would continue but its growing pains were far from over. The supporting cast also went through an overhaul. Although Lew Gallo and Jack Zaremba were gone, the brass wisely saw fit to keep Frank Overton (as Maj. Stovall) and Barney Phillips (as Doc Kaiser). Those two gifted character actors would continue to provide strong support throughout the rest of *12 O'Clock High's* run. However, Phillips' participation in the second season was limited due to his commitment to work in the Fox feature *The Sand Pebbles* (1966). He was on location in Taiwan and Hong Kong from November 1965 through February 1966. To maintain continuity, Barry Cahill made five appearances as Capt. "Doc" Douglas, the 918th's interim medical officer.

Joining Paul Burke as new additions to the series were two familiar television actors: Chris Robinson, as Technical Sergeant Alexander "Sandy" Komansky, Gallagher's flight engineer; and Andrew Duggan as Brigadier General Edward Britt, the new wing commander and Gallagher's boss. Like Paul Burke, Robinson had previously appeared in the first season of *12 O'Clock High* (though in an unrelated role) and was invited back.

Chris Robinson was born in a log cabin near Ft. Lauderdale, Florida, on 5 November 1938. After attending Hollywood High School in California, Robinson studied theater arts at Los Angeles City College. His big break in movies came when he played the title beast in the horror feature *Beast from Haunted Cave* (1959). He kept building experience and his résumé by doing small parts in films such as *Diary of a High School Bride* (1959), *The Young Savages* (1961) and *Birdman of Alcatraz* (1962) as well as episodic television including QM's *The New Breed*. While under contract to Revue, Robinson appeared in many of the studio's TV series including *Wagon Train, Arrest and Trial* and *The Alfred Hitchcock Hour*. During this period, *TV Guide* appraised Robinson's niche as portraying "kooks and beatniks." Legendary columnist Hedda Hopper reported that by 1964, Robinson had guest starred on more than 100 TV series, performed in approximately 30 stage plays and, on weekends, made a documentary film about Andros Island in the Bahamas.

Chris Robinson

"One of the first things that Quinn did before we started the show," Robinson recalled, "was set up a screening room at Fox [and] run *12 O'Clock High* the movie and two of the first year episodes to acquaint me with what had gone on."

Born in Franklin, Indiana, on 28 December, 1923, Andrew Duggan attended Indiana University, where he received his bachelor of arts degree in 1943. He served in the Army Air Force until 1946. Duggan made his stage debut at the Shubert Theatre in New Haven, Connecticut, in 1947. From 1952 to 1953, he was part of the national touring company of *Paint Your Wagon*. Duggan's first feature film was the

Andrew Duggan

big-screen adaptation of Rod Serling's TV drama *Patterns* in 1956. Usually cast in authoritarian roles, Duggan's other films included *Sundown* (1957), *The Chapman Report* (1962) and *Seven Days in May* (1964). In addition to guest-starring on many popular TV shows, Duggan co-starred in the Warner Bros. series *Bourbon Street Beat* (1959-60) and *Room for One More* (1962).

Robert Dornan was born 3 April 1933 in New York City. His uncle was Jack Haley, who played the Tin Man in MGM's classic *The Wizard of Oz* (1939). After attending Loyola University, Dornan enlisted in the Air Force and served as a fighter pilot. He appeared in a 1960 episode of TV's *Men Into Space* ("Verdict in Orbit") and the movies *X-15* (1961) and *The Great Impostor* (1961) before starring in the low-budget air adventure *The Starfighters* (1964). During the first season of *12 O'Clock High*, Dornan appeared uncredited in several episodes. In #35 "Then Came the Mighty Hunter," Dornan flew right seat with Col. Gallagher, credited as simply Co-Pilot. For one episode, #37 "Big Brother," his character was called Capt. Mike Johnson, and then it was back to Co-Pilot. Finally in #47 "Target 802," Dornan's character was given the familiar name of Bob Fowler, at first a lieutenant but then promoted unceremoniously to captain in episode #51 "Which Way the Wind Blows."

SHAKING UP THE PRODUCTION TEAM

Before production wrapped on the first season, Quinn Martin sought a new producer to replace the departing Frank Glicksman. Martin asked writer Harold Jack Bloom to take the job. Bloom declined. "I was enamored with Europe," Bloom admitted, "and at every opportunity I would run off, so I didn't want to be tied down."

Instead, effective 31 March 1965, William D. Gordon became the producer of *12 O'Clock High*. Born 4 January 1918, Gordon began his career as a radio scriptwriter in 1936, and eventually acted, directed and produced for television. He directed the Mutual Network's first live TV shows in 1939, and then served as an infantry officer during World War II. Gordon found his way to Hollywood, where he broke in by acting in series such as *Maverick, Rawhide* and *Law of the Plainsman*. Perhaps his best-known performance was in the legendary *Twilight Zone* episode "Eye of the Beholder" (original air date 11 November 1960). He portrayed a doctor, obscured by shadows, who reassured his despondent patient that her physical "deformity" didn't make her less of a person. In the denouement, viewers saw the patient as a gorgeous young woman, while the medical staff all had Neanderthal brows, flared nostrils and drooping upper lips. Writer-producer-director Doug Heyes cast his old friend Bill Gordon as the doctor. Forty years later, Gordon's character was immortalized by Sideshow Collectibles as a 12-inch action figure. Heyes came through again by recommending Gordon for the job of consultant on the short-lived Civil War drama *The Americans* (1961). From there, Gordon began writing scripts for TV series such as *Bonanza, Thriller* and *Alfred Hitchcock Presents*.

Between 1963 and 1965, Gordon served as associate producer of QM's *The Fugitive*. He also found time to pen the script for episode #16 of Revue's *Kraft Suspense Theater*, titled "The Action of the Tiger" (original air date 20 February 1964). The one-hour drama, set during World War II, followed the exploits of an Eighth Air Force bomber crew shot down over France and their pilot's subsequent journey back to England. Interestingly enough, Revue had notions of using the episode as the back-door pilot for a weekly series about the exploits of a bomb group.

"I had been with Quinn for better than two years," Gordon said. "He knew that I had been an officer. He knew that I understood the military. He liked what I had done on *The Fugitive* and just thought I was the guy for the job."

Less than two weeks after Bill Gordon was named the producer of *12 O'Clock High*, William Koenig came on board as script consultant. Koenig had written for popular shows of the day, including *Bonanza* and *The Fugitive*. It was his association with Bill Gordon on *The Richard Boone Show*—Gordon was story supervisor, Koenig was story editor—that brought him to *12 O'Clock High*.

Other new members of the production team included:
• Frank V. Phillips, who took on the responsibilities of director of photography. Phillips had put in a lengthy stint on the dean of TV westerns, *Gunsmoke*. Just prior to joining *12 O'Clock High,* Phillips photographed the pilots for *The Wild, Wild West* and *Please Don't Eat the Daisies*.

• George B. Chan joined the staff as art director. Chan's career began in 1945 as a set designer at Twentieth Century-Fox. During his tenure at Fox, he worked on the 1949 feature version of *12 O'Clock High*. From there, Chan moved to Universal and its numerous TV series including *The Virginian* and *Tales of Wells Fargo*.

• Robert Huddleston, already part of the QM family, having worked on *The Fugitive*, became unit production manager.

• Jack Sonntag was appointed production supervisor for Fox TV following the death of Gaston Glass on 11 November 1965. Sonntag had recently been assistant to the producer on Fox's *Long, Hot Summer* series. More importantly, Sonntag had been an assistant director and production manager for Four Star when the company's shows were filmed at Fox Western Studios.

FORMAT CHANGES

While season one of *12 O'Clock High* tracked the Eighth Air Force's efforts to create an effective daylight bombing program during 1942 and early 1943, season two moved the chronology forward. Stories would now focus on wartime Europe from mid-1943 through May 1944, just prior to the D-Day landings in Normandy. An ABC press release announced, "With increased activity indicated for the 918th Bomber Group, a subtle change will take place in the men who fly and those who form the ground crews. The stories, too, will be different. There will be greater emphasis on action-adventure, but with verity and without diminution in the area of character." To address its insistence on a more youthful attitude, ABC press materials noted that "*12 O'Clock High* will dramatize the 918th as a young men's team fighting a young man's war."

However, the refocus on action-adventure was not purely a decision made by ABC, Fox or Quinn Martin. Instead, the choice was made largely by freshman producer Bill Gordon. "I studied the first season," Gordon said, "and concluded that the failure of the series had been because it tended to be too intellectual, kind of psychiatry in the cockpit. Based on that and my judgment of Paul Burke's ability and his appeal, I decided on action and adventure and going for a younger audience. Kids that were too mature to play soldier any longer I thought would respond to the zoom of the engine and the boom of the guns. Maybe that's why [Martin, Fox and ABC] hired Paul Burke and Chris Robinson, because they had an appeal to a younger audience and were more action-adventure guys."

Plans for advancing the series' chronology forward included providing the bombers of the 918th with long-range fighter cover from North American P-51 Mustangs. Although the P-51 was introduced in #22 "The Ticket," season two introduced the 511th Fighter Group, a unit attached to the 918th for escort duty. ABC press materials heralded the arrival of another new character, Lt. Col. Jerry Troper, commander of the 511th. Described by ABC as "a fantastically able flying officer in his late 20s," Troper would be introduced in episode #38 "The

Hotshot." But by then, the character had developed into a bitter, thirtysomething grouch played by Hollywood heavy Warren Oates. Although the Mustangs would appear time and again on *12 O'Clock High*, Col. Troper disappeared after his introductory episode. It wasn't until the third season that Troper's replacement, Maj. John Davidson, played by Mark Roberts, would be introduced.

Meanwhile, out at Chino Airport, a second B-17 was brought in to serve as a companion to 44-83684. The wingless fuselage of B-17 44-83316 was cleaned up and given the serial number 863 on its tail. Initially, 44-83316 was positioned strategically behind the control tower to give the illusion of another B-17 without revealing its missing wings. It was used later for several "crash and burn" sequences such as in episodes #46 "Between the Lines" and #68 "The All-American."

As a relatively inexpensive way to spruce up the uniforms worn during the second season, an American flag patch was added to the right shoulder of the A-2 and shearling jackets. However, at first the costumers missed a glaring discrepancy. The initial batch of flags showed the contemporary 50 stars instead of the historically accurate 48 that would have been used during World War II. The problem was corrected but 50-star patches continued to pop up throughout the second and third seasons.

INTO THE SECOND SEASON

When Bill Gordon signed on as producer of *12 O'Clock High*, he knew the job would be a huge challenge.

"I stepped into a desperate situation with my eyes wide open," said Gordon. "There were no scripts, there was no budget, there was no replacement for Lansing and, of course, I had no control over the terrible time slot and no defense against negative publicity. Eventually, in the eleventh hour, I had one script which Quinn had commissioned.

"When [Quinn] commissioned the script," Gordon added, "he didn't know what he was going to be doing, but he did know that he would add two characters named Gallagher and Komansky."

A lot was riding on the pivotal episode in which Gen. Savage was killed and Col. Gallagher assumed command. The task fell to Harold Jack Bloom, who penned four first-season scripts and turned down the job of producing Year Two.

Bloom's script was called "The Loneliest Place in the World," which was exactly where Gallagher found himself: dropped into a command position he didn't want and facing a furious Sgt. Komansky, who blamed Gallagher for Savage's death. Screenwriter Bloom was charged with solving the most difficult challenge facing the series to date: how to dramatize Gen. Savage's death when the actor who portrayed Savage had been dismissed and wanted no part of the project. The answer: some clever sleight-of-hand. As Savage's crippled B-17 plunged to earth during the episode's teaser, a brief scene on the flight deck showed only Savage's right shoulder and arm, allowing an extra to play the part. Then, following confirmation of Savage's death, Brig. Gen. Britt ripped Savage's photograph from the organizational wall chart in his office so quickly that Savage's face was never seen. Although the seams showed, the segment did its best to make a smooth transition into the second season.

From there, *12 O'Clock High* re-introduced viewers to Joe Gallagher. The new C.O. of the 918th had matured significantly from the brash, self-absorbed Joe Gallagher introduced in episode #1 "Golden Boy Had Nine Black Sheep." Back in the premiere segment, Capt. Gallagher showed cowardice, arrogance and a lack of understanding of his leadership responsibilities. Gen. Savage gave Gallagher a good swift kick in the rear and the young pilot gradually improved his performance. In Gallagher's second appearance, episode #24 "End of the Line," now-Maj. Gallagher continued to butt heads with Savage, this time over the death of a fellow pilot. With Gallagher's track record, it's a wonder that he ever got promoted, much less earn Savage's job. But then, life moves quickly in war and television.

Life would have to move very fast in order for *12 O'Clock High* to get on track for season two. Paul Burke arrived in March 1965. Chris Robinson was signed a mere two weeks before production was slated to start on 1 June 1965. The first printed draft of Bloom's script was dated 26 May 1965.

"We were actually in pre-production before I was ever permitted to buy a second script," lamented Bill Gordon. His first two script purchases were "The Hotshot" by Robert Lewin, and William Anderson's and William Hamilton's "Sabotage" (eventually retitled "Rx for a Sick Bird").

And so filming on Year Two began at Fox Western Avenue and Chino Airport. The budget was now $132,000 per segment, the same as Fox's *Daniel Boone* and the studio's new show *The Long, Hot Summer*. By comparison, the top-budgeted shows that season were *Jackie Gleason and His American Scene Magazine*, at $180,000 per episode, and *The Hollywood Palace*, at $187,000.

Almost from the start, there was tension on the *12 O'Clock High* set. Gordon recalled the conflict: "Paul Burke was the lead. I'm not sure that he ever really believed he was a star. Chris Robinson always believed he was and felt that he ought to be featured in the series. When there was tension on the set, it would have been between Paul and his insecurities and Chris and his ego. They didn't get on too well."

Chris Robinson picked up the story: "About six episodes in, the guard at the gate, Paul Burke's stand-in, all kinds of people were coming to me and saying, 'You know, you're killing him. He is so weak. No one can believe that a tech sergeant is standing up to the colonel like that. You're too strong. You're going to take over this show. It's going to be your show by the end of the year.' If you noticed the first six or seven episodes, I had really strong parts. And when word began to get back to him, an edict went out because Paul Burke owned a piece of the show. They cut me down to next to nothing. For the remainder of that year and the following eight months it was 'Yes sir,' 'No sir,' jump in the jeep and drive him off. I found out exactly what happened because, just as the scuttlebutt had come to me from the guard at the gate to Burke's own stand-in, to agents, to viewers, what had happened came back to me. At that point I was devastated."

As for the rest of the regulars, Bill Gordon commented, "Frank Overton was a quiet guy who just did his job. Barney Phillips and I went way back into radio; he used to work for me as an actor. Barney was a sweetheart. Andy Duggan was one of the most professional performers I've ever worked with."

While the soundstages hummed with activity, Gordon spent long hours in his office pounding away at his typewriter. Gordon wrote just one teleplay during year two (#45 "The Jones Boys"). When the first freelance script was submitted to him, Quinn Martin insisted that Gordon doctor it overnight. "That set a pattern which followed me through the series," said Gordon. "No script satisfied Quinn until I had rewritten it. I never was able to convince him to let me okay one script, even a below-par script, in order to let me get one ahead. So I was always under the gun."

Alan Armer, Gordon's former boss on *The Fugitive*, said Gordon "was such a perfectionist that if he found a better way of doing something, even after he was finished with it, he would come back and rewrite it because he wanted it to be just as good as it could be."

"The best scripts that got through the production okays were those that Bill managed to get through with minimum interference," said Gordon's wife Maurine. "Often as late as possible."

"I was often still rewriting an episode when we got into production," Bill Gordon admitted. "Because of this I was always constantly reminded, 'We're in trouble, we're in trouble, we're in trouble.' There was always friction between my superiors and me."

Third season script consultant Jack Hawn said, "[Gordon] would lock himself in his office and not emerge for maybe 24 hours or more. Always facing a deadline, that left little time for any rewriting. Bill was the only one who knew what the episode was about. He wrote almost everything from scratch and it almost always was top drawer. Nonetheless, the executive producer would get frantic as deadlines approached."

Clearly, the continuous rewriting had repercussions on the production team and with the schedule. Art director George Chan said, "The scripts after the first five episodes would generally be late—sometimes as late as the day before the actual filming. Under those circumstances, we were required to exercise all kinds of ingenuity to come up with something to shoot for the first day of filming."

Gordon took a protective management approach to buffer his production staff from front office politics. "I felt I had to safeguard my company against any knowledge of the problems I was having on the creative end," he said. "Thanks to perhaps the best crew I've ever worked with, I was able to run it. I never was a take charge, gung-ho type of a guy. Everybody knew I wouldn't put up with any hanky-panky, but I ran a very loose company with an emphasis on having fun at the job."

With so much time spent at Fox Western studios, wife Maurine gave Bill Gordon an organ for his office "where he could enjoy it when he had time." Gordon was a talented piano and organ player. The sound of his music would drift throughout the office complex.

"He would sit in his office and play the organ, which was so bizarre," commented Alan Armer.

Rewrites were—and still are—one of the cogs in the Hollywood production machine. "Writers hate rewrites," said Jack Turley, who wrote or rewrote four episodes of *12 O'Clock High*, "because everyone, including the doorman at the studio, makes suggestions." Turley noted that a good sense of humor could help a writer through the rewrite process. "I used to say that the story editor changes men into women, dogs into horses, and moves the whole thing to Alaska."

THE SECOND SEASON TAKES OFF

Print ads that ballyhooed the new fall season featured both Paul Burke and Chris Robinson in full flight gear with the headline "Turn on the Adventure." Subsequent ABC ads clustered all the network's Monday night programming in one ad under the headline "Monday Night's All Excitement on ABC."

As was done the previous season, ABC and the Department of Defense generated a promotional campaign that put *12 O'Clock High* and *Combat!* on "tens of thousands" of recruiting posters. Some local ABC affiliates took it upon themselves to drum up a little drama of their own. Enterprising promotion managers staged "simulated invasions using National Guard troops complete with jets and tanks."

The highly anticipated transition episode of *12 O'Clock High*, "The Loneliest Place in the World," made its debut on 13 September 1965 in the series' new berth of Monday at 7:30 p.m. ET. The competition at that hour consisted of two game shows on CBS (*To Tell the Truth* and *I've Got a Secret*) while NBC offered *Hullabaloo* and *The John Forsythe Show*. Sponsors for the second season included Armour and Company; Beecham Products; Bristol-Meyers; Brown & Williamson Tobacco Corporation; Consolidated Cigar Sales, makers of Muriel Cigars; Ford Motor Company and its Mercury Comet; Sunbeam Corporation; and Zenith Radio Corporation. Among the products touted were Kool cigarettes, Macleans toothpaste and Brylcreem men's hair product.

"Quinn Martin's classy production touch is the chief attribute for this war series," noted *Variety* on the start of Year Two. "Otherwise it shapes as a traditional military [series], with plots and portrayals in the familiar groove." Joe Gallagher might have been a more pleasant character, but the responsibilities of command were just as much a burden on him as they had been for Gen. Savage.

The marked difference between the two characters might have made Gallagher seem like a lightweight by comparison, but no two leaders are alike. As Paul Burke noted years later after reviewing some episodes, "I saw heaviness and great, great concern for men that were being killed."

"Burke may cut a wider swath of fan favor [than Robert Lansing]," noted *Variety* at the time. "But in line with the character he plays it's a less authoritative lead." Gallagher was a young colonel, fallible and concerned about his men. The character's mien reinforced ABC's push for a more youth-oriented action series.

As the second season continued, some viewers shelled Burke. Wrote one angry fan, "While *12 O'Clock High* is still a good show, some of the impact has been lost through Paul Burke's ineffectiveness as the bomber commander. Why hire a pussycat to do a tiger's job?"

Burke was flabbergasted. "I went into that show and the hate mail started likeyou wouldn't believe," he said. "Not only from Bob [Lansing]'s fans but from my own." The press was equally ill-tempered, sometimes giving the impression that Burke had muscled his way into the role. *Los Angeles Times* columnist Hal Humphrey noted that a few critics "made him look like the hissing villain in an old melodrama."

Then Robert Lansing unknowingly added fuel to the fire. His press agent discovered a secret that completely undercut the ABC Network's insistence that the revamped *12 O'Clock High* needed a younger actor in the lead role. Curious about his client's unceremonious dismissal from the series, the clever agent did some investigating and stumbled across an interesting fact: Paul Burke, the new star of *12 O'Clock High*, was actually two years *older* than Robert Lansing. To be fair, the difference between the two leading men was more a matter of style than of age. Lansing's screen presence was highly mature, overarching, and often brooding. By contrast, Burke emanated a lighter, younger yet equally serious personality on camera. Despite actually being older than Lansing, Burke *appeared* younger, which was exactly what the network required.

Burke took it all in stride. "I knew it was a calculated risk to follow an actor as strong as Lansing," he said at the time. "It's like telling patrons of an old established restaurant that beginning tomorrow there's to be a new cook, but I never heard of the press getting on a guy for something he didn't do."

Despite some bad raps from the press and big changes in cast and crew, *12 O'Clock High* gradually regained its altitude. "[The show] took on a different tone," noted Frank Phillips, "but they surrounded themselves with pretty good character actors." The second season boasted some standout performances, including #35 "Then Came the Mighty Hunter," with Beau Bridges, and #53 "Back to the Drawing Board," which earned guest star Burgess Meredith a standing ovation from the crew.

As the season progressed, viewers learned more about Joe Gallagher's background than they ever did with Gen. Savage. Gallagher's faults and neuroses had been loudly broadcast during his first-season appearances on *12 O'Clock High*. During year two, viewers met Gallagher's brother (#37 "Big Brother") and father, a Pentagon staff officer (#42 "Grant Me No Favor"). Gallagher's back story was further detailed as other characters were introduced, such as a resentful childhood friend (#36 "The Idolater") and a bitter officer whom Gallagher helped expel from West Point (#49 "The Slaughter Pen").

Despite the advances in character development, low ratings continued to plague the series. Arbitron ratings for the second season debut shaped up this way:

7:30-8:00

NETWORK	SHOW	RATING	SHARE
ABC	*12 O'Clock High*	11.5	24
CBS	*To Tell the Truth*	14.5	30
NBC	*Hullabaloo*	13.5	28

8:00-8:30

NETWORK	SHOW	RATING	SHARE
ABC	*12 O'Clock High*	15.2	27
CBS	*I've Got a Secret*	17.7	32
NBC	*John Forsythe*	16.6	30

The first 30-market Nielsen ratings, released on 24 September 1965, placed *12 O'Clock High* as the 26th most popular show on the air. Two Nielsen reports, issued 1 and 8 October, respectively, saw *12 O'Clock High* fall completely out of the top 40. During the key November ratings period, the show again failed to crack the top 40. The time period was consistently dominated by CBS with its long-running game shows *To Tell the Truth* and *I've Got a Secret*.

CLIFFHANGER

Thomas W. Moore, president of ABC-TV, promised a group of affiliate representatives that the network would have a "brand new opening in January" by launching its "second season." ABC would introduce four new shows, two of them from Fox: *Batman* and *Blue Light*. Although *Blue Light* performed fairly well against potent competition, *Batman* became an unprecedented smash and a pop culture touchstone. Both series helped shore up ABC's sagging audience share.

"Ratings improved just enough to keep everybody hopeful," William Gordon explained. But at midseason, story editor William Koenig left *12 O'Clock High*. "Bill was an excellent story man," said Gordon, "but he just could not relate to the series." Koenig went on to a comparable staff position with *The Wild, Wild West*, then wrote for Fox's *The Felony Squad* and became an associate producer on Universal's *The Name of the Game* (1969–71).

Philip Saltzman replaced Koenig, bringing with him a solid background in writing for TV series such as *Hawaiian Eye, Stoney Burke* and *Run for Your Life*, and serving as story consultant on *Redigo* (1963-64). He joined *12 O'Clock High* as story consultant and was soon bumped up to associate producer. However, Gordon felt that while Saltzman was a talented writer, he never seemed happy in the job. Saltzman left at the end of season two. Gordon added, "He later became an excellent producer for Quinn Martin." Saltzman went on to produce other QM series such as *The FBI* (1969–73), *Barnaby Jones* (1973–80) and *A Man Called Sloane* (1979–80).

Production on Year Two wrapped in early March, leaving the cast and crew wondering if they still had jobs. Bill Gordon put his downtime to good use. Obtaining scripts in a timely manner had always been a problem. He pleaded with Quinn Martin to let him buy three scripts so that if the network renewed *12 O'Clock High* they would be ahead of the game.

"It would have cost $12,000 to buy three scripts, but he wouldn't go for it," Gordon remembered. "So I broke the rules." Gordon asked technical advisor Jim Doherty and two other writer friends to submit scripts "on spec"—on speculation without guarantee of payment. Even though speculative writing violated the Writers Guild of America guidelines, "they all went for the deal." Gordon also wrote a script on spec.

The first version of ABC's 1966–67 fall schedule put Screen Gems' *Iron Horse* in *12 O'Clock High's* current 7:30 p.m. Monday slot and Warner's *House of Wax* in its previous 10:00 p.m. Friday berth. There was no mention of *12 O'Clock High*. Subsequent reshuffling of the schedule had another new series, *The Milton Berle Show*, filling the 10:00–11:00 slot. Trade papers called *12 O'Clock High* "a question mark."

Finally, by the end of March, ABC locked its fall schedule. There on Fridays at 10:00 p.m., was *12 O'Clock High*. "I don't believe the series was ever actually canceled," Gordon said. "There were a lot of questions about renewing, but I have no idea what went on between Quinn Martin and ABC."

At least when the show was picked up, the company had four scripts ready for approval. The catch? "I couldn't admit it," Gordon confessed. "I couldn't submit them all at the same time without admitting I had broken the rules about writing on spec."

But that wasn't the only snag he confronted. "The biggest question we faced," said Gordon, "was whether to continue in what was the obsolescent black and white or go into more expensive color."

END OF THE LINE

In early May 1966, Leonard Goldberg, ABC's programming chief, announced that ABC's primetime schedule for 1966–67 would be full color.

Goldberg set a tough goal for his network. Where the CBS and NBC networks had been racing toward color broadcasting, ABC lagged far behind.

When Walt Disney's contract with ABC expired in 1961, he moved his show to NBC because ABC lacked the capability to telecast in color.

Grasping that the ability to "tint up" its schedule was critical, ABC tested the waters by broadcasting a total of one hour of primetime programming in color: 30 minutes each of *The Jetsons* and *The Flintstones*. The following season ABC increased its color output to three hours weekly. During the 1964-65 season, ABC reverted to only one hour of color each week, and again, the genre was animation: *The Flintstones* and *The Adventures of Jonny Quest*. The network attributed its lack of color programming to overall corporate belt-tightening. Similarly, although the pilot film for Fox's *Voyage to the Bottom of the Sea* was originally filmed in color, the series' first year was broadcast in black and white. Estimates at the time projected that filming in color would have boosted the cost of each *Voyage* episode by $20,000 per segment or roughly $600,000 over the season. Simply put, there weren't enough color TV sets in American households to justify the added cost.

All that would change quickly. A survey conducted by NBC showed that the number of American homes with color TV had tripled between 1965 and 1967. As of 1 April 1965, 3,210,000 homes had color TV. Two years later, 10,390,000 households were equipped with color receivers. As expected, NBC pushed its suppliers so that all but a handful of its primetime series were in color during the 1965–66 season. Following suit, CBS announced in May 1965 that starting with the 1966–67 season, all of its primetime programming would be in color.

All three networks set their sights on having a full-color primetime lineup for the fall 1966–67 season.

FOX, QM AND ABC FIND SUCCESS

ABC had not yet given up on World War II. Not only did the network's venerable *Combat!* switch to color for its fifth and final season, but ABC also introduced the half-hour adventure series *The Rat Patrol*. CBS offered up the second season of *Hogan's Heroes* and launched the only other new WWII series, MGM's *Jericho*.

Production at Twentieth Century-Fox was going at full throttle. Fox was now the leading provider of episodic series to all three networks. Fox was also back to making hit movies, including *The Bible, The Blue Max, Fantastic Voyage* and *Our Man Flint*. In fact, where Fox was once forced to rent out its own stages to raise money, the studio now had to pay other lots to use their work space. As a result, the Fox TV series *Batman, The Felony Squad* and *The Green Hornet* were all filmed at Desilu's Culver City studios, formerly the David Selznick lot.

QM Productions was also growing. In addition to three network series—*The Fugitive, The FBI* and *12 O'Clock High*—ABC ordered a fourth QM show, *The Invaders*, as a mid-season replacement for 1967. All four series generated a company record of $21 million in production money. The company also had 300 employees on its payroll.

Among the newest QM employees was Adrian Samish who, along with Arthur Fellows, was made a company vice president. At QM Productions, Samish's principal responsibility was the approval of scripts, directors and the overall quality of all QM series. Prior to joining QM, Samish was vice president of current programming for ABC-TV West Coast and head of NBC-TV's daytime programming. He also had a history of producing shows such as *Atom Squad* (1953–54), *First Love* (1954–1955) and *Northwest Passage* (1958–59).

Samish also had a history of rubbing people the wrong way. He frequently caused friction with creative talent, particularly the writers and producers of shows to which he was assigned. His most infamous confrontation was with science fiction writer Harlan Ellison. Samish met with him for a story conference on Ellison's script for *Voyage to the Bottom of the Sea*. Samish allegedly said, "Writers are toadies. You'll do as you're told." The sanitized version of what happened next has it that Ellison lunged at Samish, but the executive dodged, slipped out of his chair and suffered a broken pelvis when a huge model of the Seaview submarine fell on him.

Alan Armer, producer of QM's *The Fugitive*, *The Invaders* and *Cannon*, related how Samish came to QM. "At one point, Quinn offered the job of the number-two position at QM Productions to me. I decided that I didn't want to sit in an office. I wanted to be working, on the soundstages, out on location. So I turned the job down. Adrian Samish said to me later that he was sweating out my decision because the only way he was going to get the job was if I turned it down. When I turned it down, Quinn brought in Adrian, whom I guess he had worked with on other ABC shows."

Before long, Samish became a thorn in the side of QM's stable of producers. According to Armer, after reading a first draft script Samish would send the producer his critique, a page of notes generally filled with nitpicky changes. Most producers would fix the points that seemed important and the rest would be forgotten. Then, Samish would send another memo. The producers would complain to Quinn Martin and Martin would arbitrate the situation.

"Adrian Samish was not a beloved character at QM," said Alan Armer. "Everybody sort of resented him because he was kind of a super editor who didn't have the taste, knowledge or expertise to be in that critical position."

FLYING COLORS

During a 1965 roundtable discussion of the move toward TV programming produced in color, Fox's William Self said, "Some programs, like *12 O'Clock High*, will probably never go into color because of their extensive use of black-and-white action footage shot during World War II." However, once that minor obstacle was overcome, Self added, "If the network and the sponsor are willing to spend the extra money for color, which averages about 15 percent more than black and white, then that's the way it will be done."

When ABC renewed *12 O'Clock High* for a third season, it was with the explicit understanding that QM Productions would find a way to make the show in color. Economically, the change was imperative. Artistically, it was a different story.

"It was a mistake," said William Spencer, who had set the series' moody black-and-white tone during the first season. "World War II was in black-and-white. It's hard to make color look down and dirty and grim."

Filming *12 O'Clock High* in color may have sounded like a fairly simple task. After all, the show was shot on soundstages or on location at Chino Airport. The unenviable task fell to third-season director of photography Robert C. Moreno. He began his five-decade career as an assistant cameraman at MGM. Moreno served in the Navy during World War II, attached to the Army Air Force as a cartographer in a B-17. His first TV series was *The Adventures of Ozzie and Harriet,* which he joined as first assistant cameraman when it premiered in 1952. Moreno worked his way up to director of photography on *Ozzie and Harriet* and helped the long-running sitcom navigate the transition from black-and-white to color for its final season (1965–66).

Though Moreno wasn't happy with the decision for *12 O'Clock High* to go to color, he did the best he could. One of his changes was in lighting the B-17 cockpit mock-up. He rigged the key light, which highlighted the actors in the scene, to move up and down so that shadows in the flight deck would move as well. "That is what would actually happen in a real cockpit," Moreno explained.

With that problem solved Moreno turned his attention to another issue. The raids, the bombings and the dogfights had to be depicted in color. The best-known source of color combat footage featuring B-17s was the 1944 documentary *Memphis Belle.* Other period documentaries, such as *Combat America* (1944), also provided excellent resources. However, two key uses of footage would prove problematic. First, scenes featuring the enemy—such as fighter planes and anti-aircraft gun emplacements—were filmed in black and white. So were the process plates used behind the B-17 mock-up.

12 O'Clock High was renewed for a third year in late March 1966. The projected start-up date was late May. That gave the staff roughly two months to scour film archives on two continents for color footage. "The results were amazing," Bill Gordon reported at the time. "There just wasn't any around." Gordon and Quinn Martin were unable to locate any film at the J. Arthur Rank studio in England, which was collecting color footage from the war, or from the German film bank Transit Film Vertrieb.

Fortunately, the U.S. Air Force had color footage from the Peenemünde V-2 rocket site. Like the Luftwaffe footage already being used in *12 O'Clock High,* the V-2 color footage had been captured by Allied forces at the end of the war. It was stored at the film depository at Wright-Patterson Air Force Base in Dayton, Ohio. Film editor Patrick Kennedy was dispatched to the base, where he not only examined 320 feet of Peenemünde color film but also found 39 reels of Allied film. In nine days of research, Kennedy also looked at unused footage shot for *Memphis Belle* and *Combat America,* plus B-25 and P-47 training films. Meanwhile, a well-placed advertisement netted color shots of a B-17 crash landing and a Luftwaffe fighter attack. An ABC press release noted that "while *12 O'Clock High* now has the largest color film library of the air war in Europe— over 600 different sequences—Gordon and Kennedy are attending veterans' reunions to find out if any of the Air Corps men attending took cameras along on their combat missions."

Unfortunately, color footage of Luftwaffe fighter squadrons eluded the producers. They were forced to continue using the mass takeoff and attack scenes featured in the first two seasons. Somehow, the footage had to at least give the impression of color. Computer colorization of film was years in the future. Hand-tinting the black-and-white film was an option, but far too expensive. The producers had no choice but to tint the footage sky blue, blend it with the color footage and hope the seams didn't show too badly. The background plates of B-17s in formation, used for process shots, were also tinted blue. Robert Moreno recalled that "the plates for process shots were either in color, or were black-and-white plates colored blue, which made no sense at all."

In addition, new footage was shot of the P-51D on loan from the Ontario Air Museum. The beautifully restored Mustang, known as *Spam Can,* was flown around Chino Airport and filmed performing a variety of maneuvers from a series of different angles and ranges.

Heralding the switch to color, QM and Fox created a network teaser to herald each episode. ABC declared that all its programming would carry a brief, tailored announcement that the following show was broadcast in color. For example, Fox's *Batman* opened by showing the Batman logo with the words "in color" superimposed over the picture. The visual was underscored by a sampling of the show's theme song. For *12 O'Clock High,* color footage from *Memphis Belle* was used depicting a B-17 in flight, white contrails streaming from its engines. QM's house announcer, Dick Wesson, then told viewers, "Next—*12 O'Clock High*—in color."

Paul Burke realized years later that the lack of color footage forced the writers to make many episodes take place almost entirely on the ground. "Our air combat was cut down considerably—and that was the excitement of that show," Burke later told *TV Collector* magazine.

FINAL APPROACH

When ABC renewed *12 O'Clock High,* network programmers returned the series to the 10:00 p.m. Friday berth it held during Year One. The competing shows on NBC and CBS were, respectively, the sophomore western *Laredo* and the second hour of *The CBS Friday Night Movie.* Friday night has historically been a death sentence for TV series, including the venerated *Star Trek,* which breathed its last network gasp in that 10:00 slot during the 1968–69 season.

Moreover, the move only alienated viewers. *Variety* noted that "with no unpredictable shows against it, *High* should cut a respectable niche among the late-hour Friday night adult viewers." But after a season in the 7:30 p.m. "family hour," where a retooled *12 O'Clock High* was meant to appeal to a younger audience, the series was now thrown back into a more "adult" time period. Would *12 O'Clock High* be slam-bang action or well-constructed drama? ABC press notes for the 1966–67 season emphasized that the new time slot was designed "to attract more adult televiewers." Further reassurance was issued in an ABC release: "With increased activity planned for the 918th Bomber Group, the emphasis will be on action-adventure, but there will be no diminution in the amount of attention focused on the men who fly and those in the ground crews."

Along with a change in time and approach, the story timeline of *12 O'Clock High* would also be adjusted once more. ABC outlined the direction: "Attention will be focused on the general military situation in Europe from 1943 through 1945, but liberties will be taken with historical chronology. D-Day, the landings in Normandy, are on the planning board."

William D. Gordon re-upped as producer on 2 May 1966. The official announcement was accompanied by the news that *12 O'Clock High* would air 26 segments in color and that Gordon would pen a two-part story. Gordon quietly pulled out the scripts he commissioned on spec, and then quickly assigned writers to script the first 17 segments. ABC made a similar arrangement with Fox's new series *The Green Hornet.* Initially the network ordered 17 *Hornet* episodes, then bumped up the full-season total to 26 segments.

The third season budget ballooned to $180,000 per segment. Bill Gordon remembered that, in those days, such a price tag was "considered almost outrageous." Gordon explained that the increase was mainly attributable to the need for additional time to prepare the lighting for filming in color. He added, "Dressing a set was more expensive because you had to be color conscious." Spending that much money came with additional pressures. A letter from one of the top executives at Fox proved gratifying to Gordon and let him know he was doing his job right. The note said that "in *12 O'Clock High* he saw more production money on the screen than any other project he knew about."

One of the biggest expenses, week in and week out, was the cost of hauling cast, crew and equipment out to Chino. Looking for ways to cut costs, the QM team had what must have sounded like a good idea: why not recreate the 918th operations center in a convenient, nearby location? That's exactly what happened. A scaled-down version of the complex was built at Fox Western Studio. Using the same type of facelift that created Archbury Street, the mini-base was created in an open area between administration buildings and soundstages. Plenty of stock footage was available showing various activities at Chino; it would be just a matter of using the Chino footage to establish location, and then cutting to the new base set. Unfortunately, the seams were obvious and the result was disorienting, to say the least.

Production of *12 O'Clock High*'s third season began on 23 May 1966. Fox Western continued to be home base for *12 O'Clock High* and *Daniel Boone*, as well as the freshman ABC series *The Monroes*. The cast remained mostly intact. Barney Phillips was back on board as Doc Kaiser. Andrew Duggan's appearances were sporadic, though, because he was filming the Fox feature *In Like Flint* (1967). In Duggan's absence, Richard Anderson made four guest appearances as temporary wing commander Brig. Gen. Philip Doud.

THE SECOND FRONT

Producer, William D. Gordon…at least that's how the credits read. But an act of subterfuge, was brewing behind the walls of QM Productions. It began innocently enough…

Signing on as associate producer was veteran TV scripter Don Ingalls, who had just done the same job on the cult favorite series *Honey West* (1965–66). Ingalls entered the business on *Have Gun, Will Travel* as a writer and, later, a producer. From there he had a rocky experience with *The Travels of Jamie McPheeters* (1963-64). Citing "creative differences" with the network, Ingalls quit *McPheeters* after only a few months on the job. Upon resigning, Ingalls said, "A network can't dictate artistic policy—not to me."

The job on *12 O'Clock High* seemed like a natural fit for Ingalls, who flew B-17s during the war. "I loved the show because I had a nostalgic feeling for that time," Ingalls said. However, "it was an uncomfortable show to work on."

The reason?

"I was brought on the show to take [Gordon's] job away from him," Ingalls admitted. "But I didn't know that. After I was on a while, Bill didn't produce the show. He wrote. Bill was a compulsive re-writer. He was in his office till 10:00 every night re-writing, re-writing, re-writing. We could never get anything out of his office, couldn't get the story out of the typewriter. In TV the name of the game is getting it out. He insisted on re-writing everything. He was never satisfied with the end product."

Because Gordon spent so much time rewriting, "the show was really not being produced," Ingalls said. "The show sort of ran by itself."

Executive producer Quinn Martin frequently summoned Ingalls to lunch meetings at the legendary Hollywood eatery Musso & Frank's. There, at Martin's table—first one on the left through the door—Martin would complain about his issues with Gordon. Recalled Ingalls, "I'd say, 'Jesus Christ, I'm not the producer.' And he'd say 'Take the damn job away from him.' That sort of highlighted my relationship with Quinn Martin." Ingalls hung on as long as he could, but was never able to push out his friend Bill Gordon. However, before the season ended, Ingalls quit "because it wasn't my kind of a job."

For Ingalls, the high point of his stint on the series was a joke that back-fired miserably. ABC would, on a regular basis, send around a program practices liaison to monitor potentially objectionable content—in other words, a censor.

"The program practices person was sort of a spinster-looking lady of about 50 who used to come in and sit for dailies," Ingalls said. "We always knew when she was coming because the network would send us something. This one afternoon, and I don't know the bastards that did this, but some guy in editing put in about 30 seconds of a porno show right in the middle of one of our airplane scenes. That blew the hell out of everything. Both editors were fired and the rest of us did a lot of explaining."

After *12 O'Clock High*, Don Ingalls went on to write and produce TV series such as *Star Trek, Marcus Welby, M.D., The Name of the Game, The Sixth Sense, Night Gallery, The Bold Ones, Serpico, Police Story* and *T. J. Hooker.* By Ingalls' own reckoning, he wrote some 400 hours of network programming.

To pick up the slack left by Ingalls' departure, Bill Gordon brought in writer Jack Hawn. Hawn had been a sportswriter, specializing in boxing, for the *Hollywood Citizen-News.* He decided to try writing a script on spec for QM's *The Fugitive* and mentioned it to his friend George Latka, a boxing referee. Latka's old college buddy was none other than Bill Gordon, who at the time was associate producer on *The Fugitive* and a huge boxing fan. The script didn't sell but Gordon liked Hawn's writing style and kept him in mind. A year later, Hawn sold a script to Gordon which became *12 O'Clock High* episode #68 "The All American."

"I was paid $3,500 for the script," Hawn recalled. "I took my wife to Europe, and when we returned, Bill offered me the job as story consultant. I didn't hesitate. I resigned from the *Citizen* and took the job." Hawn soon discovered that Gordon had rewritten his script from cover to cover, but still gave him full credit. "In fact, that's what he did for most of the writers," Hawn said.

Hawn explained his job responsibilities this way: "As story consultant, I attended dailies, interviewed a few writers and passed along suggestions to Bill, which, I'm sure, he pretty much ignored. I was being paid for sitting in the office and reading scripts mainly. I sold another script to *12 O'Clock High,* but it wasn't produced."

CASUALTY OF THE RATINGS WAR

In August 1966, ABC announced that *12 O'Clock High* would be "one of 12 advance premiere shows in ABC-TV's complete color schedule, beginning its new run on an evening that also includes the debut appearances of *The Green Hornet, Time Tunnel* and *The Milton Berle Show.*" So ABC staged a sneak attack in the ratings war and premiered their chosen few one week ahead of CBS and NBC. With its "advance premiere" concept, ABC "had the field virtually to itself for a single week." As part of that assault, *12 O'Clock High* flew into its third season on Friday, 9 September 1966 at 10:00 p.m. ET.

Major sponsors for year three included Armour and Co.; Miles Laboratories, Inc.; and R.J. Reynolds Tobacco Co. through Grey Advertising, Inc. In a promotional move, Paul Burke became a pitchman for Kentucky Tavern Bourbon. Burke, looking debonair in newspaper and magazine ads, was touted as the star of *12 O'Clock High*.

Variety seemed unaware of any problems in its review of the third season opener, #62 "Gauntlet of Fire": "*High* is of the gritty and no-nonsense school of war drama, and is consistent and believable. Men die and leaders are not always right. The acting all down the line is firstrate, and the scripting is engrossing."

Despite the praise, *12 O'Clock High* fared poorly in its return to Friday night. *Variety* reported that the premiere color episode brought a disappointing Arbitron overnight rating of 12.0 and a 27.0 share for the first half hour followed by a 13.7 rating and 31 share for the second half. Things only got worse. The Nielsens for the two-week period ending 9 October found *12 O'Clock High* placing 91st out of 92 shows. The only series that finished lower—Fox's *Tammy Grimes Show*—had already been cancelled. A week later, *12 O'Clock High* was officially on ABC's critical list.

An unfavorable time slot was only part of the problem. "Defections" by local affiliates were another matter. All three networks clearly preferred their affiliates to carry the network's programs when they were broadcast. That way, network programming would be able to earn more accurate ratings. Networks preferred having 90 percent of their affiliates airing a show. However, local affiliates sometimes found it more profitable to run their own programming and sell commercial time to local sponsors than it was to carry network programming. The network would then provide local stations with a 16mm film print of the show to run on a delayed basis to fit its own program schedule. And the local affiliate came out ahead because it also received compensation from the network.

12 O'Clock High's Friday night slot was the perfect opportunity for local stations to pre-empt the ABC lineup and run a movie instead. For example, in the Greater Cleveland, Ohio, market, of the five ABC affiliates listed by *TV Guide* only three carried *12 O'Clock High* on Fridays at 10:00 p.m. Only one of the two defectors ran the show on a delayed basis, Saturday at 10:00 p.m., and that broadcast was in black-and-white. Despite all the hand-wringing and hard work to produce *12 O'Clock High* in color, not all ABC affiliates were equipped to transmit in color. As a result, in some smaller markets the signal still reached viewers in black-and-white.

More potent than the effect Nielsen ratings had on *12 O'Clock High* was a burgeoning sociopolitical factor: the Vietnam War. As the number of "advisors" and US troops in Southeast Asia increased, protests against the war intensified. The anti-war sentiment brought with it not only apathy toward depictions of war in the media but also a rejection of them.

"There was no question about it," said Bill Gordon. "The anti-Vietnam protests and the general anti-war sentiment worked against *12 O'Clock* rating-wise, and perhaps the cliché of World War II." Erik Barnouw, in his literate and insightful book *Tube of Plenty*, noted that the memory of the Second World War was fading. According to Barnouw, a network executive wondered if younger baby boomers even knew who de Gaulle and Hitler were. Moreover, confusion allegedly resulted because the former Axis powers, Germany and Italy, had become members of NATO.

Finally, on 2 November 1966, ABC made the dreaded announcement: as of January, the network would drop *12 O'Clock High* from its schedule. Ironically, it was cancelled on the same day as Robert Lansing's latest series, *The Man Who Never Was*, which had just premiered that fall. Summing up *12 O'Clock High's* stint on ABC, *Variety* said: "Quinn Martin's production auspices were, typically, first-class, but trite characterization and plots kept this plane jockey meller at low-level flight from the very start. In three years, ABC tried a number of time periods for this one, so Martin must have been doing something wrong. Looks like a good bet, however, for [Fox] in the rerun market."

Without missing a beat, ABC announced the next day that *12 O'Clock High's* vacant time slot would be filled with the return of *The Avengers*, the cult British import that proved to be a surprise mid-season hit just a year earlier.

Twentieth Century-Fox TV clearly saw the potential in syndication and pounced on the opportunity. No sooner had the cancellation been announced, than Fox sold *12 O'Clock High* to local stations in key markets including WPIX in New York, KCOP Los Angeles, WTCN Minneapolis and KPTV Portland.

Ending on a bright note, *12 O'Clock High* was honored by the American Cinema Editors with its annual Eddie award. The recipient was Jodie Copelan for her work on episode #68 "The All-American."

AFTERLIFE

Throughout Quinn Martin's career as a packager of drama for television, the premises of his work centered on variations of cops and robbers. *12 O'Clock High* carried through on that essential theme of good guys versus bad guys but set it against a global backdrop.

As part of ABC's Second Season housekeeping drive, which sent *12 O'Clock High* packing, QM Productions' *The Invaders* was tapped to join the network's lineup in January 1967. Like *12 O'Clock High*, *The Invaders* was an anomaly in QM's oeuvre. It was science fiction, but still told the story of a "good guy" (a human Paul Revere-type) versus "bad guys" (aggressors from outer space). After *The Invaders* shut down in 1968, Quinn Martin applied solid ratings appeal plus advertising backing from Ford to keep his *The FBI* healthy for years to come. Martin used *The FBI* as a foundation to subsequently sell *Dan August* (1970–71), *Cannon* (1971–76), *Banyon* (1972–73), *The Streets of San Francisco* (1972–77),

Barnaby Jones (1973–80), *The Manhunter* (1974–75), *Caribe* (1975), *Bert D'Angelo, Superstar* (1976), *Most Wanted* (1976–77), *Tales of the Unexpected* (1977), *The Runaways* (1978–79) and *A Man Called Sloane* (1979–80).

"Quinn deserved his success," said Alan Armer. "He was an extremely bright guy. Before he started producing, Quinn had done some writing so he was comfortable with scripts. He always went for incredible production values. Quinn wasn't afraid to spend money, so his shows had the classiest look in town. And he was proud of the way his shows looked. Quinn didn't do shows that were artsy craftsy; he did shows that were meat and potatoes. But, he knew how to do that kind of show and he did them beautifully."

Following the sale of QM Productions, Martin pursued a number of projects in drama and education. At the time of his death on 5 September 1987, it was estimated that QM Productions had created more than 2,000 hours of television programs.

After completing *12 O'Clock High*, Paul Burke's subsequent movie roles included *Valley of the Dolls* (1967) and *The Thomas Crown Affair* (1968). He continued to guest-star on television series such as *Police Story, Magnum, PI* and *Medical Center*, and was a regular on *Dynasty* (1982–84, 1986–87), the daytime soap *Santa Barbara* (1984) and a Canadian-produced series, *Hot Shots* (1986–87). After retiring from acting, Burke became involved in community affairs. He also joined the Commemorative Air Force, an organization dedicated to preserving warplanes of the past. Burke donated the cigarette lighter he used during the series to the 918th Bomb Group Living Memorial. The lighter is engraved with the name Col Joe Gallagher, 918th Bomb Group and the Eighth Air Force logo.

Chris Robinson moved back to his home state. "I wanted to bring my kids up in a smog-free environment, and I loved Florida and the tropic winds," said Robinson. He continued to act on television, guest starring on *Hogan's Heroes, The Man from U.N.C.L.E.* and *Voyage to the Bottom of the Sea*. Robinson also made the rounds of QM shows, including *The Invaders, Cannon* and *The Streets of San Francisco*. Still interested in filmmaking, Robinson assembled a feature film project and showed it to Quinn Martin. Martin then hired him to direct episodes of *Cannon* and *Barnaby Jones*. Meanwhile, his acting career took him to daytime television. He appeared on *General Hospital* from 1978 to 1986. After a brief stint on *Another World*, Robinson was cast in *The Bold and the Beautiful*, in which he appeared until 2002. One of his three sons, Taylor, also acted in the series. Robinson returned to *General Hospital* for a brief time in 2002. In 1982, Robinson opened an Indian trading post, cultural museum and cultural center in Page, Arizona, which he operated with Native Americans for eight years. Robinson returned to California in 1990 to open Robinson Galleries, an art gallery and fine art publishing house.

Frank Overton appeared in *The Invaders* #5 "Genesis." His final television appearance was as Elias Sandoval in *Star Trek* #25 "This Side of Paradise." The episode co-starred Jill Ireland, who had been in *12 O'Clock High* #38 "The Hotshot" and #55 "The Survivor." Overton succumbed to a heart attack in Pacific Palisades, California, on 24 April 1967.

Over the years, Barney Phillips displayed a gift for both drama and comedy through continuing roles on shows as diverse as *The Felony Squad* (1967–68) and *The Betty White Show* (1977–78). Drawing on his deep experience in radio, Phillips provided the voice of genie Shazzam in the 1967–68 animated series of the same name. A year later, he voiced the legendary Porthos in "The Three Musketeers" segment of *The Banana Splits Adventure Hour* (1968–70). He subsequently did voices for other cartoons such as *Devlin* and *Jabberjaw*. Phillips continued performing until his death on 17 August 1982.

Andrew Duggan appeared in movies like Fox's *In Like Flint* (1967) but did most of his work for the small screen. He co-starred in the Fox western *Lancer* (1968–70) and starred as the family patriarch in *The Homecoming: A Christmas Story* (1971), the pilot for the long-running series *The Waltons*. After portraying Dwight D. Eisenhower in three separate made-for-TV movies, Duggan switched parties and played Lyndon B. Johnson in *The Private Files of J. Edgar Hoover* (1977). Duggan died of throat cancer on 15 May 1988 in Westwood, California.

Even before Bob Dornan joined the cast of *12 O'Clock High*, he was deeply involved in social and political concerns. Demonstrating his commitment to human and civil rights, Dornan marched with the Rev. Martin Luther King and registered voters in the south. He also flew 12 food-relief flights into Biafra in 1969. For hosting and producing his own public affairs TV programs from 1965 to 1976, Dornan was presented with two Emmy Awards. Dornan originated the POW/MIA bracelet worn by more than 13 million Americans during the Vietnam War. Staunchly conservative Dornan served in Congress from 1977 to 1983 and again from 1985 through 1997. While serving on committees and subcommittees relating to national security, Dornan championed such defense programs as the B-1 Lancer, which earned him the nickname "B-1 Bob."

Some time after *12 O'Clock High* was dropped, Bill Gordon received a call from Quinn Martin. Martin had been watching the show in reruns and said, "We made some damn good pictures, didn't we?" Gordon continued to write, direct and act in a variety of television shows. While penning scripts for Universal's TV factory, Gordon hooked up with his old *12 O'Clock High* compatriot Jim Doherty. Doherty had retired from the military and turned to writing and producing shows such as *Dragnet* and *Adam-12,* both done at Universal. The two friends became a writing team and turned out multiple scripts for Universal's long-running *Ironside* (1967–75). Next, the duo spent a season as script consultants and writers for Paramount's *Barbary Coast* (1975–76) series, which was created and produced by Bill's old friend Doug Heyes. Then they settled in for a five-year run as story editors and, later, producers on MGM's police drama *CHiPs*. The two remained close friends until Doherty's death on 27 September 1985. Gordon retired after *CHiPs* and wrote two novels about the Civil War. He died in Thousand Oaks, California, on 12 August 1991.

Dominic Frontiere pumped out a bundle of theme songs for mid-sixties TV series such as *That Girl, The Flying Nun, The Rat Patrol, Iron Horse* and QM's *The Invaders*. He graduated to the big screen and had a huge commercial hit with the theme from Clint Eastwood's *Hang 'Em High* (1968). During the 1970s, Frontiere orchestrated album cuts for pop artists such as Chicago and Dan Fogelberg. In 1980, his work on *The Stunt Man* won a Golden Globe for Best Original Score. A decade later he was nominated for a second Golden Globe for Best Original Song, "The Color of the Night," from the 1994 movie *Color of Night*.

Following his stint on *12 O'Clock High*, director of photography Bob Moreno continued to work in TV and motion pictures. His credits included *Lassie, The FBI, Police Woman, Murder, She Wrote, Hotel* and several cruises on *The Love Boat*.

12 O'Clock High launched a 15-year relationship between art director George Chan and QM Productions. He also worked on *The Fugitive, The Invaders, Dan August, Cannon, Barnaby Jones, Caribe* and *The Streets of San Francisco*. Chan reunited with many QM alumni on the filmed-in-Boston *Spenser: For Hire* (1985–88).

Story consultant Jack Hawn was paid regularly for another six months after *12 O'Clock High* shut down production. He sold half a dozen scripts to other series including *Adam-12*, which was produced by fellow *12 O'Clock High* alum Jim Doherty. In 1968, Hawn resumed his career as a print journalist and retired from *The Los Angeles Times* in 1991 after 21 years in sports and entertainment. As of 2004, he was still actively writing for his local weekly newspaper.

Fox Western Avenue studios were leveled and replaced with a retail shopping plaza that buzzes with activity. To the east, Chino Airport still looks very much the same as it did when trucks and buses hauled actors and movie-making equipment out there four decades ago. The identifiable line of eucalyptus trees that bordered the airfield was removed years ago because, ironically, they were a hazard to air traffic. The building that served as the 918th's operations center is now the Chino Airport Lounge. A photo of how it looked back in the

1960s hangs on the wall opposite the bar. Across from the lounge, the briefing shack, officers club and other components of the 918th HQ area are long gone, now just an open field.

B-17G serial number 44-83684, which gave life to the *Piccadilly Lily,* later appeared in *The Thousand Plane Raid* (1969). Using his political strength, Bob Dornan helped Planes of Fame obtain formal title to it from the Air Force. The plane has not flown since 1975 but today bears nose art identifying it as *Piccadilly Lily II* and remains a star attraction of the Planes of Fame collection at Chino Airport. Plans are to restore 44-83684 to airworthy condition. The restoration process is estimated to cost $1 million.

The Television Series
Episode Guide

12 O'Clock High (1964–67)

KEY TO LISTINGS

CHRONOLOGICAL NUMBER OF THE EPISODE IS FOLLOWED BY ITS TITLE AND PRODUCTION NUMBER.

OAD	Original air date; when the episode was first broadcast.
RERUN	The date on which ABC repeated that episode. N/R indicates that the episode was not rerun by the network.
W	Writer of the episode.
TP	Author of the teleplay for that episode; indicates the script was based on another source.
STORY	Author of the source material for the teleplay of that episode.
D	Director of the episode.
TDY	Term for US military Temporary Duty or, in this case, the guest stars and above-the-line talent for a particular episode.
PERSONNEL FILE	Insights into the characters' backgrounds and personal lives.
DEBRIEFING	Details of the mission.

INTELLIGENCE REPORT Insight on the production process.

FLIGHT LINE Notes of significant dates that track the timeline of World War II.

TOBY SIGHTING Whether or not an episode features the Toby mug.

FIRST SEASON

BROADCAST SCHEDULE
Friday 9:30 pm EST, 18 September 1964 – 18 December 1964
Friday 10:00 pm EST, 25 December 1964 – 10 September 1965

Production run: 32 60-minute episodes filmed in black-and-white

CONTINUING CAST

Brig. Gen. Frank Savage	Robert Lansing
Maj. Harvey B. Stovall	Frank Overton
Maj. Gen. Wiley Crowe	John Larkin
Maj. Joseph "Joe" Cobb	Lew Gallo
Maj. Donald "Doc" Kaiser	Barney Phillips
Lt. Gen. Pritchard	Paul Newlan
Sgt. Nero	Bert Remsen
Liz Woodruff	Hazel Court
Maj. Harry Rosen	Jason Wingreen
Gen. Homer Stoneman	John Zaremba

KEY PRODUCTION CREDITS

EXECUTIVE PRODUCER	Quinn Martin
PRODUCER	Frank Glicksman
ASSISTANT TO THE EXECUTIVE PRODUCER	Arthur Fellows
ASSOCIATE PRODUCERS	Charles Larson
	Al C. Ward
DIRECTORS OF PHOTOGRAPHY	Meredith Nicholson
	Eugene Polito, ASC
	William W. Spencer, ASC
	Paul Vogel, ASC
MUSIC COMPOSED AND CONDUCTED BY	Dominic Frontiere
	Fred Steiner
MUSIC SUPERVISOR	Lionel Newman
PRODUCTION MANAGER	Gaston Glass
UNIT PRODUCTION MANAGER	Howard Alston
ART DIRECTORS	Jack Martin Smith

ART DIRECTORS	Hillyard Brown
	Gordon Gurnee
	Richard Y. Haman
SET DECORATORS	Walter M. Scott
	Glen Daniels
	Stuart Reiss
FILM EDITORS	Marston Fay
	Walter Hannemann, ACE
	Anthony Wollner, ACE
	Jerry Young
POST-PRODUCTION SUPERVISOR	John Elizalde
POST-PRODUCTION COORDINATOR	Robert Mintz
SUPERVISING SOUND EFFECTS EDITOR	Ralph Hickey
SOUND EFFECTS EDITORS	Jack Jackson
	Bates Mason
SUPERVISING MUSIC EDITOR	Leonard A. Engel
MUSIC EDITOR	Kenneth Runyon
ASSISTANT DIRECTORS	Jack Aldworth
	Fred Simpson
	Victor Vallejo
	Paul Wurtzel
ASSISTANT TO THE PRODUCER	John Conwell
CHIEF ELECTRICIAN	Camden Rogers
	Harry Sunby
PRODUCTION MIXERS	Jack Lilly
	Karl Zint
IN CHARGE OF PRODUCTION	Quinn Martin for
	QM Productions
IN ASSOCIATION WITH	William Self for Twentieth
	Century-Fox Television, Inc.

THE FIRST SEASON (OVERVIEW)

#1	18 September 1964	"Golden Boy Had Nine Black Sheep"
#2	25 September 1964	"Follow the Leader"
#3	2 October 1964	"The Men and the Boys"
#4	16 October 1964	"The Sound of Distant Thunder"
#5	23 October 1964	"The Climate of Doubt"
#6	30 October 1964	"Pressure Point"
#7	6 November 1964	"Decision"
#8	13 November 1964	"The Hours Before Dawn"
#9	20 November 1964	"Appointment at Liege"
#10	27 November 1964	"Interlude"

#11	4 December 1964	"Here's to Courageous Cowards"
#12	11 December 1964	"Soldiers Sometimes Kill"
#13	18 December 1964	"The Suspected"
#14	25 December 1964	"An Act of War"
#15	1 January 1965	"Those Who Are About to Die"
#16	8 January 1965	"In Search of My Enemy"
#17	15 January 1965	"The Albatross"
#18	22 January 1965	"The Lorelei"
#19	29 January 1965	"Faith, Hope and Sgt. Aronson"
#20	5 February 1965	"To Heinie, With Love"
#21	12 February 1965	"The Clash"
#22	26 February 1965	"The Ticket"
#23	5 March 1965	"The Trap"
#24	12 March 1965	"End of the Line"
#25	19 March 1965	"The Threat"
#26	26 March 1965	"Mutiny at 10,000 Feet"
#27	2 April 1965	"The Mission"
#28	9 April 1965	"The Cry of Fallen Birds"
#29	16 April 1965	"V for Vendetta"
#30	23 April 1965	"POW," Part One
#31	30 April 1965	"POW," Part Two
#32	7 May 1965	"The Hero"

14 May 1965	RERUN – #4	"The Sound of Distant Thunder"
21 May 1965	RERUN – #6	"Pressure Point"
28 May 1965	RERUN – #10	"Interlude"
4 June 1965	RERUN – #7	"Decision"
11 June 1965	RERUN – #12	"Soldiers Sometimes Kill"
18 June 1965	RERUN – #13	"The Suspected"
25 June 1965	RERUN – #20	"To Heinie, With Love"
2 July 1965	RERUN – #21	"The Clash"
9 July 1965	RERUN – #18	"The Lorelei"
16 July 1965	RERUN – #22	"The Ticket"
23 July 1965	RERUN – #23	"The Trap"
30 July 1965	RERUN – #27	"The Mission"
13 August 1965	RERUN – #16	"In Search of My Enemy"
20 August 1965	RERUN – #30	"POW," Part One
27 August 1965	RERUN – #31	"POW," Part Two
3 September 1965	RERUN – #25	"The Threat"
10 September 1965	RERUN – #3	"The Men and the Boys"

#1 "GOLDEN BOY HAD NINE BLACK SHEEP" (7303)

OAD: 18 September 1964
RERUN: N/R
W: Al C. Ward
D: Don Medford

Gen. Savage orders Capt. Joe Gallagher into his office and demands to know why Gallagher aborted a mission—again. Without a satisfactory answer, Savage dismisses the captain. Outside the operations building, Gallagher runs into Gen. Crowe, an old friend of the family. Gallagher tries to tell Crowe about his displeasure with Savage. In Savage's office, Crowe informs the General that the 918th is on for a very special mission—two bombers with top crews to be ready at a moment's notice to bomb the harbor at Bordeaux. That said, Crowe asks Savage why he refused to sign papers promoting Gallagher to major, a potential career faux pas considering Gallagher is a West Pointer and his father is a two-star general at the Pentagon. Savage counters by saying that he will promote Gallagher when the captain deserves it. The next day, the 918th goes up but Wing sends out a recall—which Savage apparently chooses to ignore. Gallagher, however, is watching his gauges and with two engines running hot, chooses to break formation and abort. Back on the ground, an enraged Savage storms into Gallagher's quarters and gives the captain the dressing down of a lifetime. Savage vows to assign Gallagher every incompetent in the outfit and gives him two weeks to mold a crack combat unit flying in a plane to be named the *Leper Colony*. Gallagher begins the arduous challenge of shaping up his special charges, but meanwhile, Crowe says he'll give Savage a break and give Gallagher a desk job at Wing. Savage contends that Gallagher and the others are good soldiers who just need discipline. Through the grapevine, Gallagher hears of the job on Crowe's staff and tells Savage he wants it. Savage reluctantly agrees but tells the captain that he and his crew are on combat status and will fly the next day's mission. Gallagher, determined to get home safely, drives his crew to do their best, mission after mission. Savage even commends Gallagher for the job he's done—then tells the captain that his transfer has come through. Savage is disappointed when Gallagher says he still wants the new assignment. The general is even more disillusioned when Gallagher says he wants the two-plane mission so he can have a meritorious record when he leaves the 918th. The mission goes on as planned and hits the target. But when FWs attack, their gunfire rips through the *Leper Colony*, badly wounding both Gallagher and his co-pilot. Despite the pain and loss of blood, Gallagher brings the plane over the channel and back to base. That's the kind of maturity Savage was looking for all along, and he rewards Gallagher by finally promoting him to major—which qualifies him to command a squadron and not a desk.

Gen. Savage, Gen. Crowe, Maj. Stovall, Maj. Cobb
Capt. Joe Gallagher ⸱⸱⸱⸱⸱⸱⸱⸱⸱⸱⸱⸱⸱⸱⸱⸱⸱⸱⸱⸱ Paul Burke
Lt. Blake ⸱⸱⸱⸱⸱⸱⸱⸱⸱⸱⸱⸱⸱⸱⸱⸱⸱⸱⸱⸱⸱⸱⸱⸱⸱⸱⸱⸱⸱⸱⸱⸱⸱⸱ Joby Baker
Lt. Michaels ⸱⸱⸱⸱⸱⸱⸱⸱⸱⸱⸱⸱⸱⸱⸱⸱⸱⸱⸱⸱⸱⸱⸱⸱⸱⸱⸱⸱ Bruce Dern
Lt. Kelly ⸱⸱⸱⸱⸱⸱⸱⸱⸱⸱⸱⸱⸱⸱⸱⸱⸱⸱⸱⸱⸱⸱⸱⸱⸱⸱⸱⸱⸱⸱⸱⸱⸱ Paul Comi
Lt. Crandall ⸱⸱⸱⸱⸱⸱⸱⸱⸱⸱⸱⸱⸱⸱⸱⸱⸱⸱⸱⸱⸱⸱⸱⸱⸱⸱⸱⸱⸱ Burt Douglas

TDY

- Bruce Dern (born 4 June 1936 in Winnetka, Illinois) trained at The Actor's Studio in 1959, then jumped into work on episodic television. Early guest appearances on *Naked City, Sea Hunt* and *Thriller* led to his only regular series work on *Stoney Burke* (1962-63). Turning his talents to the big screen, Dern worked in numerous westerns and biker movies. He gained a hefty dose of notoriety for shooting and killing John Wayne's character in *The Cowboys* (1972). Dern appeared in the cult sci-fi classic *Silent Running* (1972). His work in *Coming Home* (1978) earned Dern an Oscar nomination. He was married to actress Diane Ladd and is the father of actress Laura Dern, who received her own Oscar nomination in 1992. Dern appeared in three additional episodes of *12 O'Clock High*.

- The son of motion picture engineer/inventor Pierino Comi, Paul Comi (born 1932) made his unbilled film debut in *The Young Lions* (1958). He became a solid supporting player in movies and on dozens of TV series including *Star Trek, The Twilight Zone* and *The Wild, Wild West*. Comi had continuing roles on *Two Faces West* (1960–61) and *Ripcord* (1961–62) and the soap opera *Capital* (1985). This was Comi's first of four appearances on *12 O'Clock High*.

- Joby Baker (born 26 March 1934 in Montreal) made his first movie, *Target Zero* (1955), while he was in the Army. After discharge, he did comedy routines, appeared in three *Gidget* movies and the Disney films *Bullwhip Griffin* (1967) and *Blackbeard's Ghost* (1968). On TV he guest starred on *Combat!, Ben Casey* and *The Dick Van Dyke Show*. He co-starred in the sitcoms *Good Morning World* (1967–68) and *The Six O'Clock Follies* (1980).

Personnel File

- Crowe says to Savage, "Nobody ever has a meeting with you. It always has to be a collision."
- Savage's A-2 jacket has a cigarette pouch on its left sleeve.
- Gallagher says that he "lost two brothers before this war gets warm yet, and it taught me to know what it's like to be the last, shining hope in a military family." The implication is that all his brothers are dead, yet we meet Preston Gallagher in season two.

- Savage reiterates that Gallagher is a West Point graduate with three years' active service, and that he is the son of Maj. Gen. Max Gallagher.

DEBRIEFING
- Oxygen masks and flight helmets are used.
- Gallagher's first plane is *Could Bees.*
- On the first mission, Savage's call sign is Red Fox Charlie One; for the special mission, he's Able Leader.
- Savage says the attacking fighters are Fw 190s.

INTELLIGENCE REPORT
- The script describes Joe Gallagher as a "blond man in his twenties." That's quite a difference from the dark-haired, thirtysomething Paul Burke.

TOBY SIGHTING
- Toby mug is on the mantle of the Officers' Club.

#2 "FOLLOW THE LEADER" (6011)

OAD:	25 September 1964
RERUN:	N/R
W:	Beirne Lay, Jr.
D:	William A. Graham

On a mission, the *Piccadilly Lily* is ripped by gunfire from an Fw 190, killing Gen. Savage's navigator, whose best friend was bombardier Lt. Robert Mellon. Gen. Crowe is not happy with Savage's progress on establishing the effectiveness of precision daylight bombing. But Savage has an idea: Instead of the bombardier on each plane dropping his bombs at will, Savage wants to coordinate the group's efforts on the timing and accuracy of the lead bombardier. The general's choice: his man, Lt. Mellon. With Crowe's reluctant approval, Savage explains his plan to Mellon. Inflamed eardrums prevent Savage from leading the first mission with Mellon as lead bombardier. Maj. Cobb flies in his place. First reports are not good. It seems that Mellon dropped early and destroyed an area with a Dutch school at ground zero. Under pressure from high command and the Dutch embassy, Crowe demands an explanation from Cobb and Mellon. Without a satisfactory rationale, Crowe orders the experiment terminated. But Savage demands another chance to prove that the technique will work and Crowe caves in to his old friend. When Mellon meets his girlfriend Jill at The Star and Bottle, another airman mocks him for his tragic error. The guilt begins to get the best of Mellon. He's not even consoled by Savage's report that mechanical failure caused the bombs to drop early. The General empathizes with Mellon's concerns over bombing children; he sends boys out to die every day. Despite Mellon's protest, Savage orders the lieutenant to fly the next day's mission. Over the target area, FWs attack the group and drill the *Piccadilly Lily's* nose, wounding Mellon just before he makes the drop. Summoning all his remaining strength, Lt. Mellon crawls to the bombsight, lines up the target and drops the bomb load. In the base hospital ward, Savage tells the bedridden Lt. Mellon that the strike was a success. Mellon asks the general why he picked him for the lead bombardier assignment. Savage replies that he knew he could rely on Mellon to do the job. The lieutenant thanks Savage for making him go through the trial. Then Savage says they should both thank Gen. Crowe for his confidence.

Gen. Savage, Maj. Stovall, Gen. Crowe, Maj. Cobb, Doc Kaiser,
Sgt. Nero, Gen. Pritchard
Lt. Robert Mellon ·························· Andrew Prine
Lt. Bishop ······························· Paul Carr
Lt. Zimmerman ······················ Jud Taylor
Jill ·· Judy Carne
Capt. Gately ····················· Dan Barton

TDY
- Andrew Prine (born 14 February 1936 in Jennings, Florida) went from The Actor's Studio to become one of the busiest young leading men of the 1960s and '70s. Prine was a regular in *The Wide Country* (1962–63), *The Road West* (1966–67) and *W.E.B.* (1978). He also appeared in the cult sci-fi epic *V* (1983) and its sequel, *V: The Final Battle* (1984). Prine later appeared in #45 "The Jones Boys."

- Paul Carr (born in 1934 in New Orleans) has done it all—westerns, war, sci-fi, crime—and done it believably. Carr had recurring roles in *Days of Our Lives* (1965–66), *General Hospital* (1969), *The Doctors* (1976–77), *Buck Rogers in the 25th Century* (1981) and *Generations* (1989–91). He subsequently made two unrelated appearances in #33 "The Loneliest Place in the World" and #58 "The Hollow Man."

- Bert Remsen (1925–1999) made the first of three appearances as Sgt. Nero. Remsen built a sizeable resume as an actor until he broke his back in an on-set accident. After he recovered, Remsen stayed in the industry as a casting director. He resumed acting and became a regular on *Gibbsville* (1976), *It's a Living* (1980–81) and *Dallas* (1987–88).

- Judy Carne (born 27 April 1939 in England) made an indelible impression on American society as the "sock-it-to-me" girl on *Rowan and Martin's Laugh-In* (1968–70). Carne was also a regular in the sitcoms *Fair Exchange* (1962–63), *The Baileys of Balboa* (1964–65) and *Love on a Rooftop* (1966–67).

During the 1970s, her personal life fell apart, capped by a car wreck that resulted in a broken neck. She appeared in two unrelated roles in #35 "Then Came the Mighty Hunter" and #48 "Falling Star."

PERSONNEL FILE

- We get a hint that Savage and Crowe's relationship has some history, because Savage reminds Crowe that the latter once risked an entire crew on him. Fifteen years earlier, a plane Savage was flying stalled, killing the rest of the crew. An inquiry never resolved the matter, but fortunately Crowe persuaded Savage to fly again.
- Savage and Stovall stand on the tower waiting for the group to return. The general becomes nostalgic and tells Stovall how, when he was a boy, mail planes used to fly over the farm and he used to wave at them. All he wanted to do was fly. Savage (to Stovall): "Never got around to a lot of other things: marriage, kids. Just quick landings and takeoffs. I suppose I've missed out on something." Stovall: "Yes sir. I think you have."
- Savage's A-2 jacket has the AAF patch on the left shoulder, but no cigarette pouch.
- Stovall admits that although he is the only grandfather in the group, he wishes he was young enough to fly.
- Stovall wears wire-rim glasses; subsequently, he wears heavy, black plastic frames.

DEBRIEFING

- On Savage's second mission, his crew reports a Junkers ready to pounce, then Focke-Wulfs.
- Savage flies the *Piccadilly Lily*. Its nose art on the port side has the image of Lily left of the name "Piccadilly Lily." Later in the series, Lily is to the right.
- The flight deck is very different than in subsequent episodes. Savage is filmed from both port and starboard sides, which was not done later.
- Oxygen masks and flight helmets are used.
- On both missions in this episode, Savage uses the call sign Yellow Jacket.

INTELLIGENCE REPORT

- The published script for this episode is credited to Paul Monash and Beirne Lay, Jr.
- This episode is the only time the full-size B-17 does not have a ball turret.
- As the *Piccadilly Lily* taxis back from a mission, it circles around a P-38. There is at least one promotional photo of Lansing standing at the wing of the Lightning.
- The Star and Bottle exterior is actually the Old Writers' Building at Fox Hills studio.
- Savage's office has a layout similar to what was used in the balance of the

episodes, but its construction and details are very different.

- The briefing and interrogation hut looks like the inside of an airplane hangar; it's huge. And there must be 200 extras inside during Act I.
- When the group is back at base, Savage uses his "taxi hail" whistle to get Doc Kaiser's immediate attention for his wounded crew. Lansing perfected the whistle by hailing cabs while working as a doorman in New York City before breaking into show biz.

Sally Kellerman and Robert Lansing

#3 "The Men and the Boys" (7304)

OAD:	2 October 1964
Rerun:	10 September 1965
W:	Harold Jack Bloom
D:	William A. Graham

Capt. Wade Ritchie defies Savage's orders and breaks formation to provide cover for the crew that bails out of his best friend Lt. Tom Lockridge's badly damaged B-17. Ritchie's waist gunner Jonesy is shot up by an attacking fighter and, back at the base, he must be taken out of the plane on a stretcher. Lockridge's crew is still unaccounted for. Once they are on the ground, Savage wants an explanation for Ritchie's actions and—without a satisfactory answer— launches court-martial proceedings against the captain for disobeying a direct order in the face of the enemy. To everyone's relief, especially nurse Libby MacAndrews, Lockridge and the other survivors of his crew return to base. But Lockridge is outraged at the news that Ritchie is being court-martialed after saving their lives. Behind Lockridge's back, Lt. MacAndrews confronts Savage about the situation and tries to give the general a richer understanding of the friendship between Ritchie and Lockridge. Savage learns how unpopular his decision makes him when the group's morale plummets, ultimately failing on its missions. Morale doesn't look to get any better when Ritchie's trial finds him guilty. But after Jones dies on the operating table, Lockridge sees that Savage has been right all along: by going after Lockridge and his crew, Ritchie put his own crew in danger, as well as the lives of the other men in the formation. Crowe wants a maximum effort to complement an RAF strike on an oil storage depot 12 miles south of Rennes. That means every plane and every pilot available is to go up. Much to Crowe's surprise, Savage assigns Ritchie as his co-pilot. After a successful bomb run, Savage's plane is hit, crippling one engine and knocking out the general. The shoe is on the other foot as the rest of the group contemplates heading for home and leaving Ritchie, now flying Savage's plane. Lockridge tells the rest of the group to stay with the general's plane. Savage comes to long enough to order the group back home but directs Ritchie to fly at treetop level to prevent fighters from striking underneath. The maneuver works and they are assured of getting home when a flight of P-47s meets them. Back at the base, Savage is taken off the *Piccadilly Lily* on a stretcher but stops to tell Crowe that Lockridge has what it takes not only to be a top pilot but someday a group commander.

Gen. Savage, Maj. Stovall, Gen. Crowe
Lt. Tom Lockridge ························· Glenn Corbett
Capt. Wade Ritchie ······················ Lou Antonio
Lt. Libby MacAndrews ··············· Sally Kellerman
Liz Woodruff ································ Hazel Court
Jonesy ·· Alan Reed, Jr.
Pete ·· James Noah
Mike ··· James Secrest
Prosecuting Attorney ················ Lyle Sudrow
Defense Attorney ······················· Lew Brown

TDY

• Glenn Corbett (1930–1993) was an affable leading man who broke into movies in the late 1950s. That led to a starring role in *It's a Man's World* (1962–63). Corbett replaced George Maharis for the final year of *Route 66* (1963–64). He also had continuing roles on *The Road West* (1966–67), *The Doctors* (1976–77), *The Young and the Restless* (1982–83) and *Dallas* (1983–84).

• Lou Antonio (born 23 January 1934 in Oklahoma City, Oklahoma) began acting on the New York stage during the late 1950s, but hit his stride doing episodic television during the 1960s. He performed both drama and comedy equally well in guest roles, then found continuing parts on *The Snoop Sisters* (1973–74), *Dog and Cat* (1977) and *Makin' It* (1979). Antonio turned to directing and has Emmy nominations for his efforts in *Something for Joey* (1978) and *Silent Victory: The Kitty O'Neill Story* (1979).

• Sally Kellerman (born 6 June 1938 in Long Beach, California) broke into TV in the early 1960s in sitcoms and cop shows. But then, two science fiction projects helped her career take off. Kellerman appeared in episodes of the original *Outer Limits* (1963–64) and the second pilot for *Star Trek*, "Where No Man Has Gone Before" (OAD 22 September 1966). From there, her TV appearances wound down as her film career picked up. She earned an Academy Award nomination for her role as "Hot Lips" in the movie *M*A*S*H* (1970). Her rich voice has been used effectively on television commercials for Clairol, Volvo, and Hidden Valley Ranch.

- This episode marks the first "special appearance" by Hazel Court (born 10 February 1926 in Birmingham, England) as Liz Woodruff, Savage's love interest. In the 1950s, Court became a sex symbol in her native England by appearing in a series of horror movies such as *Devil Girl from Mars* (1954), *The Curse of Frankenstein* (1957) and *The Man Who Could Cheat Death* (1959). In America, Court co-starred in the series *Dick and the Duchess* (1957–58) and found plenty of work on series such as *Thriller, Burke's Law* and *Adventures in Paradise*. Court would next appear in #9 "Appointment at Liege."

PERSONNEL FILE
- Liz Woodruff (Hazel Court) invites Savage to her flat and makes dinner for him; he admits his doubts and misgivings. She assures him that he's just human. They cuddle and kiss; it's definitely a romantic relationship.
- We learn that Liz's brother works at the Air Ministry. Although we never meet him, he is referred to again in #9 "Appointment at Liege."
- The characters of Lt. Lockridge (played by Glenn Corbett) and Lt. MacAndrews (played by Sally Kellerman) reappear in #15 "Those Who Are About to Die."

DEBRIEFING
- On the first mission, Savage's call sign is Red Fox Leader; for the second mission, it's Arrowhead Leader.
- P-47s come to the rescue at climax of Act IV.
- Savage's plane is the *Piccadilly Lily*.
- Savage's A-2 jacket has a cigarette pouch on its left sleeve.
- Crews do not use oxygen masks. Pilots and co-pilots do not wear flight helmets.
- During the time span of season one, Rennes was targeted by the Eighth Air Force on 8 March 1943 and 29 May 1943.

INTELLIGENCE REPORT
- Music behind the title presentation has an echo. The score is bland, with nothing to punctuate the action.
- This episode reflects a primary theme of the novel and movie: leadership. Savage questions his decisions: "penny wise or pound foolish."

FLIGHT LINE
- By expressing his support for daylight precision bombing, Gen. Crowe gives

viewers a sense of where the initiative stands. The situation is far from controlled at the time of this episode. Crowe says that the time may come "in a year when our air cadets are trained and our factories have built planes for them to fly." He adds that "We can't win this war this year, or maybe in five years."

#4 "THE SOUND OF DISTANT THUNDER" (7305)

OAD:	16 October 1964
RERUN:	14 May 1965
W:	Edward J. Lakso
D:	Don Medford

Peter Fonda

Savage has doubts about his new bombardier, Lt. Andy Lathrop, an awkward, homespun young man from Tennessee. But in combat, Lathrop proves himself a sure-fire bombardier and a courageous soldier. When Savage's plane is hit, the general orders a bailout. Just as Savage gets ready to leave the cockpit, an electrical explosion dazes him. Lathrop helps the general into a chute and makes sure Savage jumps safely, then follows him. Recuperating in the hospital, Savage reflects on Lathrop's ability and potential. In fact, Savage bets Crowe that Lathrop will become a group commander. Savage begins his Pygmalion campaign by tutoring Lathrop in the finer points of tactics. Savage suggests that Lathrop take time off and go to London. In the big city, teetotaler Lathrop hears the music and laughter from a pub called The Golden Cup, and goes inside where he discovers the pleasure and power of cognac. The tipsy lieutenant finds himself in a barroom brawl but is rescued by Mary Lean, daughter of the pub's owner. Mary takes Lathrop into the family's quarters, where he passes out on the sofa and sleeps all night, oversleeping so that he misses that day's mission—and a first-meeting with Gen. Crowe. Savage is perplexed by Lathrop's behavior and outraged when it seems that the lieutenant wants to throw away his military career by requesting permission to wed Mary. The general confines Lathrop to base for one month, but after two weeks, the lieutenant steals a jeep, drives to London and proposes to Mary. Just as she accepts, an air raid siren sounds. Mary tells Lathrop to go back to the base while she seeks refuge in a basement shelter. Lathrop gets in the jeep and looks up as a German plane slams into the Leans' building. Frantic, Lathrop rushes inside and down to the basement where he finds that Mary has been killed. MPs find the stolen jeep and report it to Savage, who tracks down Lathrop. The lieutenant is now on the receiving end of a bomb run and knows firsthand the loss, pain and destruction that he causes every time he drops a load of bombs. Lathrop contends that he's not made of the same stuff as Savage and can't kill people. Savage counters by pointing out that the bombing will, in the long run, save lives by shortening the war. The general's words work because, next day, Lathrop is back in the briefing hut for another mission.

Gen. Savage, Maj. Stovall, Gen. Crowe, Doc Kaiser, Maj. Cobb
Lt. Andy Lathrop ·························· Peter Fonda
Mary Lean ······························· Jill Haworth
Tom Lean ······························· Hedley Mattingly
Lt. Smith ······························· John Alderman
Jeep Driver ······························· Charles Kuenstle

TDY

• Peter Fonda (born 23 February 1939 in New York City) helped redefine America—and Hollywood—for the baby boom generation with his groundbreaking film *Easy Rider* (1969). The son of actor Henry Fonda (1905–1982), Peter briefly did episodic TV in the early 1960s, and then branched out into features. After hitting the big time with *Easy Rider*, Fonda did a slew of low-budget action films, including *Fighting Mad* (1976), *Dirty Mary, Crazy Larry* (1974) and *Race With the Devil* (1975). Fonda emerged from that strange period as one of America's finest actors in films such as *Ulee's Gold* (1997), *The Limey* (1999) and *The Passion of Ayn Rand* (1999).

Paul Wurtzel on Peter Fonda: "On the weekend, [Fonda] had been wearing shorts, riding a motorcycle on the beach at Malibu. He hit sand, came off and peeled himself like a grape on the pavement. He had to come into work Monday and wear a fleece-lined high-altitude outfit. We were shooting out at Chino, which gets to be, like, 110 degrees in the summer. Fonda had this suit on and the sweat was running down, the salt and sweat burning all this scraped skin. But he never complained a bit. Everyone really had to salute him."

• Jill Haworth (born 15 August 1945 in Sussex, England) began her acting career in the epic film *Exodus* (1960). She holds a special place in fandom for her role in the classic *Outer Limits* episode "The Sixth Finger" (OAD 14 October 1963). In addition to film and TV, Haworth created the role of Sally Bowles on Broadway in *Cabaret* (1966). She made three subsequent appearances on *12 O'Clock High* in episode #20 "To Heinie, With Love" and as Lt. Fay Vendry in episodes #38 "The Hotshot" and #40 "Runway in the Dark."

• Hedley Mattingly (1915–1998) served in the RAF during World War II. He did Shakespeare at the Old Vic, performed for 11 years with Theatre Royal

Windsor, and then worked on Canadian TV before heading for Hollywood. His regular series roles were on *The Travels of Jamie McPheeters* (1963–64) and *Daktari* (1966–69).

PERSONNEL FILE

- Savage came to the air corps right off the farm.
- Savage says that Crowe took the time and trouble to push him early on when he needed it.

DEBRIEFING

- Crew does not use oxygen masks. The pilot and co-pilot do not wear flight helmets.
- Target is St. Etienne. The Eighth Air Force did not bomb the marshalling yard at St. Etienne until 26 May 1944.
- Lathrop just transferred in from the 912th.
- First mission: Savage's code name is Red Robin One.

INTELLIGENCE REPORT

- The set used as the cellar of The Golden Cup was reused, shot from the reverse angle, in #23 "The Trap."
- Another excellent score from Dominic Frontiere. It's atypical, somber when it needs to be, but Andy has his own comic theme.
- The sequence of a German bomber slamming into a building was used later in episodes #23 "The Trap" and #39 "Show Me a Hero, I'll Show You a Bum."

#5 "THE CLIMATE OF DOUBT" (7308)

OAD:	23 October 1964
RERUN:	N/R
W:	Harold Jack Bloom
D:	Don Medford

After a French Resistance (FFI) cell is broken, freedom fighter Nicole Trouchard promises her mentor, Henri Lau, that she will get to England and contact Gen. Crowe. Meanwhile, Crowe asks Savage to join him that evening at the Gramercy Hotel for a meeting about sending the group on one mission over two successive targets. The room to which Savage reports is

Viveca Lindfors and John Larkin

occupied by Mme. Trouchard, apparently an old acquaintance of Crowe's. Gen. Crowe explains that the FFI needs to have confidence in its leaders; they have to be shown that their contributions are valued by the Allies. By hitting two trouble spots, Crowe believes the FFI will be given the courage to keep fighting the Nazis. Savage contends that the Eighth Air Force is so short of men and planes that such an experimental mission is frivolous. He also sees that Nicole is more than a military ally, that there is a history—and a chemistry—between Nicole and Crowe. Gen. Crowe won't give in and orders Savage to plot the mission. The more Savage thinks about it the more he wonders if Crowe is set on the mission because it's the right thing to do or because of his feelings for Nicole. Savage asks British Intelligence officer Col. Charles to investigate Nicole's efforts. Are they genuinely for the Resistance movement or out of love for Henri Lau? Savage takes his suspicions directly to Nicole and asks her about her relationship with Lau and her feelings for Crowe. She is insulted by his questions and the lack of trust they imply. The mission goes on but, despite heavy losses, does only minimal damage to the target. What's worse, the lackluster showing reflects badly on Gen. Crowe, who faces a hearing that could jeopardize his career. At the inquest, Crowe reiterates his stand that the mission was intended to strengthen relations with the French which, when the time comes, would save American lives during the Allied invasion of the continent. Then, Crowe is asked point blank whether or not his decision was affected by his feelings for Mme. Trouchard. Crowe admits that he is, indeed, in love with Mme. Trouchard. After the inquest is recessed for the day, Col. Charles tells Savage that his sources confirm that Henri Lau was indeed killed. That evening, Nicole calls on Savage to plead with the general to help save his friend's career. When the hearing reconvenes, Savage takes the stand and confirms his dispute with Crowe's decision but contends that Crowe rose above personal relationships to rely on his own judgment to do what's best for his men, his service and his country. That said, the inquest is dismissed with no further action taken against Gen. Crowe. Later, Crowe tells Savage that Nicole was killed in action. Crowe reflects on what a waste war is, but then if hadn't been for the war, he would not have met—or lost—Nicole.

Gen. Savage, Gen. Crowe, Maj. Cobb, Maj. Stovall
Nicole Trouchard ·························· Viveca Lindfors
Brigadier General ······················· David White
Major General ···························· Carl Benton Reid
Col. Harry Charles ····················· Bernard Fox
Dorathy Hall ······························ Mitzi Hoag
Sgt. "Pineapple" Kanaka ············ Ralph Hanalei
Henri Lau ································· Jacques Roux
Co-Pilot ·································· Jack Powers

TDY

- Viveca Lindfors (1920–1995) starred in films in her native Sweden, and then continued her career in the U.S. With a successful movie and TV career, Lindfors dropped out of television for a decade. Her triumphant return to the medium resulted in a 1990 Emmy win for her guest appearance in an episode of *Life Goes On*. Lindfors is the mother of actor Kristoffer Tabori.

- David White (1916–1990) served with the Marines during World War II. He was a regular in only one series but the role was unforgettable. White will always be known as Larry Tate, Darrin Stevens' boss on *Bewitched* (1964–72). Other TV appearances included *The Alcoa Hour*, *Alfred Hitchcock Presents*, *Have Gun, Will Travel* and *Remington Steele*.

- Bernard Fox (born 11 May 1927 in Port Talbot, Glamorgan, Wales) is widely recognized for his role of Dr. Bombay on the long-running sitcom *Bewitched* (1967–72). He also had the recurring role of bumbling Col. Crittendon on *Hogan's Heroes* (1965–70). *Andy Griffith Show* fans know him from three appearances as the meek but well-meaning Malcolm Merriweather.

PERSONNEL FILE

- Crowe said that his wife Martha had been dead five years before he looked at another woman, who happened to be Nicole. Nicole lost her husband, too. Crowe and Nicole had met two years earlier just before the fall of France.
- Savage and Crow were both at Langley Field two years earlier.
- Savage tells Nicole, "Wiley Crowe is the best friend I have or ever hope to have."

DEBRIEFING

- Savage's plane is *Piccadilly Lily*.
- Oxygen masks are used. However, during an interphone call to his crew, Savage rips off the mask and continues his conversation. The general doesn't replace it until a couple of scenes later. Then, the next time he needs to give an order to his co-pilot, he rips it off again.
- Savage's call sign is Ramrod. He calls Red Flanker Two as it spirals down out of control. He also calls Blue Flanker One, which goes down in flames. The general then orders Blue Flanker Two to take over as Blue Flanker Leader.
- The targets are, at first, a troop replacement depot in Normandy and an ammunition dump nearby. But then Crowe says the target is the Rouen marshalling yards.
- During the time period covered in season one, the Eighth Air Force B-17s targeted Rouen on 17 August 1942, 5 September 1942, 12 December 1942, 8 March 1943, 17 March 1943 (recalled) and 28 March 1943.

- This episode also has an underlying theme of leadership, reflecting a subject from the novel and movie.
- The set used for Nicole's hotel room is the same one used as the hotel room shared by Savage and Stovall in #23 "The Trap."
- The plane in which Sgt. Kanaka flies has the call number 713; the lead 3 has been partially painted over. The fuselage of the plane has only the national emblem.
- Peter Deuel has an unbilled, bit part as a member of Sgt. Kanaka's crew. Deuel returned with screen credit in #9 "Appointment at Liege" and #32 "The Hero."

FLIGHT LINE

- At the hearing, Crowe says: "We haven't been in this war long enough to have many precedents."

Elen Willard

#6 "PRESSURE POINT" (7307)

OAD: 30 October 1964
RERUN: 21 May 1965
W: John T. Dugan
D: William A. Graham

Gen. Crowe prepares Savage for Sen. Clayton Johnson's visit to the 918th. Sen. Johnson is in England to evaluate the effectiveness of long-range daylight strategic bombing and determine whether or not the program will continue. Both men know that Sen. Johnson has no love for the Army Air Corps, but Crowe doesn't realize that there is personal animosity between Johnson and Savage. Fifteen years earlier, Savage asked Johnson's daughter Arlene to marry him. Because of the senator's attitude toward aviators, Johnson stepped in and broke up the relationship. Johnson's first stop is the base hospital, where he meets bedridden Staff Sgt. Edward Pryor, who was injured when his plane made a belly landing. Later, Sgt. Pryor is visited by his fiancée, April Barrett. She explains her morning sickness and wonders when Savage will give them permission to marry. Meanwhile, Sen. Johnson meets with Gen. Crowe and Gen. Pritchard in Savage's office to express his disapproval of bombing policies and practices. In answer to Johnson's grave concerns about heavy losses, Savage reveals his answer: "Project Porcupine," arming key aircraft with 20mm cannon and ammunition in the bomb bays instead of bombs. Savage is disappointed when Maj. Rosen, group meteorologist, reports that the continent will be closed down for a week. That means the general won't have an opportunity to show what his new tactic can do before Johnson's committee reaches a decision. Suddenly, Maj. Rosen notifies Savage that there may be a break in the weather over Northern Germany. Savage orders Sgt. Nero to rig eight Porcupines by the next morning. The Vicar of Archbury meets with Gen. Savage about his parishioner April Barrett and Sgt. Pryor. It seems that Pryor has been telling April that the general refuses to grant permission to marry—but Maj. Stovall verifies that Pryor never submitted a request. The general suggests that Pryor face up to his responsibilities and deliver his decision in one week. Savage then orders Maj. Cobb to replace Pryor as his ball turret gunner because he doesn't trust the sergeant. After Crowe hears about Savage's proposed mission, he demands to see the general and reminds Savage of Clayton's stance. When Savage replies that this mission may be their only chance to keep the program alive, Crowe reluctantly gives his blessing. With *Piccadilly Lily* temporarily out of action, Savage leads a raid on Hamburg in Maj. Cobb's plane. But as soon as Sen. Johnson hears of the mission, he tells Gen. Pritchard to order a recall. The senator adds grimly that Savage's defiance spells the end of long range bombing—and of Gen. Savage. By the time Savage receives the recall, the 918th is in the thick of a heated air battle with Me 109s. Flak rips into the plane, knocking out the number three engine and trapping Sgt. Pryor in the ball turret. Back at Wing HQ, the reports come back that the 918th has struck Hamburg. Johnson is outraged by the insubordination and vows that Savage and Crowe will be stripped of command. But, the senator may not get his chance: the group is headed back to base but Savage's plane was reported going down. However, Gen. Pritchard is amazed that Project Porcupine allowed the 918th to successfully hit a target in Germany and return without a single loss. Even the strike photos demonstrate that the group clobbered docks and tankers. But the general isn't out of it yet. His plane is coming in low on fuel, the right landing gear is jammed, one engine gone and another running hot, and Sgt. Pryor still trapped in the ball turret. Savage obeys Gen. Crowe's orders to bail out, but while the co-pilot flies the plane, Savage works furiously to manually lower the landing gear. With no guarantee that the gear is locked, Savage resumes control and brings the plane in for a safe landing. Later, Sgt. Pryor submits a formal request to marry April, which Savage gladly approves. Gen. Crowe escorts Sen. Johnson to say farewell to Savage. Johnson's opinion has been changed and he sheepishly admits that aircraft and precision daylight bombing will undoubtedly help shorten the war.

Gen. Savage, Maj. Stovall, Maj. Cobb, Gen. Crowe, Gen. Pritchard,
Sgt. Nero, Doc Kaiser
Senator Clayton Johnson ············ Larry Gates
S/Sgt. Edward Pryor ···················· Robert Doyle
April Barrett ····························· Elen Willard
Maj. Harry Rosen ······················ Jason Wingreen

Vicar of Archbury	Brendan Dillon
Capt. Sherman Mewlay	Robert Hogan
Sgt. Jim Loren	Jud Taylor
Lt. Tom O'Leary	Bill Cort

TDY

- Larry Gates (1915–1996) capped a career on stage, in films and on TV with a 1985 Emmy nomination for his continuing role on *The Guiding Light*. His rich resume included appearances on *The Twilight Zone, The Invaders* and *Then Came Bronson*. Gates played President Herbert Hoover in the 1979 miniseries *Backstairs at the White House*. His film credits include *Invasion of the Body Snatchers* (1956), *Cat on a Hot Tin Roof* (1958) and *The Sand Pebbles* (1966). Gates returned in #46 "Between the Lines."

- Robert Doyle (1938–2000) kept busy playing troubled youths in two episodes of *The Outer Limits,* three *Fugitives* and two *Voyage to the Bottom of the Seas*. His only regular series work was in *Lanigan's Rabbi* (1977). Doyle made two additional, unrelated appearances on *12 O'Clock High*.

- Robert Hogan (born 28 September 1936 in New York City) has been a regular on the series *General Hospital* (1966), *Peyton Place* (1968–69), *Days of Our Lives* (1970–71), *The Don Rickles Show* (1972), *The Manhunter* (1974–75), *Richie Brockelman, Private Eye* (1978), *Operation Petticoat* (1978–79), *Secrets of Midland Heights* (1980–81), *Another World* (1987–89), *As the World Turns* (1991–92) and *One Life to Live* (1995–98).

- Jason Wingreen (born 9 October 1919 in Brooklyn, New York) made the first of three appearances as Maj. Rosen, meteorological officer for the 918th. Wingreen built a career out of portraying clerks, public servants and various employees in the service sector. He had continuing roles on *The Rounders* (1966–67), *All in the Family* (1971–79) and *Archie Bunker's Place* (1979–1983).

PERSONNEL FILE

- Gen. Savage tells Maj. Stovall, "The last time I spoke to Clay Johnson, Major, he said to me 'Savage...do you know what I should have done the first night I met you? I should have picked up my gun and I should have shot you through the head.'"
- Savage has known Johnson since 1927 when the senator was a member of the House of Representatives. Savage wanted to marry his daughter, Arlene. He asked her to marry him, and she said yes, but the senator stepped in to break the engagement. Although Savage had just received his commission, Johnson wanted him to resign it. The general recalled that Johnson said "flying was a

game for the emotionally immature. He said anyone who went into it showed a dangerous pattern of irresponsibility."

· In the script for this episode, Gen. Pritchard's first name is George.

DEBRIEFING

· "Project Porcupine" was based on the YB-40, an enhanced B-17 heavily armored and heavily armed with 14 .50-caliber machine guns. The experiment failed because the YB-40 was tail-heavy and couldn't keep pace after the bombers dropped their loads.

· Seldom seen new footage shows gunner Pryor operating inside the ball turret.

· Savage's call sign is Tightrope Red.

· Oxygen masks and flight helmets are used.

· Cobb's B-17 has call number 3713 on the tail and only the national insignia on the fuselage.

· Pryor's B-17, which crashes, is *April Showers.*

INTELLIGENCE REPORT

· Archbury tower is not the one that audiences were accustomed to seeing. It was actually an original Cal-Aero structure out at Chino.

· The teaser recycles footage from the movie, showing the B-17 belly landing and ambulances racing to its rescue.

· This episode was originally slated to air on 9 October 1964.

FLIGHT LINE

· Senator Johnson is no dummy about the daylight bombing program. He says authoritatively that the success of long-range bombing depends on long-range fighters.

#7 "DECISION" (7310)

OAD:	6 November 1964
RERUN:	4 June 1965
TP:	Clair Huffaker
	& Jack Turley
STORY:	Clair Huffaker
D:	William A. Graham

Gen. Crowe tells Savage that the Nazis' flying bomb program must be stopped at any cost. Crowe orders the 918th on a strike against a factory in Lyonne that manufactures precision parts—an ideal site for producing gyro

John van Dreelen

guidance systems. The group's rotation schedule taps Savage's old friend Maj. John Temple for duty. This means Temple will be completing his 25th mission. The 918th bombs the target but Maj. Temple's plane, *Lucky Lady*, runs out of luck: flak damages one of its engines, making the plane an easy target for Luftwaffe fighters. *Lucky Lady* is shot up so badly that Temple orders a bailout. Temple and five of his crew are captured by Germans under the command of Col. Alfred Hoeptner. Temple's men are confined in the middle of the factory complex, a target zone—clearly in violation of the Geneva conventions. Col. Hoeptner admits he will use the airmen as a shield for three days until a train arrives that will transport vital machinery out of the area. A broadcast by Lord Haw Haw notifies the Americans where Temple's men are located and what could happen if the 918th pays another "visit" to the factory. Feeling down, Savage offers to buy Maj. Stovall a drink at the Officers' Club. They start to play a game of darts, but when the darts accidentally fall on the floor, Savage hits on an idea. The general wants to see every scrap of information about the factory complex and sends up a photo reconnaissance plane. When Temple sees the recon flight he orders his men to form a human arrow facing the building where the machinery is located. With the aerial photos in hand, Savage sells Gen. Crowe on a single B-17 bombing the factory building identified by Temple's men. But Crowe tells Savage that if his idea doesn't work, 100 more B-17s will be right behind for a saturation raid. The next day, Savage prepares for his mission but meanwhile, Col. Hoeptner plays a shell game: he saw Temple's men aimed at the factory building and has moved the machinery to a location across the compound. Savage agrees to a request from Lt. Peters, his bombardier, to make two passes over the target. When Savage's first salvo hits, Temple and his men overtake their captors. Instead of killing Hoeptner, Temple just knocks him flat. After Temple orders his men to get out of the compound, he commandeers a gasoline transport truck and crashes it into the new storage building. As Temple sets the gas on fire, Col. Hoeptner shoots him. Lt. Peters sees the fire Temple started, alerts the general and suggests they bomb there, too. The general orders Peters to drop on the other structure, and he scores a direct hit. Back at the base, Savage learns the second strike was successful and at the same time tries to compose a letter to the widow of a man who was a soldier, a hero and a friend.

Gen. Savage, Maj. Stovall, Gen. Crowe
Maj. John Lawrence "Jack" Temple Tim O'Connor
Col. Alfred Hoeptner ·················· John Van Dreelen
Lt. Ross Kinner ···························· Hunt Powers
Sgt. Hugo Ernest Weinstock ····· Kip King
Sgt. Roland Chester Nichols ····· Steve Harris
Cpl. Dennis Kenneth Moody ·· Buck Taylor
Lt. Peters ································· Peter Duryea
Aide ······································· Walter Friedel

TDY

- Tim O'Connor (born 3 July 1927 in Chicago, Illinois) worked his way up through the ranks of stage acting, first in his home town and then in New York City. Raves for his performance in *The Crucible* put him on the map. In the early 1960s, the *Journal American* newspaper called O'Connor the busiest actor in New York City. A continuing role on the prime-time soap *Peyton Place* (1964–68) brought him public notice. From there, he guest starred on shows such as *M*A*S*H, The Outer Limits, TJ Hooker* and *Knight Rider*. He was also a regular on *Buck Rogers in the 25th Century* (1979–80).

  Tim O'Connor on "Decision"—On the walk with Savage around the 918th's HQ area: "I read the script over first, laying out the relationship. I realized I would have to drive the scene, so I would have to put some twist on it. It just lays out as an easy, comfortable banter, but I wanted to give it more than was written." On the shoot at Chino Airport: "I remember a long drive to the location. The path we walked on was made of wood, a couple of inches off the ground. It had been there for some time as part of the set." On the first escape attempt: "I raced back to grab one of the crew. I leaned over him, spun him and threw him over neat as can be. That was a stunt man. He used my pulling to make it look easy." On flattening Col. Hoeptner: "My character's earlier actions gave me a sense of strength and immense control. When I socked the major, they knew that he was down. They knew why because the character knew how to throw a punch because he was strong and athletic throughout the show." On the explosive finish: "I drove the truck, and then did a deadfall just before it hit. I was allowed to do it because I am very athletic and could do it."

- John Van Dreelen (1922–1992) carved a niche portraying members of the aristocracy or the military of various European countries, real or fictitious. A native of the Netherlands, Van Dreelen's series work included *Combat!, I Spy, Men Into Space, It Takes a Thief* and *The Man from U.N.C.L.E.* His English-language films included *13 Ghosts* (1960), *The Leech Woman* (1960), *Von Ryan's Express* (1965) and the musical remake of *Lost Horizon* (1973). This was the first of six appearances by Van Dreelen on *12 O'Clock High.*

- Buck Taylor (born 13 May 1938 in Hollywood, California) is the son of comedic actor Dub Taylor. He began his career as a stuntman and gymnast. Taylor is best known for his role of Newly O'Brien on *Gunsmoke* (1967–75). He also appeared in the family oriented Fox western *The Monroes* (1966–67).

- Clair Huffaker (1926–1990) co-wrote this episode. The dénouement, in which Maj. Temple turns a German truck into a flaming vehicle of destruction, is reminiscent of another Huffaker work, her script for the 1967 John Wayne-Kirk Douglas movie *The War Wagon*. Huffaker's *War Wagon* screenplay was based on her 1957 novel *Badman*.

PERSONNEL FILE
- Savage and Temple's friendship goes back to when they faced each other in a West Point boxing tournament. "Trying to beat each other's brains out," Savage says. "Funny way for a friendship to start." Crowe notes that Savage went through a pile of red tape to get Temple transferred to the 918th.

DEBRIEFING
- Crews do not use oxygen masks.
- Savage flies the *Piccadilly Lily*.
- Temple's plane is *Lucky Lady*.
- On the initial mission, Savage uses call sign Blue Troop Leader. For the pinpoint run, he uses Spearhead.

INTELLIGENCE REPORT
- This episode provides an excellent walking tour of the HQ set at Chino Airport. From the Briefing-Interrogation shack, Savage and Temple walk south in front of the Officers' Club and base hospital.
- In both the title presentation and the end credits, John Van Dreelen is billed on-screen as John Van Dreelan.

FLIGHT LINE
- Savage writes a condolence letter to Temple's wife. It's dated June 15 but the year is out of frame.

TOBY SIGHTING
- Toby mug is on the mantle in the Officers' Club.

Fritz Weaver and Glynis Johns

#8 "THE HOURS BEFORE DAWN" (7309)

OAD:	13 November 1964
RERUN:	N/R
W:	Donald S. Sanford
D:	Don Medford

At a briefing in London with Gen. Crowe and Gen. Stoneman, Savage is told that his scheduled mission is being abruptly changed to throw off German intelligence. Savage will be the only one with the details of the new mission and will put the strategy into action the next day only after the group is airborne. Savage is not happy with the risk and the melodramatics surrounding the mission but hunkers down to memorize the details. Once Savage is set, he leaves for the base but is detoured by an air raid. An exploding bomb impacts Savage's car and he crashes into a tree. Savage is knocked unconscious but is rescued by taxi driver Doker Drew and his passenger, Jennifer Heath. Ms. Heath lives nearby and reluctantly allows Savage to use her telephone. The bombing continues as Ms. Heath and Savage run inside. As a window glass implodes and the chandelier plummets, Ms. Heath has a panic attack which is only stopped when Savage knocks her unconscious. When she comes to, Ms. Heath shows Savage the phone. Before Savage can make a call, he and Ms. Heath are surprised by Col. Peter Raff, a wounded Nazi flier. Savage tries to work with Ms. Heath to overcome the intruder but she refuses, claiming to be "strictly neutral." Raff rips the phone cord out of the wall, orders Ms. Heath to bandage his wound and then makes himself at home. A troop of Home Guard volunteers, accompanied by Doker, approaches the Heath home. They know her phone is out of order and Doker's cab has been stolen by a German flier. Ms. Heath blithely sends the group away. Then, Raff locks his two captives in the basement where they exchange philosophies of life, of giving up and never surrendering. Just then, Raff orders Savage upstairs to change uniforms with him so he can effect his escape. Savage takes advantage of the situation to try to disarm his captor. As they fight, Ms. Heath turns up ready to clobber Raff with a club. But before she can strike, Raff shoots her. Raff and Savage continue the struggle until the general comes into possession of the handgun and kills the German. Savage is able to repair the phone and call the Home Guard, which takes Ms. Heath to the hospital and drives Savage back to base.

Gen. Savage, Gen. Crowe, Gen. Stoneman
Jennifer Heath ···························· Glynis Johns
Col. Peter Raff ···························· Fritz Weaver
Doker Drew ···························· John McLiam
Maj. Tod Colin ···························· Maurice Dallimore
Col. Meyers ···························· Robert Brubaker
Policeman ···························· Gil Stuart
Sgt. Albert Reed ···························· Eric Micklewood

TDY

- Glynis Johns (born 5 October 1923 in Pretoria, South Africa) is the fifth generation of a show business family. She debuted on stage at 12 and made her first film at 15. Johns matured into an attractive woman and a gifted actress. Along the way, she was nominated for a Best Supporting Actress Oscar for her performance *The Sundowners* (1960) and won a Tony for her performance in the 1973 Broadway production of *A Little Night Music*.

- Fritz Weaver (born 19 January 1926 in Pittsburgh, Pennsylvania) has successfully created intellectual, strong-willed characters on stage, in movies and on TV. On Broadway, Weaver portrayed Sherlock Holmes in the 1965 musical *Baker Street* and won a Tony in 1970 for *Child's Play*. During the spy cycle of the 1960s, Weaver was frequently cast on series such as *The FBI*, *Mission: Impossible* and played the suave, arch-villain Andrew Vulcan in the pilot for *The Man from U.N.C.L.E.* (OAD 22 September 1964). His films include *Fail-Safe* (1964), *Marathon Man* (1976), *Black Sunday* (1977) and *Creepshow* (1982).

- John McLiam (1918–1994), a native of Alberta, Canada, parlayed his craggy features and everyman bearing into a lengthy career in features such as *My Fair Lady* (1964), *In Cold Blood* (1967), *Cool Hand Luke* (1967) and *First Blood* (1982). His TV appearances included *Honey West, The Twilight Zone, The Gallant Men* and *The Outer Limits* plus continuing roles on *The Men from Shiloh* (1970–71) and *Two Marriages* (1983–84).

- Robert Brubaker (born 9 October 1916 in Robinson, Illinois) began his performing career in radio at KMPC in Hollywood. Brubaker had featured roles on *The Sheriff of Cochise* (1958), *Days of Our Lives* and *Gunsmoke* (1974–75). Perhaps his most unsung role was in the pilot for *The Man from U.N.C.L.E.* (OAD 22 September 1964) as a THRUSH agent who penetrates U.N.C.L.E. headquarters. Brubaker fired his gun at the unflappable Napoleon Solo (Robert Vaughn), who was spared by a full-length sheet of bullet-proof glass, which splintered into an eerie network of spiderwebs.

PERSONNEL FILE
- Even though Savage and Crowe are best friends, in the teaser Savage blows his stack at Crowe, who takes it in stride and tells Savage to straighten his tie. Savage discounts Crowe's "big brother attitude." But that pretty much sums up their relationship.
- Savage tells Jennifer that he came from a small farming community.
- Crowe reminds Savage that Stoneman is a stickler for military discipline.

DEBRIEFING
- Initially, the target is Hamburg, then it's changed to Dortmund. The Eighth Air Force did not bomb Dortmund until 22 June 1943.

INTELLIGENCE REPORT
- The room in which Savage crams for the mission is the same one used as a hotel suite in #23 "The Trap."
- According to the script for this episode, Jennifer Heath is "going down in flames and doesn't give a damn."

• In this episode, Gen. Stoneman is a lieutenant general. When he next appears, in #26 "Mutiny at Ten Thousand Feet," he is a major general.

#9 "APPOINTMENT AT LIEGE" (7311)

OAD:	20 November 1964
RERUN:	N/R
TP:	Charles Larson
Story:	John McGreevey
D:	Don Medford

Nancy Kovack

Maj. Gus Denver has a death wish. On his last tour with the 918th, Maj. Denver was shipped stateside while his crew flew with a new skipper on another mission—their final mission, over the city of Liege. When Denver reports to Maj. Stovall for his second hitch with the 918th, he obsesses over losing his crew—being an orphan, they were the only family Denver knew—and his plans for revenge on Liege. Stovall expresses concern to Savage, telling the general he thinks Denver came back to die. Knowing Maj. Stovall isn't prone to melodramatics, the general shares Stovall's feelings. Meanwhile, Crowe has handed down orders for a bombing raid at 8,000 feet over the rail yards at Maastricht in Eastern Belgium. Because of the low level and heavy flak, Savage is relieved to learn that bad weather has postponed the mission. Before taking off for the alternate target, Savage talks with Denver; his friendly conversation indirectly suggests that Denver not jeopardize his green crew. Up in the air, the oxygen and radio systems on Denver's plane go out. Denver breaks formation to allow his bombardier, Lt. Jake Benning, to strike a target of opportunity. Just then, a burst of flak hits the belly of *Gus's Revenge,* killing Lt. Charlie Vale. He dies in the arms of his best friend, Lt. Benning, who then suffers a breakdown. Back at the base, Savage interprets Denver's actions as a suicidal attempt to fight his own private war and grounds the major. On the other hand, Gen. Crowe sees Denver's actions as a commendable act of initiative and selfless heroism. With such divergent opinions, Savage and Crowe clash but Gen. Crowe insists that the Maastricht raid is still on. After Savage's collision with Crowe, he can use some cheering up and Liz Woodruff's surprise visit does the job. In the Officers' Club, Denver runs into gorgeous Lt. Irene Cooper who, in her way, is as dissatisfied with life as Denver is. Two kindred souls, they find comfort in each other—until Savage uses psychology to get Denver to face the truth. Then, Denver bolts from the shelter of Irene Cooper and breaks down in front of Savage and Gen. Crowe.

After Denver is hospitalized, Crowe notes the value of finding the truth and sticking to it. Crowe adds that the Maastricht raid is postponed until Savage feels the odds are better.

Gen. Savage, Maj. Stovall, Gen. Crowe, Maj. Cobb
Maj. August "Gus" Denver ········· Gary Lockwood
Lt. Irene Cooper ···························· Nancy Kovack
Liz Woodruff ································· Hazel Court
Sergeant ·· Wynn Pearce
Lt. Col. Ed Chandler ··············· Burt Metcalfe
Lt. Jake Benning ························· Peter E. Deuel
Lt. Charlie Vale ·························· Yale Summers
Radioman ···································· Jonathan Lippe

TDY

• Gary Lockwood (born John Gary Yusolfsky on 21 February 1937 in Van Nuys, California) started in the business as a stuntman. Bit parts in *Warlock* (1959) and *Tall Story* (1960) led to a co-starring role in the TV series *Follow the Sun* (1961–62) and *The Lieutenant* (1963–64). Roles in two sci-fi legends have kept Lockwood in the public eye for nearly four decades: astronaut Frank Poole in *2001: A Space Odyssey* (1968) and Gary Mitchell in the second pilot for *Star Trek,* "Where No Man Has Gone Before" (OAD 22 September 1966). Lockwood made two subsequent appearances on *12 O'Clock High.*

• Nancy Kovack (born 11 March 1935 in Flint, Michigan) played scheming sirens with such delight and verve that she's always a pleasure to watch. For example, Kovack's socialite character tried to steal newlywed Darrin Stevens away from his bride, Samantha, in the pilot of *Bewitched* (OAD 17 September 1964). She also appeared in *Burke's Law, Star Trek, I Dream of Jeannie* and *Jason and the Argonauts* (1963).

• Peter E. Deuel (1940–1971) later shortened his name to Peter Duel and used his amiable charm to perform both comedy and drama in regular series parts on *Gidget* (1965–66), *Love on a Rooftop* (1966–67) and *Alias Smith and Jones* (1971–72). While working on the latter show, Duel took his own life. He appeared again in episode #32 "The Hero."

• Yale Summers (born Roy Reed Neuvohner on 26 July 1933 in New York City) graduated from Cornell with a degree in government. Summers sold real estate until he was spotted by a Hollywood talent scout. That led to his film debut in *Mad Dog Coll* (1961) and subsequent roles on TV in *The Lieutenant, The Outer Limits* and *Land of the Giants.* He appeared on

Daktari (1966–68) and the soaps *General Hospital* and *Return to Peyton Place.*

• Jonathan Lippe (born Jonathan Goldsmith on 26 September 1938 in New York City) built a career on playing tough guys with an attitude. He appeared in a handful of movie roles but had an extensive resume of TV work including *Mannix; Mission: Impossible; The Wild, Wild West* and *The Streets of San Francisco.* In the late 1970s, he dropped the name Lippe and continued acting under his birth name.

PERSONNEL FILE
• Liz and Savage actually kiss. They have a date planned for the coming Saturday. Scripts throughout the first season have no real character description for Liz Woodruff (played by Hazel Court). Again we hear about her brother (the first time was in #3 "The Men and the Boys"), who works at the Air Ministry. Liz then tells Savage that she and her brother decided the day was too nice for a widow to stay at home. It's the one-year anniversary of her husband, Miles, being killed in North Africa.
• Crowe calls Col. Chandler by his first name, Ed, during the episode. Chandler returns in #21 "The Clash" and #25 "The Threat."

DEBRIEFING
• Denver hopes for Spitfires to show up and escort them home.
• On the first mission, Savage uses call sign Leader.
• At 10,000 feet, Denver orders the crew on oxygen. They put on their masks but a problem with the system forces them to abandon use of oxygen.
• Savage's crew uses oxygen masks, but the general rips off his mask before going for his throat microphone.
• Denver's plane is named *Gus's Revenge.*
• The mission calls for the 918th to rendezvous with the 911th for their attack on the sub pens.
• The Eighth Air Force did not strike Maastricht until 18 August 1944.

INTELLIGENCE REPORT
• Two scenes dovetail perfectly with the series' novel and movie predecessors. First, following a conversation with Col. Chandler, Savage asks Crowe: "Was I ever that bright-eyed and bushy tailed?" Crowe replies, "The day I asked you to take over the 918th from Col. Davenport."

Later, after Savage pulls an all-night planning session, Stovall tells him, "You keep on punishing yourself, sir, you'll have plenty more [nightmares]. I saw it happen to Col. Davenport." Savage says, "Col. Davenport's crack-up. You were close to him. Did you see it coming?" Stovall replies, "Now that I look back at it I suppose I should have been able to. I'd watch him fighting with Pinetree and I'd think, 'Somewhere this man's lost the ability to judge himself. He thinks he's thrifty but he's a miser; he can't spend lives any more. He won't make room for anyone who can.' He was too compassionate, too stubborn for the job. I suppose in the end, that's what broke him." That, in a nutshell, was how Col. Keith Davenport was relieved of command and Gen. Frank Savage became C.O. of the 918th.

At the heart of this episode are parallel storylines about two men on the edge: Savage and Denver. One finds the strength to rise above, the other breaks under pressure.

- The character of Maj. Gus Denver (Gary Lockwood) reappears in #29 "V for Vendetta." Lockwood made a third, unrelated appearance in #36 "The Idolater."
- The character of Col. Chandler appears later in #21 "The Clash" and #25 "The Threat."

FLIGHT LINE

- Liz says she has a knack for remembering anniversaries (but doesn't divulge hers and Savage's), although she says the last time he phoned her was more like August. So this episode must take place in September or October 1942.

TOBY SIGHTING

- Toby mug is on the mantle, but someone has put his 50 mission cap on its head.

Dana Wynter and Robert Lansing

#10 "INTERLUDE" (7306)

OAD:	27 November 1964
RERUN:	28 May 1965
W:	Dean Riesner
D:	William A. Graham

Gen. Crowe sees how the burden of combat and command have burned out Savage, so he orders Savage to take a one-week leave and forget about the war. An act of calculated happenstance pairs Savage in the same train compartment with Wren Lt. Ann Macrae. Their relationship gets off to a rocky start: Savage's idea of relaxation is smoking a cigar, which doesn't sit well with the prim lieutenant. Things get worse when Savage accidentally causes Lt.

Macrae's priceless, rationed bacon to fly out of the train window. When the train arrives at Inverness, Savage uses his rank to appropriate a canned ham from an army depot. But when Lt. Macrae has apparently disappeared, the general gives the ham to a young boy. Next, Savage boards a ship that will take him to Dunfergus, an island off the coast of Scotland. That evening, Savage is seated in the dining room at the same table with Lt. Macrae, who promptly leaves in a huff. When the chief steward verifies Savage's story, Lt. Macrae insists on apologizing. Alone in her cabin, Ann Macrae must take medication to relieve severe abdominal pain. By the time the ship docks, Ann and Savage have put their animosity aside. Her father, Adam Macrae, invites the general to their home for breakfast. From there, Ann and Savage build affection for each other that quickly turns to romance. Ann's pain continues and, although she has not yet told Savage, her father learned of her serious illness through a Wren comrade. Mr. Macrae cautions his daughter not to be selfish with her emotions, so she backs away from her plans to leave with the general. That night, Ann regretfully breaks up with Savage. Next day, Savage meets up with the ship's chief steward who presents the general with another canned ham, which Savage quickly delivers to the Macraes. Savage is met at the door by the family's physician, Dr. Gunn, who tells Savage that Ann is dying from carcinoma. Mr. Macrae confirms that Ann came home to die. She hears Savage and asks to see him one last time. In the midst of awkward small talk, Ann presents the general with a clan scarf. He, in turn, gives her his pilot's wings. They embrace, kiss and say their goodbyes. To herself, Ann bids farewell to Frank Savage, her love. The general goes out to the Macrae's backyard and walks to a small garden that Ann planted. He kneels down beside the flower bed and begins to weep. Back at the base, Savage hits the flight line and admits that Crowe was right: you have to get away once in a while. As Savage boards his B-17, he puts on the scarf and tucks it into his shirt.

Gen. Savage, Gen. Crowe	
Lt. Ann Macrae	Dana Wynter
Adam Macrae	Rhys Williams
Dr. Gunn	Jack Raine
Chief Steward Macutcheon	Arthur Malet
Captain of Work Detail	Ken Berry
Ticket Seller	Ashley Cowan
Sgt. Dawson	Don Spruance
Lt. Peg Butterford	Molly Roden
Eddie	James Wixted
Sam	Roy Dean

TDY

• Dana Wynter (born Dagmar Winter on 8 June 1930, in Berlin, Germany) brought a quiet, self-assured elegance to roles on the stage, in film and on

TV. She did live drama during television's Golden Age, then turned to filmed dramas such as *Burke's Law, The Rogues* and *It Takes a Thief.* Wynter's only continuing TV role was co-starring with Robert Lansing in the short-lived spy drama *The Man Who Never Was* (1966–67). This is the first of Wynter's two unrelated appearances on *12 O'Clock High.*

- Rhys Williams (1897–1969) portrayed a succession of sympathetic character roles in *Mrs. Miniver* (1942), *The Bells of St. Mary's* (1945) and *How Green Was My Valley* (1941). On TV, he guested on *Dr. Kildare, Mission: Impossible* and played completely against type as a mad scientist on *The Wild, Wild West.* He was back in character in his second *12 O'Clock High* episode, #61 "Siren Voices."

- *F-Troop's* Ken Berry (born 3 November 1933 in Moline, Illinois), makes the first of two guest shots on *12 O'Clock High.* Berry also starred in *The Andy Griffith Show's* successor, *Mayberry R.F.D.* (1968–71) and *Mama's Family* (1983–90).

- James Wixted (born 8 September 1961 in Santa Monica, California) later took the professional name Michael-James Wixted. He appeared on the Henry Fonda series *The Smith Family* (1971–72) as the Smiths' youngest son who, as Alex McNeil writes in *Total Television*, "inexplicably spoke with a British accent." Wixted also appeared in the pilot for Fox's series *Swiss Family Robinson* (1975–76).

PERSONNEL FILE
- Walking along the beach, Ann asks Savage about his childhood. As Savage reflects on his love for flying, which started when he was a little boy, a soft version of the *12 O'Clock High* theme takes over and underscores his passion for flight.
- Savage reveals that he was born on a farm. As a little boy he "flew" diskers, harrows, combines, milking stools—any kind of farm implement. Barnstormers Ted King and His Flying Circus would come by every year. That's what he lived for. Savage remembers the sights, sounds and smells of those planes as they taxied and took off. "There wasn't anything else for me. Not ever."

DEBRIEFING
- In the teaser, Savage flies *Piccadilly Lily.*

INTELLIGENCE REPORT
- Lt. Macrae and Lt. Butterford are in the Women's Royal Naval Service, familiarly known as Wren.

- Dana Wynter wears the same uniform she wore in the 1960 Fox feature *Sink the Bismarck!* in which Wynter portrayed 2nd Officer Anne Davis. Using the off-the-rack costume accounts for the disparity between her uniform's insignia and Wynter's character being referred to as a lieutenant.
- The train compartment shared by Ann Macrae and Savage is the same set that was used later in #25 "The Threat."
- The Macrae house is the same façade as the Conboy cottage in #61 "Siren Voices" and the Swedish tavern in #71 "To Seek and Destroy."
- There is a remarkable richness and detail to the photography, as Savage and Ann walk through the countryside and the interior of the Macrae home.

FLIGHT LINE
- Mr. Macrae says "This is no talk for a bright spring morning." That would mean this episode took place sometime in spring 1943.

#11 "HERE'S TO COURAGEOUS COWARDS" (7315)

OAD:	4 December 1964
RERUN:	N/R
W:	Al C. Ward
D:	Don Medford

Hungry for a taste of aerial combat, Cpl. Ross Lawrence gets his buddy Sgt. Jimmy Smith to let him stow away on a mission. When Lawrence blasts a Focke Wulf, the mission commander, Maj. Joe Morse, naturally assumes one of his regular crew made the kill. When Morse learns that typewriter jockey Lawrence shot down the fighter, the major tries to convince him to train for combat. Much to Morse's surprise, the corporal turns down his offer. Morse wants to know how he can get to Lawrence and has a friend check into the corporal's records. It seems that Lawrence served time for being a conscientious objector. Meanwhile, Savage questions the heavy losses his group has sustained flying under Maj. Morse and wonders if Morse's marathon run of 35 missions has taken its toll. When the general confronts Morse, the major uses the issue of Lawrence's conscientious-objector status to deflect further criticism. In turn, Savage meets with Lawrence for details. The corporal explains that at the time, he felt war was wrong. Then he questioned his motivations and enlisted to prove to himself whether it was a matter of ethics or cowardice. After another mission, Morse's co-pilot, Capt. Wilson, knows that the major is hanging on by a thread. In that frame of mind, Morse storms into the orderly room and gives Lawrence an ultimatum: transfer to gunnery school. But the corporal refuses to give in. Savage still thinks Morse should be grounded and gives the major the opportunity to name his own successor. When Savage is ordered by Bomber Command to put up a maximum effort, he needs men—and looks with disappointment at Lawrence. Finally, the general orders

Lawrence to undergo an intensive training program and be put on combat status with Morse's crew. On the next mission, Capt. Wilson convinces Morse to let him take over. After the group hits the target, fighters attack but Lawrence can't bring himself to fire—until Sgt. Smith is killed. Then he opens up and downs a string of German fighters. Back at the base, Savage offers his condolences to Lawrence on the loss of his friend and then congratulates Morse on a job well done. Morse admits to the general that he is finally ready to step down and take a desk job.

Gen. Savage, Maj. Stovall
Cpl. Ross L. Lawrence ·············· Brandon de Wilde
Maj. Joseph "Joe" Morse ············ Gerald O'Loughlin
Capt. Wilson ······························ Dabney Coleman
Sgt. Jimmy Smith ························ Jimmy Hawkins
Sgt. Meadows ···························· John Newton
Ground Crew Chief ···················· Michael Harris

TDY

- Gerald S. O'Loughlin (born 23 December 1921 in New York City) served in the Marines during World War II, which may have helped hone the type of gruff, no-nonsense characters that became his specialty. He was a regular on *The Doctors* (1965–66), *Men at Law* (1971), *The Rookies* (1972–76), *Automan* (1983–84) and *Our House* (1986–88).

- Brandon de Wilde (1942-1972) will always be remembered for his Oscar-nominated performance as the boy who shouted "Come back, Shane" in the classic western *Shane*. He made his acting debut at age 9 in the Broadway play *The Member of the Wedding* and its subsequent 1952 film version. His other films included *Blue Denim* (1959), *Hud* (1963) and *In Harm's Way* (1965). On TV, de Wilde had the title role in *Jamie* (1953–54) and appeared in *Combat!*, *Night Gallery* and the classic 1961 *Thriller* episode "Pigeons from Hell."

- Like Brandon de Wilde, Jimmy Hawkins (born 13 November 1941 in Los Angeles) was a very successful child actor who worked steadily into his twenties. He's most closely associated with the holiday classic *It's a Wonderful Life* (1946), but became familiar to TV audiences with regular roles in *Annie Oakley* (1953–57) as Annie's kid brother, Tagg, and a variety of interchangeable roles on *The Donna Reed Show* (1958–66). Hawkins also did two Elvis movies, *Girl Happy* (1965) and *Spinout* (1966).

PERSONNEL FILE

- Gen. Crowe does not appear but is mentioned.

DEBRIEFING

- Morse's B-17 is named *Terrible Tillie*.
- Crew does not use oxygen masks. Morse and his co-pilot do not wear flight helmets.
- Savage says that continued heavy losses could jeopardize the future of daylight precision bombing.
- Replacements earmarked for the 918th have been reallocated to the 926th.

INTELLIGENCE REPORT

- The plot of this episode is reminiscent of one vignette in the movie and the novel, about office clerk Sgt. McIllhenny stowing away for a taste of combat.
- A draft of the script for this episode, dated 24 September 1964, included a female character, Peggy Livingston. Fox promo material credits the role of Peggy to Noreen Corcoran. It is not known if her scenes were never filmed or if they wound up on the cutting room floor.
- Footage recycled from the feature includes the belly landing and rescue vehicles racing out to the airfield.
- The soundstage tower set is used.

TOBY SIGHTING

- Toby mug is on the mantle of the Officers' Club.

#12 "SOLDIERS SOMETIMES KILL" (7314)

OAD: 11 December 1964
RERUN: 11 June 1965
TP: Edmund H. North &
           Charles Larson
Story: Edmund H. North
D: Sutton Roley

Lt. Ryan finds a disheveled, disoriented Savage wandering around London and brings him back to base. As Doc Kaiser examines the general, Savage only recalls bits and pieces of the previous night. A matchbook with the name Barbara Talbot scrawled on it provides a link—which becomes more ominous when Savage sees the newspaper headline that announces Ms. Talbot has been

Victoria Shaw

murdered. Savage later runs into Ryan and tries to get a better sense of what went on the night before. The general goes to light up a smoke and can't find his cigarette lighter, so Ryan obliges and gives him a light. According to Ryan's account, there was an air raid and Savage got back into a cab after arguing with the cabbie. Savage ran out of money, so Ryan got the cabbie's name and address. Inspector Thorne of Scotland Yard shows up to speak with Savage about Ms. Talbot's murder. From what Thorne has gathered, Ms. Talbot spent her last few hours with an American airman, so he'd like to review the group's personnel files. Thorne goes on to explain that a cigarette lighter with the insignia of the 918th group was found in Ms. Talbot's flat. That evening, Savage goes to London to look up the cabbie he tangled with, and then pays a visit to Redgrave's Club, which is closed. At the club, he meets Nicholas Redgrave, who is aghast that Savage would dare to show his face there again. With Redgrave's prompting, Savage's memory slides back to his chance meeting with Ms. Talbot. He remembers that they got off on the wrong foot but wound up dancing together and she delivered a tearful treatise on the heartbreak of war, at which point they left the club together. Something clicks with Savage and he takes a cab to Scotland Yard. Inspector Thorne says that Redgrave told him he had called Ms. Talbot's flat after midnight and that Savage answered the phone. After the general leaves the Yard, Thorne has one of his men follow Savage. Stovall comes to London to tell Savage that Pritchard has relieved Savage from the upcoming SHAEF meetings and to report back to base. Savage takes the time to explain the spot he's in. Meanwhile, Thorne phones Savage to tell him that a handyman has confessed to the crime. Just as Savage and Stovall pack up to leave for the base, Morrison the cabbie shows up and tells Savage that he called for the cab from Ms. Talbot's flat. Savage insists on revisiting Ms. Talbot's flat, hoping that something would further jog his memory. Savage asks the man who's been tailing him to call in Scotland Yard for permission. The man does so and escorts the general inside. Once Savage sees a portrait of Ms. Talbot, more memories of a romantic evening come back to him. After an idyllic date, she suddenly wanted him out immediately. Savage deduced that she drugged him, and she confessed that it was her job to lure him there for blackmail purposes. The general's reverie is shattered by the real murderer: aristocratic Nicholas Redgrave, a Nazi sympathizer, who is now determined to get rid of Savage. The two scuffle but just then, Inspector Thorne and his men break in and shoot Redgrave. At last, Stovall collects Savage and, just as they pile into a taxi, another air raid stalls their exit.

Gen. Savage, Maj. Stovall, Doc Kaiser
Inspector Thorne .... John Williams
Nicholas Redgrave .... Murray Matheson
Barbara Talbot .... Victoria Shaw
Lt. Patrick J. Ryan .... Tom Skerritt
Padget .... Terence Vliet

Maitre d'	Patrick O'Moore
Archie Morrison	Barry Macollum

TDY

- John Williams (1903–1983) launched his career on the British stage at 13 years of age and, over the years, developed a readily identifiable persona as an urbane authority figure. His defining role was as Inspector Hubbard in the stage, screen and TV versions of *Dial M for Murder*. Williams also appeared in Hitchcock's *To Catch a Thief* (1955), *D-Day the Sixth of June* (1956), *The Solid Gold Cadillac* (1956), *Witness for the Prosecution* (1958) and dealt with a fairly sedate Jerry Lewis in *Visit to a Small Planet* (1960). On television, Williams specialized in law enforcement roles on series such as *Ironside*, *Alfred Hitchcock Presents* and *The Wild, Wild West*. For a complete change of pace, Williams filled in for the ailing Sebastian Cabot as a manservant in nine episodes of *Family Affair* (1967).

- Murray Matheson (1912–1985) specialized in portraying well-bred gentlemen on both sides of the law. Australian-born Matheson began acting onstage, then moved to film and became a fixture on television in series such as *Thriller, Checkmate* and *Alfred Hitchcock Presents*. Matheson played completely against type with his role as the Clown in the 1961 *Twilight Zone* episode "Five Characters in Search of an Exit." His only continuing TV role was on *Banacek* (1972–74).

- Victoria Shaw (1935–1988) began as a model in her native Australia. She appeared in films during the 1950s and moved to TV with guest roles in series such as *77 Sunset Strip, Kraft Suspense Theatre* and the pilot for *The Man from U.N.C.L.E.* Shaw appeared later in episode #61 "Siren Voices."

- Edmund H. North (1911–1990) served in the Signal Corps during World War II, then resumed his screenwriting career. North shared the Oscar with Francis Ford Coppola for the story and screenplay of the Fox war epic *Patton* (1970). He also wrote *The Day the Earth Stood Still* (1951), *Cowboy* (1958), *Sink the Bismarck!* (1960) and *Meteor* (1979), his final film.

- Director Sutton Roley logged 2,000 hours flying B-25s during World War II.

PERSONNEL FILE

- Stovall tells Savage that, before the war, he had been a practicing attorney.
- Chandler is mentioned by Stovall as an alternate to attend the SHAEF meetings.

INTELLIGENCE REPORT

- A murdered beauty, the flashback structure of the script and a portrait of Ms.

Talbot in her flat combine to make this episode reminiscent of the 1944 Fox film *Laura*. This is one of the best constructed and most engaging scripts of the entire series.

- Although he doesn't appear in this episode, the script includes Maj. Rosen, weather officer of the 918th.
- The base PX is shown, which is actually one of the original Cal-Aero buildings located parallel to Merrill Avenue.
- The local newspaper is the *Archbury Journal.*

#13 "THE SUSPECTED" (7313)

Michael Callan

OAD:	18 December 1964
RERUN:	18 June 1965
TP:	Jack Turley & Charles Larson
Story:	Ken Pettus
D:	Don Medford

American war correspondent Clifford B. Moran has been scouring the 918th for a story and he may finally have one. He thinks one of Gen. Savage's gunners, Sgt. James Driscoll, is actually George Turner. A decade earlier, Moran covered the trial for which Turner was convicted of murdering his stepfather. Turner was sentenced to prison but subsequently escaped. Driscoll and his pregnant wife, Meg—Savage's former company clerk— celebrate their one year wedding anniversary by hosting the general at a small party. The next day, Moran shows up in Savage's office with an order from SHAEF that authorizes the reporter to interview an average enlisted man. Moran naturally wants Driscoll and meets with the sergeant to outline his plans. The reporter offers Driscoll a cigarette from his case—then has the case dusted for fingerprints. From there, Moran questions Meg and finally confronts Driscoll, calling him "Turner." Moran is convinced that Driscoll is his man and, over a beer in a pub, advises the sergeant to give up. Moran leaves the pub and, shortly afterward, so does Driscoll. Both men are spotted by Cpl. Wagner, a clerk in the 918th. The next morning, the top story on the radio and newspaper headlines is Moran's death in a subway accident...and Driscoll is AWOL. When Cpl. Wagner reports what he saw the night before, Savage races to the Driscolls' flat, only to learn that they've left. The general is both relieved and elated when he learns that Meg has just had her baby. Savage goes to the hospital, offers his congratulations and then tries to find out more about Driscoll's meeting with Moran. Later, Savage is told that a pickpocket has confessed to trying to steal Moran's wallet, causing him to topple from the underground platform. Things are complicated once again when Philip Fraser, a private investigator, shows up with the results of the fingerprint sampling Moran ordered. As the group gets ready for a raid on Frankfurt, Savage explains to Driscoll that he is going to follow through with Moran's plan and send the prints to St. Louis for comparison. The 918th bombs Frankfurt successfully, but afterward Luftwaffe fighters swarm in on the group and Savage's plane is forced to drop out of formation. Spotting an easy target, another German fighter swoops down and shoots up the cockpit, badly wounding the co-pilot and causing Savage's eyes to be scratched. The general wants to land the plane but orders a bail out. All the crew jumps except for Driscoll, who moves forward to the flight deck. There, Driscoll admits Moran was right about him, although he denies his actions 10 years earlier were murder. Savage tries to reason that if Driscoll runs now he will keep running every time another Moran shows up. With that, Driscoll turns to face his responsibilities to himself and his new family, and helps the partially-blinded Savage guide the plane to a landing. Confined to the base hospital, Savage is visited by Driscoll, who is now using his real name. Turner has agreed to go back for a retrial and Savage offers the judge advocate's services.

Gen. Savage, Maj. Stovall, Doc Kaiser, Maj. Rosen
Sgt. James Driscoll ···················· Michael Callan
Clifford B. Moran ···················· Edward Binns
Meg Driscoll ···················· Antoinette Bower
Philip Fraser ···················· John Orchard
Cpl. Harvey Wagner ·················· Nick Blair
Egan [UNCREDITED] ············ Robert Dornan

TDY

• Michael Callan (born Martin Calinieff in 22 November 1935 in Philadelphia) began his career as a comic, singer and dancer, appearing on Broadway in *West Side Story*. Under contract to Columbia, his first film was *They Came to Cordura* in 1959 followed by *The Victors* (1961) and *Cat Ballou* (1965). Callan may be best remembered for his role in the special effects epic *Mysterious Island* (1961). His TV appearances include *The FBI*, *The Fall Guy*, *Charlie's Angels* and the sitcom *Occasional Wife* (1966–67). Callan made a second appearance in #57 "Decoy."

Michael Callan on "The Suspected": "It was a fun show and I enjoyed doing it. [Director] Don Medford had been a fighter pilot. I was a young actor so I went to him for advice on what it was like to fly in combat."

• Edward Binns (1916–1990) went from Broadway to films to a busy career on television series such as *Combat!*, *The Fugitive* and *The Untouchables*. His regular series roles were on *Brenner* (1959, 1964), *The Nurses* (1962–63) and *It Takes a Thief* (1969–70). Binns' feature films included *Fail Safe* (1964), *Patton* (1970), *Judgment at Nuremberg* (1961) and the made-for-TV movie *Fireball Forward* (1972). He also did many commercials, voice-overs and narrations.

- Canadian-born Antoinette Bower added a touch of sultry allure to the many action and mystery series in which she was featured during the '60s and '70s. Bower may be best remembered for her role in the *Star Trek* Halloween episode, "Catspaw" (OAD 27 October 1967). Other notable appearances included *I Spy*, *Combat!*, *Thriller*, *Have Gun, Will Travel* and *The Man from U.N.C.L.E.* She also appeared in the miniseries *The Thorn Birds* (1983). Bower returned in episodes #19 "Faith, Hope and Sgt. Aronson" and #54 "25th Mission."

DEBRIEFING
- Robert Dornan—who would play Gallagher's co-pilot Bob Fowler during the second and third seasons—makes an unbilled appearance here as Egan, Savage's co-pilot on the Frankfurt mission.
- On the mission to Frankfurt, Savage's B-17 tail number is 3713, fuselage markings K WW. Driscoll says to Savage, "It's going to seem strange not flying the *Lily.*"
- During the mission to Frankfurt, Savage's co-pilot reports that the ship is at 10,000 feet. In turn, Savage orders the crew to go on oxygen. Savage and the co-pilot do not wear flight helmets.
- Savage's call sign over Frankfurt is Blackjack Dealer.
- The Eighth Air Force did not bomb Frankfurt until 17 August 1943.

INTELLIGENCE REPORT
- Fox promotional materials list the role of Philip Fraser (John Orchard) as Mike Fraser.
- Dominic Frontiere does that marvelously suspenseful "step" progression music cue while Savage tries to land his plane.

#14 "AN ACT OF WAR" (7302)

OAD: 25 December 1964
RERUN: N/R
W: Donald S. Sanford
D: William A. Graham

Maj. Cobb reports that his mission successfully destroyed the factory at Metz.

But intelligence officer Maj. Herrick reports that the Germans are still shipping airframes out of the Metz factory. Savage wants answers so he orders Cobb, Herrick and photo interpretation specialist Lt. Canello to his office. Canello examines the strike photos and agrees with the reports that the factory was successfully hit. Later, Gen. Crowe meets with Savage in private and gives Savage 72 hours to get the job done once and for all. Savage takes the adage "if you want something done right, do it yourself" to heart. He orders a B-17 stripped of all guns, bombsight and anything else not essential to flight. Then Herrick briefs Savage on the most effective way to reach the target with minimal enemy interference. Savage takes only Canello along, and orders Stovall not to tell Crowe about the mission until they've taken off. Flying at treetop level in the stripped-down B-17, Savage and Canello see a dummy target but then locate the real factory. German spotters see the bomber and send up anti-aircraft fire. A shell hits the B-17 and the plane spirals down in flames. Savage manages to crash- land the plane in the French countryside. He is hurt and Canello is dead. Savage leaves the plane and is attacked by Monsieur Cadol, a woodchopper. Cadol swings his ax, punctures the plane's hull and fuel spews out. A spark sets the fuel on fire and the plane turns into an inferno. Savage tries to rescue Cadol but must save himself from the flames. The whole incident was witnessed by Cadol's mute young son, Paul. Now in possession of vital tactical information, Savage makes his way cross-country toward England. He stops to rest in a barn and is confronted by Paul Cadol. Savage tries to communicate with the boy and, after he discovers that Paul is mute, decides to tie him up and push on alone— until a German patrol approaches. Paul throws them off the trail and then leads Savage to a kangaroo court that finds the general guilty of murdering Paul's father. One of the group, Malot, sparks lynch fever but another man, Verenne, intervenes to prevent the hanging until Belloc, their leader, arrives. Savage urges Paul to stand up for what's right and explain to the group that he was trying to save his father, not kill him. When Belloc finally arrives, the boy acknowledges the truth. Malot makes an emotional plea that everyone in the group has lost family and property to the American bombings, and therefore the general should die. Just as the mob moves to lynch Savage, Paul ignites a diversionary fire that gives Savage a chance to break free. Once outside, Paul leads Savage to the Maquis leader, Janville, who arranges air transportation to take the general home. At the base, Crowe good-naturedly orders Savage not to conduct any more intelligence work in person.

Gen. Savage, Maj. Stovall, Maj. Cobb, Gen. Crowe, Sgt. Nero
1st Lt. Mario Canello ·················· Norman Fell
Maj. Dwight Herrick ·················· John Kerr
Paul Cadol ····························· Michael Davis
Belloc ································· Emile Genest
Malot ································· Al Ruscio

Verenne	Jay Novello
Janville	Marcel Hillaire

TDY

- Norman Fell (1924–1998) served as an aerial gunner in World War II. After studying at The Actor's Studio, Fell appeared in numerous live TV dramas. In Hollywood, he co-starred with Robert Lansing on *87th Precinct* (1961–62). Later, Fell was paired with Mary Ann Mobley in the pilot for *The Girl from U.N.C.L.E.;* both actors were replaced by Noel Harrison and Stefanie Powers, respectively, after the series sold. But Fell is best remembered as Mr. Roper, the grouchy, homophobic landlord on *Three's Company* (1977–79) and its spin-off *The Ropers* (1979–80). Fell's other continuing roles were on *Joe and Mabel* (1956), *Dan August* (1970–71) and *Needles and Pins* (1973).

- Émile Genest (1921–2003) worked on TV and in film in his native Canada before making the move to Hollywood. He appeared in a trio of Disney features, *Big Red* (1962), *The Incredible Journey* (1963) and *Nikki, Wild Dog of the North* (1961). His TV appearances included episodes of *Combat!*, *Garrison's Gorillas* and *The Man from U.N.C.L.E.*

- Jay Novello (1904–1982) was born in Chicago but made a career of portraying people of various European nationalities. He broke into films in the 1930s and quickly built a massive resume of credits in both movies and TV. Novello's films included *The Lost World* (1960), *The Mad Magician* (1954) and *Atlantis, the Lost Continent* (1961). On TV, he appeared in Disney's *Zorro, My Three Sons, The Andy Griffith Show* and was a regular on *McHale's Navy* (1965–66).

DEBRIEFING

- In the teaser, Savage and Stovall stand in front of the B-17 with tail number 3713.
- Maj. Cobb's B-17 is *So-Wot.*
- Maj. Herrick suggests that Savage take up a P-47 for his recon flight instead of a B-17.
- Savage and Canello do not use oxygen masks because they're flying at tree-top level. Also, they both wear 50 mission caps, not flight helmets.
- The plane in which Savage wakes up after the crash is number 23308 B.
- The Eighth Air Force did not bomb Metz until 25 April 1944.

INTELLIGENCE REPORT

- The sequence where Savage's B-17 is hit by anti-aircraft fire, exploding a port engine, is taken from the 1943 RKO feature *Bombardier*. However, for this episode the image was flopped, or reversed. In *Bombardier,* the B-17 flies from screen left to screen right; in this episode, it flies screen right to screen left.

- Fox promo material credits the character of 1st Lt. Mario Canello as simply Lt. Mario.
- Savage's A-2 jacket does not have a cigarette pouch on its left sleeve.

#15 "Those Who Are About to Die" (7316)

OAD:	1 January 1965
RERUN:	N/R
W:	Harold Jack Bloom
D:	Abner Biberman

Glenn Corbett

Savage is troubled by projected losses for a particularly grueling mission. The target is a heavily defended aircraft plant in the Rhone valley, surrounded by 500 AA guns and defended by three fighter squadrons. Complicating the mission: fighter escort will leave the group 120 miles short of the target, which is nearly the extent of the B-17s' range, leaving almost no fuel for evasive action. At the last minute, weather reports indicate that fog is too heavy over the target to fly the mission. All leaves and passes are cancelled until the mission is rescheduled. Lt. Tom Lockridge has one more mission to go before he completes his tour of duty, but he's grounded until Doc Kaiser is sure he's over a bout of hepatitis. Lockridge confesses to his girlfriend, nurse Libby MacAndrews, that he is afraid the other guys in the outfit will think he's a goldbrick, pretending to be sick in order to skip the rough mission. Later, Libby asks Savage to order Lockridge not to fly. Savage appreciates Libby's concerns but won't interfere on the grounds that his intervention would not affect a combat professional such as Lockridge. With the men confined to base and the mission hanging over their heads, a series of petty fights and arguments breaks out. When news of the breakdown in morale reaches Gen. Crowe, he calls a meeting with Savage and Doc Kaiser to determine whether or not the 918th is fit to fly such a critical mission. Kaiser believes that the stress of waiting for the weather to break will cause reduced efficiency on the mission. Hearing that, Crowe wants to reassign the mission to another group. Over Crowe's and Kaiser's objections, Savage insists on having his men see the mission through. Savage believes that shouldering the mission is a matter of group pride that will help keep the 918th an effective fighting unit. That night at the Officers' Club, Libby tries to talk Lockridge—who's been discharged—out of going on the mission. Savage takes up where Libby left off, trying to point out that his recurring symptoms may mean he's still not up to speed. Axis Sally's broadcast further stirs the rumor mill. On behalf of the other men, Parmalee expresses the tension they all feel. Lockridge steps in and adds that the general has the same feelings, too. Savage admits to the men that he turned down Crowe's offer to let another group fly the mission. Just then, Stovall says that the weather changed and that the target will be clear the next morning. The mission goes on with Lockridge piloting a B-17 and leading a formation. After Lt. Parmalee's plane takes a hit from flak, Savage orders Lockridge to cover Parmalee's ship. Despite one of Lockridge's best friends being hit, he resumes command with assurance and authority. The mission is a success with minimal losses. However, it results in collateral damage: Parmalee suffers an emotional breakdown, and Libby and Lockridge's relationship is on the rocks.

Gen. Savage, Maj. Stovall, Maj. Cobb, Gen. Crowe, Doc Kaiser
Lt. Tom Lockridge ·························· Glenn Corbett
Lt. Libby MacAndrews ··············· Sally Kellerman
Lt. Steve Parmalee ······················· Tom Skerritt
T/Sgt. Mason Rutherford ·········· Dee Pollock
Lt. Carl Jensen ······························· George Brenlin
M/Sgt. Leo Hale ·························· Ken Lynch
Lt. Bill Muncie ····························· Robert Yuro
Maj. Jack C. Lloyd ······················ Phillip Terry
Voice of Axis Sally ························ UNCREDITED

TDY
- Tom Skerritt (born 25 August 1933, Detroit, Michigan) appeared in five episodes of *12 O'Clock High,* good experience for his role as commander of the Navy's fighter pilot training school in the movie *Top Gun* (1986). Skerritt toiled in television on shows such as *Combat!, Gunsmoke, The Time Tunnel* and *My Three Sons.* He made his film debut in Robert Redford's first movie, *War Hunt* (1962). Other films included the hits *M*A*S*H* (1970), *Alien* (1979) and *The Turning Point* (1977). He returned to series work with continuing roles on *Ryan's Four* (1983), *Cheers* (1987–88) and *Picket Fences* (1991–96).

- Ken Lynch (1910–1990) had a surly appearance and gravelly voice that made him perfect for tough guy roles in westerns, detective shows and sitcoms. Lynch's diverse résumé included *Bat Masterson, The Munsters, The Untouchables, The Twilight Zone, The Andy Griffith Show, The Dick Van Dyke Show* and *Gomer Pyle, USMC.* His continuing roles were on *The Plainclothesman* (1949–1954) and *McCloud* (1970–77).

- Robert Yuro (born 1 August 1932 in New York City) kept busy on TV in action roles on *Combat!*, *The FBI*, *The Invaders* and *Kolchak: The Night Stalker*.

PERSONNEL FILE
- Savage raises his voice to his superior officer, Crowe, who reminds his friend of what he's doing.

DEBRIEFING
- The target is a heavily defended aircraft plant in the Rhone valley.
- Savage's call sign is Arrowhead Leader.

INTELLIGENCE REPORT
- The voice of Axis Sally is not provided by June Foray, who did so in later episodes.
- The characters of Lt. Tom Lockridge and Lt. Libby MacAndrews appeared earlier in #3 "The Men and the Boys."
- There are parallel plots between Lockridge-Libby and Savage, and Savage and Crowe. Libby wants Savage to ground Lockridge for his own good; Crowe wants to ground the 918th for its own good.
- Act IV features another nice tour around the Chino Airport buildings.

TOBY SIGHTING
- Toby mug is on the mantle of the Officers' Club.

#16 "IN SEARCH OF MY ENEMY" (7317)

Hazel Court

OAD:	8 January 1965
RERUN:	13 August 1965
TP:	Stanford Whitmore
Story:	Jean Holloway
D:	Don Medford

A cocktail party becomes uncomfortable when Liz Woodruff introduces Savage to Maj. Peter Gray, who's just been assigned to the 918th, and Mrs. Gray—who had been the general's fiancée. The next day, Savage takes a walk to the neighborhood where the Grays have rented a flat and meets Ann Gray. They exchange pleasantries but it's clear that Mrs. Gray still has strong feelings for Savage. From there, Savage reports to

Pinetree, where Gen. Crowe discusses a key target, the rail junction at St. Avord. Aerial photos reveal clustered, camouflaged areas that could be gun emplacements. Savage convinces Crowe to let him hit the rail yard and then fly a low-level photo recon mission for a closer look at the target zone. The most qualified pilot to lead the mission is Maj. Gray. But Gray thinks that Savage assigns him so the general can spend time with his wife. The major's suspicions are given credence by Doc Kaiser, who tells Gray that the only woman Savage was ever serious about was Ann Goss—who is now Mrs. Ann Gray. After the mission is underway, Crowe informs Savage that he's just learned G-2 believes the camouflage actually conceals prototype flying bombs, which means a hot reception for the 918th. Back at the base, Gray vents his displeasure over the "milk run" turning into a massacre. But Lt. Fowler gets the photos and gives all credit for success of the mission to Gray's command of the group. That night, Savage shows up at the Grays' flat, as the major had invited him, but Ann is completely unaware of the appointment. To complicate matters, Gray has not yet come home from the base. Again, their small talk leads to analysis of what went wrong. Seeking comfort, Ann embraces the general—just as Peter enters the flat. Briefing for the next day's mission reveals the target is once more St. Avord. Unexpectedly, Savage names himself as group leader despite his game leg. Gray and Maj. Hayes will lead the other two squadrons. Before takeoff, Gray admits to Hayes his concerns about the general's intentions. Up in the air, the 918th rendezvouses with the 911th, 915th and 926th for a maximum effort. Their strength is quickly tested by attacking FWs. Maj. Hayes' ship is hit and he's badly wounded. In light of the heavy enemy fighter strength, Savage refuses to allow Hayes' ship to break formation and return to base. Gray questions the kind of man who would refuse medical attention to a friend. Gray's co-pilot, Lt. Macall, reminds the major that Savage is a commanding officer even if it means letting a friend die. After a successful bomb run, Savage attends another of Liz's cocktail parties where he meets Maj. and Mrs. Gray. They've had a long talk and looked inside themselves for the answers on how to deal with their relationship and with Savage.

Gen. Savage, Maj. Stovall, Gen. Crowe, Maj. Cobb, Doc Kaiser
Ann Goss Gray ···························· Barbara Shelley
Maj. Peter Gray ···························· Steve Forrest
Liz Woodruff ···························· Hazel Court
Maj. Jake Hays ···························· Roy Thinnes
Lt. Macall ···························· John Milford
Capt. Butcher ···························· Don Penny
Lt. Grenfell ···························· Burt Douglas
Lt. Fowler ···························· Bob Kanter
Corp. Weatherby ···························· Jo Helton

TDY

- Steve Forrest (born William Forrest Andrews on 29 September 1924 in Huntsville, Texas) is the younger brother of actor Dana Andrews. Forrest appeared in many dramatic anthologies during the 1950s, and continued in guest roles throughout the '60s. His first continuing TV role was in the made-in-England series, *The Baron* (1966). Forrest's next series, *SWAT* (1975–76) was propelled by a hit theme song. Regrettably, *SWAT* was cancelled over violence-related issues. However, *SWAT* was revived in 2003 as a feature film in which Forrest made a cameo. Samuel L. Jackson assumed Forrest's role of "Hondo" Harrelson.

- Barbara Shelley (born in 1933 in London, England) worked on both sides of the Atlantic. She's known for fantasy films such as *Village of the Damned* (1960), *The Gorgon* (1964), *Dracula, Prince of Darkness* (1966) and *Five Million Years to Earth* (1967). Her TV work includes the British series *The Avengers, The Saint* and *Danger Man,* plus the U.S. series *Route 66, The Man from U.N.C.L.E.* and *The Wackiest Ship in the Army.*

- Roy Thinnes (born 6 April 1938 in Chicago) is best known for his role as architect David Vincent, who tried to warn an unbelieving world about a takeover by space aliens in QM's *The Invaders* (1967–68). In addition, he had recurring roles on six other series: *General Hospital* (1963–66), *The Long, Hot Summer* (1965–66), *The Psychiatrist* (1970–71), *From Here to Eternity* (1980), *Falcon Crest* (1982–83) and the 1991 revival of *Dark Shadows.* Thinnes made a second, unrelated appearance in #66 "A Distant Cry."

- With his rugged appearance and gruff delivery, John Milford (1929–2000) was in demand as the heavy in westerns. He appeared in *Lawman, The Texan, The Rifleman* and *Have Gun, Will Travel,* among many others. He was a regular on *The Lieutenant* (1963–64), *The Legend of Jesse James* (1965–66) and *Enos* (1980–81). This was the first of his two appearances on *12 O'Clock High.*

PERSONNEL FILE

- Maj. Gray asks Kaiser if Savage is married. The doctor replies that "there was only one woman he was ever that serious about. An English girl. Beautiful. Ann...something." Gray fills in the blank with "Ann Goss." "Ann Goss," Kaiser replies. "You know the lady?" So where does that leave Liz Woodruff?
- Ann calls Savage a "born flier," whereas her husband is a "volunteer warrior."

DEBRIEFING

- Gray's call sign is Arrowhead Leader.
- The Lt. Fowler flying the photo recon plane is not the Lt. Fowler played by

Robert Dornan in season two.
- Crowe says the mission will go on with 918th rendezvousing with elements of the 911th, 915th and 926th.
- Savage's call sign is Pack Leader "…to Blue and Green Wolves."
- At 10,000 feet, Gray orders the crew to go on oxygen. We see only Lt. Macall put the oxygen mask up to his face, then the scene dissolves.
- Attacking fighters are FWs.
- The Eighth Air Force did not bomb St. Avord until 5 February 1944.

INTELLIGENCE REPORT
- This was the first episode of *12 O'Clock High* in its new time slot of 10:00 pm.
- The soundstage tower set was used.

#17 "THE ALBATROSS" (7312)

OAD:	15 January 1965
RERUN:	N/R
W:	Richard Landau
D:	William A. Graham

Acting is everything to Lt. Joey Kane, who shares his dreams of Hollywood stardom with his English girlfriend Angie. Lt. Kane has completed his 25th mission and is slated to tour in a morale-building show. Facing a shortage of pilots, Savage asks a favor of Lt. Kane. The general needs a co-pilot to fly a mission with him and wants Kane for the job. Much to everyone's surprise, Kane accepts. During the mission, German fighters attack Savage's plane, fouling up its oxygen system. When the general orders Kane to investigate, another fighter rips into the plane, hitting the oxygen tanks, which ignite and burn Lt. Kane's face. In Kane's chosen profession, his face was his fortune; but at the moment, Kane is emotionally bankrupt. Stewing in self pity, Kane builds a wall, isolating himself from everyone, even Angie. Doc Kaiser wants Kane to get back into real life but Savage gives in to Kane's pleas to ease his way back. Two of Kane's friends, Lt. Ankers and Lt. O'Toole, want to cheer him up so they arrange for a luau in his honor. The party features a roast pig, which causes Lt. Kane to sink into a maudlin discourse about his connection to the entrée. Meanwhile, Savage asks Angie, who has distanced herself from her reclusive lover, to try to bring Kane out of his self-inflicted cage. When Angie visits Kane in his hospital room, he cracks. The lieutenant pulls off his bandages to display his injuries, then commandeers a B-17 and takes off for one final mission. Since Kane put on a headset, Savage reasons the lieutenant wants someone to try to stop him. Savage radios Kane and tries to get the lieutenant to face up to himself. Finally, Savage tells the lieutenant that he's been like an albatross around the general's neck, but now he's cutting Kane loose. At the last second Kane pulls out of a power dive and returns to the base. Later, Kane—minus his bandages—reports to Savage. Now that the lieutenant has the inner man repaired, he's going to see a plastic surgeon to repair his outer self.

Gen. Savage, Maj. Stovall, Doc Kaiser
Lt. Joseph Timothy "Joey" Kane   Robert Drivas
Angie ·· Janine Gray
Lt. Ankers ···································· Martin West
Lt. O'Toole ································· Paul Lukather
Sentry ·· Don Eitner
Nurse ··· Dale Hogan

TDY
- This episode marked the first of two appearances on *12 O'Clock High* by Robert Drivas (1938–1986). Drivas had the ability to project a very dark, disturbed side of a character. His first feature role was with Paul Newman in *Cool Hand Luke* (1967). One of his standout performances was as renegade scientist Morgan Midas, obsessed with melting diamonds to provide him with super-speed in the 1966 *Wild, Wild West* episode "The Night of the Burning Diamond." Drivas found a home on Quinn Martin shows. He appeared on *The Fugitive* and multiple episodes of *The FBI*. A 1976 episode of QM's *The Streets of San Francisco* titled "Underground" was planned as a spin-off series featuring Drivas as a Serpico-style undercover cop.

- Janine Gray (born in 1942 in Bombay, India) had a brief but memorable career in features such as *The Americanization of Emily* (1964) and on TV in *The Avengers, T.H.E. Cat, Hogan's Heroes* and *The Man from U.N.C.L.E.*

- Don Eitner (born 29 November 1934 in San Marino, California) earned a part in an MGM movie before he graduated high school. Early in his career, Eitner appeared in such low-budget sci-fi gems as *Kronos* (1957) and *Queen of Blood* (1966). He stayed in demand as a supporting player and eventually found himself with recurring roles on *Dynasty* and *Dallas*. He returned to *12 O'Clock High* in #27 "The Mission."

DEBRIEFING
- Oxygen masks are used.
- Savage uses the call sign Leader "…to Wolf Pack."

INTELLIGENCE REPORT
- Seldom-seen views aboard the B-17 show the crawlspace from nose to bomb bay, and the area from the flight deck to bomb bay.
- If the exterior tower set looks different that's because it is. The tower used in

this episode is an original from the Cal-Aero days at Chino.
- Lansing does that "taxi call" whistle of his to get Kane to listen to him.
- The door to Doc Kaiser's office does not have his name on the window.

#18 "The Lorelei" (7319)

Rip Torn

OAD:	22 January 1965
Rerun:	9 July 1965
W:	Albert Aley
D:	Don Medford

Gen. Crowe assigns Col. Mark Royce as temporary deputy commander of the 918th. Crowe wants Savage to evaluate Royce for his suitability as a potential group leader. Royce, who has flown 45 missions and received numerous medals, is more than qualified but displays a very superstitious personality. An eerie mood falls over the group when a bomber named *Lorelei* returns to base after a mission, apparently in good shape but with its entire crew dead. That night, over drinks with Royce, Savage briefly meets Mrs. Royce who is deeply involved with Bundles for Britain. When Crowe orders a maximum effort for the next day, Savage assigns Royce to fly *Lorelei*. Royce is reluctant to take on the "ghost" ship but changes its name to *Four Leaf Clover II* and rounds up his new crew, which thinks the plane is a jinx. Even though Royce takes a rabbit's foot with him, his plane's controls jam and he's forced to break formation. Royce manages to bring the plane back to base but after the crew piles out, he notices that the nose art has been rubbed away to reveal the name *Lorelei*. Against Royce's objections, Savage orders Royce to lead the group flying *Lorelei*. This time, the bomb release mechanism fouls up so that the entire group misses its target. In London for a SHAEF conference, Savage is intercepted by Mrs. Royce, who tries to persuade the general to give her husband a fair evaluation so he can command a group of his own. She believes the decision should be a personality contest, and is insulted when the general doesn't see it her way. Back at the base, Savage gives Crowe his evaluation of Royce as being unsuitable for group command because of the colonel's reliance not only on fate but also on others around him as crutches. Not having those crutches could result in tragedy if he was alone in a command role. Royce leads the next mission, but engine trouble forces him to abort, head for home and prepare to ditch. Despite being mechanically unable to drop the bomb load, Royce orders a bail out. After the crew is out of the plane, the engines suddenly start up and *Lorelei* keeps flying. Savage takes up *Piccadilly Lily* in pursuit of *Lorelei* and shoots down the runaway bomber. Back on the ground, Royce has been assigned temporarily to SHAEF. He admits his dependence on others and wants to be flying again soon.

Gen. Savage, Maj. Stovall, Gen. Crowe, Doc Kaiser, Maj. Cobb
Col. Mark Royce .... Rip Torn
Carol Royce .... Diana van der Vlis
Lt. Danton .... Bruce Dern
Sgt. Cryder .... Paul Sorenson
Lt. Myrowitz .... Barry Russo

TDY
- Rip Torn (born 6 February 1931 in Temple, Texas) is a powerful and flexible actor. He can go from over the top parody in *You're a Big Boy Now* (1966) to sinister in *Coma* (1978) to his sensitive portrayal of poet Walt Whitman in the TV special *Song of Myself* (OAD 13 February 1974). Torn was President Richard Nixon in the miniseries *Blind Ambition*. He appeared in *RoboCop 3* (1993), both *Men in Black* movies and was the voice of Zeus in Disney's *Hercules* (1997).

- Diana van der Vlis (1935–2001) was a regular on the soaps *Ryan's Hope, The Secret Storm* and *Where the Heart Is*. Her prime time appearances included *Checkmate, The Rogues, Route 66* and *T.H.E. Cat*.

- Paul Sorensen (born 1926 in Kenosha, Wisconsin) specialized in roles that not only used his burly stature but also engaged his stage training. Sorensen did well in westerns with appearances on *Cheyenne, The Westerner* and *Have Gun, Will Travel*, among many others. He moved forward to crime shows such as *The Rogues, Burke's Law* and *The Untouchables;* sitcoms such as *Bewitched, My Three Sons* and *The Brady Bunch* and a recurring role on *Dallas* (1979–86). Film roles included *Hang 'Em High* (1968), *Smokey and the Bandit* (1977) and *Star Trek III: The Search for Spock* (1984).

DEBRIEFING
- After the initial mission, Savage complains to Crowe that he could have used three full squadrons.
- Royce changes the B-17 named *Lorelei* to *Four Leaf Clover II*.
- Savage's call sign is Badger Leader; Royce is Red Badger One.
- Neither Savage's nor Royce's crews use oxygen masks. Savage and his co-pilot do not wear flight helmets.
- FWs attack the formation.
- Royce's first call sign is Blue Jay leader; his second call sign is Red Dog leader.

- Nice shot of the brick fence posts along Merrill Avenue at Chino Airport.
- A great cloud-shadow effect on the *Piccadilly Lily* flight deck as the plane goes through a cloud bank.
- The soundstage tower set was used.

Sorrell Booke

#19 "FAITH, HOPE AND SGT. ARONSON" (7318)

OAD: 29 January 1965
RERUN: N/R
W: Charles Larson
D: Laslo Benedek

Gen. Savage returns from a mission so badly wounded by flak that Doc Kaiser thinks he's had it. Hours of surgery pull the general through, but Kaiser hesitates on removing a shard of flak near Savage's heart. Instead, he recommends calling in a coronary specialist, Dr. Simon Lewis. Sgt. Herschel Aronson, confined to the base hospital, is devastated when his lifelong friend, Sgt. Sol Barstein, dies. Barstein's death creates a vacancy so that Gen. Savage can be placed in a bed. Sgt. Aronson's grief takes over his life and shakes his deeply religious nature. But his new neighbor, Gen. Savage, gets him to open up and talk about why he is abandoning his convictions. Aronson confesses that, in respect to God's wishes, he has kept his body a temple of purity, not smoking, drinking or fornicating. Determined to make up for lost time, the sergeant signs himself out of the hospital and heads for Archbury. At the cinema, Aronson meets Ivy Wescott. They want to see the movie but are too early for the first show. It begins to rain, so Ivy suggests they go to her flat. Once there, the two become incredibly uncomfortable. Aronson has never been alone with a woman and Ivy has never been alone with a man. He follows his impulse and does what he thinks any man would do: he kisses her. Ivy admits how sheltered her life is. Aronson relates to this clear parallel and becomes protective of her. As he leaves her flat for the afternoon, Aronson stumbles down a flight of stairs and winds up back in the base hospital. After hearing Aronson's story, Savage commends the sergeant for sticking to his core beliefs. Aronson seems to have regained his faith—until he learns that the plane carrying Dr. Lewis has crashed, killing the man who was Savage's only hope. Aronson is discharged, and he meets Ivy at the main gate, prepared for a wild night of debauchery. As they leave, the guard at the base gate tells Aronson they need someone with type AB blood for Savage's surgery. Of course, the sergeant does and he realizes he's fighting a higher power. Aronson returns to the hospital and offers his blood. After the operation, Doc Kaiser tells him that the general will be fine and thanks Aronson. In turn, Aronson gives thanks to God for seeing him through his crisis of faith. Following a three-week recovery, Savage returns to command. He acknowledges Aronson's request to marry Ivy and gladly approves.

Gen. Savage, Maj. Stovall, Gen. Crowe, Maj. Cobb, Doc Kaiser

Sgt. Herschel Aronson	Sorrell Booke
Lt. Jenkins	Phyllis Love
Ivy Wescott	Antoinette Bower
Sgt. Gruenwald	James Frawley
Sgt. Sol Barstein	Joseph Perry
Sgt. Fry	Charles McDaniel

TDY

- Sorrell Booke (1930–1994) was a gifted, stage-trained actor who will, ironically, always be remembered for his farcical performance as Jefferson Davis "Boss" Hogg on *The Dukes of Hazzard* (1979–85). His legacy runs the gamut from gritty drama to sitcoms, including *Naked City, M*A*S*H, Columbo, Dr. Kildare, The Patty Duke Show* and *All in the Family.*

- Phyllis Love (born 21 December 1925 in Des Moines, Iowa) built up a reputation for strong, dramatic performances in series such as *Ben Casey, The Outer Limits, Alfred Hitchcock Presents* and multiple appearances on QM's *The FBI.*

- James Frawley (born in 1937) had a respectable run as an actor guest starring on series such as *The Outer Limits, My Favorite Martian* and *Voyage to the Bottom of the Sea.* Soon Frawley veered away from acting and directed multiple episodes of *The Monkees* (1966–68), for which he won the 1967 Emmy for Outstanding Directorial Achievement in Comedy. He continues to direct episodic TV such as *Ed, Smallville* and *Ally McBeal.*

PERSONNEL FILE

- Doc Kaiser asks Stovall and Cobb for their blood types; both are O. Savage is AB.
- The glass window on the door of Doc Kaiser's office reads Dr. Donald Kaiser.
- Doc Kaiser studied under Dr. Lewis.

DEBRIEFING

- Cobb's B-17 is *Nervous Nellie.*

- Crowe has talked Pritchard into holding off on the Ruhr strike because Crowe knows that Savage wants to fly the mission.
- In the teaser, Savage flies *Piccadilly Lily* back to base.

INTELLIGENCE REPORT
- Working title of this episode was "The Nebbish."
- Gen. Pritchard does not appear but his name is mentioned.
- *Command Decision* stock footage is used showing a B-17 landing on one wing, spinning and blowing up.
- The Star and Bottle is closed; it was wrecked in the bombing.
- At the Archbury Cinema, Ivy and Aronson see posters for *The Mark of Zorro*, a 1940 Twentieth Century-Fox film.
- The soundstage tower set is used.

Keir Dullea

#20 "To Heinie, With Love" (7321)

OAD:	5 February 1965
RERUN:	N/R
TP:	Gilbert Ralston & Charles Larson
Story:	Gilbert Ralston
D:	Ralph Senesky

Savage's crew is eager to meet its newest member, Lt. Kurt Mueller. But Mueller gets off on the wrong foot by shunning the crew's attempts at making him feel welcome. On his first mission in the *Piccadilly Lily*, navigator Mueller and bombardier Lt. Magill exchange words, capped with Magill calling Mueller "heinie." A flak burst throws Mueller on the deck and his wallet spills out. Magill opens it and sees a picture of a man saluting in front of a Nazi flag. Mueller tries to recover his wallet and a fight breaks out. Savage notices that the nose guns aren't firing, so he sends his co-pilot to investigate. With the fight broken up, Mueller grabs the .50-caliber gun and promptly shoots down an enemy fighter. Back at the base, Savage's feuding navigator and bombardier report to his office where they reluctantly divulge what happened. The general asks for Mueller's wallet and questions him about the photos. The snapshots are of his mother and his late father, a member of the German American Bund. Under orders from Gen. Crowe to make another strike on a target he thought he had destroyed, Savage comes up with a new approach using a single B-17. Because of heavy overcast and the mountains surrounding the target, the navigator will be key to the success of the mission. Savage explains the issues surrounding Mueller and adds that the lieutenant is probably the best navigator he's ever had—but qualifies that by saying Mueller's background bothers him. On a nature walk, Mueller meets an attractive, young deaf woman, Nora Burgess, and loses track of time. The mission takes place as planned but when the *Lily* emerges from the cloud cover it's miles away from the target. With the *Lily* exposed, German fighters move in and Magill is shot by German fire. Meanwhile, Mueller assumes Magill is dead and frantically works to get the plane back home. Back at the base, medics arrive to take care of Magill but they're too late. A medic says that Magill bled to death but a simple tourniquet could have saved his life. Naturally, the rest of the crew assumes Mueller let Magill die on purpose. Savage sees his crew falling apart and is ready to have Muller transferred. Mueller seeks solace in the country, where he shares his burden with Nora. She gives Mueller the strength to return to base where Savage alerts him that he's on for the next day's return to Eitzen. Mueller gets the *Lily's* crew right on target and the bombs drop—for except the incendiaries, which are stuck in the bomb bay. A second attempt to dump the load succeeds partially, with the exception of one incendiary that flies loose into the radio room. Muller throws the bomb out of the plane, burning his hands severely in the process. Released from a stay in the hospital, Mueller returns to the barracks—and a surprise party thrown by the *Lily's* crew and Nora. He appreciates the sentiment and joins in the celebration.

Gen. Savage, Gen. Crowe, Gen. Pritchard
Lt. Kurt Mueller ·············· Keir Dullea
Nora Burgess ·············· Jill Haworth
Lt. Morgan Pike ·············· Ralph Williams
Lt. Wynn Magill ·············· Stewart Moss
Sgt. Robert Bergen ·············· Bard Stevens
Lt. Daniels ·············· Jimmy Hayes

TDY

· The signature role for Keir Dullea (born 30 May 1936 in Cleveland, Ohio) was Dave Bowman in the groundbreaking *2001: A Space Odyssey* (1968) and its 1984 sequel, *2010*. Dullea made a name for himself with the independent feature *David and Lisa* (1962) and subsequent art films such as *The Naked Hours* (1964). Of the latter film, Dullea said, "This role is a big departure for me and I had to go to Italy to do it. It's [the] first time I do not play a neurotic." Dullea also reprimanded the industry for "pigeonholing" actors by their perceived capabilities. "Television will type [cast] you even faster than films. It's worse in the TV industry and eventually I avoided doing any more TV work."

· Screenwriter Gilbert Ralston (born 1912) is best known for penning the script for the original *Willard* (1971), adapted from his 1968 novel *Ratman's Notebook,* and its 1972 sequel *Ben.* He also did a smattering of TV work including scripts for *Naked City, Alfred Hitchcock* and the pilot for *The Wild, Wild West.*

- Stewart Moss (born in 1938 in Chicago, Illinois) debuted on television in 1964 and worked steadily in films and TV for nearly three decades. Among his appearances in the 1960s were *Star Trek, The Invaders* and *Hogan's Heroes.* He was a regular on *Fay* (1975) and *Beyond Westworld* (1980). One of his acting projects was the unsold 1973 pilot for a TV version of *Catch-22* starring Richard Dreyfuss as Yossarian. Moss' other guest appearances included *Hart to Hart, Magnum P.I.* and *Remington Steele.*

PERSONNEL FILE
- Savage relates an incident in 1934 when a girl he knew tried to demonstrate at a Nazi rally and they beat her to death. She died in his arms.

DEBRIEFING
- Savage flies *Piccadilly Lily;* we see its nose art. The fuselage has only national designation.
- Savage's call sign is Arrowhead Leader.
- Crew does not use oxygen masks.
- Crowe reflects on a raid by the medium bombers of the 909th.
- Target is the Eitzen rail junction. Eitzen was not an official target of the Eighth Air Force.

#21 "THE CLASH" (7320)

OAD:	12 February 1965
RERUN:	2 July 1965
TP:	Jack Turley & Mike Adams
Story:	Mike Adams
D:	Josef Leytes

Flying back from a mission, Savage's plane is so badly shot up that he must turn command over to Maj. Cobb and drop out of formation. Seeing the lone aircraft limping along, a single Me 109 moves in for the kill. Savage's crew is able to down the fighter but not before it does critical damage to the B-17, forcing Savage to ditch in the Channel. When the general surfaces, he spots a life raft and swims to it. Savage sees a man floundering in the water and drags him aboard. The other person is Col. Hans Dieter, the German flier who shot down Savage's plane. Col. Dieter's arms are badly injured. Savage wants to radio for help but Dieter pulls a gun and orders the general to move away from the radio.

Dieter doesn't intend to sit out the war in an Allied POW camp, so he orders the general to row toward Norway. Fog and a torrential rain storm prevent Air-Sea Rescue planes from seeing the raft. Surviving the elements together doesn't create a bond of friendship between the two combatants. When they approach a small, rocky island, Savage leaps overboard and swims for shore. The tide carries in the raft, but Dieter spills out and his foot gets stuck in the rocks on the bottom of the bay. Seizing an opportunity, Savage tries to retrieve the raft but Dieter shoots him in the arm. The two strike a bargain: Dieter will throw away his gun if Savage rescues him. But the deceitful German only pretends to give up his weapon. Improvising, Savage uses a handful of sand to blind Dieter, then runs for shelter. The colonel shoots blindly, missing Savage, but he believes that he has killed the general. Savage waits until dark and moves in on his adversary. The general grabs a flare gun and fires it to startle Dieter, then wrestles with the colonel. In the struggle, Dieter's gun goes off, killing the German. Savage sets off the raft's emergency distress beacon and lights a signal fire. Air-Sea Rescue spots the general and lands to pick him up. At the base hospital, Savage gives Dieter's wallet, which includes photos of the German's family, to Stovall and asks him to send it and a condolence letter to the colonel's widow.

Gen. Savage, Maj. Stovall, Maj. Cobb, Gen. Crowe, Doc Kaiser, Maj. Rosen
Col. Hans Dieter ·························· Albert Paulsen
Col. Chandler ······························ Burt Metcalfe

TDY
- Albert Paulsen (1925–2004) displayed a tremendous range of acting ability, perhaps best demonstrated by his two roles on *Combat!* He played a German foot soldier in the debut episode "Forgotten Front" (OAD 2 October 1962) and then, just one month later, rose up the ranks to play a German general desperate to break away from the Reich in "Escape to Nowhere" (OAD 20 November 1962). The native of Ecuador won an Emmy in 1964 for "One Day in the Life of Ivan Denisovich" on *The Bob Hope Chrysler Theater*. His continuing roles were on *A World Apart* (1971), *Doctor's Hospital* (1975–76), *Stop Susan Williams* (1979) and *General Hospital* (1988). Paulsen appeared again in #40 "Runway in the Dark."

PERSONNEL FILE
- Savage reveals that he grew up on his family's 40-acre farm in Ohio. He belonged to 4-H and raised a prize heifer.

DEBRIEFING
- On the mission in the teaser, Cobb's call sign is Bonus One; Savage's is Peoria.
- Gen. Crowe makes Stovall acting C.O. of the 918th in Savage's absence.

- The island where Savage and Dieter wash up is west of the Trondheim sub pens.

INTELLIGENCE REPORT

- Achieving the flow of this seafaring yarn was a complex job. Long shots of Savage and Dieter in the raft were actually done out on the Pacific. Some water work was done in a tank at Twentieth Century-Fox studios. Scenes with dialogue were done in a soundstage against a process screen.
- The printed script credits the teleplay to Jack Turley and Meyer Dolinsky from a story by Meyer Dolinsky. Prolific screenwriter Dolinsky was known to use pseudonyms, including Mike Dolinsky and Michael Adams.
- Chandler is now a full colonel. The script for this episode describes Chandler as Gen. Crowe's aide.

Earl Holliman

#22 "THE TICKET" (7322)

OAD:	26 February 1965
RERUN:	16 July 1965
W:	Al C. Ward
D:	Josef Leytes

Gen. Crowe outlines a major underground mission that hinges on the 918th taking out the Braubourg dam. Savage contends that the target is impossible for a B-17 to reach, but suggests that a P-51 has the speed and maneuverability to do the job. Crowe agrees, but with one condition: Savage must find the right pilot for the job. Savage thinks his man is Lt. Paul Steiger, a flier from a rural background, who flaunts the fact that he has nothing to live for. Steiger's background in flying fighters and bombers makes him the ideal candidate. When Savage pitches the mission, he accepts without blinking. That evening Steiger sees his girlfriend, Myra, and buys some sweepstakes tickets that she's selling. Myra tries to lead Steiger toward a commitment in their relationship but he backs away and starts training for his mission the next day. After explaining the complexities of the mission to Steiger, Savage is amazed at how coolly the lieutenant takes it. But, just after Steiger gives his firm commitment to the project, Myra rushes in to tell him that he's won the top sweepstakes prize of £20,000. This puts a different spin on his thinking. Now Steiger's crew, who justifiably thought his attitude was a little weird, offers to celebrate with him. After a few drinks, some of the other pilots let a few words slip about Steiger's mission. Myra questions Steiger, but all he can talk about is his new-found wealth and the high-flying life it will buy them. Steiger's vision of the future soon gets in the way of his training, to the point where he asks Savage for permission to marry Myra before the big mission. The general tries to make Steiger understand that thousands of people will be depending on him and refuses to grant permission. The training continues, as does Steiger's binging on booze and gambling. Myra grows angry and intolerant of Steiger's excesses because they cover a new fear that he's never shown before. Steiger replies that he's afraid now because he finally has something to live for. Savage gives in and authorizes Steiger's request to be married, then restricts the lieutenant to the base until takeoff. On the morning of the mission, Savage leads a flight of B-17s to act as decoys for Steiger's P-51. Steiger rendezvouses with the group but at his scheduled point of descent, he freezes. Savage radios Steiger to convince him to go through with the mission. Steiger does and delivers a direct hit that smashes the dam. With the mission behind him, Steiger marries Myra. At the wedding, Savage buys all the sweepstakes tickets she has and intends to pass them out to his other pilots, hoping that Steiger's brand of luck will strike again.

Gen. Savage, Maj. Stovall, Gen. Crowe
Lt. Paul H. Steiger ·························· Earl Holliman
Myra Bentley ······························· Elen Willard
Lt. Lou Crain ······························· Donald Harron
Lt. Morgan ································· Jud Taylor
Sergeant ···································· Hal Riddle
Corporal ···································· Glen Sipes

TDY

· Earl Holliman (born 11 September 1928 in Delhi, Louisiana) is best remembered for his role as Angie Dickinson's boss on *Police Woman* (1974–78). After serving in the Navy, Holliman studied acting and broke into films in 1953. Three years later, his performance in *The Rainmaker* (1956) won Holliman a Golden Globe. Other movies included *Giant* (1956), *Gunfight at the OK Corral* (1957) and *The Sons of Katie Elder* (1965). His first TV appearance was a live production of *Playhouse 90* co-starring with Dean Jagger, Academy Award winner for the film version of *12 O'Clock High*. Holliman appeared in the pilot for *The Twilight Zone* (OAD 2 October 1959). His other continuing series roles were in *Hotel de Paree* (1959–60) and *The Wide Country* (1962–63).

Earl Holliman on "The Ticket"—on the Chino location: "First thing in the morning, the airfield set at Chino was really cold and kind of foggy." On working with Robert Lansing and director Josef Leytes: "Bob Lansing was a sweet guy. Joe [Leytes] spoke with an accent. Joe had an image in his head; he wanted Bob to stand in a certain place, near an airplane wing. But

Lansing didn't like to work that way, so Bob seemed very uptight with Joe." On the P-51 mock-up: "I remember sitting in the mock-up and stagehands shaking the plane to give the illusion of flying." On co-star Elen Willard: "I found out years later that she had quit acting because it was such an emotionally painful experience for her."

- Elen Willard had a short career but delivered some very credible performances in series such as *Combat!; The Twilight Zone; Have Gun, Will Travel* and *The Man from U.N.C.L.E.*

- Donald Harron (born 19 September 1924 in Toronto, Ontario, Canada) also appeared in episodes #30 and #31 "POW," parts one and two, and #46 "Between the Lines." His series television work included *The Outer Limits, The Time Tunnel* and *The Man from U.N.C.L.E.* Harron published several humorous books and became very active in broadcasting in his native Canada, hosting his own program, *The Don Harron Show* (1983–85).

- Jud Taylor (born 25 February 1940) also appeared in the pilot episode, "Follow the Leader" and #6 "Pressure Point." Shortly after completing this installment, Taylor turned to directing episodic television such as *Star Trek, T.H.E. Cat* and *The Man from U.N.C.L.E.* He excelled at his new craft and was soon an A-list director of pilots and made-for-TV movies such as *Tail Gunner Joe* (1977) *The Great Escape II* (1988) and *The Old Man and The Sea* (1990).

PERSONNEL FILE
- Crowe calls Savage the "best group commander in England."

DEBRIEFING
- Crews do not use oxygen masks.
- Steiger's B-17 crew is surprised to see a P-51 on a bomber base.
- The concrete enclosure that conceals the P-51 is at Chino. It appears later in #46 "Between the Lines," #60 "Day of Reckoning" and #62 "Gauntlet of Fire."
- The P-51 has no nose art, no call number and only the national insignia.
- On the Braubourg mission, Savage uses the call sign Able Leader.

INTELLIGENCE REPORT
- The Braubourg dam mission is similar to that in the 1954 film *The Dam Busters,* based on the book by Paul Brickhill.
- This episode marks the first appearance of the P-51 mock-up.
- Stock footage of the dam bursting came from the 1955 Fox film *Rains of Ranchipur.*

· Although early model P-51s were used by the RAF, Mustangs were not in common use by the USAAF during the time covered by season one.

#23 "THE TRAP" (7323)

OAD:	5 March 1965
RERUN:	23 July 1965
W:	Richard L. Newhafer
D:	Ralph Senesky

Savage and Maj. Stovall are in London for an important meeting with SHAEF regarding a difficult target. Unable to sleep, the general goes out for a walk but is detoured by an air raid. An air raid warden directs Savage and four other people to seek shelter in the cellar of an abandoned building. Outside, a bomb blast buries the air raid warden. Inside, the group settles in and introduces themselves: Eleanor Nichols, pregnant and unmarried; Lady Constance, a noblewoman who's fallen on hard times; Dr. Lewis Glenway, a member of the idle rich; and Bert Higgs, a young cockney back in London to join the military. As the bombing continues, a Heinkel slams into the building, delivering a wave of rubble—and a ticking bomb armed with a delayed action fuse. Glenway has a panic attack causing Savage to punch him. Then, the general, maintaining his composure, decides to disarm the bomb with Higgs' assistance. Meanwhile, Stovall searches everywhere for Savage. Finally, at a hospital, Stovall's story is overheard by the badly-wounded air raid warden, who tells where he left the general. Stovall and a team of air raid wardens find the building and start digging. While the bomb continues to tick, Miss Nichols goes into labor and Glenway confesses that he is not a doctor, just a poseur who drifts through life in a series of roles. Lady Constance steps in and delivers the baby. Continuing to work on the bomb, Savage is distracted by a rat. The general deduces that there must be another way out, and discovers a coal chute leading up. He convinces Higgs—who is claustrophobic—to make the climb and tells the rescuers to stop digging. Without Higgs to assist Savage, Glenway lends a hand, allowing the general to pull out the detonator. The rescue team brings everyone to safety. Stovall is ready to cancel Savage's meeting, but the general retorts that after what he's been through, nothing is hopeless.

Gen. Savage, Maj. Stovall	
Lady Constance	Hermione Baddeley
Bert Higgs	John Leyton
Dr. Lewis Glenway	David Frankham
Eleanor Nichols	Dinah Anne Rogers
Air Raid Warden	Jack Raine

Civil Defense Worker ················· Ashley Cowan
Civil Defense Worker ················ George Pelling

TDY

- Hermione Baddeley (1906–1986) brought a delightful touch to matronly British characters in films such as *Mary Poppins* (1964), *The Unsinkable Molly Brown* (1964) and *Marriage on the Rocks* (1964). She provided the voice for Madame Adelaide Bonfamille in Disney's *The Aristocats* (1970). Her regular TV roles were on *The Cara Williams Show* (1964–65), *The Good Life* (1971–72), *Maude* (1974–77), *Little House on the Prairie* (1977–79) and *Shadow Chasers* (1985).

- David Frankham (born 26 February 1926 in Kent, England) should get an award for best hysterical screaming. He lets loose in this episode when he faces the prospect of being trapped with a live bomb. But, by far, his best work was the relentless fit unleashed during the *Star Trek* episode "Is There in Truth No Beauty?" (OAD 18 October 1968). Frankham appeared later in #49 "The Slaughter Pen" and #71 "To Seek and Destroy."

- John Leyton (born 17 February 1939 in Frinton-On-Sea, Essex, England) is probably best known by American audiences for his role in the short-lived World War II series *Jericho* (1966-67). But Leyton had quite a career outside the States. In the early 1960s, he had a string of hit pop records, including "Cupboard Love," "Johnny Remember Me," "Tell Laura I Love Her" and "I'll Cut Your Tail Off." Leyton artfully segued into acting with roles in films such as *The Great Escape* (1963), *Guns At Batasi* (1964), *Von Ryan's Express* (1965), *Every Day's a Holiday* (1965), *The Idol* (1966) and *Krakatoa, East of Java* (1969).

DEBRIEFING

- The target is Strausbourg. The Eighth Air Force did not bomb Strausbourg until 1 April 1944.

INTELLIGENCE REPORT

- The set used for Savage's and Stovall's hotel room is the same one used in #5 "The Climate of Doubt."
- The set used for the cellar was used previously in #4 "The Sound of Distant Thunder," but shot from the reverse angle.
- Fox promo material credits the script to Richard L. Newhafer, Chester Krumholz & Charles Larson.
- The sequence of a German bomber slamming into a building was used earlier in #4 "The Sound of Distant Thunder" and again in #39 "Show Me a Hero, I'll Show You a Bum."

#24 "END OF THE LINE" (7324)

OAD:	12 March 1965
RERUN:	N/R
W:	Dean Riesner
D:	Sutton Roley

Joe Gallagher's head cold keeps him out of a mission to St. Nazaire. After a distress signal comes from his plane, Gallagher learns that Larry Hollander, the pilot who took his place, was killed. Gallagher blames himself for Hollander's death and sees to wrapping up Hollander's personal affairs—including telling Hollander's fiancée, May Hudson, that he's dead. To help bring Gallagher out of his funk, Savage offers him a secret mission: piloting a specially outfitted B-17 to drop a commando team and provide air support for a mission to liberate a captured underground leader. Gallagher accepts but still takes it upon himself to personally break the news to Miss Hudson, even when it means missing a key briefing about the commando raid and keeping his girlfriend, Lt. Claire Cummings, waiting. Next day, Gallagher begins training for the mission and also starts a precarious relationship with May, which alienates Claire Cummings and throws off his focus on the mission. Gallagher's concentration suffers so much that, during a practice run, he nearly clips the parachuting commandos by pulling up too fast and losing control, eventually ditching the B-17. After a dressing down by Savage, Gallagher gives May £300 to save her Aunt Nell's shop. He then breaks off their relationship and makes up with Claire. But then, Gallagher gets an emergency phone call from Aunt Nell: May supposedly tried to commit suicide. Gallagher races to May's apartment, where she confesses that she's carrying Hollander's baby. Gallagher says that he'll make things right for her and goes straight to Savage for permission to marry May. Stovall tries to set up a meeting between May and Savage but Aunt Nell says that her niece isn't home. She's out at a pub. Next day, Savage tells a perplexed Gallagher that he and Stovall found May at the tavern in the company of another man. Savage presents further evidence by having Capt. Whitelaw read a British Intelligence profile of May, which includes a lengthy arrest record and a stint as an exotic model. Gallagher confronts May and encourages her to have a checkup at the base hospital to make sure the baby is healthy. Under pressure, May breaks down and confesses there is no baby. Gallagher walks out and, with his mind clear, goes back to the base and prepares for the mission.

Gen. Savage, Maj. Stovall, Gen. Crowe	
Maj. Joe Gallagher	Paul Burke
May Hudson	Sarah Marshall
Lt. Claire Cummings	Barbara Feldon
Nell Forrester	Florence Sundstrom

Capt. Whitelaw	Ben Wright
Capt. Carmichael	Michael St. Claire
Lt. Lewin	Charlotte Stewart
Lt. Dinardo	James Douglas

TDY

- Sarah Marshall (born 25 March 1933 in London, England) is the daughter of actors Herbert Marshall (1890–1966) and Edna Best (1900–1974). Marshall appeared on live, dramatic TV anthologies in the 1950s. From her film debut in *The Long, Hot Summer* (1958), she went to the grade-C Roger Corman picture *Teenage Caveman* (1958). She worked steadily on series such as *Hong Kong, Thriller, The Rogues* and *The Wild, Wild West*. She was also in the miniseries *Scruples* (1980).

- Barbara Feldon (born 12 March 1932 in Pittsburgh, Pennsylvania) will be forever remembered as Maxwell Smart's long-suffering partner Agent 99 on the hit comedy *Get Smart* (1965–70). But at the time this episode was filmed, Feldon was best known for her role pitching Top Brass men's hair grooming product. In the commercial, Feldon lay seductively on a tiger skin rug and enticed male viewers to "sic 'em, Tiger." While on retainer with Revlon, Feldon also did ads for Five Day Deodorant pads and was rolled up in a carpet for Chemstrand. The ads led to dramatic roles on TV including *Flipper, The Nurses, Dupont Show of the Week* and *East Side, West Side*. Feldon also made frequent appearances on the daytime game show *Missing Links*.

- Ben Wright (1915–1989) served in the King's Royal Rifle Corps from 1940–1946. The next year, he moved to Hollywood and appeared in many films for Fox during the 1950s. He provided the voice for Roger in Disney's *101 Dalmatians* (1961) and narrated Fox's massive *Cleopatra* (1963). Wright's most notorious part was as Zeller, the Nazi who pursues the Von Trapp family in Fox's *The Sound of Music* (1965). He was a very familiar face and voice on TV in such series as *Combat!, The Outer Limits, The Twilight Zone, The Man from U.N.C.L.E.* and *Voyage to the Bottom of the Sea*. Wright later appeared in #73 "The Ace."

PERSONNEL FILE

- Gallagher and Hollander were at West Point together. Hollander used to spend summers at the Gallaghers' summer home in Connecticut.
- Maj. Cobb is mentioned.

DEBRIEFING

- Gallagher's plane is still called *Leper Colony* as it was in #1 "Golden Boy Had Nine Black Sheep."

- As Gallagher practices flying for the mission, Savage and Stovall watch from the airfield. In the background is the Cal-Aero tower. Later, Stovall and Savage watch from the Cal-Aero tower catwalk.
- During the time period covered by season one, the Eighth Air Force bombed the port and U-boat base at St. Nazaire on 9 November 1942, 14 November 1942, 17 November 1942, 18 November, 23 November 1942, 3 January 1943, 16 February 1943, 1 May 1943, 29 May 1943 and 28 June 1943.

INTELLIGENCE REPORT
- Archbury Cinema is shown, last seen in #19 "Faith, Hope and Sgt. Aronson."
- When Gallagher ditches, stock footage of the water landing is pulled from the Fox feature *Captain Eddie* (1945). The footage would be reused in several subsequent episodes.

#25 "THE THREAT" (7325)

OAD:	19 March 1965
RERUN:	3 September 1965
W:	Jack Turley
D:	Ralph Senesky

Axis Sally predicts that Gen. Savage will have a fatal accident that afternoon. Just then, an explosion at the motor pool sends metal shards smashing through the windows of the Officers' Club. Everyone, including itinerant barber "Gilly" Bright, races outside to see what happened. Savage receives a minor cut and is treated at the hospital, where Doc Kaiser introduces him to the base's newest nurse, Lt. Dietrich. Kaiser orders Dietrich to give Savage a tetanus vaccination but the overworked nurse accidentally fills the hypodermic with morphine—and is stopped in the nick of time by the doctor. Col. Reed from G-2 arrives to investigate the explosion and to check out everyone who has access to the base. Crowe wants Savage to leave the base, but Savage insists on staying to help keep up morale. Axis Sally's next broadcast mentions the 13th and a cryptic message about Savage putting out a fire. The next day, Savage leads the 918th on a mission to destroy a strategic railhead. On the mission, German fighters approach but do not attack the formation. After the group lands, Axis Sally makes another broadcast, boasting how she asked German fighters to leave the *Piccadilly Lily* alone because she still had something special for Savage. Col. Reed announces that he plans to take three suspects into custody, one of them is Nurse Dietrich. Reed has discovered that she is of German descent. Her brother was a flier with the 918th and Lt. Dietrich moved mountains to be assigned to the 918th. That night, as Savage leaves the base hospital, he's almost run down by a speeding jeep driven by Cpl. Jones, who has been recording the Axis Sally broadcasts for the general. Jones is cleared but as Friday the 13th approaches, another suspect emerges: barber

Gilly Bright. On Friday, the operations building is surrounded by guards. Even Maj. Stovall wears a sidearm. With all the security, no one thinks twice about allowing Gilly in to give Savage a shave and a haircut. After Axis Sally makes another broadcast Savage decides he's had enough of the tension and suggests that he and Gilly take a trip to a remote fishing spot for some relaxation. Savage feels that he's in the clear and wants a good night's sleep in order to be fresh for the next day. Gilly also prepares for the trip by packing his rod and reel—and gun. Savage and Gilly meet at the train station, find their seats—in compartment #13—and begin their adventure. Just before 1:00 p.m.—thirteen hundred hours—Gilly pulls out his gun and aims it at the general. Gilly's concentration breaks and Savage lunges at him. The two fight it out in the cramped compartment, breaking windows and pushing open the outer door. Finally, Savage is able to elbow Gilly in the stomach, sending the barber flying out the open door. Back at the base hospital, Savage is alive but suffers from a broken rib. G-2 finds Gilly's body and a notebook with the names of German spies in the UK.

Gen. Savage, Maj. Stovall, Gen. Crowe, Doc Kaiser
Gilbert "Gilly" Bright ················ Laurence Naismith
Col. Stuart Reed ···························· Harold Gould
Lt. Adrienne Dietrich ··············· Stanja Lowe
Corp. Jones ································· Jack Grinnage
Corp. Smith ······························ Don Spruance
Col. Chandler ···························· Burt Metcalfe

TDY
- Laurence Naismith (1908–1992) served with the Royal Artillery during World War II. Resuming his film career after the war, Naismith appeared in *The Dam Busters* (1954), *The Man Who Never Was* (1956) and *Sink the Bismarck!* (1960). He worked on episodic TV series on both sides of the Atlantic, including *Danger Man, The Protectors, The Fugitive* and *The Invaders*. Naismith's later films included *Young Winston* (1972), *The Valley of Gwangi* (1969) and *Diamonds are Forever* (1971).

- Harold Gould (born Harold V. Goldstein on 10 December 1923 in Schenectady, New York) followed an atypical career path. He started teaching drama and then went into acting as a profession. Gould created memorable performances on stage, in films and on TV, and excelled in light comedy. His continuing roles on TV included *He and She* (1967–68), *Rhoda* (1974–78), *The Feather and Father Gang* (1977), *Park Place* (1981), *Foot in the Door* (1983), and *Under One Roof* (1985).

PERSONNEL FILE
- Maj. Cobb is mentioned, as is Maj. Rosen, the weather officer.

DEBRIEFING

- At first, Gen. Crowe wants the mission to be led by the 927th but Savage persuades him into letting the 918th take the lead.
- Crew does not use oxygen masks.
- Savage's mission call sign is Royal Coachman.

INTELLIGENCE REPORT

- This was the last episode to feature John Larkin as Gen. Wiley Crowe.
- The voice of Axis Sally was performed by June Foray, best known as the voice of Rocky, the Flying Squirrel. Foray would continue to recreate Axis Sally in later episodes.
- After completing this episode, Burt Metcalfe moved behind the camera as part of the team that produced Fox's *M*A*S*H*. Metcalfe was the only producer who stayed with the series for its entire CBS run, from 1972–83.
- The train compartment in Act IV is the same set used in #10 "Interlude."

#26 "MUTINY AT TEN THOUSAND FEET" (7326)

OAD: 26 March 1965
RERUN: N/R
W: Harold Jack Bloom
D: Sutton Roley

Lt. Tony Kemp has come up with a plan to bail out of the war. Savage heatedly dresses down Maj. Towson, who suffered a nervous breakdown after completing a mission. Kemp uses the incident to plant doubts in the minds of the other airmen about Savage's ability to command. Kemp blackmails Sgt. Phil Reese, who enlisted under an assumed name, into helping him execute his plan for desertion. Kemp uses his friendship with Nurse Amy Patterson to break into the pharmacy and steal drugs. Meanwhile, Doc Kaiser and Gen. Stoneman confront Savage about the general possibly suffering from combat fatigue. Kemp interrupts the meeting to offer his crew to Gen. Savage, whose last crew just finished its 25th mission. Having access to Savage and Savage's plane is the key to Kemp's plan. He needs to convince enough members of the 918th that Savage is over the edge so that he, as co-pilot of the general's plane, can take over and fly to neutral Switzerland so he can sit out the rest of the war. Kemp's scheme gets some unexpected help when Savage's plane suffers damage on a mission and Savage refuses to abort. Afterwards, Kemp plants the stolen drugs on Savage's seat in the cockpit so that the other crew members will find them. Later, at The Star and Bottle, Kemp publicly asks Nurse Patterson to identify the drugs. She says they are amphetamines and sedatives—a potentially lethal combination. During the next mission Savage announces that his plane will divert from formation in order to drop propaganda leaflets near Innsbruck. After the drop, flak damages two engines. Savage orders the navigator to plot a course for Nazi-occupied France instead of neutral Switzerland. Seeing his chance, Kemp talks the rest of the crew into believing that Savage has cracked up so that he can seize control of the ship. Savage plays devil's advocate and conducts a mock court-martial trial, asking each crewman what led him to believe the general's command needed to be relieved. When all of the "testimony" points to Kemp as the instigator, Sgt. Reese confesses the plan. Kemp retaliates by shooting Reese, and a struggle breaks out between pilot and co-pilot for control of the plane. After Kemp is knocked out, the bombardier helps Savage get the plane under control and they head for home.

Gen. Savage, Doc Kaiser, Gen. Stoneman
Lt. Tony Kemp ···························· Larry Blyden
T/Sgt. Phil Reese ······················· Robert Brown
Lt. Ray Thatcher ······················· John Kerr
Liz Woodruff ··························· Hazel Court
Sgt. Laz Coleridge ····················· Jess Pearson
Lt. Amy Patterson ····················· Lee Meriwether
Lt. Murray Epstein ···················· Stuart Margolin
Maj. Andrew "Andy" Towson ···· James Dobson

TDY

· Larry Blyden (1925–1975) came to national attention with his powerful portrayal of Sammy Glick in the 1959 *Sunday Showcase* production of "What Makes Sammy Run?" His stage career garnered Blyden three Tony nominations and a win in 1972 for *A Funny Thing Happened on the Way to the Forum*. Blyden's flair for comedy helped him land two sitcoms, *Joe and Mabel* (1955–56) and *Harry's Girls* (1963–64). Then he turned to another career path: game show host on a string of shows including *Personality* (1967–69), *You're Putting Me On* (1969), *The Movie Game* (1969–72) and *What's My Line* (1972–75). Blyden died in 1975 from injuries suffered in an auto accident.

Frank Aletter on Larry Blyden: "Blyden and I came out of Downey's Restaurant on 8th Avenue, many, many years into our friendship. He put his arm around me and said, 'Morph (a name Larry and Ray Walston and I made up and always called each other), I've never told you one of the reasons why I love and envy you so much. You have the capacity to get up in the morning and take what the day throws at you, deal with it, for good or bad, and go to bed again that night satisfied. I have to chase the day with everything I've got.' My reply 'Morph, I have always envied your ability to get up in the morning and chase the day with everything you've got.' Therein was the strongest relationship I ever had in my life. I still wish that I could have done it his way."

"It was that quality in Larry that made him so perfect for playing Sammy Glick in 'What Makes Sammy Run.' It was that quality that got him all those parts—the schemer, hustler and con man. No, he was not those people. He was the kind and considerate friend who, when I tore all the ligaments in my ankle playing softball in the Broadway Show League, picked me up and took me down to his apartment in the Village where he lived with his wife, Carol Haney, and they waited on me, hand and foot."

- Robert Brown (born 17 November 1927 in Trenton, New Jersey) is best known for his role as virile timber baron Jason Bolt in *Here Come the Brides* (1968–70). He competed for the lead role of Napoleon Solo in *The Man from U.N.C.L.E.* He guest starred on *Bewitched, Mannix* and *Star Trek.* Brown also had the lead in the 1971 syndicated series *Primus.*

- John Kerr (born 15 November 1931 in New York City) is a Harvard and Columbia-educated attorney. Since his parents were in show biz, Kerr gravitated toward performing. His most memorable role was in the film version of *South Pacific* (1958). Kerr's regular series roles were on *Arrest and Trial* (1963–64), *Peyton Place* (1965–66) and *The Streets of San Francisco.* This was Kerr's second appearance on *12 O'Clock High.*

- Lee Meriwether (born 27 May 1935 in Los Angeles) made the first of three *12 O'Clock High* appearances in this episode. After being crowned Miss America 1955, She worked in small parts on TV until she scored her first feature, *The 4-D Man* (1959) with Robert Lansing. From there, she starred in the first in a long line of soaps including *The Clear Horizon, The Young Marrieds* and *All My Children.*

  Lee Meriwether on "Mutiny at 10,000 Feet": "I had not worked on a Quinn Martin show at that point, but I don't recall reading for the role. I was thrilled because I knew Bob was doing the series. I also worked with him on a live jury show where I convinced the jury that Bob was guilty. To get the part on *12 O'Clock High* was wonderful, but I wasn't his girlfriend. In fact, there wasn't even any byplay between us."

- Stuart Margolin (born 31 January 1940 in Davenport, Iowa) netted two Emmys for his role as Angel Martin, the eccentric ex-con on James Garner's series *The Rockford Files.* Margolin had appeared previously with Garner on the western *Nichols* (1971–72) and later in the 1981 revival of *Maverick.* Margolin has also successfully expanded his involvement in the industry to writing, composing music and directing.

PERSONNEL FILE
- Lt. Patterson tells Kemp that Gen. Crowe was transferred to Washington the

day before.
• This is the last appearance of Liz Woodruff.

DEBRIEFING
- The plane in which Kemp and Reese fly is named *Girl Friend.*
- Savage flies *Piccadilly Lily*.
- The crew does not use oxygen masks. The general and Kemp do not wear flight helmets.

FLIGHT LINE
- Savage says the date of the mutiny is 24 February 1943.
- Gen. Stoneman is now a major general. In his initial appearance, episode #8 "The Hours Before Dawn," Stoneman was a lieutenant general.
- The door to Doc Kaiser's office has his name, Maj. Donald Kaiser, painted on the glass window.

#27 "THE MISSION" (7327)

OAD:	2 April 1965
RERUN:	30 July 1965
W:	Samuel Roeca
D:	William A. Graham

Gen. Savage has the green light for a mission he planned: the Eighth Air Force will bomb Hamburg as a diversion while the general leads a flight of seven planes to bomb a key oil supply line in the Saar basin. Savage orders Maj. Stovall to assemble a crew that includes Lt. Michaels and Lt. Gunther. With a shortage of gunners, the general requests Flight Officer Joe Waller, but Stovall tells Savage that Waller is in the guard house for having started a fight in the NCO club. The general frees Waller to bring him in on the mission as right waist gunner. Savage is curious about Waller's military record. He washed out of pilot training only to be certified as a bombardier, but prefers to serve as a gunner. After Waller acknowledges the general's order, he asks who the left waist gunner will be. When Savage tells him it's Lt. Maglie, the general sees how irritated Waller becomes. That night at The Star and Bottle, Lt. Gunther approaches Savage to request that he be transferred to another plane. Gunther's reason: he won't fly with "Washout" Waller. It seems that Gunther blames then-bombardier Waller for freezing over a target, resulting in the deaths of the rest of the plane's crew. Savage orders Gunther to fly with whomever comes up on the rotation schedule, and the mission goes on. As expected, Waller and Maglie go at it in the waist, but Michaels breaks things up just in time for them to fight off the Luftwaffe. When German fighters close in and take out the bombardier, Savage orders Waller to assume the job—sitting right next to the navigator, Lt. Gunther. Waller hits the target, but one bomb is caught in the rack and does not release. The armed bomb must be jettisoned before the plane can land. Waller tries to free the bomb and gets nothing but grief from Gunther and Maglie. Even when Gunther is hit by German fire, he won't accept help from Waller. Finally, Savage is convinced that the bomb can't be dislodged so he orders a bailout. Waller disobeys, instead offering to pilot the plane so the general can make it to safety. Although the general commends Waller for his performance on the current mission, Savage criticizes him for his bad attitude, the real reason for his checkered military career. The general insists Waller bail out, but instead Waller goes back to work on the stuck bomb. The wounded Gunther, left behind in the waist, crawls to the bomb bay, where Waller is feverishly working. With no other option apparent, Waller shoots the bomb loose and it tumbles into the Channel. On the ground, Savage informs Waller that he will have to report the refusal to follow orders but that the general will put in a good word so he can have another lead bombardier…with the rank of Lieutenant.

Gen. Savage, Maj. Stovall
Flight Officer Joe Waller ············ Burt Brinckerhoff
1st Lt. Gunther ···························· Chris Robinson
Lt. Michaels ································ Bruce Dern
Sgt. Maglie ································· Rudy Solari
Lt. Farrell ·································· Robert Hogan
Capt. Dirksen ······························ Forrest Compton
Willie ······································ Ted Gehring
Sgt. Cord ··································· Ray Kellog
Radioman ···································· Don Eitner

TDY

• Burt Brinckerhoff (born 25 October 1933 in Pittsburgh, Pennsylvania) started his career playing young loners on *Naked City, Target: The Corruptors* and *The Defenders*. In the early 1970s, Brinckerhoff switched over to directing and had a very successful career with episodic series and made-for-TV movies, including multiple episodes of *ALF, Remington Steele* and *Scarecrow and Mrs. King.*

• Rudy Solari (1934–1991) brought a streetwise intensity to roles on *The Detectives, The Gallant Men, The Fugitive* and *The Outer Limits*. His continuing roles were on *Redigo* (1963), *The Wackiest Ship in the Army* (1965–66) and the *Dirty Dozen* knock-off, *Garrison's Gorillas* (1967–68). Solari would make another appearance in #74 "Six Feet Under."

• Forrest Compton (born 15 September 1925 in Reading, Pennsylvania) is best remembered for his supporting role as Col. Gray in the long-running sitcom *Gomer Pyle, USMC* (1964–69). Other primetime appearances included *77 Sunset Strip, Hogan's Heroes* and QM's *The FBI*. Compton was also featured on the soaps *The Brighter Day* (1961–62), *The Edge of Night* (1971–84) and *As the World Turns* (1992).

· Ted Gehring (1929–2000) made his first primetime acting appearance in this episode. Gehring would return in episode #45 "The Jones Boys." Other guest appearances included *Get Smart, Daniel Boone* and the *Star Trek* episode "Assignment: Earth" (OAD 29 March 1968), which also featured Robert Lansing. His continuing series roles were on *The Family Holvak* (1975), *Little House on the Prairie* (1975-76) and *Alice* (1979–81).

DEBRIEFING
· The plane Savage flies has only national insignia on fuselage; nose art is not shown.
· Lt. Michaels says, "I sure have pulled a GONWEC," then explains that the acronym means Goofed Off and Nobody Will Ever Care.
· Savage uses the call sign Blue Fox One.
· Crew does not use oxygen masks.
· The Eighth Air Force did not bomb Hamburg until 25 June 1943.

INTELLIGENCE REPORT
· The Archbury tower used in this episode was recreated on a soundstage.
· Brinckerhoff does a sly job of delivering sardonic jabs at his persecutors.
· Stovall's, Waller's, Michaels' and Maglie's A-2 jackets all have the AAF patch on the left shoulder.

Dana Wynter and Robert Lansing

#28 "THE CRY OF FALLEN BIRDS" (7328)

OAD:	9 April 1965
RERUN:	N/R
TP:	Edward J. Lakso & Charles Larson
Story:	Edward J. Lakso
D:	Walter Grauman

Returning to base following a mission, *Piccadilly Lily* has two engines out, forcing Savage to make an emergency landing. Gen. Savage is barely able to pull up the *Lily's* nose in order to miss crashing into the landmark manor house owned by Lady

Catherine Hampshire. Savage plans to tear down the home to clear his runway approach. Stoneman counters by saying that Lady Catherine has already filed charges against Savage for buzzing her home. Fuming, Savage sets out to make his point to Lady Catherine. Their encounter is far from cordial, with Savage overly aggressive and Lady Catherine understandably defensive. Lady Catherine registers complaints with Stoneman and the mayor of Archbury. Meanwhile, she calls in her friend, RAF Group Captain Derek Evans, for advice. Evans, who has romantic designs on Lady Catherine, believes she has become a prisoner of her ancestral home. Still, he promises to investigate Lady Catherine's legal options. A mission over Blaustadt heavily damages Savage's plane, so much so that he crashes into the countryside surrounding Lady Catherine's home. *Piccadilly Lily* is destroyed and the general is badly hurt, so Doc Kaiser commandeers the manor house to use as a field hospital. Kaiser doesn't want to risk moving the general, so he leaves Savage there and sends in nurses to watch over him. For three days, Savage lies in a semi-conscious state; during that time, Lady Catherine sees the general in a new light. In fact, during a quiet moment together, they kiss. Later, Group Captain Evans drops by to bring official approval for removing the manor. Evans is surprised to see that Catherine has gone out of her house to tend to a bird that has fallen from its nest. He is even more surprised to learn Savage is still there. Evans explains his perception of Catherine as a woman who needs a man to lean on but who instead uses the manor house as a crutch. When Savage packs up to return to the base, Catherine expresses her love for him. But, the general says he will sign the orders to demolish the manor. She feels betrayed by Savage, but then Mayor Hickey shows her that the birds outside her home have left their nest. She understands his meaning and realizes her future lies in London with Evans.

Gen. Savage, Maj. Cobb, Doc Kaiser, Gen. Stoneman
Lady Catherine Hampshire ········ Dana Wynter
Group Captain Derek Evans ····· Lloyd Bochner
Bridget Foote ······························· Nora Marlowe
Mayor Hickey ······························· John McLiam
Corp. Smith ································· Don Spruance

TDY

- Lew Gallo was impressed by Dana Wynter, both on and off the set. "Dana Wynter did one of the most beautiful things," Gallo said. "When she finished her show, she came back with gifts for the cast and some of the crew. She said it was one of the most wonderful experiences she had ever had. Most of the people who came on the show, who were serious about their work, felt pretty much the same way."

- Lloyd Bochner (born 29 July 1924 in Toronto, Canada) may be best recognized in fandom for the *Twilight Zone* episode "To Serve Man" and its entertaining spoof in *The Naked Gun 2 1/2: The Smell of Fear* (1991). Bochner also gained fame for his role as the husband of Joan Collins' character on *Dynasty* (1981–82). Other continuing roles were on *Hong Kong* (1960–61), *The Richard Boone Show* (1963–64) and *Santa Barbara* (1984–85). Bochner's best work includes the *Wild, Wild West* episode "The Night of the Puppeteer" (OAD 25 February 1966) in which he plays two very different shades of the same character. He appeared in two additional episodes of *12 O'Clock High.*

• Nora Marlowe (1915–1977) portrayed maids, housekeepers and workaday women on series such as *M Squad, Family Affair* and *Longstreet.* She had continuing parts on *Law of the Plainsman* (1959–60), *My Living Doll* (1964–65), *The Governor and J.J.* (1969–70) and *The Waltons* (1972–77). Her films included *Westworld* (1973), *The Thomas Crown Affair* (1968) and the much-applauded made-for-TV movie *Queen of the Stardust Ballroom* (1975). Marlowe made a second appearance in #35 "Then Came the Mighty Hunter."

• Director Walter Grauman was a television pioneer, setting up the Armer, Grauman & King production company in the early 1950s with Alan Armer, who would become a QM producer, and actor Walter Woolf King. Grauman helmed the pilot and many subsequent episodes of QM's hugely successful *The Fugitive* (1963-67).

PERSONNEL FILE
• When Savage is told the target is the university town of Blaustadt, Germany, he says he has an old friend there, a professor. The professor went back to visit his home and was caught up in the Nazi takeover. He was unable to leave the country.

DEBRIEFING
• Crew does not use oxygen masks.
• On the first mission, Savage uses call sign Red Fox Leader; his co-pilot, Maj. Cobb, uses Red Fox One.
• On the second raid, Savage uses the call sign Blue Wolf Leader.

INTELLIGENCE REPORT
• Walter Grauman staged a wild montage sequence, embodying Savage's feverish nightmare. It's a torrent of scenes depicting the general tossing, turning and fighting with his nurses, interlaced with shots of bombs falling, planes exploding and an airplane crashing.
• The soundstage tower set was used in the teaser.

#29 "V FOR VENDETTA" (7330)

OAD: 16 April 1965
RERUN: N/R
W: Al C. Ward
D: William A. Graham

Gary Lockwood

Acting wing commander Gen. Hoagland flies in for what he considers to be an urgent meeting with Savage. Hoagland is troubled by Savage's prima donna-like approach to fighting the war outside the box of military regulations. After the day's mission, Maj. Gus Denver is relaxing in the officers club when Maj. Bragg, Hoagland's aide, tells him that the general wants a meeting with him. Meanwhile, Hoagland is in a marathon session with Savage, demanding to know why on the past eight missions he's diverted the 918th six times to strike the vigorously defended Focke-Wulf factories at Mannheim. Savage defends his actions by pointing out that Hoagland has never had combat experience and therefore can't relate to the decisions a group commander must make. It comes out that Hoagland and Savage both wanted command of the 918th, but now that Hoagland is temporarily wing commander he can make sure the group is run according to his by-the-book approach. When it's Denver's turn to meet with Hoagland, the general tries to find out Denver's view of why Savage has, in his opinion, ignored the primary target to strike Mannheim, a target that Bomber Command thinks can't be hit because of the potential for unacceptable losses. Savage is incensed that Hoagland is interrogating his people and urges the desk-bound Hoagland to get a taste of combat. On the next mission, Hoagland flies right seat with Savage to bomb the rail yards outside Eindhoven. Hoagland scoffs at Savage's prediction that the mission will be grueling—until the group is hit by a swarm of FWs and Savage's plane is badly damaged. Savage orders a bail out and the first man to jump is Hoagland—just before Savage gets the plane under control and cancels the bail order. Hoagland is left in mid-air, where an FW flies by and shoots him. Denver, also along on the mission, begins to wonder if Savage meant for Hoagland to die as part of a vendetta. As a result, Denver avoids Savage to the point of failing to follow orders on a mission. Naturally, Savage demands to know what's bothering the major and Denver explains his suspicion. Complicating Denver's position is a letter that each member of the crew received from the Inspector General's office seeking information about Hoagland's death. Denver requests a meeting with an IG officer, then seeks shelter in the base hospital. There, Savage tries to persuade Denver to fly a mission to the Rhine River shipyards, but the major doesn't want to fly any more—especially with Savage, who may try to kill him the way Denver thinks the general tried to get rid of Hoagland. Savage counters by saying that Hoagland was a good man in his field, which wasn't aerial combat. The general continues by saying that, as a leader, he must sacrifice the lives of good men every day so that more good men may not have to die. Savage understands that Denver ran away from the harsh realities of war before but doesn't want him to do it again. The general also can't let talented pilots waste away on the ground, and tells Denver that he will fly the next day. Denver goes up, but when bad weather obscures the primary and alternate targets, he knows they're headed back for Mannheim. The mission is a success but Denver's plane is hit by flak so badly that the rest of his crew is killed. Denver suffers a panic attack and tells Savage that he's going to bail out but the general says that fighters will tear him apart just as they did Hoagland. Denver composes himself and brings his plane safely back to base. Later, Savage reveals that Hoagland's death was ruled a combat casualty. Denver's testimony was not the clincher that the defense hoped for, in part because the major is now determined to face his personal demons.

Gen. Savage, Maj. Stovall, Doc Kaiser, Gen. Pritchard
Maj. August "Gus" Denver ········ Gary Lockwood
Gen. Brad Hoagland ··················· Lin McCarthy
Maj. Bragg ······························· Ken Berry
Lt. Perkins ································ Mike Doherty

TDY
- Linwood (Lin) McCarthy (1918–2002) used the GI Bill after serving during World War II to study acting at Geller's Theater Workshop in Los Angeles. McCarthy broke in during the era of live TV drama, then grew with the medium to become a specialist in playing intelligent, well-educated professionals. Guest appearances included *The Invaders, Stoney Burke* and *Mission: Impossible.* His only regular series role was on *The Blue Knight* (1976). McCarthy also appeared in the miniseries *Winds of War* (1983).

- Mike Doherty later appeared as an MP in episodes #39 "Show Me a Hero, I'll Show You a Bum" and #42 "Grant Me No Favor."

DEBRIEFING
- Crews do not use oxygen masks.
- Savage's call sign on all missions is Red Dog Leader.
- Savage gives Denver "his old job back" as senior squadron C.O.
- Stovall gets a message from the 614th that Gen. Hoagland has hitched a ride

with them to reach the 918th.

- Eindhoven in the Netherlands was not bombed by the Eighth Air Force until 14 February 1944.

INTELLIGENCE REPORT
- The character of Maj. Denver (Gary Lockwood) appeared earlier in #9 "Appointment at Liege." Lockwood made another appearance on *12 O'Clock High*, portraying an unrelated character in #36 "The Idolater."
- In episode #9, Denver is out for revenge because his crew was lost over Liege; in this episode we're told it was Mannheim.
- We get a nice tour of the B-17 mock-up as Denver crawls through his plane looking for survivors.

#30 "POW," PART ONE (7329-1)

OAD:	23 April 1965
RERUN:	20 August 1965
W:	Al C. Ward
D:	Don Medford

Robert Lansing and Alf Kjellin

Gen. Savage reprimands three of his crewmen—Moxey, Baby and Doc— just before they take off on a mission, and promises more trouble when they get back. Getting back may take longer than the general anticipates: over the target, German fighters inflict so much battle damage that Savage must order a bail out. Ironically, the general, along with Moxey, Baby and Doc, are captured and interred in Stalag 12 along with other American, British and French airmen. The commandant is Luftwaffe Col. Richter; his second-in-command is SS officer Capt. Staufman. Col. Richter tells Savage that no one has successfully escaped from Stalag 12 on his watch and he intends to keep a perfect record. Unknowingly, Richter ignites a battle of wills between Savage and himself. Since Savage is isolated, the prisoners create a diversion to allow second-ranking POW Group Capt. Brail to sneak in to tell the general about the prisoners' escape tunnel and plans to break out. The escape attempt occurs on schedule, but Richter's men are waiting and gun down the first few escapees. Savage later tells the POWs that he wants to keep thinking of new escape plans to defy the cunning Col. Richter. Richter establishes a ritual of going for a morning drive with Savage; he believes that special treatment will help erode morale among the other POWs. Morale plummets after Richter confines the POWs to their barracks during Allied air raids under penalty of death. When Baby runs outside during a raid, Savage stands up for him and prevents Richter's men from shooting him. That action wins support for Savage and his escape plans. Savage hits on a bold scheme that calls for forged documents, fake German uniforms—and the kidnapping of Col. Richter. With the next escape on for the following morning, Savage and Doc talk about the strength of the human spirit. The general concludes that if only one of the POWs gets back home, the effort will be worthwhile.

Gen. Savage
Col. Max Richter .... Alf Kjellin
Group Capt. Morris Brail .... Donald Harron
Capt. Staufman .... John van Dreelen
"Moxey" .... James Farentino
"Doc" .... Peter Haskell
"Baby" .... Jim Shane
Flight Lt. Forrester .... James Forrest
Lt. Regis .... Don Penny
Lt. Smith .... Stephen Brooks
Guard .... Sasha Harden
Guard .... Henry Rico-Cattani

TDY

- Alf Kjellin (1920–1988) began acting in his native Sweden. He continued performing in Hollywood, then directed his first movie in 1955. From there, Kjellin successfully pursued both facets of the industry. His acting credits include work on TV series such as *I Spy, Combat!* and *Mission: Impossible,* and films such as *The Victors* (1963), *Assault on a Queen* (1966) and *Ice Station Zebra* (1968). Kjellin returned in #53 "Back to the Drawing Board."

- James Farentino (born 24 February 1938 in Brooklyn, New York) began his career on the New York stage, then worked on series like *Naked City, The Defenders* and *The Reporter.* Farentino signed a long-term contract with Universal that put him in shows such as *Laredo, Ironside, Run for Your Life* and his first two series, *The Bold Ones: The Lawyers* (1969–72) and *Cool Million* (1972–73). Farentino also appeared in *Dynasty* (1981–82), *Blue Thunder* (1984) and *Mary* (1985–86). He received an Emmy nomination for his portrayal of Simon Peter in the 1977 miniseries *Jesus of Nazareth.*

- Peter Haskell (born 15 October 1934 in Boston, Massachusetts) put off law school to appear in an off-Broadway play. From there, Haskell racked up a significant run of credits in TV series such as *Combat!, The Green Hornet,*

The Outer Limits and *The Man from U.N.C.L.E.* Haskell had continuing roles on *Bracken's World* (1969–70), *Rich Man, Poor Man* (1976–77), *Ryan's Hope* (1982–83), *Search for Tomorrow* (1983), *Rituals* (1983–85), and *The Law and Harry McGraw* (1987–88).

• Stephen Brooks (born 12 August 1942 in Cincinnati, Ohio) had continuing roles on *The Nurses* (1963–64), QM's *The FBI* (1965–67), *The Interns* (1970–71) and the soap *Days of Our Lives* (1980–81). Guest appearances included *Star Trek*, *The Invaders* and *Ghost Story*.

• Donald Harron's bravura performance in this, his second *12 O'Clock High* appearance, is in stark contrast to the cowardly clerk he portrayed later in episode #46 "Between the Lines."

DEBRIEFING
• Savage's call sign is Blue Robin One.
• Savage says he will not fly *Piccadilly Lily* on the mission.

INTELLIGENCE REPORT
• The gritty and foreboding outdoor set of Stalag Luft 12 is the same complex used to represent the Nazi concentration camp at Dachau in *The Twilight Zone* episode "Death's Dead Revisited," (OAD 10 November 1961). Don Medford also directed that episode. In his book *The Twilight Zone Companion*, author Marc Scott Zicree relates producer Buck Houghton's disclosure that the set was originally built on MGM's Lot 3 to use in the pilot for a western series.
• In the big-budget Fox film *Von Ryan's Express* (1965), about escaping POWs during World War II, Maj. Fincham (Trevor Howard) says, "If only one gets out, it's a victory," a sentiment which is echoed at the conclusion of "POW," part one. Savage talks with Doc and says, "If only one of us gets back, it'll be worth it. And it'll make others try again." It seems like a couple of writers had lunch at the Fox commissary and shared a few story ideas.

#31 "POW," PART TWO (7329-2)

OAD: 30 April 1965
RERUN: 27 August 1965
W: Al C. Ward
D: Don Medford

Gen. Savage takes a key step in launching his escape plan by requesting that Col. Richter release the POWs from confinement to barracks. When the colonel agrees, Savage signals the men that the escape is on. Back in Savage's quarters, he

Robert Lansing, Don Penny, James Forrest and Jim Shane

again meets covertly with Brail and other leaders of the escape to work out the final details. Next morning, the plan is launched: five hand-picked POWs—Moxey, Baby and Doc, plus Lt. Regis and Lt. Forrester—suit up in phony German uniforms. While attention is focused on putting out a fire started by other POWs, the bogus Germans—plus Gen. Savage—sneak into the stalag's fire engine and roar out of camp. At the motor pool, the next phase is thrown off when Regis tangles with a German guard and dislocates his shoulder. As a contingency plan, Regis drives the fire engine in the other direction to throw off pursuers. The others then take Col. Richter's staff car and go through the routine of picking up the commandant for his daily drive with Savage. They are successful, but Regis is picked up and returned for questioning by Capt. Staufman. Soon the SS officer has deduced where the escapees are headed and sends out an alert. The escaping prisoners are pursued by guards at a checkpoint who shoot out the staff car's gas tank. When they pull over and stop, Richter exits the car and stumbles, badly cutting his leg. Savage announces that he's going to the nearby town of Luneberg to find their underground contact, Dr. Karl Ehrlich, and arrange for a way home. Ehrlich schedules their departure for the next day but the men must make their way north to the village of Cuxhaven on the North Sea coastline no later than 1800 hours. To help ensure that someone gets through, Savage splits up the group: Lt. Forrester is to go solo; Moxey, Baby and Doc will team up, and the general will go with Col. Richter. Savage helps the colonel limp until it's clear that the general may not make the rendezvous. So he frees Richter, hops a freight train for a short distance, and then jumps off. Col. Richter is rescued and taken to a German hospital. There, Capt. Staufman arrogantly tells the commandant that he is now in charge of capturing the escapees and executing them. Moxey, Baby and Doc stop in the woods for a rest but when a German patrol surprises them they wind up in a life or death fight in which Baby is killed. The four remaining POWs rendezvous at a designated, bombed-out church and wait for the fishing boat that will take them home. Staufman, Richter and a patrol have followed the trail to Cuxhaven and conduct a building-to-building search. The Germans corner their prey, but the POWs have one last hope: three hand grenades. Lt. Forrester is wounded by gunfire but Savage, Moxey and Doc throw their grenades and charge the Germans. Only Richter survives, and his battle of wits with Savage erodes into an old-fashioned shootout in which the general guns down his oppressor. The survivors pile into the waiting fishing boat and set out to sea, where they are picked up by a British destroyer.

Gen. Savage
Col. Max Richter ·························· Alf Kjellin
Group Capt. Morris Brail ········· Donald Harron
Capt. Staufman ························· John Van Dreelen
"Moxey" ···································· James Farentino
"Doc" ······································· Peter Haskell
"Baby" ······································ Jim Shane
Flight Lt. Forrester ··················· James Forrest
Lt. Regis ·································· Don Penny
Lt. Smith ································· Stephen Brooks
Dr. Erlich ································· Oscar Beregi
Guard ······································ Sasha Harden
Guard ······································ Henry Rico-Cattani
Merchant Seaman ····················· Norbert Siegfried
Guard ······································ Kurt Landen
Guard ······································ Chris Anders

TDY
· Oscar Beregi, Jr. (1918–1976) used his stocky appearance for both comic and commanding roles. On TV, he guested on *Mr. Ed, Hogan's Heroes, The Twilight Zone, The Untouchables* and *The Wild, Wild West*. Along with appearances in big-budget features *My Fair Lady* (1964) and *Judgment at Nuremburg* (1961), he was also in *The Incredible Mr. Limpet* (1964) and The *Christine Jorgensen Story* (1970). And you shouldn't miss his comic turns in *Young Frankenstein* (1974) and *Everything You Always Wanted to Know About Sex (But Were Afraid to Ask)* (1972).

Intelligence Report
· Act IV takes place in the fishing village set on MGM's backlot.
· Fox documentation of episodes #30 and #31 also refers to them as "The POW Story," Part I and II.

#32 "The Hero" (7331)

OAD: 7 May 1965
Rerun: N/R
W: Albert Aley
D: Ralph Senesky

Savage's old friend and mentor, highly decorated World War I fighter ace Col.

Paul "Pappy" Hartley, is flying in his second war, but this time he's flying a desk. Hartley hitches a ride from the States with a transport crew to his new position with SHAEF. The plane's pilot gives the veteran some flight time and when the plane is attacked by FWs, Hartley's old fighting spirit bubbles up once more. Instead of taking evasive action, Harley deliberately engages the enemy. The pilot and co-pilot are badly shot up but the colonel manages to bring the B-17 in for a perfect landing. At the Officers' Club, Savage and Hartley catch up on the previous 15 years. Hearing about Hartley's flying exploits makes Savage convince Stoneman to give his friend a chance to lead the 920th, a new group made up of green pilots. Until the new group is activated, Hartley is assigned to the 918th for evaluation and indoctrination. On the major's first practice run, he is reluctant to relinquish control of the plane to his bombardier. Then when a German E-boat is spotted, he orders the crew to strafe and sink the patrol vessel. Although Gen. Stoneman commends Hartley for his kill, Savage is disappointed by the colonel's lone-eagle approach to aerial combat. Savage explains that it's a different war, fought with teamwork, not individual showboating. That said, the general assigns Hartley to combat status on the next mission to bomb the sub pens at St. Nazaire. After the group has a successful bomb run, they are attacked by German fighters. It's against Hartley's instincts to just sit and take machine gun fire so he peels away from the formation and limps back to base. Savage holds Hartley's future in his hands and orders him to become a team player or wash out of the program. Having Hartley as part of the team is crucial for Savage, who wants the colonel to lead one wave of a complex raid. Shortly after Hartley takes off with the first flight, Stoneman confronts Savage with news from the co-pilot of the plane Hartley originally hitched a ride with. The co-pilot has recovered sufficiently and reveals that Hartley intentionally attacked the enemy, a serious charge especially for someone who is up for command of a group. Savage leads his flight toward the rendezvous with Hartley's flight. Reviewing the situation, the general orders Hartley to abort his end of the mission. Only minutes from the target, Hartley disobeys and flies directly into a blanket of enemy flak that rips his plane apart. Hartley orders the crew to bailout but stays at the controls and crashes into an ammo dump. The local newspaper account that praises Hartley's heroism makes Savage realize he couldn't separate Hartley the man from Hartley his idol.

Gen. Savage, Maj. Stovall, Maj. Cobb, Doc Kaiser, Gen. Stoneman
Col. Paul J. "Pappy" Hartley ····· James Whitmore
Lt. Mason ················· William Court
Capt. Franklin ················ William Arvin
Lt. Ditchik ················ Peter E. Deuel
Lt. Hearn ················ Jimmy Hayes
Lt. Miller ················ Glenn Sipes
Capt. Wayland ··············· James Beck
Radio Operator ··············· Nigel McKeand

TDY

- James Whitmore (born 1 October 1921 in White Plains, New York) is hilarious in *Kiss Me Kate* (1953) and gives solid dramatic support to *The Asphalt Jungle* (1950), *Battle Cry* (1955) and *Tora! Tora! Tora!* (1970). Whitmore received an Oscar nomination for his second film, *Battleground* (1949). He starred in the groundbreaking film *Black Like Me* (1964). Whitmore also appeared in the sci-fi classic *Them* (1954) and wore John Chambers' Oscar-winning makeup in *Planet of the Apes* (1968). Continuing roles on TV included *The Law and Mr. Jones* (1960–62), *My Friend Tony* (1969) and *Temperatures Rising* (1972–73). Uncanny recreations of Will Rogers, Teddy Roosevelt and Harry Truman in one-man shows have kept Whitmore busy for decades. He returned in an unrelated, though similar, role in #73 "The Ace." His son, actor James Whitmore, Jr., appeared in the TV series *Black Sheep Squadron* (1976–78).

PERSONNEL FILE

- Col. Hartley calls Savage "Franklin."
- Hartley and Savage haven't seen each other in 15 years. Savage says Hartley is one of the two men who taught him everything he knows about flying; without Hartley, he probably wouldn't have his star or be in the Air Corps. Hartley was there when Savage made his first flight, complete with shaky landing.
- We hear again that Stoneman is a stickler for military protocol. He frowns on Hartley not saluting Savage.

DEBRIEFING

- Crews do not use oxygen masks.
- FWs attack the transport.
- The 920th is a new group with green pilots.
- Cobb's call sign on the St. Nazaire mission is Fox Leader.
- Savage's call sign is Red Leader.
- The B-17 at Chino Airport has serial number 3713.

INTELLIGENCE REPORT

- The sequence where Hartley's plane slams into the munitions dump is stock footage taken during Project Aphrodite test flights. The program was designed to use radio-controlled B-17s as flying bombs to knock out extremely tough targets, such as submarine pens and V-1 launch sites. The footage was used again in #36 "The Idolater."
- Savage gives a straightforward explanation to Hartley that the Air Corps' mission during WW II is to kill in wholesale lots as quickly and efficiently as possible.
- The local newspaper is still called the *Archbury Journal.* We last saw a copy in #12 "Soldiers Sometimes Kill."

Toby Sighting
• Toby mug is on mantle in the Officers' Club.

Second Season

Broadcast schedule
Mondays 7:30 pm ET, 13 September 1965 – 5 September 1966

Production run: 29 60-minute episodes filmed in black-and-white

Continuing Cast
Col. Joseph Anson Gallagher	Paul Burke
Maj. Harvey B. Stovall	Frank Overton
T/Sgt. Alexander "Sandy" Komansky	Chris Robinson
Maj. Donald "Doc" Kaiser	Barney Phillips
Brig. Gen. Edward Britt	Andrew Duggan
Lt. Gen. Pritchard	Paul Newlan
Lt. Bob Fowler	Robert Dornan
Capt. Douglas	Barry Cahill
Col. Frank Bailey	Robert Colbert
Capt. Phyllis Vincent	Lee Meriwether
Lt. Fay Vendry	Jill Haworth

Key Production Credits
Executive Producer	Quinn Martin
Producer	William D. Gordon
Assistant to the Executive Producer	Arthur Fellows
Associate Producer	Philip Saltzman
Story Editor	William Koenig
Director of Photography	George T. Clemens, ASC
	Richard H. Kline
	Kenneth Peach, ASC
	Frank V. Phillips, ASC
Music Composed andCconducted By	Dominic Frontiere
Production Manager	Gaston Glass
Production Supervisor	Jack Sonntag
Unit Production Manager	Robert Huddleston
Assistant to Producer	John Conwell
Art Directors	Jack Martin Smith
	George B. Chan
Set Decorators	Walter M. Scott
	Glen Daniels
	Frank Wade

FILM EDITORS	Jodie Copelan, ACE
	Walter Hannemann, ACE
	Stanley E. Rabjohn
POST-PRODUCTION SUPERVISOR	John Elizalde
SOUND EFFECTS EDITOR	Carl Mahakian
	Chuck Overhulser
	John Post
	Tom Post
MUSIC EDITOR	Ted Whitfield
	Ken Wilhoit
ASSISTANT EDITOR	Michael Brown
	O. Nicholas Brown
	Charles Perry
	John Post
ASSISTANT DIRECTOR	Jack Aldworth
	Robert Daley
	Al Westen
CASTING	Patricia Rose Mock
POST PRODUCTION COORDINATOR	Robert Mintz
CHIEF ELECTRICIAN	John Baron
	Patrick R. Blymyer
	Burt Jones
	Wilbur Kinnett
PRODUCTION MIXER	Jack Lilly
	Alfred Overton
IN CHARGE OF PRODUCTION	Quinn Martin for
	QM Productions
IN ASSOCIATION WITH	William Self for Twentieth
	Century-Fox Television, Inc.

THE SECOND SEASON (OVERVIEW)

#33	13 September 1965	"The Loneliest Place in the World"
#34	20 September 1965	"Rx for a Sick Bird"
#35	27 September 1965	"Then Came the Mighty Hunter"
#36	4 October 1965	"The Idolater"
#37	11 October 1965	"Big Brother"
#38	18 October 1965	"The Hotshot"
#39	25 October 1965	"Show Me a Hero, I'll Show You a Bum"
#40	1 November 1965	"Runway in the Dark"
#41	8 November 1965	"I Am the Enemy"
#42	15 November 1965	"Grant Me No Favor"
#43	22 November 1965	"Storm at Twilight"

#44	29 November 1965	"We're Not Coming Back"
#45	6 December 1965	"The Jones Boys"
#46	13 December 1965	"Between the Lines"
#35	20 December 1965	**RERUN**
#47	27 December 1965	"Target 802"
#48	3 January 1966	"Falling Star"
#49	10 January 1966	"The Slaughter Pen"
#50	17 January 1966	"Underground"
#51	24 January 1966	"Which Way the Wind Blows"
#52	31 January 1966	"The Outsider"
#53	7 February 1966	"Back to the Drawing Board"
#54	14 February 1966	"25th Mission"
#55	21 February 1966	"The Survivor"
#56	28 February 1966	"Angel Babe"
#57	7 March 1966	"Decoy"
#58	14 March 1966	"The Hollow Man"
#59	21 March 1966	"Cross-Hairs on Death"
#60	28 March 1966	"Day of Reckoning"
#61	4 April 1966	"Siren Voices"

11 April 1966	RERUN – #37	"Big Brother"
18 April 1966	RERUN – #38	"The Hotshot"
25 April 1966	RERUN – #42	"Grant Me No Favor"
2 May 1966	RERUN – #36	"The Idolater"
9 May 1966	RERUN – #46	"Between the Lines"
16 May 1966	RERUN – #39	"Show Me a Hero, I'll Show You a Bum"
23 May 1966	RERUN – #40	"Runway in the Dark"
30 May 1966	RERUN – #41	"I Am the Enemy"
6 June 1966	RERUN – #45	"The Jones Boys"
13 June 1966	RERUN – #43	"Storm at Twilight"
20 June 1966	RERUN – #48	"Falling Star"
27 June 1966	RERUN – #49	"The Slaughter Pen"
4 July 1966	RERUN – #47	"Target 802"
11 July 1966	RERUN – #50	"Underground"
18 July 1966	RERUN – #52	"The Outsider"
25 July 1966	RERUN – #53	"Back to the Drawing Board"
1 August 1966	RERUN – #61	"Siren Voices"
8 August 1966	RERUN – #56	"Angel Babe"
15 August 1966	RERUN – #57	"Decoy"
22 August 1966	RERUN – #54	"25th Mission"
29 August 1966	RERUN – #58	"The Hollow Man"
5 September 1966	RERUN – #34	"Rx for a Sick Bird"

#33 "THE LONELIEST PLACE IN THE WORLD" (8301)

OAD: 13 September 1965
RERUN: N/R
W: Harold Jack Bloom
D: Richard Donner

Returning from a mission, Gen. Savage's plane trails smoke and shows signs of battle damage. Its radio is out so no one knows if the plane has wounded aboard. A B-17 lagging behind the group requests permission to join the formation. No one from Savage's crew responds. Flying in *The Leper Colony,* deputy group commander Joe Gallagher takes the initiative to give the outrider permission and the plane merges with the group behind Savage's plane. Suddenly, the pilot

Chris Robinson and Paul Burke

of the intruder plane barks commands in German and his gunners open fire on Savage's plane. The general is mortally wounded. The plane is damaged so badly that it drops out of formation and spirals out of sight. That night, Gen. Britt from SHAEF pays a visit to the 918th and tells the squadron commanders that the underground reports Savage is dead. The only survivor is Sgt. Komansky, the flight engineer. Britt remains on base to determine who will succeed Savage: Gallagher, Col. Bailey or Lt. Col. Heindorf. Komansky returns to base as the flag is lowered to half-mast and Savage's desk is cleared out. Acting commander Gallagher asks Komansky if Savage had any chance of survival. Komansky reports that none of the crew had a chance and that the group left them all to die, implying that he holds Gallagher responsible for Savage's death. Sgt. Komansky seems to create hard feelings wherever he goes, and Col. Bailey objects to Gallagher assigning Komansky to his crew. Later, Gallagher meets Gen. Britt for drinks and runs into Komansky and his date, the beautiful Suzanne Arnais, who happens to be a good friend of Gen. Britt. Mlle. Arnais is writing a story on Komansky's rescue. Gallagher meets with Britt to tell the general that he doesn't want Savage's job. On the next mission, another straggler shows up and does not identify itself. Gallagher orders his men to shoot it down, which they do—but the underground identifies the crash victims as Americans. Gallagher is burdened with the pain of having ordered the deaths of 10 men and tries to drink away the pain. Slightly tipsy, he goes into town hoping to make romantic headway with Mlle. Arnais. Komansky also shows up at her flat and goads Gallagher into a confrontation, which leads to the colonel grabbing the sergeant—violating the Articles of War. The next day, Col. Bailey's plane is scrubbed so Gallagher chooses Komansky to be his flight engineer. On the mission, the nose of Gallagher's plane takes a burst of flak that kills the co-pilot and forces Gallagher to drop back and leave Heindorf leading the group. From his new level below the group, Gallagher can see another straggler and warns the others. Gallagher engages the infiltrator in a deadly game of chicken and Komansky is able to shoot down the opposing plane. After hearing Gallagher's explanation of his actions, Britt promotes Gallagher to full colonel and cuts an order making him commander of the 918th. Komansky admits to having provoked Gallagher the night before. Britt leaves the two men to straighten things out.

Col. Gallagher, Maj. Stovall, Sgt. Komansky, Brig. Gen. Britt
Suzanne Arnais ···························· Claudine Longet
Lt. Col. Frank Bailey ················· Robert Colbert
Lt. Col. Chic Heindorf ············· Paul Carr
M/Sgt. Caber McVaigh ············· Leo Gordon
Capt. Lowell ····························· William Arvin
Maître d' ································· Jack Raine
Duty Sergeant ·························· Ken Baechel
German Pilot ···························· Chris Howard
Right Waist Gunner ···················· Charles Kuenstle

TDY

• Claudine Longet (born 29 January 1942 in Paris, France) carved a niche for herself during the early 1960s war cycle by appearing in shows such as *Combat!, McHale's Navy* and *The Rat Patrol.* The attractive, young vocalist married popular singer Andy Williams. Longet's marriage—and her life— went downhill fast when she shot her lover, skier Spider Sabitch, in 1976.

• Robert Colbert (born 26 July 1931 in Long Beach, California) has two series that keep him in the minds of fans: *Maverick* (1960), in which he filled in for AWOL James Garner and producer Irwin Allen's sci-fi series *The Time Tunnel* (1966–67). Colbert appeared in two other Irwin Allen projects, *Land of the Giants* (1968) and the made-for-TV *City Beneath the Sea* (1971). He also had a 10-year run on the soap *The Young and the Restless* (1973–83).

• Leo V. Gordon (1922–2000) didn't just act like a tough guy, he lived like one too. Gordon did a four-year stretch in San Quentin. After his release, Gordon studied acting in New York City, but found his calling as the heavy in countless westerns such as *Maverick, Bat Masterson* and *The Rough Riders.* Gordon continued to act but branched out into writing screenplays for movies, such as *Wasp Woman* (1960) and *Attack of the Giant Leeches* (1959), and TV series, including 21 segments of *Adam-12.*

PERSONNEL FILE
- Britt walks into Savage's office and pulls what is supposed to be Savage's photo from the org chart; however, Duggan's hand artfully covers the image so we can't see who it is.
- Gallagher checks Komansky's service record. Komansky was one of the first chosen to be flight engineer on a B-17. He qualified for Officer Candidate School but went AWOL for a week instead.
- Suzanne promptly becomes the first of "Joe's Girls."
- A script revision of 1 June 1965 changed Maj. Gen. Britt to Brig Gen. Britt.
- Britt lost his right leg in a plane crash during the First World War.
- Britt says he has two daughters about Suzanne's age.
- Britt gives his own eagle insignia to Gallagher.
- Gen. Pritchard does not appear but is mentioned by Britt.
- Col. Bailey appeared later in #37 "Big Brother."

DEBRIEFING
- Gallagher's call sign on the first mission is Red Leader.
- Next mission, his call sign is Ramrod; Col. Heindorf is Blue One.
- The mission in Act IV shows a different view of the flight deck.

INTELLIGENCE REPORT
- Working title of this script was "Pirate XIII."
- The airmen do not wear flag patches on their A-2 or shearling jackets.
- The pilot of the Nazi B-17 that shoots down Savage boldly wears a signet ring adorned with a swastika.
- During the mission in Act IV, viewers are shown a seldom seen three-quarter view of the flight deck, looking forward from behind the pilot, which includes the control panel.

#34 "RX FOR A SICK BIRD" (8305)

OAD: 20 September 1965
RERUN: 5 September 1966
W: William C. Anderson & William D. Hamilton and Marc Huntley
D: Richard Donner

G-2 officer Brig. Gen. Creighton escorts resistance leader Ilka Zradna to a meeting with Gallagher. Creighton also presents Gallagher with a briefcase

Gia Scala

containing sealed orders for a top secret mission to drop Ms. Zradna on the continent. The next morning, Flight 262 takes off and the mission is on. Gallagher chews out his maintenance chief, Sgt. Podesta, for having the worst maintenance record in the wing. Then, as the colonel informs Capt. Zoller, the Polish liaison officer, that Zradna is airborne, Gallagher gets a message that Flight 262 has aborted and gone down. The radio communications between Flight 262 and the 918th are monitored off the base by Sgt. Hansen—who partners with Capt. Zoller to covertly demoralize the group. Hansen works on the enlisted men and causes a rift between the maintenance crews and the air crews so that when Komansky shows up, the sergeant and Podesta break into a fistfight. Gallagher breaks up the scuffle and then busts both Komansky and Podesta down to private. The good news is that Zradna survived the crash and she is ordered confined to base. Gallagher knows he must get morale up again so he orders Komansky to find Podesta and shake hands. As Komansky searches for Podesta, he chases a shadowy figure away from the armorer's shed, then finds a case of .50-caliber ammo that had been tampered with and a knife that belongs to Sgt. Podesta. Gallagher goes to Wing to tell Creighton that the 918th doesn't have a maintenance problem; it has a sabotage problem. Creighton acknowledges this and tells Gallagher that a team of Germans has infiltrated Bomber Command and that G-2 is on to them and is poised to shut down the group. In fact, Creighton has called in CIC Maj. Adams to help. They know about tampering with .50-caliber ammo with explosive charges that go off intermittently. Gallagher doesn't want his men to fly with that potential hazard, but Creighton counters that the Germans want just that reaction. Major Adams explains that he has carefully placed his men in the 918th and that Podesta is one of them. Back at the base, Komansky finds Podesta dead. The major takes Podesta's place working under-cover. But when Zoller complains to Gallagher about the lack of information he's receiving, Zoller lets slip that he knows an intelligence major is on the base. Although Gallagher tries to talk Creighton out of jeopardizing Zradna's life, the general insists on scheduling another attempted drop to trap Zoller. On the day of the mission, Sgt. Hansen hands off a thermos of coffee to another German agent, who puts it on board Gallagher's plane. Hansen is arrested by CIC agents and Zoller is shot by MPs. On board the *Piccadilly Lily*, Gallagher asks where the thermos came from. A gunner says that typically, either Hansen or Pierson would bring the coffee. Gallagher orders the gunner not to open the thermos, then runs outside, grabs a rifle and shoots Pierson as he attempts to flee. With the saboteur ring smashed, the *Piccadilly Lily* takes off and drops Ilka as planned.

Col. Gallagher, Maj. Stovall, Sgt. Komansky
Ilka Zradna ·· Gia Scala
Brig. Gen. Dave Creighton ······················· J.D. Cannon
M/Sgt. Tony Podesta ································· Tige Andrews
Technician Third Grade Ed Hansen ······· Don Quine
Sgt. Pete Pierson ···································· Tom Stern
Capt. Zoller ·· Hans Gudegast
Maj. Ken Adams ·· Paul Comi
Sgt. Clem Garnet ····································· Charles Kuenstle
Technician Fourth Grade Thibideaux ···· James Brolin
Capt. Chuck Langgaard ·························· John Crowther

TDY

• Gia Scala (1934–1972) is probably best recognized for her role as resistance fighter Anna in the epic *Guns of Navarone* (1961), good practice for her role in this episode. She also played exotic beauties in such TV series as *Hong Kong*, *The Rogues* and *It Takes a Thief*. Scala died of a drug overdose.

• J.D. Cannon (born 24 April 1922 in Salmon, Idaho) began his career in New York City doing live TV dramas and locally-based film productions such as *Naked City*, *The Defenders* and *The Nurses*. Roles in the movie *Cool Hand Luke* (1967) and guest shots on *Combat!*, *The Invaders* and *The Wild, Wild West* led to his most visible role as Chief Peter B. Clifford on *McCloud* (1970–77).

• Tige Andrews (born Tiger Androwaous on 19 March 1923 in Brooklyn, New York) was mentor to the undercover cops known as *The Mod Squad* (1968–73). However, he is most recognized by fans for his performance as a Klingon in the *Star Trek* episode "Friday's Child" (OAD 1 December 1967). Andrews also had steady work on *The Phil Silvers Show* and *The Detectives*.

• Don Quine (born 1939 in Fenville, Michigan) dropped pre-med studies in favor of drama. Roles on Broadway led to guest shots on *Rawhide, Dr. Kildare* and *The Fugitive*. At the time of this episode, Quine was a regular on Fox's *Peyton Place*. Later, he co-starred on the long-running series *The Virginian* (1966-68). He appeared again in #55 "The Survivor."

· Hans Gudegast (born 3 April 1939 in Kiel, Germany) is now known as Eric Braeden. But in the early 1960s, he still used his birth name and starred in war dramas. During this period, he was seen frequently as Captain Dietrich on *The Rat Patrol*, but also appeared in *Jericho, Garrison's Gorillas* and made multiple appearances on *Combat!* He was also able to take advantage of the spy cycle, appearing in *Mission: Impossible* and *The Man from U.N.C.L.E.* He changed his name in 1970 and appeared in movies such as *Colossus: The Forbin Project* (1970) and *Escape from the Planet of the Apes* (1971). He began a marathon run as Victor Newman on *The Young and the Restless* in 1980.

· Thirty years later, James Brolin (born 18 July 1940 in Los Angeles) would star in his own aviation series, *Pensacola: Wings of Gold* (1997-2000). But at the time, Brolin was a Fox contract player. He had minor roles in other Fox TV series including *Batman, The Monroes* and *Voyage to the Bottom of the Sea*. Brolin was also in various features, including *Dear Brigitte* (1965), *Our Man Flint* (1966) and *Fantastic Voyage* (1966). Perhaps his most unusual assignment was making the test film for *Planet of the Apes*. Brolin was outfitted in prototype simian makeup and created the role of Cornelius (portrayed by Roddy McDowall in the actual film). Following his stint at Fox, Brolin soared to leading man status with roles in the hit TV series *Marcus Welby, M.D.* and *Hotel*.

PERSONNEL FILE
· Ilka becomes another one of "Joe's Girls." They say goodbye in the bomb bay of the *Piccadilly Lily*. Ilka asks Gallagher, "How do you like your coffee in the morning?" Fairly racy stuff for the family hour back in 1965.
· The character Sgt. Garnet (played by Charles Kuenstle) appeared later in #38 "The Hotshot" and #44 "We're Not Coming Back." Sgt. Garnet was written in the script for #35 "Then Came the Mighty Hunter," but did not actually appear in the episode. Charles Kuenstle also portrayed the unnamed Right Waist Gunner in #33 "The Loneliest Place in the World."
· Although neither Gen. Britt nor Doc Kaiser appear in this episode, both are mentioned.

DEBRIEFING
· Gallagher's plane is the *Piccadilly Lily*. V HP is on the starboard fuselage, 3713 V on the tail.

- This script was originally sold by William Anderson and William Hamilton under the title "Sabotage."
- Neither the script nor the Fox promo material gives credit to writer Marc Huntley.
- The old bomb-in-the-thermos trick was used in a 1956 *Playhouse 90* teleplay "Forbidden Area" by Rod Serling, based on a novel by Pat Frank.
- In the teaser, we see Sgt. Pierson working with an unseen saboteur who wears a prominent gold serpent ring. Another Nazi agent in Act IV has one as well.
- A-2 and shearling jackets now have U.S. flag patches on the right sleeve. The exception is Maj. Stovall, whose jacket has only the Army Air Force emblem on his left shoulder throughout the second season. Gallagher's patch has 48 stars; Komansky's has 50.
- A script revision dated 13 July 1965 changed the character name Maj. Ken Chandler to Maj. Ken Adams. In the third season, another character named Ken Chandler would make two appearances.

#35 "THEN CAME THE MIGHTY HUNTER" (8306)

OAD:	27 September 1965
RERUN:	20 December 1965
W:	Jack Paritz
D:	Laslo Benedek

New arrival Corp. Steve Corbett begs to be turned loose in combat. After Komansky checks Corp. Corbett's phenomenal gunnery school record, he goes to bat for the newcomer and recommends Corbett as Gallagher's new waist gunner. Corbett gratefully—and eagerly—accepts the assignment. At Wing HQ, Gallagher meets with Gen. Britt to strategize another attack on the factory at Hagensburg, which has proven to be a tough target to reach. Gallagher's plan is to use bad weather as a shield, then fly three B-17s down through the cloud cover, drop their bombs and fly back out of sight again. Britt agrees and the 918th begins an intensive training and coordination program with the RAF. Corbett is given his first chance to fire at a plane-towed target sleeve—but when the crucial time comes, his gun jams and the other gunners laugh at him. Komansky relates with Corbett the underdog and tries to get Corbett to become one of the guys. The two enlisted men hit the Denby Lion pub that night and Corbett is smitten with the owner's daughter, Gillian Denby, a sweet English girl. Steve has such a good time with Gillian that he's tired for the next day's practice mission. He's still sharp enough to spot German fighters out on patrol but when it comes time to squeeze the trigger, he freezes. And when the right waist gunner is shot, Corbett can't even bring himself to help him. But when Gallagher orders Corbett to fire, he hits an enemy plane and watches it burst into flames. After the *Piccadilly Lily* lands, Corbett won't leave the plane. Gallagher goes into the waist and listens to the corporal confess that he is only 15 years old. Corbett is confined to the base hospital. When he gets permission to eat in the mess hall, he never shows up. Distraught that he killed a man in combat, he goes into town to see Gillian, and she offers him shelter. Instead of calling the MPs, Komansky figures Corbett went to the Denby's pub and goes there to find him. Komansky talks him into coming back to the base with him, then covers for him to get things right with Gallagher. The next day, the mission continues—with stowaway Corbett on board the *Piccadilly Lily.* When the radio operator and both waist gunners are hit, Corbett grabs a .50-caliber gun and starts downing the Luftwaffe single handedly. After the mission, Gallagher reprimands Corbett and turns him over to the MPs. In confidence, the colonel tells Komansky that, before Corbett is discharged, he wants the lad promoted and recommended for a Silver Star.

Col. Gallagher, Maj. Stovall, Sgt. Komansky, Brig. Gen. Britt, Doc Kaiser

Corp. Steven Corbett	Beau Bridges
Corp. Billy Smith	Ted Bessell
Sgt. Ben Rodale	Tom Skerritt
Gillian Denby	Carol Both
Flora	Judy Carne
Mavis Denby	Nora Marlowe
Patient	William Christopher
Co-Pilot	Robert Dornan
Maj. Martin Percy	Willard Sage
Annabelle	Jane Wilde
Gunner	John Garwood
Abbott	John Hanek
Beegeebird	Rick Newton
Wing Commander Robertson	James Beggs [UNCREDITED]

TDY

• Beau Bridges (born 9 December 1941 in Hollywood, California) must have had an intense sense of déjà vu working in this episode. Just one year earlier, he essayed a virtually identical part in *Combat!* episode #60 "The Short Day of Private Putnam." The son of actor Lloyd Bridges (1913–1998), Beau kicked around TV in the early 1960s and made his Broadway debut in 1966. From there, Bridges focused on a film career and has become one of America's finest actors in movies such as *Norma Rae* (1979), *The Fabulous Baker Boys* (1989) and *Out of the Ashes* (2003).

• Ted Bessell (1935–1996) is best remembered as Donald, boyfriend of Ann

Marie (Marlo Thomas) on the hit comedy *That Girl* (1966–71). He seemed to come from nowhere to land co-starring roles in *It's a Man's World* (1962–63) and *Gomer Pyle, USMC* (1965–66). After toiling in a succession of short-term sitcoms, Bessell turned to directing episodic television.

- William Christopher (born 20 October 1932 in Evanston, Illinois) found the role of a lifetime as Father Mulcahy on the landmark series *M*A*S*H* (1972–1983), even though the part was played by another actor in the pilot.

PERSONNEL FILE
- Gallagher implies that Komansky has kept a wall around himself to keep people at a distance; the sergeant's relationship with Corbett may be a breakthrough. Gallagher says part of his job is helping his people grow. He calls Komansky "the best flight engineer in the service."
- Komansky tells Corbett that he also enlisted when he was underage to escape school and the cops.
- Gallagher tells Stovall to assign two new men to Gaines' group and three to Bailey's group.

DEBRIEFING
- Gallagher says that bombing the factory at Hagensburg is "suicide."
- Hagensburg was not an official target of the Eighth Air Force.
- Gallagher's call sign during the practice mission is "Readygo Leader."
- On the mission, stock footage shows a bombardier wearing a flight helmet, head down over the bombsight. The next scene is a man, with hair exposed, no helmet, pushing the release button.

INTELLIGENCE REPORT
- Twentieth Century-Fox studio chief Darryl F. Zanuck enlisted underage.
- Working title of this script was "Almost a Man."
- The script included the character Sgt. Clem Garnet, who also appeared in episodes #34 "Rx for a Sick Bird," #38 "The Hotshot" and #44 "We're Not Coming Back."
- Sgt. Rodale's jacket has no flag patch. Corbett has a 48-star flag on his right shoulder and an Eighth AF emblem on left shoulder.
- The pub Komansky and Corbett go into is the same one used as the tavern in #71 "To Seek and Destroy" and as the meeting room from #67 "Practice to Deceive."

#36 "THE IDOLATER" (8308)

OAD:	4 October 1965
RERUN:	2 May 1966

Lee Meriwether

TP:	Gerald Sanford
	& Marc Huntly
Story:	Gustave Field
D:	Laslo Benedek

Buzzing the 918th's field is hardly the way for replacement pilot Lt. Josh McGraw to start off with new C.O.—and old friend—Joe Gallagher. Both men grew up together, and both men are Army brats. But McGraw resents the colonel because Gallagher has always been held up to him as a role model. When Gallagher invites McGraw to join him on a dinner date with Capt. Phyllis Vincent, McGraw takes the opportunity to try to move in on her. Gallagher sees through McGraw's flirtation, but it has no bearing on his decision to break up McGraw's crew to give them combat indoctrination. Naturally, McGraw resents the move and as the 918th begins hitting a series of bridges in Poland, he takes advantage of every opportunity to undermine Gallagher's authority. Phyllis observes McGraw's upper level backstabbing at Wing HQ and tells Gallagher what she sees. For the next leg of the bombing campaign, Gallagher reassigns McGraw's crew to its own plane. The scheming McGraw breaks formation and uses his plane to knock out another in the series of bridges. When Gallagher confronts McGraw for what other commanders would call insubordination, McGraw brings up his long-standing resentment of Gallagher and vows to be his own man no matter what. The last straw comes after McGraw takes his plane up for a flight check and his gunners shoot down *Bed Check Charlie,* a Luftwaffe recon plane that Bomber Command feeds with bogus information. Britt wants the immature pilot put under arrest but Gallagher wants the general to let him handle his pilots in his own way. Back in Gallagher's office, the colonel faces McGraw with the crib notes McGraw used to hit the solo target. Gallagher orders McGraw to explain his actions to Gen. Britt, who allows the colonel to decide McGraw's fate. Gallagher lets McGraw decide whether to stay or be transferred. Surprisingly, McGraw takes the tougher route and chooses to stay with the 918th. McGraw joins his crew for the final leg of the campaign, but his plane is badly damaged by flak. Instead of falling back as Gallagher orders, McGraw orders the crew to bail out. The group misses its target so McGraw decides to fly his crippled plane into a tunnel that supports the final bridge. In doing so he destroys the bridge and his plane. Back at base, Gallagher waits for the final word on survivors before he personally writes a notification letter to McGraw's father.

Col. Gallagher, Sgt. Komansky, Maj. Gen. Britt
Lt. Joshua Melton "Josh" McGraw ⋯ Gary Lockwood
Capt. Phyllis Vincent ⋯⋯⋯⋯⋯⋯ Lee Meriwether
Lt. Guy Kelly ⋯⋯⋯⋯⋯⋯⋯⋯⋯ Robert Hogan
Russian Major ⋯⋯⋯⋯⋯⋯⋯⋯ Albert Szabo
Gallagher's Co-Pilot ⋯⋯⋯⋯⋯⋯ Robert Dornan
Lt. Nick Constantinius ⋯⋯⋯⋯⋯ Paul Mantee
Lieutenant ⋯⋯⋯⋯⋯⋯⋯⋯⋯⋯ Jerry Ayres

TDY

• Paul Mantee (born Paul Marianetti on 9 January 1931 in San Francisco, California) holds a special place with sci-fi fans for his starring role in *Robinson Crusoe on Mars* (1964). While Mantee never broke into leading man territory, he gave it a shot with the campy Bond wannabe film *A Man Called Dagger* (1967). Television was where he found more opportunities and he guest starred in series such as *The FBI, Jericho, SWAT* and multiple episodes of *Mannix*. His recurring roles were on *Cagney and Lacey* (1986–88) and the soap *Capitol* (1982–83).

• This was Lee Meriwether's second of three appearances on *12 O'Clock High*. Within a year, Meriwether was cast as a regular in the Fox series *The Time Tunnel* (1966–67). She also filled in for Julie Newmar as Catwoman in the big screen version of Fox's TV phenom *Batman* (1966). Meriwether later returned to QM, co-starring with Buddy Ebsen in the long-running series *Barnaby Jones* (1973–80). She also assumed the role of Lily in *The Munsters Today* (1988–1991).

Lee Meriwether on #36 "The Idolater": "I loved working with Paul Burke. We had a kissing scene first thing in the day and I had never met Paul. It was excruciating and I'm sure it was for him. But he got us through with his sense of humor. I didn't get to know Gary Lockwood very well on this show. But he and I worked together later on *Barnaby Jones* and we became good friends.

"Because [director] Laslo Benedek had worked with me, I got the movie *Namu, the Killer Whale* (co-starring Robert Lansing) because I looked like the wife of cinematographer Lamar Boren. At the time, she was a stunt-women. So Laslo said, 'I know the perfect person for the part.'"

PERSONNEL FILE

• Britt's daughter, Martha, is a nurse at Abberfeldy Rehabilitation Center in Scotland.

- The script for this episode identifies Ed Britt as a major general. In the episode, Britt's uniform has two stars yet he's credited as a brigadier general.
- The character of Capt. Phyllis Vincent appears later in #52 "The Outsider." In this episode, she says she works for Gen. Britt. However, in "The Outsider," she works for Gen. Pritchard.

DEBRIEFING
- When McGraw's plane first lands at the 918th, stock footage shows it to be the *Piccadilly Lily.*
- Gallagher's call sign is Bingo Leader. McGraw is Bingo Six.

INTELLIGENCE REPORT
- The stock shot of a B-17 slamming into the hillside and blowing up was first used in #32 "The Hero."
- McGraw's A-2 shoulder patch has 50 stars.
- *Command Decision* stock footage is used again.

#37 "BIG BROTHER" (8302)

OAD: 11 October 1965
RERUN: 11 April 1966
W: Jack Turley
D: Jerry Hopper

Tough-as-nails Col. Pres Gallagher welcomes his kid brother Joe and the crew of the *Piccadilly Lily* to the airstrip at Magadar, Africa, where Pres commands the 105th Infantry. Joe Gallagher needs fuel to get back in the air and complete the second leg of his group's shuttle raid. While Pres is glad to see his kid brother, he seems to have a chip on his shoulder about cooperating with "flyboys." In fact, his unit surgeon, Maj. Lecroy, and Nurse Betty Russo are concerned about Preston's overall health, with stress and exhaustion taking their toll on the C.O. Joe talks with Col. Bailey, deputy commander of the 918th, who tells Joe that Pres used fuel earmarked for their planes to keep his own trucks moving. When Joe confronts his older brother, Pres admits he has the fuel and has ordered the bombers destroyed to eliminate targets for the Luftwaffe. German tanks are headed their way so Pres plans on moving out his entire unit and wants nothing to attract enemy fire. Joe and Pres get into it and, as feared, Pres collapses. Acting commander Maj. Dutton allows Joe to radio for additional fuel. As the plane ferrying in the fuel approaches the runway, German fighters attack it and cause the plane to explode on impact. Meanwhile, Pres comes to and changes his stand. He tells Joe to take back the gasoline. Then, Pres outlines his strategy, which is quite a long shot: set a trap for the advancing Germans, while Bailey uses the remaining fuel to fly three B-17s to another base, pick up a bomb load and return in time to hit the German column. Joe remains with Preston to spring the trap. The next day, Preston waits until the Germans are almost on top of them, then launches his assault with tanks and artillery. Bailey arrives with his flight of B-17s and bombs the rear of the German column. Together, the air and ground assault effectively stop the advance. The 918th is free to complete its mission and Pres goes back to leading his troops.

Col. Gallagher, Sgt. Komansky
Lt. Col. Pres Gallagher ············· Jack Lord
Col. Frank Bailey ······················ Robert Colbert
Lt. Betty Russo ························· Julie Adams
Maj. Dutton ···························· Bernard Fox
Maj. Paul Lecroy ······················ Douglas Henderson
Capt. Strader ·························· Harry Millard
S/Sgt. Clyde Webhorn ············· Robert Sorrells
M/Sgt. John Orland ················· Ken Lynch
Sgt. Oscar Bessie ···················· Robert Biheller
Lieutenant ···························· William Swan
Sergeant ······························· Ted Markland
Scout Officer ························· Trevor Cuming
German Officer ······················ Hans Heyde
Capt. Mike Johnson ················ Robert Dornan

TDY

• Jack Lord (1920–1998) surely deserves a place of honor in the TV hall of fame for his role as steely, sharp-witted detective Steve McGarrett in *Hawaii Five-O* (1968–80). His film appearances were nominal, although he established the continuing character of Felix Leiter in the first James Bond movie, *Dr. No* (1962). Lord worked hard in guest appearances on *Route 66*, *The Untouchables* and *Have Gun, Will Travel* before he won the title role on *Stoney Burke* (1962–63).

• Julie Adams (born Betty May Adams on 17 October 1926 in Waterloo, Iowa) worked small parts in a number of forgettable movies in the early 1950s until she met *The Creature from the Black Lagoon* (1954). She played in live TV dramas and then appeared in guest spots on *Checkmate, Dr. Kildare* and *77 Sunset Strip*. Her continuing roles on TV were in *Code Red* (1981–82), *The Jimmy Stewart Show* (1971–72) and two soaps, *General Hospital* and *Capitol*.

• Robert Sorrells (born 29 June 1930) was a familiar face on TV. So familiar that police easily caught up with him after he shot two bar patrons in 2004. Known mostly for westerns, Sorrels turned in an admirable performance in the *Twilight Zone* episode "The Mighty Casey" (OAD 17 June 1960). His only recurring role was on *Ensign O'Toole* (1962–63). Sorrells appeared again in #53 "Back to the Drawing Board."

PERSONNEL FILE
- Joe says there were three Gallagher brothers; Jeff was killed the previous year. Pres is the oldest.
- Pres reveals that Joe's nickname is "Danzo," a corruption of Joe's middle name, Anson.
- Komansky asks why Joe Gallagher is in the air and Pres is on the ground. Joe says that an instructor at West Point told him, "Never walk when you can ride."
- Col. Bailey appeared earlier in #33 "The Loneliest Place in the World." Bailey is deputy commander of the 918th.
- Robert Dornan plays Gallagher's co-pilot, but the character is named Capt. Mike Johnson.

DEBRIEFING
- Gallagher flies *Piccadilly Lily.*
- Bailey tells Gallagher that Stukas hit and bombed them just after they landed.

INTELLIGENCE REPORT
- The *Command Decision* stock shot is reused, showing a B-17 spinning on runway and exploding into a fireball.
- The airmen have flag patches on their A-2 jackets. Gallagher and Bailey have 48-star emblems. Komansky has both the 48-star flag and Army Air Force patch on his left shoulder.
- Process photography—the same technique used to simulate flight in the B-17 mock-up—is used to depict motion as Joe and Pres drive in a jeep.
- The exterior of the Magadar village area was located at the Fox Ranch. It was used again in #46 "Between the Lines." The set also appears briefly in the 1966 Fox feature *Our Man Flint.*

FLIGHT LINE
- This story arc actually begins in #44 "We're Not Coming Back" and concludes in #38 "The Hotshot." Chronologically, this is Part Two.
- In this episode, Gallagher recaps the plot of episode #44, where his crew lands in Yugoslavia to make repairs.
- The RAF actually launched the concept of shuttle raids. Beginning 20 June 1943, planes left England, bombed Germany, reloaded in North Africa, bombed Italy and then returned to England.

#38 "THE HOTSHOT" (8303)

OAD: 18 October 1965
RERUN: 18 April 1966
W: Robert Lewin
D: Richard Donner

Pulitzer Prize winning journalist Roy Saxon has been brought in by SHAEF to report on the final leg of the 918th's shuttle raid from Wesselhaven to Magadar, Africa and back to bomb the oil storage depot at Saarbrucken. The key to successfully concluding the mission lies with veteran pilot Lt. Col. Jerry Troper of the 511th Fighter Squadron. Col. Troper will meet the 918th over Saarbrucken with his squadron of new P-51 Mustang long-range fighter planes—which are faster and have more range than any other Air Corps fighter. With the 918th airborne, each aircraft's gunnery station is posted with a silhouette of the P-51. German Me 109 fighters attack the group and a fierce aerial battle ensues, which soon includes the 511th's Mustangs. Col. Troper shows up five minutes after the scheduled rendezvous and fails to follow Eighth AF identification procedures. In the heat of combat, Sgt. Komansky shoots down a P-51. Outraged, Troper is determined to find the responsible gunner, even if it means working over Col. Gallagher. Komansky admits to Gallagher that he's responsible and is ready to face the consequences. Gallagher insists on viewing the gun camera film. On his way to meet Gen. Britt, Gallagher meets Lt. Fay Vendry, who delivers an intelligence report to his office and coyly maneuvers the colonel into a dinner date. At the Officers' Club, Britt explains that an order will attach the 511th to the 918th. The goal is to show that long-range fighter cover works. This means Gallagher will have to work closely with Troper. Troper continues to act like a boor by interrupting Gallagher's date with Lt. Vendry and whisking her away. This gives Gallagher time to watch the gun camera films. The films reveal why Troper's squadron was late meeting the 918th: he diverted to strafe a rail yard. When the flyers of the 511th drift in for an early-morning training mission called by Gallagher for all pilots, he is appalled by their lack of military discipline—and the fact that everyone ordered to attend is not present, including Col. Troper. Gallagher puts Troper under arrest and assigns his men to learn everything about B-17s, in and out of combat. Gen. Britt orders the first real mission with long-range escort to be flown on the marshalling yards at Würzburg. Just then, Fay arrives with a very intoxicated Troper, who passes out on the floor of Gallagher's office. Gallagher grounds Troper and gives the lead to Maj. Marriott, deputy squadron commander. For the initial phase of the mission, P-38s fly with the group. Then they peel off and are replaced by P-51s. While the bombers fly through flak, the 511th tangles with the Luftwaffe, led by the 918th's old nemesis, Col. Falkenstein. When the planes return to base with no losses, Maj. Marriott and his men have a new-found respect for Gallagher and his B-17s. Britt tells Roy Saxon that the end of his story is the fighter pilots. But Troper still hasn't caught on to the concept of teamwork and is left behind by the rest of the 511th.

Col. Gallagher, Maj. Stovall, Sgt. Komansky, Brig. Gen. Britt
Lt. Col. Jerry Troper ···················· Warren Oates
Lt. Fay Vendry ···························· Jill Haworth
Alyce Carpenter ························· Jill Ireland
Roy Saxon ································· Walter Brooke
Lt. Bukich ································· George Brenlin
Col. Falkenstein ························· Gunnar Hellstrom
Maj. Marriott ···························· William Bryant
Sgt. Garnet ······························· Charles Kuenstle
Capt. Mike Johnson ················· Seymour Cassel
Waiter ···································· Tom Symonds

TDY

• Warren Oates (1928–1982) found a home playing quirky, free-spirited characters. Among his many guest appearances on TV westerns are *The Rebel, Tombstone Territory* and *Wanted: Dead or Alive*. Somehow, Oates also found time to do fantasy series, such as *Thriller, The Twilight Zone* and *The Outer Limits*. Oates became a member of director Sam Peckinpah's stock company, appearing in *Major Dundee* (1965), *The Wild Bunch* (1969) and *Bring Me the Head of Alfredo Garcia* (1974). He recreated two signature roles in TV incarnations of *True Grit* and *The African Queen*. His only recurring role was in *Stoney Burke* (1962–63).

• Jill Ireland (1936–1990) relocated from her native England to Hollywood with her then-husband, actor David McCallum. She guest starred in four episodes of McCallum's hit series *The Man from U.N.C.L.E.* (1964–67). She also appeared in the *Star Trek* episode "This Side of Paradise" (OAD 3 March 1967) along with Frank Overton.

• Walter Brooke (1915–1986) had a small part with an enduring line in *The Graduate* (1967), in which he advises Dustin Hoffman's character to "go into plastics." Other films included *Marooned* (1969), *Tora! Tora! Tora!* (1970) and *The Andromeda Strain* (1971). His name and face carry an impact with martial arts fans because of his regular part on Fox's *The Green Hornet* (1966–67). He also kept busy with the daytime soaps *One Man's Family* (1950–52), *Three Steps to Heaven* (1953–54), *The Brighter Day* (1956–58) and *Paradise Bay* (1965–66).

• Seymour Cassel (born 22 January 1935 in Detroit, Michigan) made his first appearance on film in John Cassavetes' independent film *Shadows* (1959). That started a relationship with the filmmaker that spanned seven films over 25 years. Cassel is now one of the busiest actors working in independent films. Back in the day, Cassel did episodic TV to help make his break. He guest starred on shows such as *Batman, Combat!* and *My Three Sons*. This was the first of five appearances on *12 O'Clock High*.

PERSONNEL FILE
- Stovall introduces Britt as "our new wing commander."
- Britt says to Saxon, "I've just been given this wing to command. This is my first major mission and I didn't want you in on it."
- Gallagher calls Troper "the best fighter pilot I've ever seen."
- Lt. Fay Vendry, Gallagher's flame-of-the-month, reappears in episode #40 "Runway in the Dark."
- Because the chronology of the episodes is off, viewers are left wondering how Gallagher knows Col. Falkenstein. The two airmen had a brief encounter in "We're Not Coming Back," which was broadcast out of order as episode #44.

DEBRIEFING
- Returning from the shuttle raid, Gallagher's call sign is Shuttle Leader; Troper is Constable Leader.
- During the time period covered by season two, the Eighth Air Force bombed Saarbrucken on 4 October 1943.
- On the training mission, Troper uses the call sign Hemstitch Leader; on actual mission, Marriott uses Hemstitch One.
- The Eighth Air Force did not bomb Würzburg until 21 July 1944.
- The 511th is stationed at Hollypool.

INTELLIGENCE REPORT
- Gallagher uses flash cards to test Troper's ability to recognize planes. The cards resemble those from Milton-Bradley's *12 O'Clock High* card game.
- Someone at QM Productions must have liked the title of this episode. Episode #9 "Appointment at Liege" was originally sold by John McGreevey as "The Hot Shot."
- Richard Donner directed the movie *X-15* (1961), which co-starred Robert Dornan, who played Gallagher's co-pilot, Bob Fowler.
- Fox promotional material bills the role of Maj. Marriott (William Bryant) as Maj. Greentree.

FLIGHT LINE
- Gallagher says the shuttle from England to Africa and back again took three days. The story arc began in episode #44 "We're Not Coming Back" and continued in #37 "Big Brother." Chronologically, this episode is the conclusion.

Lois Nettleton

#39 "Show Me a Hero, I'll Show You a Bum" (8309)

OAD: 25 October 1965
RERUN: 16 May 1966
W: Robert Hamner
D: Richard Donner

Newsman Kirby Wyatt tips off up-and-coming journalist Susan Nesbit to some breaking news: The *Piccadilly Lily*—badly damaged, co-pilot dead and Col. Gallagher out cold—is being flown back to base by Sgt. Komansky. For Nesbit, the story could be a career maker either way: The death of Gen. Max Gallagher's son or his heroic rescue by Komansky. With guidance from Maj. Stovall via the radio and a semi-conscious Gallagher, Komansky brings the plane in for a landing. Nesbit races to the 918th and gets Wyatt to use his influence to keep the other reporters away from Komansky. Meanwhile, the reluctant hero is counseled by Doc Kaiser about his feelings of guilt over self-preservation versus a selfless act of courage. Determined not to play the hero, Komansky decides to go on the next day's mission instead of traveling to London for a press reception. Komansky flies with Maj. Benson's crew. When a bomb sticks in the bomb bay and Komansky kicks it loose, the men start kidding him about his heroic stature. Komansky freezes at the thought of being labeled a hero. At the NCO club, Nesbit steals Komansky away and takes him for a walk on the outskirts of the base. She persuades Komansky to take a field commission if it's offered to him and, in the process, leads him to believe that she cares for him. The sergeant is puzzled: Gallagher hasn't even mentioned the possibility of a commission. The next day, Komansky calls in sick, skips the mission and goes AWOL to London in search of Susan to clarify where they stand. He finds her dressed for an evening out in the company of Wyatt. Susan begs Komansky to wait nearby for her, which he does. Wyatt follows the sergeant and tells Komansky that Susan has been using him to further her own ambitions. They begin to argue and when an MP appears, Komansky slugs him and runs away. During an air raid that evening, Kirby escorts Susan back to her flat, where Gallagher shows up looking for Komansky. Susan admits it was her idea to use Komansky—and Gallagher and his family name—for her own gain. Just then, Komansky shows up at the door. Gallagher advises the sergeant to give himself up. Komansky agrees but wants a minute alone with Susan. After the colonel and Wyatt leave, Komansky says he overheard what she said and knows she was using him. He leaves Susan alone, and joins Gallagher in the hallway just as a German bomber slams into the building, burying Susan under rubble and a fallen beam. Later, in a ceremony at the base attended by Susan and Wyatt, Komansky is awarded the Silver Star. Gallagher asks Susan to wait for the ending before she writes a story.

Col. Gallagher, Maj. Stovall, Sgt. Komansky, Doc Kaiser
Susan Nesbit ·· Lois Nettleton
Kirby Wyatt ··· Lloyd Bochner
T/Sgt. Vern Chapman ················ Burt Reynolds
Pamela Hurley ································· Anne Whitfield
S/Sgt. Weber ································· Michael McDonald
Sgt. Roberto ································· Steven Bell
Maj. Benson ································· Lee Farr
GI Reporter ································· Ira Barmak
MP ································· Mike Doherty
Civilian Reporter ························ Shawn Michaels
Control Officer ························ Charles McDaniel
Air Raid Warden ························ Pat O'Hara

TDY
- Although Lois Nettleton (born in 1929 in Oak Park, Illinois) has two Emmy awards to her credit, her heart has always been in the theatre. She trained at Chicago's Goodman Theatre and at The Actor's Studio, which led to performances on Broadway and at the Shakespeare Festival in Stratford, Connecticut. Nettleton had continuing roles on *The Brighter Day* (1954–56), *Accidental Family* (1967–68), *All That Glitters* (1977) and *You Can't Take It With You* (1987–88).

- Burt Reynolds (born 11 February 1936 in Waycross, Georgia) was still years away from his breakout performance in *Deliverance* (1972) and his controversial Cosmopolitan centerfold. Reynolds revealed a much darker side of Sgt. Chapman in #45 "The Jones Boys."

PERSONNEL FILE
- Susan Nesbit (Lois Nettleton) describes Komansky as "an orphan kid," and "a lone wolf type...he's always in hot water."
- Susan knows that Joe Gallagher is Gen. Gallagher's son.
- Sgt. Chapman (Burt Reynolds) offers a facetious toast to Komansky: "To the man that was the flight engineer when the general bought the farm."
- Although he does not appear, Gen. Pritchard is mentioned.

DEBRIEFING

- In the teaser, P-51s chase German fighters away from *Piccadilly Lily*.
- Gallagher's call sign is Chicago Leader.
- At the airfield there are two B-17s in profile, one close up and one in the background.

INTELLIGENCE REPORT

- The title of this episode is adapted from the closing line of World War II ace Greg "Pappy" Boyington's autobiography, *Baa Baa Black Sheep:* "If this story were to have a moral, then I would say, 'Just name me a hero and I'll prove he's a bum.'"
- Great direction by Richard Donner. There is a very detailed shot set in the alley toward other side of Archbury Street set. When Wyatt confronts Komansky, we see in the background a woman airing laundry in her second floor window. There is also smoke billowing from the chimney.
- The sequence of a German bomber slamming into a building was used earlier in #4 "The Sound of Distant Thunder" and #23 "The Trap."
- The script and Fox promo material credits the script to Robert Hamner and William Koenig.
- The Archbury Street set stands in for London.

FLIGHT LINE

- Special order dated 10 June 1943 from the President authorizes the Silver Star for Komansky.

#40 "RUNWAY IN THE DARK" (8311)

OAD:	1 November 1965
RERUN:	23 May 1966
W:	Robert Lewin
D:	Robert Douglas

Col. Gallagher is handed a politically sensitive mission: Airlift Arn Borg, a revered Norwegian Resistance leader, to England so he can deliver vital documents in person. The night mission calls for using the King Frederick Lighthouse as a marker for landing in Norway. Gallagher assigns Capt. "Chub" Willis, his best navigator, to get him to the rendezvous point. During the mission, a second beacon throws Willis off course, and Gallagher's plane is hammered by flak. Willis gets them back on course and Gallagher does a power approach to get in quickly. With the engines running, Gallagher goes out to meet Borg, who insists that his son Christian accompany him. This goes against Gallagher's orders, but the colonel gives in when Borg counters by refusing to leave without Christian. As German gunfire nips at their heels, Gallagher ushers Borg and his son aboard.

Once Borg and his son are secure at the 918th, Arn Borg produces maps of a Nazi installation. To Gallagher, the importance of Borg's information was exaggerated; further, the colonel questions Borg's motives because he dragged his son along. The Borgs are billeted on base but that night, Arn writes a note to his son, slugs a guard and flees. The next morning, Christian finds the message from his absent father. Britt needs to reconcile inconsistencies between Borg's drawing and other maps of the area, so he orders a recon flight. Gallagher shows the resulting photos to Christian, but the boy is leery about helping him because the colonel didn't trust his father. After Gallagher explains that people are saying Borg is a traitor, Christian tells the colonel about the Nazi buildup in Norway. Just before Gallagher takes off on a mission to bomb the installation, Borg returns. Borg explains that he suddenly realized that, by selfishly taking his son, he betrayed his people. The only way he could rectify his disloyalty, Borg realized, was by destroying the Nazi facility himself. Borg volunteers to go along and leads Gallagher to the target for a successful raid that wipes out a fuel depot. Borg agrees to accompany Gallagher to take out a second installation, after which he will parachute back into Norway to resume the battle there. Christian wants to go with his father but Gallagher explains that his place is in England where Borg can grow up to be part of the future that his father is fighting to create.

Col. Gallagher, Sgt. Komansky, Maj. Gen. Britt
Arn Borg ·· Albert Paulsen
Lt. Fay Vendry ···························· Jill Haworth
Christian Borg ···························· Pat Cardi
Capt. "Chub" Willis ···················· Jack Weston
Cynthia Finlay ···························· Dinah Anne Rogers
British Officer ···························· Gil Stuart
Mr. Dahlgren ···························· Peter Bourne
Co-Pilot ······································ Robert Dornan
Sven ·· Donald Ein

TDY

• Pat Cardi (born Patrick Cardamone on 2 May 1952 in Patchogue, New York) was apparently a casting director's favorite at QM Productions because he also appeared in *The FBI*, *The Fugitive* and *The Invaders*. A year later he would co-star as cave boy Breer on the sitcom *It's About Time* (1966–67) from the creators of *Gilligan's Island*. Cardi also appeared in *Battle for the Planet of the Apes* (1973).

• Jack Weston (1924–1996) had a way with comedy but is better known for his role as a sinister heavy in *Wait Until Dark* (1967). Other movies include *The Incredible Mr. Limpet* (1964), *The Thomas Crown Affair* (1968) and *The*

The Four Seasons (1981). His TV roles ranged from *Peter Gunn* to *Bewitched* to *Burke's Law*. Weston co-starred with a bunch of chimps on *The Hathaways* (1961–62).

- Gil Stuart (1919–1977) also appears as an RAF Wing Commander in #42 "Grant Me No Favor." Stuart was a utility player who appeared as three additional, unrelated characters in #8 "The Hours Before Dawn" (Policeman), #67 "Practice to Deceive" (Shullendorf) and #78 "The Hunters and the Killers" (Barkeep).

PERSONNEL FILE
- Gen. Britt wears the two stars of a major general but is still credited as a brigadier general.
- Gallagher calls his co-pilot (Robert Dornan) Bob.
- Although Gen. Pritchard does not appear, he is mentioned.
- In Act IV, Gallagher calls the British Officer (Gil Stuart) by the name Group Capt. Stuart.

DEBRIEFING
- On the practice run, Gallagher's call sign is Columbine. The RAF control center is Cameo Victor.
- The target is near Trysil, Norway.

INTELLIGENCE REPORT
- Fay Vendry (Jill Haworth) appeared earlier in #38 "The Hotshot."
- The part of Mr. Dahlgren is credited on-screen as Norwegian Civilian.

William Shatner and Peter Marko

#41 "I AM THE ENEMY" (8312)

OAD:	8 November 1965
RERUN:	30 May 1966
W:	Anthony Spinner
D:	Robert Gist

German-born Maj. Kurt Brown drives himself and his crew to destroy Germans—not only by bombing railroads, factories and submarine pens, but by killing German civilians. Despite this disturbing outlook, Brown is an outstanding pilot, so much so that

Gen. Britt wants to give him command of the 82nd Bomb Group. But Brown wants no part of command; he would rather keep bombing Germans. Later, in The Star and Bottle, Gallagher asks Brown to escort Elizabeth Hoffman, a lonely young woman, back home. In Elizabeth's flat, after he tries to take advantage of her, she tells Brown that they both share an intense sense of loneliness. With that in common, they begin a relationship that seems doomed from the start: she is German. Furious, the major confronts Gallagher, who tells him that Elizabeth has been cleared by G-2. Gallagher then tells Brown that if Brown's hatred of Germans was carried to its logical conclusion then he would have to exterminate himself, too. This revelation causes Brown to have a breakdown on his next mission, which causes him to go back to Elizabeth and explain himself. The source of Brown's hatred of Germans is a long-standing death wish for himself. The closer Brown grows to Elizabeth, the more human he becomes. Brown realizes his iron façade is caving. Now that he has someone to live for, he requests to be relieved from flight duty. Gallagher needs good pilots. He again asks Brown to examine his motives and make his choice based not on fear but instead on his new-found love. Brown flies on the next mission. After Gallagher's plane is crippled by flak, the colonel orders Brown to take the lead. Brown successfully leads the group on an effective bomb run but then flak rips into his plane and he is hurt badly. The group returns to base and Brown pulls through in surgery. Elizabeth is angry with Gallagher for making Brown fly again, but Gallagher tells her that Brown is proud of what he's done—and that she gave him the desire to keep flying.

Col. Gallagher, Maj. Stovall, Sgt. Komansky, Maj. Gen. Britt, Doc Kaiser

Maj. Kurt Brown	William Shatner
Elizabeth Hoffman	Elen Willard
Capt. Forbes	Peter Marko
Co-Pilot	Robert Dornan
Lt. Daniels	Walter Gregg
Waist Gunner	Claude Johnson
Tail Gunner	Richard Brander
Young Officer	Tom Falk
Capt. Donalsen	Tom Palmer
Capt. Davis	Adam Roarke
Davis' Co-Pilot	Richard Schuyler

TDY

• William Shatner (born 22 March 1931 in Montreal, Canada) became a pop culture icon for his portrayal of Capt. James T. Kirk on *Star Trek* (1966–69). In addition to *Star Trek,* Shatner gained notoriety in a wide variety of stage and screen appearances. For four years (1982–86) he portrayed TV supercop T.J. Hooker. His other regular series included *For the People* (1965), *Barbary*

Coast (1975–76), *Rescue 911* (1989–96), *Tek War* (1994–96) and *Boston Legal* (2004–present).

PERSONNEL FILE
- Gen. Britt wants to give Maj. Brown command of the 82nd Bomb Group.
- Maj. Gen. Britt is still credited as a brigadier general.
- Gallagher calls his co-pilot Bobby.
- On the strike in Act IV, Gallagher's call sign is Ramrod; Brown's call sign is Ramrod One.

DEBRIEFING
- The 918th has hit the sub pens at St. Nazaire for a period of four weeks.

INTELLIGENCE REPORT
- Shatner's A-2 jacket has a 50-star flag patch.

#42 "GRANT ME NO FAVOR" (8307)

Barry Sullivan

OAD:	15 November 1965
RERUN:	25 April 1966
W:	Anthony Spinner
D:	Robert Douglas

The latest in a series of brutally crippling raids on an unspecified target in Norway makes Lt. Col. Bill Christy choose to abort the mission and limp back to base. Even though three previous attempts resulted in heavy losses and casualties, Christy was the only commander not to complete the mission. Gallagher fires off a scathing letter to Gen. Britt, demanding to know how he should explain the repeated raids over a secret target. Upon receiving the note, Britt orders Gallagher to London. Gallagher expects a dressing down, but instead discovers a party celebrating Britt's promotion and the arrival of his father, Lt. Gen. Maxwell Gallagher. In private, Britt tells Joe Gallagher that Col. Christie's actions may lead to a court martial. Joe's indignation is apparent to his father, who advises Joe to drop his convictions because bigger issues are in play. Joe refuses to abandon Christie and storms out. Gen. Britt fights to keep his best group commander in line, while Gen. Gallagher pursues a hidden agenda aimed at getting his son promoted to general. News of Christie's court martial hearing pushes Gallagher to develop a plan to successfully hit the target. Suddenly the mission is taken away and handed to another group, and the 918th is assigned to training missions. Gallagher knows the group is being punished because of his position so he asks his father to get the 918th another chance. Gen. Gallagher works with Pritchard to approve Joe's strategy: send the group over one more time but have two B-17s break away and hit the target at low level. To demonstrate their commitment, Joe volunteers himself and Bill Christie for the job. The mission goes on as planned, with Col. Gallagher and Col. Christie dropping below the group. When fighters pick on Christie's plane, he feigns engine trouble to make himself a decoy so that Gallagher's plane can hit the target successfully. After the drop, the fighters pursue Gallagher, so Christie moves in to bomb the target again and clearly destroys it. Once the target is destroyed, SHAEF removes the cloud of secrecy and Gen. Gallagher discloses that the target was a secret nuclear weapons research facility. The general tells Joe that Christie will have to stand trial, but he's also been awarded the Distinguished Flying Cross.

Col. Gallagher, Maj. Stovall, Sgt. Komansky. Maj. Gen. Britt, Doc Kaiser, Gen. Pritchard

Lt. Col. Bill Christy	Frank Aletter
Lt. Gen. Maxwell Gallagher	Barry Sullivan
WAC Captain	Jacqueline Russell
Capt. Don Edwards	Don Spruance
Gallagher's Co-Pilot	Robert Dornan
Aide	Kirby Brumfield
MP Officer	Mike Doherty
Christy's Co-Pilot	Ricks Falk
Wounded NCO	Robert Hathaway
RAF Wing Commander	Gil Stuart
WAC Noncom	Charisse Eland [UNCREDITED]

TDY

• Barry Sullivan (1912–1994) geared up for this role by appearing in *Strategic Air Command* (1955) and *A Gathering of Eagles* (1963). A distinguished actor, Sullivan was at home playing authority figures in continuing TV roles on *The Man Called X* (1955–56), *Harbourmaster* (1957–58), (which co-starred Paul Burke), *The Tall Man* (1960–62), *The Road West* (1966–67) and *Rich Man, Poor Man—Book II* (1976–77).

• Frank Aletter (born 14 January 1926 in College Point, Long Island, New York) had a gift for light comedy that got him noticed on Broadway in the 1950s. Sitcoms provided all his starring vehicles: *Bringing Up Buddy*

(1960–61), *The Cara Williams Show* (1965–66) and *It's About Time* (1966–67) and *Nancy* (1970-71). Aletter also guest starred on *Fantasy Island, All in the Family* and *Kolchak: The Night Stalker.*

Frank Aletter on "Grant Me No Favor": "I remember riding out to the location airfield sitting next to Barry Sullivan, being impressed by my proximity to what I considered a legit Hollywood star. He was charming and talkative and I was impressed to watch him work.

"I was delighted to see Andy Duggan. He was a very good friend of mine in New York and a very special, kind human being. Andy and I were the only non-family beneficiaries in Larry Blyden's will and I miss them both deeply. I don't know if Larry ever did a show in this series but he was my very favorite human being in my entire career.

"I have nothing but fond memories of Paul Burke who was a thoroughgoing professional in everything he did. Don Dubbins was in 'Grant Me no Favor' also and he had been in the road company of *Mr. Roberts* with me in 1951."

PERSONNEL FILE
- Joe and his father phone Preston on his birthday.
- Gen. Gallagher says Joe is a boxing and football star.
- Britt tells Gen. Gallagher that Joe is "impertinent, he is infuriating, but at what he is now doing he is maybe the best in Bomber Command."
- Gen. Gallagher calls Gen. Pritchard by the first name Bill.
- Although Britt is promoted to Major General in this episode, the end titles still credit the role as Brigadier General.

DEBRIEFING
- Christie's initial call sign is Antelope Leader.
- Christie's plane is *Hundred Proof.*
- The mission is turned over to the 815th.
- Christie's second call sign is Ramrod Able. Gallagher is Ramrod.

INTELLIGENCE REPORT
- The character of Lt. Col. Bill Christy (Frank Aletter) returns in #62 "Gauntlet of Fire," but is portrayed by William Windom.
- Gen. Gallagher calls Gen. Pritchard by the name Bill.
- *Command Decision* stock footage is used again.

FLIGHT LINE
- When Col. Gallagher talks with his brother Preston, Joe acknowledges that he returned from the shuttle raid safely. Regrettably, because of network scheduling, the mission that Joe Gallagher referred to—the story arc from #44 "We're Not Coming Back" to #37 "Big Brother" to #38 "The Hotshot"—hadn't occurred yet.

#43 "STORM AT TWILIGHT" (8315)

OAD: 22 November 1965
RERUN: 13 June 1966
TP: Anthony Spinner
Story: James Doherty
D: Robert Gist

Maj. Stovall's day starts off with a mission gone bad and only gets worse: he receives a telegram notifying him that his only son, 1st Lt. Michael A. Stovall, has been reported missing in action. Despite the efforts of other officers to cheer him up, Stovall blames himself for the deaths of 35 men in that day's mission. Wanting to make up for the losses and avenge his son, Stovall strong-arms his old friend Gen. Britt into giving him a chance to fly combat again. When Gallagher returns from sick leave, he tries to bring up logical reasons why the major shouldn't fly—but Stovall isn't thinking logically. He gets a waiver for his age and, although he knows his vision isn't what it used to be, passes his physical. Gallagher treats the middle-aged Stovall as he would any 22-year-old flight school grad. When Gen. Britt insists that Stovall has proven himself capable and should be allowed to go on an actual mission, Gallagher schedules Stovall to fly the next day. The mission target is the refinery and oil storage facilities at Geissen, where the Germans have built a POW camp. The facts are that if even one bomber misses the target, burning oil could kill Allied prisoners—maybe even the major's son. Stovall is still raring to go—but on the mission, he has trouble staying in formation and nearly collides with another B-17. Afterwards, Stovall talks privately with Komansky, his flight engineer, who tells the major candidly that he was a lousy pilot. Despite Stovall's second thoughts, when Britt calls for a maximum effort over Geissen, Gallagher insists that Stovall fly. Gallagher assigns him to fly right seat in his aircraft. When a burst of flak knocks Gallagher out, Stovall must take the controls and fly the bomb run. The strike is successful and Maj. Stovall leads the group back to base weary, but satisfied.

Col. Gallagher, Sgt. Komansky, Maj. Stovall, Maj. Gen. Britt, Doc Kaiser
Lt. Col. Rogers ····························· Ted Knight
Capt. Phil Kelly ··························· William Cort
Charley, Stovall's Co-Pilot ········ Don Spruance
Navigator ···································· James Devine
Waist Gunner ······························ Bruce Glover
Capt. Lou Brewer·························· Ken Baechel
Young Lieutenant ······················· Ray McGrath
Officer ··· Glenn Sipes
Bombardier ······························· George Sims [UNCREDITED]

TDY

- Ted Knight (1923–1986) was still a few years away from his Emmy-winning, signature role as news anchor Ted Baxter on *The Mary Tyler Moore Show*. At this time, he was just another working actor particularly busy doing character voices for Saturday morning cartoons such as *Superman, Batman, Aquaman, Fantastic Voyage* and *Journey to the Center of the Earth*.

- Bruce Glover (born 2 May 1932 in Chicago, Illinois) joined The Actors' Studio and initially worked in the New York City area on projects such as *Blindfold* (1965) and the TV series *Hawk* and *Car 54, Where are You?* Glover's other films include *Chinatown* (1974), *Diamonds are Forever* (1972) and *The Thomas Crown Affair* (1968). He is the father of actor Crispin Glover.

PERSONNEL FILE

- The telegram from the Secretary of War to Maj. Stovall gives his full name as Harvey B. Stovall.
- Maj. Stovall is 44 years old.
- Britt and Stovall have been in the military together since at least 1928.
- Gen. Britt wears the two stars of a major general but is still credited as a brigadier general.
- Although Gen. Pritchard does not appear, he is mentioned.

DEBRIEFING

- Targets are the marshalling yards at Antwerp and the Geissen oil refinery and storage dumps.
- On the Antwerp mission, Stovall's call sign is Blue Five.
- After the strike on Antwerp, Me 109s attack.
- Over the Geissen mission, Gallagher's call sign is Red Dog Leader.

INTELLIGENCE REPORT

- Col. Rogers is acting commander of the 918th.

TOBY SIGHTING

- Toby mug is on the mantle of the Officers' Club.

#44 "WE'RE NOT COMING BACK" (8304)

OAD: 29 November 1965
RERUN: N/R
W: Philip Saltzman & Dan Ullman
D: Jerry Hopper

While airborne, Gallagher reveals to his crew that the group is on a secret mission, a pilot program called a shuttle raid. Their initial target is Wesselhaven, 200 miles deeper than any Allied aircraft has gone before. From there, the group will fly south to Africa to refuel and reload with more armaments. The return trip will include a bomb run over occupied France. The Germans monitor the 918th's course and wonder why the bombers pass by obvious targets of opportunity. Finally, the 918th hits its target and turns south, confusing the Germans even more. The maneuver also drains the Germans' fuel so that they cannot pursue the group. But, Luftwaffe Col. Falkenstein, at an observation outpost, leads a flight of cadets in pursuit of the bombers. The Me 109s lay into the *Piccadilly Lily,* wounding Gallagher's co-pilot and

Gunnar Hellstrom and Ina Balin

knocking out an engine. Gallagher has no choice but to leave the formation and land in Yugoslavia to attempt repairs. On the ground, the colonel orders Komansky to repair the engines and the rest of the crew to camouflage the plane. Their work is interrupted by a group of armed Yugoslavians, who force the crew to a cave where Gallagher meets Yellich and his daughter Mara. The colonel tries to cut a deal for Yellich's help but the old man refuses. Instead, he uses Gallagher as bait to trap and kill two patrolling Germans. The next day, Yellich tells Gallagher in confidence that he will help him fix the plane—if Gallagher promises to take Mara to safety. Meanwhile, Col. Falkenstein is determined to find the downed American crew and learn the details of their mission. Gallagher's men join forces with Yellich's partisans to raid a nearby German base to secure the supplies necessary to patch up the B-17. Once the plane is repaired, Gallagher and his crew are ready to take off. When the colonel directs Mara to go with him, she's surprised; she knew nothing of her father's wishes. Mara refuses to go because she believes if her father is left alone he will die a martyr; with her there, he will keep fighting. The *Piccadilly Lily* takes off just as Col. Falkenstein and a patrol drive up and try to stop them with small arms fire.

Col. Gallagher, Sgt. Komansky
Mara Yellich ···································· Ina Balin
Nicolas Yellich ···························· George Voskovec
Col. Falkenstein ······················· Gunnar Hellstrom

Mikhail	Michael Forest
Gen. Von Leyden	John Hoyt
Capt. Dan Lowell	William Arvin
Sgt. Clem Garnet	Charles Kuenstle
Capt. Gunter	Sasha Harden
German Soldier	Hans Heyde
Gregore	Peter Coe
German Officer	Walter Friedel
Capt. Mike Johnson	Seymour Cassel
Sophie	Gabrielle Rossillon
German Guard	Rick West

TDY

- In addition to her successful acting career Ina Balin (1937–1990) worked as an activist for the plight of Vietnamese orphans. Her performances on film included *The Black Orchid* (1958), *From the Terrace* (1960) and *The Comancheros* (1961). Balin's TV work was mainly on detective and adventure series, but she did manage some comedic roles on *Get Smart* and *The Dick Van Dyke Show*.

- John Hoyt (1905–1991) is recognized by the TV generation as an elder-statesman type. But Hoyt also had a rich history on Broadway and left a legacy of more than 60 movies. He is also remembered for his long-running series of commercials for Midas mufflers. His continuing TV roles were on *Tom, Dick and Mary* (1964–65), *Return to Peyton Place* (1972–74) and *Gimme a Break* (1982–87).

- Michael Forest (born Gerald Michael Charlebois on 17 April 1929 in Harvey, North Dakota) starred in the 1959 drive-in classic *Beast from Haunted Cave*, which was also Chris Robinson's breakthrough film. The ruggedly handsome actor wore a mini-toga as Apollo in the *Star Trek* episode "Who Mourns for Adonis?" (OAD 22 September 1967).

PERSONNEL FILE

- Komansky speaks a few words of Polish, hoping the Yugoslavs will understand. He learned a little of the language from the neighbors where he grew up.

DEBRIEFING

- Wesselhaven was not a target of the Eighth Air Force.
- Spitfires and P-38s escort the mission in the teaser.
- Capt. Lowell is Gallagher's co-pilot. On the mission he reports that Col. Bailey's squadron lost another plane. When Gallagher's plane is hit, Gallagher turns the mission over to Bailey.

- Gallagher does not use a call sign.
- Me 109s attack the 918th.

FLIGHT LINE
- This episode begins a story arc, aired out of order, that continues in #37 "Big Brother" and concludes with #38 "The Hotshot."

#45 "THE JONES BOYS" (8314)

OAD: 6 December 1965
RERUN: 6 June 1966
W: William D. Gordon
D: Robert Douglas

AWOL Lt. Jaydee Jones uses nurse Lt. Jean Warner to sneak back in time for briefing. But Jaydee does not want to fly any more and wants his brother, Sgt. Frank Jones, to help him get out. Jaydee's discontent results in a botched takeoff in which he cracks up his plane, killing the bombardier and co-pilot Larry Cahill. Lt. Jones is hospitalized, unable to recall the details, while his flight engineer, TSgt. Vern Chapman, files a purposely vague report. Sgt. Chapman doesn't want to jeopardize his current situation:

Andrew Prine

he's been stealing small arms and selling them to a British buyer. Because Gallagher can't put up a maximum effort due to a shortage of planes and spare parts, he calls a meeting at Wing HQ with Col. Ken Hunter of G-4. Col. Hunter chooses to investigate the crash of Flight 376 to prove that a lack of parts was not to blame. Gallagher hosts Hunter and calls a meeting with Lt. Jones, Sgt. Chapman and Sgt. Jones, who was maintenance chief of 376. Chapman comes forward with a story that puts the blame on the late Larry Cahill and saves Jaydee Jones. Later, Chapman tells Jaydee he wants payment for his AWOL trip into town to sell the guns. Frank Jones overhears the conversation and wants to help his little brother out of a scrape. But Chapman vows to bring everyone down into a court martial if anyone interferes. Sgt. Chapman makes Jaydee an offer: on the next mission, Jaydee will break formation and fly to Switzerland, where Chapman will split his take from selling stolen goods with Jaydee. Meanwhile, Capt. Jim Mason from the Provost Marshall's office shows up with a Briton in whose possession was found three .45s with serial numbers matching guns assigned to the 918th. Making matters worse, the Briton identifies Sgt. Chapman as his supplier. Chapman and Jaydee are already in their plane ready for the day's mission when Gallagher puts in the call to bring in the sergeant. Frank Jones puts the puzzle together, realizes what Chapman's been up to and boards the plane to stop him. Chapman knocks out Frank with a .45 and orders Jaydee to take off. With a gun in his face, Jaydee takes off while Chapman tells him where to go. As Gallagher pursues them in a P-51, Chapman mans the top turret and tries to shoot down the colonel. Just then, Frank regains consciousness and wrestles Chapman into submission. As Gallagher drives off German fighters, Jaydee heads back to the base. On the ground, Chapman and Jaydee are taken away by MPs. Frank tries to rationalize where his brother went wrong, but Gallagher says Jaydee finally grew up.

Col. Gallagher, Sgt. Komansky, Maj. Stovall
Lt. Jaydee Jones ···································· Andrew Prine
T/Sgt. Frank Jones ························· Bruce Dern
T/Sgt. Vern Chapman ················ Burt Reynolds
Col. Kendal Hunter ···················· Mark Richman
Lt. Jean Warner ··························· Susan Seaforth
Co-Pilot ······································· Burt Douglas
The Briton ··································· Noel Drayton
Capt. Jim Mason ·························· Logan Field
Sgt. Fazio ····································· Ted Gehring
Sgt. Peters ···································· John Ward
MP ·· Ed Deemer
Gunner ·· Robert Bolger
Gunner ·· Garrison True

TDY

- Mark Richman (born 16 April 1927 in Philadelphia, Pennsylvania) is now known as Peter Mark Richman. He acts, he writes, he directs and he looks debonair doing it all. On TV, his lengthy résumé includes appearances on *Swamp Thing*, *T.H.E. Cat*, *Three's Company* and *Land of the Giants*. His continuing roles were on *Cain's Hundred* (1961–62), *Longstreet* (1971–72), *Dynasty* (1981–84) and *Santa Barbara* (1984).

- Susan Seaforth (born 11 July 1943 in Oakland, California) has been a fixture on daytime soap operas since the late 1960s, primarily on NBC's *Days of Our Lives*. Primetime appearances include *Emergency!*, *Hawaiian Eye* and *The Man from U.N.C.L.E.* After marrying vocalist Bill Hayes in 1974, she changed her name to Susan Seaforth Hayes. She also appeared in episode #66 "A Distant Cry."

Susan Seaforth on "The Jones Boys": "It was shot night-for-night. I arrived about six and finished around ten the same night. It was mighty dark and I could hardly see for the moon refused to shine. I dated Andy Prine for a while. Director Robert Douglas and I had met at Warners a few years before. He was an excellent British actor who played costume-flick villains in heavy wigs."

PERSONNEL FILE
- Sgt. Chapman appeared earlier in episode #39 "Show Me a Hero, I'll Show You a Bum."
- The script identifies the co-pilot role played by Burt Douglas as Larry Cahill.

DEBRIEFING
- After Chapman's escape flight is airborne, Gallagher calls Hollypool to have a P-51 sent over.
- In the P-51, Gallagher uses call sign Ramrod.

INTELLIGENCE REPORT
- A script revision dated 13 October 1965 changed the character name T/Sgt. Chet Barrow to T/Sgt. Vern Chapman.
- Footage recycled from the *12 O'Clock High* feature includes ambulances and trucks racing to the rescue.
- Chapman consummates his deal with the Briton in the alley between sections of the Archbury Street set, which was also dressed as a Swiss village in #50 "Underground."

#46 "BETWEEN THE LINES" (8310)

OAD:	13 December 1965
RERUN:	9 May 1966
TP:	Andy Lewis
Story:	Coles Trapnell
D:	Gerald Mayer

Col. Gallagher is flying Maj. Gen. Stace and Brig. Gen. Krasker to a conference in Russia and then back to England. On the return trip, German fighters attack and cripple Gallagher's plane. The colonel orders a bail out, but only half the crew and passengers jump before he is forced to make a belly landing in an open field. Gallagher is not certain if they've landed in Russian or German territory. Gallagher, Komansky and co-pilot Capt. Pete Gargas help Gen. Stace and his spineless clerk, MSgt. Trask, evacuate before the plane explodes. Running for cover, Gen. Stace is hit by gunfire from a German fighter. Komansky rushes back inside the airplane and, as the B-17 explodes into a fireball, is naturally presumed dead. Gallagher, Gargas, Trask and the badly wounded Stace find shelter in an abandoned church. There, as Stace slips in and out of consciousness, Gallagher explains that the mission was to coordinate Russian support for the planned invasion of France. Information about Russian military strength is recorded on rice paper in a pack of chewing gum that Stace entrusts to Gallagher. Just then, the Americans discover they are sharing their shelter with someone…who turns out to be Anya, a frightened and hungry Russian peasant. Her fears are not relieved when Komansky suddenly shows up lugging a .50-caliber gun salvaged from the B-17. That night, the Americans and Anya narrowly evade a German patrol which shows up to search the village. After they've left, Gallagher puts on the uniform of a dead Nazi and reconnoiters the area. When Gallagher returns, Komansky informs him that Stace has died. The next day, the Germans return and a firefight ensues. Trask, wanting to save himself, grabs a religious icon from Anya and runs outside in an attempt to surrender. Without hesitation, the Germans cut him down. Anya goes out to distract the Germans so that the Americans can escape through the rear of the church. They almost make a clean getaway until Gallagher accidentally trips the church's bell rope, which sounds a chime. The Germans give chase and, although they shoot Gargas, Gallagher and Komansky are able to break free and are greeted by Russian troops. Once Gallagher and Komansky are reunited with Gen. Krasker, the three are flown back to England.

Col. Gallagher, Sgt. Komansky	
M/Sgt. Trask	Donald Harron
Maj. Gen. Stace	Larry Gates
Capt. Pete Gargas	Philip Bruns
Brig. Gen. Ed Krasker	Ken Drake
German Officer	Sasha Harden
German Sergeant	Norbert Meisel
Russian Major	Peter Coe
Anya	Lydia Markova
German Lieutenant	Eric Forst
Right Waist Gunner	Richard Brander
Rescue Pilot	Steve Wolfson
German Soldier	Hans Heyde

TDY

- Philip Bruns (born 2 May 1931 in Pipestone, Minnesota) seems born to play comedic roles, such as those on *Mary Hartman, Mary Hartman* (1976–77) and *Forever Fernwood* (1977–78). But he is equally adept at playing serious dramatic characters as well: Bruns has done *Sanford and Son* as well as *The Streets of San Francisco.*

- Hiding out in the church, Komansky is terrified by the rats; he admits he became afraid of them while he grew up in Oakland.
- After Gallagher and Komansky are rescued, Gallagher wants to get in some flying time as co-pilot of the rescue plane instead of relaxing.
- Although the script and the end titles identify Gargas as a lieutenant, he wears captain's bars and Gallagher addresses him as Captain.

DEBRIEFING
- The plane that Gallagher belly-lands and which subsequently explodes had triangle A and tail number 1863 but no fuselage numbers, only the national emblem. It's used again in #68 "The All American" as the plane Capt. King belly-lands at the 918th.

INTELLIGENCE REPORT
- Working title of this episode was "A Journey Toward the River."
- The exterior set of the church and the bombed-out village was located at the Fox Ranch.
- The brick bunker where Gallagher, Gargas, Stace and Trask initially take shelter was located at Chino. An overhead, long shot of it can be seen in episode #60 "Day of Reckoning." It's also featured in #22 "The Ticket" and #62 "Gauntlet of Fire."
- Gargas' A-2 jacket has a 50-star flag patch. Stace and Trask wear shearling jackets; neither one has a flag emblem.

#47 "TARGET 802" (8313)

OAD:	27 December 1965
RERUN:	4 July 1966
TP:	Sherman Yellen & Marc Huntly
Story:	Sherman Yellen
D:	Robert Douglas

When the *Piccadilly Lily* is severely battle-damaged before it can reach a target, Gallagher relinquishes command and turns back for the base. The colonel orders his bombardier, Lt. Jerry Parks, to dump their bomb load after they've reached the English Channel. Lt. Parks prepares to do so, but as soon as he opens the bomb bay doors, a mechanical failure causes the bomb load to fall immediately. Instead of hitting the channel, the bombs pound the French coastal village of Sainte Monique. Among the villagers who run for their lives are downed American fliers Capt. Bing Pollard and Maj. Hub Coefield. Back at the base Officers' Club, Axis Sally's latest broadcast denounces the 918th's devastating error, a message that Lt. Parks takes very personally. In Sainte Monique, German

Capt. Burgdorf investigates the underground railroad that helps Allied airmen escape to freedom. Burgdorf's job is made easier because the embittered villagers' sympathies have turned against the Americans. Brig. Gen. Marteen of G-2 is sent to the 918th to investigate the accidental bombing and explains to Gallagher how important the village had been as an escape route. Meanwhile, Capt. Pollard and Maj. Coefield, along with widow Claudine Corbelle and her badly wounded son Jean-Paul, have been picked up by Air-Sea Rescue and brought back to the base for treatment. Mme. Corbelle wants revenge against the fliers who killed her father and injured her son, and has brought along a gun to ensure justice is served. She overhears Gallagher tell Pollard and Coefield that his plane dropped the bombs and begins plotting her revenge. Doc Kaiser tells Gallagher how necessary—and critical—surgery is for Jean-Paul and, in turn, the colonel visits Mme. Corbelle to explain things. She agrees to go out with him and slips the gun into her purse. They have a drink at the Officers' Club, where Gallagher extends his apologies and tries to assure Claudine that the Americans will help rebuild Sainte Monique. Just then, Capt. Pollard stops by their table to demand action be taken against Lt. Parks or else he will file a report with the inspector general. After Gallagher dismisses Pollard, Claudine tells the colonel point blank that she holds him responsible for what happened. She accompanies Gallagher to a meeting on the Sainte Monique incident to be held at Wing HQ. On the drive there, she pulls her gun on him. The colonel explains how Luftwaffe cannon fire fouled his plane's bomb release which caused the accidental bombing. Suddenly, Claudine breaks down, giving Gallagher the opportunity to disarm her and return her to Doc Kaiser's care. Back at Wing, Gen. Marteen shows Gallagher updated aerial reconnaissance photos that reveal the Nazis are setting up a radar installation in the village, confident that the Americans will not bomb it again. Marteen's plan is to immediately send in a CIC radio team, which reports back that the Germans are holding hostages near the radar site. The transmission also explains that the Nazis are compiling a file of Free French operatives and storing it at the radar installation. Claudine is heartsick at the prospect of more French citizens dying but she still identifies the building on an aerial photo labeled Target 802. First, the Americans drop leaflets warning the citizens of Sainte Monique of the imminent bombing. Then Gallagher flies the *Piccadilly Lily* on a single-plane raid supported by the 511th Fighter Squadron. Bombardier Lt. Jerry Parks gets a chance to set things right and drops a single, delayed-fuse bomb right on target. Back at the base, everyone is elated that Jean-Paul's operation has been a success and he will walk again.

Col. Gallagher, Maj. Stovall, Sgt. Komansky, Doc Kaiser
Capt. Bing Pollard ·········· Lou Antonio
Brig. Gen. Stan Marteen ·········· Harry Townes
Claudine Corbelle ·········· Lisa Pera
Lt. Jerry Parks ·········· George Brenlin

Maj. Hub Coefield	Wright King
Marcel Lenoir	Jacques Roux
Jean-Paul Corbelle	Gerald Michenaud
Capt. Burgdorf	Anthony Zerbe
Fishwife	Monique Lemaire
GI Patient	Bobby Pickett
Co-Pilot	Robert Dornan
Lt. Davis	Rees Vaughn
Pierre Fecamp	Jean Del Val
Voice of Axis Sally	June Foray [UNCREDITED]

TDY

- Harry Townes (1914–2001) was one of the supreme character actors—believable, appealing and competent in a wide range of roles. Townes' career grew along with the television medium—from the Golden Age of live drama, to westerns, sci-fi and detective shows but, surprisingly, almost no comedy. Among his numerous guest appearances were *Charlie's Angels*, *The Incredible Hulk*, *Night Gallery* and *The Wild, Wild West*.

- Wright King (born 11 January 1923 in Okmulgee, Oklahoma) brought an earthy realism to his roles. King made his feature film debut in *A Streetcar Named Desire* (1951) but many baby boomers remember him as Ernest P. Duckweather on *Johnny Jupiter* (1953–54). He worked in many westerns of the era, capped by a co-starring role on *Wanted: Dead or Alive* (1960).

- Bobby Pickett is Bobby "Boris" Pickett of "Monster Mash" fame. Pickett (born Robert George Pickett on 11 February 1940 in Somerville, Massachusetts) served in the Army Signal Corps, and then went straight to Hollywood. "Monster Mash" was released in 1962 and has resurfaced every Halloween since. His other TV work included *Bonanza*, *The Lieutenant*, *The Beverly Hillbillies* and *Petticoat Junction*. He also appeared in movies such as *It's a Bikini World* (1967) and *Chrome and Hot Leather* (1971).

PERSONNEL FILE

- Although the end titles credit Robert Dornan's role as Co-Pilot, the script and Fox promo material identify the role as Bob Fowler.

DEBRIEFING

- P-47s join the single B-17 photo recon unit for fighter cover.
- Gallagher's call sign is Ramrod; Pollard's is Blue Leader.

INTELLIGENCE REPORT

- The aerial photo of Target 802 is the same photo used later to represent the

German village of Adelberg in #73 "The Ace."
· June Foray once again provides the voice of Axis Sally.

TOBY SIGHTING
  · Toby mug is on the mantle of the Officers' Club. There is a good close-up of
  the Toby as Stovall turns it around. Then, Gallagher explains the legend to
  Claudine.

Judy Carne and James Daly

#48 "FALLING STAR" (8316)

OAD:	3 January 1966
RERUN:	20 June 1966
W:	Andy Lewis
D:	Laslo Benedek

Gen. Pritchard has two men in mind for a vacant wing commander position: veteran pilot Gus "Pappy" Wexler and Joe Gallagher. With Gallagher hospitalized due to injuries from flak, Wexler is made temporary commander of the 918th. Wexler, who left the Air Corps to be a stunt pilot, has been given a second chance. Once an easygoing guy, Wexler has become a strict disciplinarian, calling for Class A uniforms and by-the-book behavior—behavior that is interpreted by Stovall and Komansky as attempts to take over the 918th for good. What Col. Wexler doesn't tell anyone is that he is suffering from flashbacks and mood swings; he's haunted by the deaths of his wife and former stunt partner. Meanwhile, Gallagher is released from the hospital and assigned temporarily to Wing HQ. Wexler sees a special mission as a critical opportunity to prove himself. However, during the mission he suffers from another flashback. When Komansky tries to help him, Wexler accuses the sergeant of insubordination and aborts the mission. Wexler asks young Lt. Booth to accompany him to see a good friend of his, Mrs. Alicia Clyde-Bryce. The situation seems almost as though Wexler is trying to create the family he lost. Gallagher confronts Wexler about his behavior in the air and their discussion reveals that neither one of them wants the wing job. They both want to fly combat. But Gallagher insists that Wexler stay down and go through a thorough physical. The special mission goes on with Booth flying co-pilot with Banazak. After the bomb run is completed, Banazak's plane gets caught in the resulting firestorm and shock wave and explodes, crashing to earth. Wexler feels responsible for Booth's death but gets no sympathy from Alicia, who begs him to give up flying and face the ghosts that haunt him. But Wexler is not ready to give up flying. Gallagher has an idea of how to beat the elusive target: one B-17 that drops a bomb delivered by a parachute to delay the explosion. Gallagher assigns himself and Wexler to pilot the plane. Just before the target, Wexler has another flashback and turns the plane off course. Gallagher has to slug Wexler and take control to deliver a perfect bomb run. Back at base, Doc Kaiser defines Wexler's problem as "traumatic amnesia" and orders him to take treatment in London. It's perfect timing because Wexler admits he's in love with Alicia and is ready to settle down.

Col. Gallagher, Sgt. Komansky, Maj. Stovall, Doc Kaiser, Gen. Pritchard
Col. Gus "Pappy" Wexler ·········· James Daly
Mrs. Alicia Clyde-Bryce ·········· Barbara Shelley
Lt. Downey Booth ·················· David Macklin
Capt. Peter Banazak ··············· Paul Comi
Lt. Bob Fowler ····················· Robert Dornan
Doris ······························· Judy Carne
WAC Sergeant ····················· Jayne Massey
Lt. Clark ··························· John Luce

TDY
- James Daly (1918–1978) brought his skills and talent from the theatre to TV and films. Daly appeared in numerous live TV dramas in the 1950s. As filmed programs dominated, he appeared on *Dr. Kildare*, *The Nurses* and *The Twilight Zone*. His performance in the *Hallmark Hall of Fame* production of "Eagle in a Cage" earned Daly an Emmy award. He put on orangutan make-up for his role in *Planet of the Apes* (1968). Daly found his career-making role as a father-figure physician on the long-running series *Medical Center* (1969–76). He was the father of actors Tyne Daly and Timothy Daly. James Daly joined other *12 O'Clock High* alums, including Gen. Savage himself, Robert Lansing, in *Wild in the Sky* (1972), which also featured Brandon de Wilde and Tim O'Connor.

PERSONNEL FILE
- Gen. Pritchard notes that Stovall knew Wexler "in the old days...for 15 years."
- Wexler was Gallagher's instructor pilot during transition training.
- Pritchard says that Gen. Britt is in Washington, D.C.

DEBRIEFING
- The mission is to destroy an underground fire-control center for flak and coastal barriers.

- One can only imagine the casting session for this episode. Someone must have said, "Get me a Dana Wynter-type." And in came Barbara Shelley.
- Before Wexler gives his first briefing, there's a shot of two B-17s on the airfield.
- The set used as Mrs. Clyde-Bryce's great room was used later in #63 "Massacre" and #64 "Face of a Shadow."
- Komansky's shearling jacket has a 50-star flag patch.
- Doc Kaiser's office has his name on the door.

Harry Guardino

#49 "THE SLAUGHTER PEN" (8317)

OAD:	10 January 1966
RERUN:	27 June 1966
W:	Dave Lewis and Andy Lewis
D:	Robert Douglas

The 918th must abort another mission to "the slaughter pen"—an invincible bunker that houses a superior new form of radar. An exasperated Gallagher tells Gen. Pritchard that the target is not a job for bombers but rather for a commando raid. Pritchard takes Gallagher to a meeting at an elite British commando training center and introduces him to Col. Percy Vivyan and Gen. Saint-John Keighley, leaders of the team that will take out the slaughter pen. The radar expert is Capt. Barney Deel, an officer whom Gallagher had a hand in getting expelled from West Point. Despite the animosity, Gen. Pritchard insists that Deel is the best man for the job. Training for the assault begins on Col. Vivyan's estate, but it gets off to a rocky start—and is complicated by the local postman spying on the activities. Deel doesn't exactly give the training his all: he's too busy romancing Vivyan's sister, Sydney. Col. Vivyan warns Deel to back away from Sydney which Deel does and seems to break off their brief affair. However, Gallagher and a squad of British commandos catch the spy and intercept a letter from Sydney to her aunt and uncle which tells of her romance and innocently gives away much of the carefully planned raid. Ironically, Col. Vivyan slowly realizes that he knew his sister was privy to too much classified information. Gen. Keighley is incensed by the behavior of both Deel and Vivyan but knows he needs them both, and gives the mission a green light for the next day. The assault begins with a naval bombardment, then Allied aircraft drop the commandos over the target. As the commandos fight their way to the bunker and secure it, the 918th finds a target of opportunity and bombs a fleet of German warships. Inside the bunker, Deel removes a piece of equipment and takes the mortally wounded German commander, Gen. Reger, out to safety. Although Reger warns Deel that the bunker is armed to explode, Deel believes he can salvage more of the radar system. He runs back inside just before the bunker explodes. With the slaughter pen out of commission, the 918th goes up the next day to bomb Hamburg.

Col. Gallagher, Sgt. Komansky, Maj. Stovall
Capt. Barney Deel ····················· Harry Guardino
Col. Percy Vivyan ····················· David Frankham
Sydney Vivyan ····················· Juliet Mills
Gen. Saint-John Keighley ········ Michael Rennie
Gen. Kurt Reger ····················· John Van Dreelen
Sgt. Angus Dunbar ················ John Alderson
Col. Peter Thom ···················· John Lasell
Col. Hans Mahler ···················· Walter Friedel
Lt. Bob Fowler ······················ Robert Dornan
Capt. Kelly ························· Rees Vaughn
Henry Smith, the Postman ······· Pat O'Hara
Capt. Eddington ···················· Ted Dudomaine
German Radarman ················ Peter Hellmann
German Radioman ················ Heinz Brinkmann

TDY

- Michael Rennie (1909–1971) exhibited a reserved, dignified presence throughout his film and TV career. Rennie made an indelible impression as Klaatu in the Fox sci-fi masterpiece *The Day the Earth Stood Still* (1951). He is also remembered for the his role of Harry Lime in the syndicated *The Third Man* (1959–60) co-starring Jonathan Harris.

- Harry Guardino (1925–1995) served in the Navy during World War II, then studied at the New York Dramatic Workshop. Guardino developed a likeable, tough-guy persona that shone in guest roles on *Checkmate*, *The Untouchables* and *The Outer Limits*. His recurring TV roles were on *The Reporter* (1964–65), *Monty Nash* (1971–72) and *The New Adventures of Perry Mason* (1973–74).

- Juliet Mills (born 21 November 1941 in London, England) is part of the Mills family that included father Sir John Mills; mother, playwright Lady Mary Mills and sister, actor Haley Mills. Juliet's already substantial career was rejuvenated by her appearance as a charming witch on the soap opera *Passions*. Previously, Mills won an Emmy award for her work in the miniseries *QB-VII*

(1974). Mills also received Golden Globe nominations for her roles in *Nanny and the Professor* (1970–71) and the movie *Avanti!* (1972). She appeared again in #61 "Siren Voices."

· John Lasell (born 1928) made a career out of portraying officious characters on TV series ranging from *I Spy* to *87th Precinct* to *My Favorite Martian*. Lasell was also a regular in the soap operas *Dark Shadows* (1967) and *As the World Turns* (1966).

PERSONNEL FILE
· The script gives Gen. Pritchard's first name as Bill.
· Fox promo material spells the role of Capt. Kelly as Kelley.

DEBRIEFING
· Wiping out the installation is key to the Allied bombing of Hamburg.
· P-38s escort the B-17s on the practice run and on the mission.
· During the practice run, Gallagher uses the call sign Daybreak. On the mission, Capt. Kelly uses Daybreak Leader.
· On the mission, Gallagher flies his P-51 and uses his Ramrod call sign. The Germans know that Ramrod identifies Col. Gallagher of the 918th.

INTELLIGENCE REPORT
· If Col. Vivyan's Brywncote manor house looks familiar, that's because you've seen it before as the Clampett mansion on *The Beverly Hillbillies*.
· The sound effect of the German radar blips is the same sound used on the Fox series *Voyage to the Bottom of the Sea*.

(Left to right) Robert Walker, Claudine Longet and Paul Burke

#50 "UNDERGROUND" (8319)

OAD:	17 January 1966
RERUN:	11 July 1966
TP:	Robert Lewin
STORY:	James Doherty & Coles Trapnell
D:	Robert Douglas

On a mission to take out a chemical factory, the 918th is duped into bombing a diversionary target and is then hit with heavy flak. Gallagher's plane is hit badly, killing the radio operator, knocking out the radio and causing a fuel leak. After ordering his crew to bail out, Gallagher follows suit. He no sooner hits the ground than he is surrounded by troops—Swiss troops, who escort the colonel to the American embassy. There, Capt. Wright informs Gallagher that because he landed in neutral Switzerland, he is now officially out of the war. But because Gallagher has vital military information, Wright unofficially arranges for Gallagher to get home by traveling incognito. Gallagher's first contact is at a sidewalk café with American George Richardson. As the colonel makes his way to the second station, a patrol of Swiss guards is escorting Karl Weigand down the street, when two men on bicycles run interference and give Weigand a chance to escape. Gallagher reunites with Richardson, who outfits him with a gun and money, then points him to a truck that will drive him out of town. However, ever since the colonel left the café, he has been shadowed by a sinister-looking Gestapo agent. At the outskirts of town, the truck slows down and Weigand jumps out of the truck bed. Once the truck has stopped the driver gives Gallagher directions and password for his next checkpoint. After the truck pulls away, Weigand points his gun at Gallagher but both men are surprised when the Gestapo agent rides up on a motor scooter. Using the element of surprise, Gallagher turns the tables and holds Weigand at bay. Once the Gestapo man leaves, Gallagher prods Weigand at gunpoint to his next rendezvous. They find the farmhouse deserted. Inside Gallagher tells his prisoner that because Weigand knows too much, he must be turned over to the Nazis. Just then, a woman enters the house. She is Liane, daughter of the underground contact. Her father had been picked up by the Gestapo that morning. Liane does not know the rest of the underground system, but since she now fears for her life, offers to take Gallagher and Weigand to someone who may be able to help. Using an ambulance as cover, Liane, Gallagher and Weigand pass a German checkpoint and meet Clioche, who tells Liane that the Gestapo killed her father. Clioche insists that Gallagher save Liane's life but also insists that Weigand be killed and orders one of his men, Francois, to take care of the deserter. Instead, Weigand turns the knife on Francois and kills him. Liane and Gallagher walk into trouble at a German checkpoint, but Weigand shows up and kills the guard and the shadowy Gestapo agent. In the next town, the trio meets Foulard, who has two German soldiers on his side. The double agents pose as the trio's captors and put them on a prison train. Another sympathetic Nazi makes sure they get off at the right stop and sends them on to the end of the line, a riverside watch shack, where they meet Leduc, the man in charge of the underground. He outlines the final step to freedom and reluctantly agrees to allow Weigand to go along. Just after Leduc leaves them, a German patrol approaches. Weigand volunteers to surrender in order to save Liane and Gallagher. The colonel feels loyalty to Weigand for saving his life and goes after him. As insurance, Gallagher gives Liane the target information and tells her to contact Gen. Britt if he doesn't return. In hiding, Gallagher overhears Weigand confirm that he is an SS officer who has successfully infiltrated the underground.

In a shootout, Gallagher fatally wounds Weigand and admits he made the fatal mistake of trusting the Nazi. After a seaplane takes Liane and Gallagher back to England, the colonel leads the 918th on a mission to wipe out the real chemical factory, and this time Gallagher dedicates the mission to everyone who helped him back to freedom.

Col. Gallagher, Sgt. Komansky
Karl Weigand ·································· Robert Walker
Liane ·· Claudine Longet
George Richardson ···················· Whit Bissell
Leduc ··· Emile Genest
Wilson Sechrist ···························· Frank Wilcox
Train Guard ································· Robert Boon
Winery Guard ···························· Sasha Harden
Capt. Peter Wright ···················· Tom Palmer
Foulard ······································· Maurice Marsac
Clioche ·· Norbert Schiller
Bridge Guard ····························· Norbert Meisel
Emile ··· Jacques Roux
German Sentry ··························· Horse Ebersberg
The Shadower ···························· Bud Walls
Patrol Captain ···························· Erik Holland
Jim, the Co-Pilot ······················ Seymour Cassel
Swiss Officer ······························ George Perina
Swiss Soldier ······························ Nickolaus Kopp
Francois ······································· Chuck Courtney

TDY

· Robert Walker (born in 15 April 1940 in New York City) proved early on that he had acting talent, but his eccentric personality may have cramped his career. It was reported in 1968 that Walker refused to wear shoes and was "not interested" in working for money anymore. "'It's just a weird means to an end,'" Walker said at the time. His eccentricities didn't appear to damage his career too badly. Fans remember his performance as the titular "Charlie X" on *Star Trek* (OAD 15 September 1966). Walker would return in #69 "The Pariah."

· Whit Bissell (1909–1981) is fondly remembered for his part in the Irwin Allen sci-fi series *The Time Tunnel* (1966–67). His *The Time Machine* (1960) is a cult favorite film, along with *Creature from the Black Lagoon* (1954) and those twins of terror *I Was a Teenage Werewolf* (1957) and *I Was a Teenage Frankenstein* (1957). TV guest appearances included *Tightrope, Land of the Giants* and *It Takes a Thief*.

- Frank Wilcox (1907–1974) is best recognized as Mr. Brewster of the OK Oil Company on *The Beverly Hillbillies* (1962–66). He also had the continuing role of Beecher Asbury on *The Untouchables* (1959–63). Guest appearances included *I Love Lucy*, *The Adventures of Fu Manchu* and *The Wild, Wild West*.

PERSONNEL FILE
- Gallagher gives his serial number: 01167087.

INTELLIGENCE REPORT
- The Archbury Street set is redressed as a Swiss village. We also get to see the rear of some studio buildings behind the façade.
- Process photography, like that used to simulate flight in the B-17 mock-up, is used at the boathouse to show the river and opposite shore.

#51 "WHICH WAY THE WIND BLOWS" (8318)

OAD:	24 January 1966
RERUN:	N/R
W:	James M. Miller
D:	Laslo Benedek

Bad weather forces the 918th to abort a mission to destroy the yards at Kiel. With seven planes lost in the effort, Gallagher is furious with the shortcomings of the Eighth's weather section. Some of the guesswork may be reduced by the arrival of Capt. Patricia Bates, a professor of meteorology, who has a scientific approach to forecasting weather. Capt. Bates and her assistant, Lt. Rogers, are assigned to the 918th to help the group successfully bomb Kiel. Bates invites Gallagher to work in her "office": a B-17 specially outfitted for studying the weather. On their first flight, German fighters attack and send the crippled ship heading for home. Following her first taste of combat, Capt. Bates decides she wants no part of the military life or of helping send men to their deaths. But surviving a German air raid on Archbury changes her mind. Using another plane, Bates goes up for further study. She hits on a plan to use cloud cover as a shield for the attacking bombers and orders the pilot to fly right into a thunderhead. As Bates tracks the storm within the cloud, the plane ices up and the pilot loses control, forcing him to ditch. With an assist from Gallagher's crew, Air-Sea Rescue picks up the survivors and Capt. Bates gives Gallagher the wrap-up on her forecast for Kiel. The colonel persuades Gen. Britt to let him apply Bates' recommendation and lead an offensive the next day. With the cloud cover, the Germans can't send up fighters or flak, allowing the bombers to do their job without losing a plane. Back at the base, Gallagher returns to find Capt. Bates waiting for him. It seems that the emotionless science of war is too much for her. She prefers the science of weather and is transferring to a desk job in London.

Col. Gallagher, Sgt. Komansky, Maj. Stovall, Maj. Gen. Britt
Capt. Patricia Bates ·················· Dina Merrill
Maj. Fitzsimmons ·················· Robert Yuro
Capt. Blodget ·················· Med Flory
Lt. Rogers ·················· Michael Macready
Capt. Bob Fowler ·················· Robert Dornan
Air Raid Warden ·················· Jack Greening
Capt. Blodget's Co-Pilot ·········· Richard Schuyler

TDY
· Dina Merrill (born 9 December 1925) and then-husband, Cliff Robertson, played arch-villains Calamity Jan and Shame on the Fox series *Batman* (1968). Merrill appeared in films such as *Desk Set* (1957), *Butterfield 8* (1960) and *The Sundowners* (1960), while pursuing roles in episodic TV such as *The Rogues, Night Gallery* and *Mission: Impossible.*

PERSONNEL FILE
· Co-pilot Bob Fowler wins his captain's bars in this episode.
· Along the same lines, Gen. Britt is finally credited as a major general.
· Komansky still wears a 50-star flag patch.
· Britt tells Bates that it's been 24 years since he was shot down by a German fighter.

DEBRIEFING
· The Eighth Air Force bombed Kiel more than 20 times between November 1942 and May 1945.

INTELLIGENCE REPORT
· Great effect of rivulets of rain shadows on the faces of the crew on the flight deck.
· Stock scene of a B-17 ditching is reused.

#52 "THE OUTSIDER" (8320)

OAD:	31 January 1966
RERUN:	18 July 1966
W:	Ellis Marcus
D:	Don Medford

While escorting the 918th, Maj. Zachary Temple's P-51 squadron tangles with attacking Me 109s. One of Temple's pilots, Lt. Harley Wilson, eagerly takes off in pursuit of a Messerschmitt. But when Wilson fires at the enemy, he inadvertently shoots up Gallagher's plane so badly that the colonel must drop out of the mission. Komansky later finds .50-caliber bullets in the waist, rather than German 20mm bullets. At the post-mission debriefing Wilson claims a kill—the fighter that attacked Gallagher's plane. But none of the other pilots can confirm it. Wilson hopes Komansky will verify his claim. Instead, Komansky bitterly informs Wilson what really happened. Later Wilson—feeling personally responsible—feels even more isolated after his buddy Lt. Mikler cancels their night out. Wilson wants to admit his error and goes to Pinetree to confront Gallagher. The colonel, Gen. Pritchard, Maj. Temple and Capt. Robbins have just watched films of that day's mission and know that Wilson was at fault. To try to make up for his error, Wilson

James MacArthur

volunteers for a photo recon mission to scout a problematic fuel storage target. That night, Wilson goes to the officers' club for a drink but is chided about his "kill" by his fellow pilots. From there, Wilson tries to find a friend at The Star and Bottle, but just doesn't fit in. The next day, Gallagher leads the P-51s on the photo recon mission but on the way home, engine trouble forces Gallagher to bail out. Wilson disobeys orders, breaks formation and rescues the colonel. Wilson's luck may be changing: for his act of heroism, Gallagher says he'll put the lieutenant in for the Distinguished Flying Cross. That night at The Star and Bottle, Wilson is the life of the party. The guys in his squadron make him feel welcome. Reporters want to interview him. Even Komansky apologizes for his outburst. The glow of fame is short-lived for Wilson because as soon as Gallagher enters the room, everyone flocks to him. The next day, it's business as usual as the 918th successfully destroys its target. As German fighters move in, Temple's men meet them head on and Wilson again breaks formation to get a kill. Because Wilson left his position, his pal Mikler is shot down. Wilson thinks he has to prove himself so he again defies Gallagher's orders and knocks down two more Messerschmitts before he himself is shot down. The Star and Bottle is quiet that evening as the few patrons who show up salute the late Lt. Wilson, someone who no one seemed to notice but a man that they would not soon forget.

Col. Gallagher, Sgt. Komansky, Lt. Gen. Pritchard
Lt. Harley Wilson ·················· James MacArthur
Maj. Zachary Temple ··············· James Callahan

Capt. Phyllis Vincent ⋯⋯⋯⋯⋯ Lee Meriwether
Lt. Don Mikler ⋯⋯⋯⋯⋯⋯⋯⋯⋯ Sammy Jackson
Lt. Gabriel ⋯⋯⋯⋯⋯⋯⋯⋯⋯⋯ Patrick Wayne
Capt. Robbins ⋯⋯⋯⋯⋯⋯⋯⋯ Dabney Coleman
Co-Pilot ⋯⋯⋯⋯⋯⋯⋯⋯⋯⋯⋯ Robert Dornan
Agnes ⋯⋯⋯⋯⋯⋯⋯⋯⋯⋯⋯⋯ Vikki Harrington
Steve Harkness ⋯⋯⋯⋯⋯⋯⋯⋯ John Newton
Right Waist Gunner ⋯⋯⋯⋯⋯ John Garwood
Barnes ⋯⋯⋯⋯⋯⋯⋯⋯⋯⋯⋯ Ollie O'Toole
Toley ⋯⋯⋯⋯⋯⋯⋯⋯⋯⋯⋯⋯ Lee Millar

TDY

- James MacArthur (born 8 December 1937 in Los Angeles) is best known for his role as "Dano" on the long-running hit *Hawaii Five-O* (1968–79), although he did not play the role in the show's pilot film. The son of actress Helen Hayes and writer Charles MacArthur, he appeared as a young leading man in Disney films such as *Kidnapped* (1960) and *Swiss Family Robinson* (1960) and *The Light in the Forest* (1958), for which MacArthur submitted to a Mohawk hair style.

- James Callahan (born in 4 October 1930 in Grand Rapids, Michigan) is known for his comedic talent, but his role in the *M*A*S*H* episode "Sometimes You Hear the Bullet" (OAD 28 January 1973) was a poignant and thought-provoking treatise on the futility of war. Callahan's continuing roles were on *Wendy and Me* (1964–65), *Convoy* (1965), *The Governor and JJ* (1969–70), *The Runaways* (1979) and *Charles in Charge* (1987–91).

- One year earlier, Sammy Jackson (died 24 April 1995) starred in the television version of the hit play and movie, *No Time for Sergeants* (1964–65), about a country boy's adjustment to life in the Air Force.

- Patrick Wayne (born 15 July 1939 in Los Angeles) is The Duke's son. Wayne started acting in his father's films, then earned roles in films such as *Shenandoah* (1965), *An Eye for An Eye* (1966)—which co-starred Robert Lansing—and as co-star of TV's *The Rounders* (1966–67). In the 1970s, Wayne worked his way up to a leading man in films such as *Sinbad and the Eye of the Tiger* (1977), *The People that Time Forgot* (1977) and Disney's *The Bears and I* (1974).

- This was Lee Meriwether's third and final appearance on *12 O'Clock High*.
   Lee Meriwether on "The Outsider": "I was with the same agent as Helen Hayes. I worked with her in *Mrs. McThing* (OAD 9 March 1958), a live television show, and had a wonderful time. So, Jimmy pumped me for that

story. I liked Andy Duggan a lot. He was so charming, so easy to talk to and went out of his way to be nice to me."

PERSONNEL FILE
- In her second appearance, Capt. Phyllis Vincent is still dating Gallagher but is now Gen. Pritchard's secretary.
- Gallagher calls Robert Dornan Bob, even though the role is credited only as Co-Pilot.
- Komansky is still wearing a 50-star flag patch.

DEBRIEFING
- During the strike in the teaser, Gallagher turns over command of the mission to Baker Blue.
- In the teaser, Maj. Temple is Bird Dog Leader; Lt. Wilson is Bird Dog Red.
- On the recon flight, Gallagher is Ramrod; Temple is Ramrod Blue.
- On the mission, Temple calls Gallagher Ramrod Leader; Capt. Robbins is Ramrod Two. Wilson is Bird Dog Four.
- The target is Kesseldorf. Kesseldorf was not an official target for the Eighth Air Force.

TOBY SIGHTING
- Toby mug is on the mantle of the Officers' Club.

#53 "BACK TO THE DRAWING BOARD" (8321)

OAD: 7 February 1966
RERUN: 25 July 1966
W: Dave Lewis and Andy Lewis
D: Gerald Mayer

After heavily overcast skies force Gallagher to scrub another mission, Gen. Britt makes him the guinea pig in an experiment. While the 918th was away on its mission, Britt had a team of engineers brought in, led by Dr. Michael Rink, who set up a field lab on the base. Dr. Rink and his team have installed a prototype Bomb Through Overcast (BTO) device on a B-17. The BTO airborne radar unit will allow planes to bomb with accuracy in bad weather, which will prevent the Germans from sending up flak or fighters. Meanwhile, the Germans take advantage of the long-range forecast for more cloud cover by working feverishly to get as many fighters airworthy as possible. On a test run, the 918th makes a successful bomb run—much to the amazement of the Germans, who want revenge. However, during the raid, Dr. Rink has a heart attack. He apparently witheld information regarding his rare heart condition and must be hospitalized. His assistant, Sgt. Zemler, takes over training the 918th how to read the radar.

During another successful mission, the Germans' ground radar picks up something and the group leader, Col. Ehrland, orders all fighters airborne. Even with the continued successful bombing missions—and the honor of having the men name the BTO plane *Rink's Raidar*—Dr. Rink doesn't feel successful. The Germans have discovered how to use a form of triangulation (using radar to track radar) and they deliver a crushing blow to the 918th and Dr. Rink's project. One third of the 918th is downed by flak and Sgt. Zemler is blinded when a burst of flak rips through *Rink's Raidar*. On the way to the operating room, Zemler figures out how the Germans beat Rink's BTO. Rink confirms that it is possible, but he is so devastated by the loss of lives during the mission that he gives up on the project. Britt thinks the whole project should be scrapped but he's outranked by Gen. Pritchard, who orders the testing to continue until airborne radar is proven to be at fault. The next day, Gallagher leads the 918th upstairs again but this time he has a strategy: after the first burst of flak, he orders his plane's radar shut off. Without the bounceback reading, the Germans lose their fix. However, the American bombers need to use airborne radar for at least five minutes from the IP in order to find the target. Komansky shames the now-reclusive Rink into going to see his convalescing comrade, Sgt. Zemler. In the hospital room, Zemler accidentally drops his tin drinking cup—which gives Rink an idea on how to confuse the German radar. Gallagher orders all the spare canteens on base to be cut up into strips, "chaff" as Rink calls it. On Gallagher's signal, each plane will drop a load of the chaff, which will give a flurry of false signals to German radar. As planned, the chaff works perfectly, allowing the group to hit its target. Back at the base, everyone celebrates the success of chaff but they agree that it is only a stopgap measure. Someone will come up with something better...maybe even Sgt. Zemler.

Col. Gallagher, Maj. Stovall, Sgt. Komansky, Maj. Gen. Britt	
Dr. Michael Rink	Burgess Meredith
Col. Felix Ehrland	Alf Kjellin
M/Sgt. Ray Zemler	Robert Doyle
Capt. Max Schiller	Robert Boon
Capt. Schmidt	Walter Friedel
MP Lieutenant	Robert Sorrells
Capt. Fowler	Robert Dornan
Capt. Douglas	Barry Cahill
Lt. Gurney	Hal Stalmaster
Lt. Butler	Richard Brander
Maj. Rice	Lee Farr
German Girl	Susan Denberg

TDY

• In those days, Burgess Meredith (1908–1997) was one busy man. The veteran character actor was most visible portraying arch villain the Penguin on Fox's smash series *Batman* (1966–68). However, Meredith was also a regular on the series *Mr. Novak* (1965–66), filling in for—coincidentally—Dean Jagger, Oscar-winner for the movie *12 O'Clock High*. Meredith earned two Oscar nominations: in 1975 for *Day of the Locust*, and in 1976 for the first of his three *Rocky* films. He won an Emmy for outstanding supporting actor in the 1977 made-for-TV movie *Tail Gunner Joe*. His other continuing series roles were on *The Big Story* (1957), *Search* (1972–73), *Those Amazing Animals* (1980–81) and *Gloria* (1982–83).

- Barry Cahill (born in Canada in 1921) started acting professionally in his teens. His movies include *Westworld* (1973), *Hang 'Em High* (1968) and the original *Grand Theft Auto* (1977). TV guest spots include *The Invaders; Baa, Baa, Black Sheep; Buck Rogers in the 25th Century* and a stint on *The Young and the Restless* (1974–75).

PERSONNEL FILE
- This is the first of five appearances by Barry Cahill as interim base physician Capt. Douglas.

DEBRIEFING
- The chaff in this episode was actually called "Window"—strips of metal foil—and effectively confused German radar.
- The Germans know that triangle A means the 918th Bomb Group.
- The target for the 918th's test of chaff is Hemmingstedt.
- Fox promo material says that at the conclusion of this episode, *Rink's Raidar* is renamed *Blip*.

INTELLIGENCE REPORT
- Scenes of the radar station exterior are lifted from the Fox film *13 Rue Madeleine* (1946).
- Two B-17s are shown on the 918th's airfield.
- The radar sound effect is once again from Fox's *Voyage to the Bottom of the Sea*.

FLIGHT LINE
- On 18 July 1944, B-17s of the Third Bombardment Division used radar to attack the oil refineries at Hemmingstedt.
- Although the actual Hemmingstedt raid was out of the chronological scope covered by season two, the first use of Window was during the 20 December 1943 raid on Bremen.

#54 "25th Mission" (8322)

Bradford Dillman

OAD: 14 February 1966
RERUN: 22 August 1966
W: Carey Wilber
D: Lawrence Dobkin

Gen. Britt shows movies of the prototype for a devastating new rocket powered fighter being developed by the Germans. The general needs his group commanders to knock out the factories at Swearingen that will mass produce the planes. The RAF couldn't destroy it at night and daylight precision bombing was met with overwhelming flak. Gallagher's solution: precision bombing at night, with the target illuminated by a pathfinder piloted by Maj. Tom Parsons, who just chalked up his 25th mission and is ready to head Stateside. When Gallagher calls him in for a meeting, Parsons asks his roommate Capt. Cowley to watch out for his girl, Naomi Rockford. Despite his extensive background in low-level flying, Parsons wants no part of the mission and goes back to his barracks. Cowley goes back to the base and demands to know why Parsons didn't show up and, in the bigger picture, what his future plans are for Naomi. Parsons' love-'em-and-leave-'em attitude angers Cowley so much that he decks the major and moves out. With Parsons out as the pathfinder pilot, Cowley volunteers—and, ironically, Parsons must train him for the job. When Britt hears that Parsons won't fly the mission, he dresses down the major for cowardice, and then informs Parsons that he miscounted his mission tally: he's only flown 24, not 25. Parsons returns to his barracks and promptly doubles over from an anxiety attack. Gallagher wants to save Parsons for the Swearingen raid, but Britt orders the colonel to send him up the next day. Despite his plane's sluggish performance and permission from Gallagher to abort, Parsons is determined to complete the mission. His crew was trying to help, too, by bringing extra ammo to help fend off the Luftwaffe. But, the added weight caused the plane to perform poorly. Parsons is so enraged that he slugs a couple of his crew members, then goes AWOL to see Naomi. After she confronts him about his lack of making a commitment and sticking to it, Parsons has another anxiety attack and collapses in the hallway outsider Naomi's flat. The major is examined by Capt. Douglas and confined to quarters pending court martial proceedings. The doc explains to Gallagher that Parsons suffers from psychosomatic trauma and can't face what's ahead. On the night of the big mission, Parsons sneaks to the airfield and overpowers Cowley, switches uniforms with him and boards the pathfinder as its pilot. Gallagher receives a radio message about Parsons' actions. A recall at night could endanger too many crews and planes so Gallagher decides to let Parsons do the job. Over the target, when the searchlights flood the night and flak rocks the sky, Parsons has another attack, leaving his startled co-pilot to cope with lining up the bomb run to make the first strike. Parsons regains his composure and takes control of the ship to successfully make the second strike. With the target lit up, Gallagher leads the group to clobber the factory. But Parsons' plane is damaged so severely that he orders the crew to bail out. Parsons and his bombardier are picked up in the English Channel and brought back to the 918th. Gallagher says the charges against Parsons will stand but that his achievement should weigh strongly in his favor.

Col. Gallagher, Maj. Stovall, Sgt. Komansky, Maj. Gen. Britt
Maj. Tom Parsons ························ Bradford Dillman
Capt. Bruce Cowley ···················· Don Galloway
Naomi Rockford ······················· Antoinette Bower
Lt. Paddy Giallella ···················· Tom Skerritt
Capt. Douglas ························· Barry Cahill
T/Sgt. Sperling ······················ Wade Graham
Capt. Fowler ························· Robert Dornan
Parsons' Co-Pilot ····················· Don Spruance
Gunner ····························· Ron Kramer
Colonel ···························· James Drake
Colonel ···························· Garth Pillsbury

TDY

- Bradford Dillman (born 14 April 1930 in San Francisco, California) won a 1975 Best Actor Emmy for his performance in the *Afternoon Playbreak* presentation "The Last Bridge of Salem." He co-starred with Peter Graves in the military series *Court Martial* (1966). Other continuing roles were on *King's Crossing* (1982) and *Falcon Crest* (1982–83).

- Lawrence Dobkin (1920–2002) portrayed Chaplain Twombley in the feature *12 O'Clock High*. Dobkin applied a lifetime of experience performing in dramatic radio, theatre, movies and TV to a second career as a director. Among his directorial projects were *The Munsters*, *Star Trek*, *The FBI*, *Charlie's Angels* and *Barnaby Jones*.

- Don Galloway (born 27 July 1937 in Brooksville, Kentucky) had the opportunity of a lifetime with his role of Sgt. Ed Brown on *Ironside* (1967–75).

His other continuing roles were on *The Secret Storm* (1962); *Arrest and Trial* (1963–64); *Tom, Dick and Mary* (1964–65); *Hizzoner* (1979); *The Guinness Game* (1979) and *General Hospital* (1985–87).

DEBRIEFING
- On his "make-up" mission, Maj. Parsons' call sign is 97 Foxtrot.
- The pathfinder plane carries napalm bombs.
- Gallagher's call sign is Ramrod.
- Swearingen was not a target of the Eighth Air Force.

INTELLIGENCE REPORT
- Parsons' jacket has 50-star flag on right shoulder and an Eighth AF patch on left shoulder.
- *Bombardier* footage is used again to depict the big raid.
- B-17 with call number 863 is behind Archbury tower.

TOBY SIGHTING
- Toby mug is on the mantle of the Officers' Club.

#55 "THE SURVIVOR" (8323)

OAD:	21 February 1966
RERUN:	N/R
W:	Philip Saltzman
D:	Alan Crosland, Jr.

Lt. John Tourneau sees fellow pilot Capt. Ernie Bradovich's B-17 in trouble and breaks formation to stay with Bradovich's plane until the group is joined by fighter escort. Bradovich blasts Tourneau's action as a violation of procedure and a compromise of the group formation. Stovall tries to counsel Bradovich on maintaining group morale and teamwork, but the captain wants to play strictly by the book. Bradovich's copilot, Lt. Ainsley, tries to make him feel like one of the guys but he gives the lieutenant the cold shoulder. During the next mission, Bradovich's plane takes a real beating and spins out of control, although the group spots one parachute. Bradovich is later brought back to base, safe and sound, but he icily brushes off inquiries about the rest of his crew. No one is happy when Gallagher orders a new crew mustered to fly with Bradovich in another plane on the next mission. In fact, the crew completely ignores Bradovich and will only respond to co-pilot Dickey or Komansky. Back in Archbury, Tourneau discovers that Bradovich is taking care of party girl Sara Blodgett, a widow who seems to care nothing about her baby. Tourneau is surprised to learn that Sara's late husband was actually a friend of Bradovich's. When Tourneau tries to get fresh with the comely young woman, she hits him repeatedly with her purse. A crowd gathers and when inquiries are made, Bradovich covers for Sara by saying he struck Tourneau. Komansky investigates and brings Sara back to Gallagher's office where she confesses that she was the assailant. Sara tells Bradovich to stay out of her life and then she leaves. Bradovich wants to keep flying and on the next day's mission, he finds his plane heavily battle-damaged and his crew wounded. The captain radios Gallagher that he can't keep up with the group and is heading back to England. With the gear up, Bradovich brings the plane in for a belly landing and then radios for an ambulance. Bradovich uses his leave to go into Archbury, where he patches things up with Tourneau and begins a new relationship with Sara.

Col. Gallagher, Maj. Stovall, Sgt. Komansky
Capt. Ernie Bradovich ·············· Don Gordon
Lt. John Tourneau ·················· Don Quine
Sara Blodgett ···················· Jill Ireland
Lt. Stan Ainsley ················· Bill Sargent
Lt. Dickey ····················· Carl Reindel
Lt. Williams ···················· Burt Douglas
Capt. Fowler ···················· Robert Dornan
T/Sgt. Braack ·················· Peter Marko
Left Waist Gunner ··············· Seymour Cassel
Barkeep ························ Tom Symonds
Tourneau's Co-Pilot ············· Wally Strauss

TDY

• Don Gordon (born 13 November 1926 in Los Angeles, California) previously co-starred as Lt. Hank Bertelli in the syndicated series *The Blue Angels* (1960), based on the exploits of the famed U.S. Navy flight team. Gordon turned in a series of intense performances on programs such as *The Twilight Zone, Johnny Staccato* and *The Untouchables*. Gordon was a regular on *Lucan* (1977–78). He also appeared in the movies *Bullitt* (1968), *Papillon* (1973) and *The Towering Inferno* (1974). He made a second appearance in #70 "The Fighter Pilot."

• After Jill Ireland divorced actor David McCallum, she married macho star Charles Bronson and appeared in many of his films throughout the 1970s and '80s. Her only regular TV appearance was on *Shane* (1966–67). Before Ireland died of breast cancer, she wrote the book *Life Wish* to inspire other women to cope with the disease. Jill Clayburgh portrayed Ireland in the TV movie *Reason for Living: The Jill Ireland Story* (1991). Ireland previously appeared in episode #38 "The Hotshot."

PERSONNEL FILE
• Stovall says that Bradovich flew 14 missions with the 966th.

- Although Doc Kaiser does not appear, he is mentioned.

DEBRIEFING
- During the mission in the teaser, Capt. Bradovich uses the call sign Red Easy; Lt. Tourneau is Red X-ray.
- On the mission in Act I, Bradovich uses the call sign Red Easy but Tourneau is Red Fox.
- On the mission in Act IV, Bradovich uses the call sign Daybreak Red Leader; after battle damage, he breaks formation and becomes Green Easy.
- Gallagher's call sign is once again Ramrod.

INTELLIGENCE REPORT
- In Act II, we see the makeshift base set for the first time. However, stock shots are still used to establish the Chino locale.
- Act IV concludes on the 918th's airstrip, but with a very atypical process shot. The background is the control tower (shown through rear projection). In the foreground are Stovall and Gallagher seated in a jeep.
- The pub interior is the same one used before in #35 "Then Came the Mighty Hunter," and later as the tavern in #71 "To Seek and Destroy" and as the meeting room in #67 "Practice to Deceive."

TOBY SIGHTING
- Toby mug is on the mantle of the Officers' Club. Maj. Stovall comes into the club on two different occasions to turn it around.

Frank Aletter

#56 "ANGEL BABE" (8324)

OAD:	28 February 1966
RERUN:	8 August 1966
W:	Preston Wood
D:	Robert Douglas

SHAEF public relations officer Maj. Budd and his team of Sgt. Prinzi and Sgt. Marven announce that after completing its 50th mission, *Angel Babe* will be reassigned to help boost stateside morale. Budd and company are on the base to film *Angel Babe's* swan song. However, flight engineer Sgt. Billy Willets has an almost supernatural connection with the B-17 and says the old girl is a fighter and won't retire. Sgt. Prinzi, a Hollywood cinematographer, sees *Angel Babe* as just another pile of tin and completely misses the affection felt for her by Willets and the rest of her crew. The call comes through for the 918th to bomb Wilhelmshaven and Hamburg, meaning the last mission for *Angel Babe*. For the mission, Sgt. Prinzi will fly in *Angel Babe* while Sgt. Marven flies with Gallagher to photograph the exterior of *Angel Babe*. But plans go awry when *Angel Babe* blows a tire on takeoff. When Maj. Budd is able to get two photographs that show Willets slugging Prinzi, he concludes there was sabotage and seeks an explanation from Gallagher. The colonel advises Budd not to pass judgment until something can be proven. Gallagher does concede by agreeing to let Budd interview both men. Willets explains he wanted to keep Prinzi from going back in the plane because the bombs might go off. Then Willets completely mystifies Budd when he tries to explain the bond he has with *Angel Babe*. It looks like *Angel Babe* will finally fly her last mission but, up in the air, mechanical trouble forces Lt. Drennan to turn back. Although it's Prinzi's job, when the next mission is scheduled the sergeant refuses to go up in *Angel Babe*. He's sure the plane will kill her crew. That kind of talk aggravates *Angel Babe's* crew. So Gallagher grounds Prinzi and reassigns Lt. Drennan to his plane while the colonel takes up *Angel Babe*. On the mission to Emden, *Angel Babe's* number-three engine goes and the ship becomes nose heavy, forcing Gallagher to drop back. Intense flak hits *Angel Babe*, wounding the co-pilot. Gallagher dives under the flak to give his bombardier the chance to hit the target. *Angel Babe* refuses to level out of the dive, but just after bombs away she soars back up again. German fighters attack and knock out another engine, but *Angel Babe* keeps flying until Gallagher lands her back at the base. After the crew gets out safely, one of the engines sparks and *Angel Babe* goes up in a ball of fire.

Col. Gallagher, Maj. Stovall, Sgt. Komansky	
T/Sgt. Billy Willets ····················	Roddy McDowall
S/Sgt. Ben Prinz ·························	Frank Aletter
Maj. Budd ·······························	Lee Patterson
S/Sgt. Harker ···························	Les Brown, Jr.
Lt. John Drennan ·····················	Tom Stern
Capt. Fowler ···························	Robert Dornan
Lt. McKennon ·························	Don Dubbins
Sgt. Bonneyman ······················	Jonathan Lippe
Sgt. Marven ···························	Michael Murphy

TDY

- Roddy McDowall (1928–1998) literally grew up on the Fox lot. A gifted child actor, he appeared in films such as *How Green Was My Valley* (1941), *The Pied Piper* (1942) and *My Friend Flicka* (1943). Soon after filming this episode, McDowall played the villainous Bookworm in Fox's smash *Batman* series. A year later, McDowall returned to Fox. This time he endured hours of makeup to be transformed into simian scientist Cornelius for the sci-fi block-buster *Planet of the Apes* (1968). McDowall also appeared in three of the movie's four sequels and in the subsequent 1974 TV series. Other continuing series roles were on *Fantastic Journey* (1977), *Tales of the Gold Monkey* (1982–83) and *Bridges to Cross* (1986).

- This was Frank Aletter's second and final appearance on *12 O'Clock High*.

Frank Aletter on "Angel Babe": "I once again enjoyed Paul Burke's company and working with him. Roddy McDowell seemed distant, but I worked with him again on *Planet of the Apes* and discovered that was him, for better or worse. I don't mean that as a negative.

"I have one interesting theory about my performance in 'Angel Babe.' I chose chewing gum as a character staple and for me, it worked, adding to the unfeeling and uncaring attitude of this wise guy I was playing. Years later, it came back to haunt me. Quinn Martin was the producer on that show and many years later, he produced *Barnaby Jones* . As it turned out, my then-wife, Lee Meriwether, co-starred with Buddy Ebsen. I had acted with Tom Palmer many years before and, at the time, he was the casting director for *Barnaby*. Lee suggested that Tom keep an eye out for something I was suitable for. She told me he was vague about using me. When I finally spoke to him, he said he didn't really know what the problem was but somebody upstairs was grumpy about actors busily chewing gum while they were acting."

- Don Dubbins (1928–1991) effectively played the everyman in roles that crossed every genre: sitcom, western, detective and fantasy. His appearances included *M-Squad*, *Petticoat Junction*, *Wanted: Dead or Alive* and *Then Came Bronson*.

PERSONNEL FILE
- Although he does not appear, Doc Kaiser is mentioned.

DEBRIEFING
- *Angel Babe* came to the 918th from the 966th.
- On the mission to Wilhelmshaven and Hamburg, Gallagher uses his call sign Ramrod; Lt. Drennan (in *Angel Babe*) uses call sign Red One.
- During the time period covered by season two, Wilhelmshaven was hit by the Eighth Air Force on 27 January 1943, 26 February 1943, 22 March 1943, 21 May 1943, 11 June 1943, 26 July 1943, 3 November 1943 and 3 February 1944.
- During the time period covered by season two, the Eighth Air Force struck Hamburg on 25-26 July 1943 and 13 December 1943.
- The final mission is to Emden.
- Capt. Fowler pilots Gallagher's plane over Emden.

- On the Emden mission, call signs are Blue Leader and Red Baker.
- During the time period covered by season two, the Eighth Air Force bombed Emden on 27 September 1943, 2 October 1943, 8 October 1943, 11 December 1943 and 3 February 1944.

INTELLIGENCE REPORT
- The premise for this episode was inspired by the last flight of the B-17 *Memphis Belle,* as told in the 1944 documentary of the same name and dramatized in the 1990 feature film.
- Working title of this episode was "The Moral Airplane."
- The text of Fox promo material for this episode calls the aircraft *Angel Face.*
- The final inferno is clipped from the last few seconds of the *Command Decision* stock footage that, when used in full, depicts a B-17 landing, spinning around and bursting into flames.
- Komansky's A-2 jacket still has a 50-star patch; so does Lt. Drennan's.

#57 "DECOY" (8325)

OAD:	7 March 1966
RERUN:	15 August 1966
W:	Lou Shaw
D:	Gerald Mayer

Paul Burke, Michael Callan and captors

Gallagher travels to a secret meeting at a Scottish castle to get the go-ahead for mounting air support for an amphibious troop landing. The clock is ticking: He only has 12 hours to get the group ready to fly. That's why Gallagher is perturbed when the pilot for his flight back, Capt. Powell, shows up late. As far as Gallagher is concerned Powell, a spoiled, rich kid, has two strikes against him:

The colonel had previously washed him out of the 918th. Guarding the briefcase that contains details of the mission, Gallagher boards the homeward bound plane with only Powell and flight engineer Sgt. Miller aboard. Once the plane is airborne, Powell bitterly explains the circumstances that led to Gallagher transferring him. The plane is suddenly jumped by German fighters, Powell—who's had virtually no combat experience—panics and Gallagher must take over. The plane is badly shot up, killing Miller, and Gallagher must ditch in the North Sea. The two survivors get into a life raft and do what they can to alert search-and-rescue parties. After rowing for a while, they spot a small island and head for it. Meanwhile, a Scottish fishing boat picks up their signal and heads for its source. A weather observation plane spots their distress flares and hears the signal. Gallagher and Powell believe help is on the way. But a third party also picks up the signal: a German U-boat, which sends an armed search party ashore. While Gallagher hurriedly buries his briefcase before the Nazis spot it, the spineless Powell surrenders to the enemy. The colonel is soon picked up as well. Both Americans are taken aboard the U-boat, where they are unexpectedly made to feel at home by the urbane Capt. Wessel. Following a gourmet lunch and a painless interrogation, Wessel orders the Americans put ashore. Back on the island, Gallagher and Powell watch in horror as the U-boat picks off the fishing boat that had come to their rescue. The American officers realize Wessel is using them as decoys to lure innocent vessels in for the kill. As an American destroyer approaches, Gallagher uses Powell's polished metal cigarette case to signal it to stay away. But the Germans see the signal first and shoot at them. Gallagher and Powell decide to row out closer to the destroyer and signal from there. Gallagher uses the cigarette case, but Powell stands up to wave his arms and is shot. The destroyer's commander gets the signal, orders evasive maneuvers and sends out depth charges that finish off the U-boat. Gallagher is picked up by the destroyer, which arranges for a plane to fly him back to base in time to lead the next mission.

Col. Gallagher, Maj. Stovall, Sgt. Komansky	
Capt. Anthony C. Powell	Michael Callan
Capt. Wessel	Carl Schell
Sgt. Johnny Miller	Steve Harris
Fisherman	John McLiam
Margaret	Dinah Anne Rogers
Capt. Bolling	Len Wayland
B-17 Pilot	Robert Ivers
Gen. Hardy	Bill Zuckert
Girl	Vikki Harrington
British Soldier	Nigel McKeand
Hammond	Eric Micklewood
German Sailor	Karl Sadler

TDY
- This was Michael Callan's second and final appearance on *12 O'Clock High*. Michael Callan on "Decoy": "That was a great death scene but we had to refilm it. The first time, I left my eyes open. Then, they told me you can't do that on television."

PERSONNEL FILE
- Held captive in the German sub, Gallagher begins to recite his serial number, "0764..." but he is cut off by Capt. Wessel. The script has Gallagher saying 0762. Neither set of numbers agrees with #50 "Underground," in which Gallagher gives his serial number as 01167087.
- Although Gen. Britt does not appear, he is mentioned.

DEBRIEFING
- The flight engineer says the B-17 in which they fly from Scotland will be ferried to the 966th.
- "Gibson Girl" was the nickname for the SCR-578 emergency transmitter. Powered by cranking a hand-operated generator, it enabled downed air crews to send out an SOS signal operating on a frequency of 500 kHz. Rescue crews could then home in on the signal and take appropriate measures.

INTELLIGENCE REPORT
- Stock shot from *Captain Eddie* of a B-17 skimming into the water is re-used.
- Scenes of Powell and Gallagher in the raft were done through process. Long shots were done on location, not in a studio tank.
- The destroyer bridge set is used again in #78 "The Hunters and the Killers."

#58 "THE HOLLOW MAN" (8326)

OAD:	14 March 1966
RERUN:	29 August 1966
W:	Gustave Field & Marc Huntly
D:	Robert Douglas

Five harrowing months in a German prison camp have left their mark on Capt. Walter Bolen. Bolen escaped and brought back critical knowledge of the deeply camouflaged synthetic oil plant at Baderheim. His pals at the 918th welcome him

Robert Drivas

back to the fold as does his girl, Ruth Wagner. Gallagher picks Bolen's brain for details on a return raid on Badenheim. But Bolen would rather get back to flying because thinking about flying was what kept up his morale during his capture. The next day, Bolen goes up for a flight check with Gallagher and Komansky but he suddenly goes into a cold sweat and recounts how the Nazis did everything they could but couldn't defeat his love of flying. Back at the base, Gallagher introduces Bolen to Captains Lewis and Stewart, who were fighter pilots on an earlier, unsuccessful mission to Badenheim but are now flying bombers. They take offense when Bolen is made flight leader, even though they both outrank him. Gallagher counters with the fact that Bolen has much more bomber flight time than both of them put together. That still doesn't sit well with Lewis and Stewart, who give Bolen a rough time on the practice run, which ends tragically when Bolen has a flashback to his POW experience and loses control, causing Stewart's plane to spin out of control and crash, killing all aboard. Bolen is taken to the hospital where he has a mental breakdown, babbling in German and experiencing hallucinations of his former Nazi tormentor and prison guards. Capt. Lewis, trying to clear Capt. Stewart's name, pays a visit to Komansky's quarters to try to sway the sergeant's allegiance from his friend Wally Bolen to Capt. Stewart. But Komansky refuses to budge. The mission to Baderheim is on so Gallagher must somehow get through to Bolen for his input on striking the target. In a lucid moment, Bolen is able to point out the details on an aerial photograph. A determined Lewis goes straight to Bolen's hospital room and there, in front of Gallagher, Komansky, Ruth Wagner and Ken Shaw, Bolen has an epiphany and realizes that he did indeed freeze that morning, killing Stewart and his crew. The next day, Gallagher flies his plane as pathfinder to mark the target but soon discovers he has a stowaway aboard: Capt. Bolen, who had hidden in the tail gunner's position. Gallagher sends Fowler back to man the guns Bolen abandoned and has Bolen stay on the flight deck to point out the target. Gallagher's crew effectively lights up the target so that the rest of the group can successfully bomb it. Afterward, Me 109s attack, shooting up Gallagher's plane and wounding the colonel. Gallagher orders Bolen to take the controls and, at that moment, the captain fully realizes that flying is his salvation and guides the plane back to base. From there, Bolen and Ruth are headed for London, where he will undergo psychological treatment.

Col. Gallagher, Sgt. Komansky, Maj. Stovall
Capt. Walter Bolen ···················· Robert Drivas
Capt. John Lewis ························ Paul Carr
Ruth Wagner ····························· Marion Thompson
Ken Shaw ································· Cec Linder
Capt. Bobby Stewart ·················· Anthony Hayes
Lt. Ed Nielsen ·························· Alan Reed, Jr.
SS Officer ······························ Curt Lowens

Doctor	Barry Cahill
Co-Pilot	Peter Baron
Reverend Blodgett, The Rector	Jack Raine
Capt. Fowler	Robert Dornan
Surgical Nurse	Laurie Mock
Waist Gunner	Richard Brander

TDY

• This was Robert Drivas' second appearance on *12 O'Clock High*. Once again, he portrays a brooding, mysterious personality and delivers another intense performance.

• Cec Linder (1921–1992) is best recognized for his role as CIA agent Felix Leiter in the gold standard of James Bond films, *Goldfinger* (1964). Although the Canadian Linder racked up significant credits in his homeland, his U.S. appearances are few. He guest starred in *SWAT*, *It Takes a Thief* and *Voyage to the Bottom of the Sea*.

• Curt Lowens (born 17 November 1925 in Allenstein, East Prussia, Germany) began acting in the early 1960s, just as the World War II cycle kicked in. Lowens found himself portraying Nazis on shows such as *Combat!*, *Jericho*, *Hogan's Heroes* and *The Rat Patrol*. His films include *Tobruk* (1967), *The Mephisto Waltz* (1971) and *The Hindenburg* (1975). He briefly had a continuing role on *General Hospital* (1989). Lowens would appear again in #61 "Siren Voices" and #67 "Practice to Deceive."

PERSONNEL FILE
• Komansky and Bolen are old friends. Komansky tells Bolen that Bolen has been trying to knock him down since they were nine years old. Later, Komansky says they grew up in Oakland together.
• Lewis and Stewart recently completed a tour as P-47 fighter pilots and have just been assigned to the 918th as bomber pilots.

DEBRIEFING
• On the training run, Capt. Bolen uses the call sign Mock-up Leader; Capt. Lewis is Mock-up Two and Capt. Stewart is Mock-Up Three.
• Gallagher's call sign to Badenheim is once again Ramrod. Lewis is simply Leader.
• Even though Badenheim is located in the same region as Mainz, it was not a target of Eighth Air Force raids.
• Me 109s attack after the raid.
• Fowler gets to blast away on the .50-caliber waist gun and he's hit by enemy fire.

• Bolen's A-2 jacket has a 50-star flag patch.

INTELLIGENCE REPORT
• Working title of this episode was "The Archbury Story."
• Actual-size wreckage is used to depict Capt. Stewart's downed plane.

TOBY SIGHTING
• Toby mug is on the mantle of the Officers' Club.

#59 "CROSS-HAIRS ON DEATH" (8327)

OAD:	21 March 1966
RERUN:	N/R
W:	Robert Lewin
D:	Alan Crosland, Jr.

Devious Everett Stone sheds his position as a merchant seaman, steals an Air Corps captain's uniform and sweet talks a secretary into cutting orders assigning him to the 918th as Capt. Tom Carpenter. Stone, now acting as Carpenter, reports to Gallagher, who assigns him as co-pilot on Capt. Vic Enright's plane, *So-Wot.* Capt. Enright's flight engineer, Sgt. Holcombe, is sure he knows who "Carpenter" really is: a man who washed out of pilot training and was then dishonorably discharged for hitting an officer. On Carpenter's first mission, Holcombe confronts him and he denies being Stone. The mission goes on, but as fighters attack, Holcombe is shot and badly wounded. Carpenter gets out of his seat to try to silence Holcombe but Enright orders him to sit down and puts him on report. It seems that Carpenter's secret is safe when Holcombe dies in surgery. On the next mission, Komansky fills in as flight engineer and Enright lets Carpenter fly back home, where he makes a very shaky landing at the base. When Carpenter's name doesn't make the base payroll, Stovall becomes suspicious. While the group is on maximum effort to bomb the tank factories at Mainz, two MPs show up on base and tell Stovall that no records exist for a Capt. Thomas Gaines Carpenter. However, fingerprints at the scene of the robbery at the tailor's shop where an officer's uniform was stolen are identified as belonging to Stone. Over the target, heavy flak keeps the group from hitting the target. Enright's plane is so battle-damaged that he orders a bail out but Carpenter refuses. Instead, he takes control of *So-Wot,* flies in low, successfully bombs the target, then heads for base, where he surrenders to the authorities.

Col. Gallagher, Sgt. Komansky, Maj. Stovall
Everett Stone/Capt. Carpenter ···· James Franciscus
Capt. Victor Enright ··············· Roger Perry
Sgt. Stan Holcombe ··············· H.M. Wynant

Doctor	··	Barry Cahill
MP Major	··	Ross Elliott
Capt. Fowler	··	Robert Dornan
Captain	··	Garth Pillsbury
Finance Officer	··	Rand Brooks
WAC	··	Victoria George
Seaman	··	Raoul Perez
Corporal	··	Paul Aaron

TDY

- James Franciscus (1934–1991) had clean-cut, Ivy League good looks and a Yale education to back them up. Franciscus played the lead in such TV series as *Naked City* (1958–59), *Mr. Novak* (1963–65), *Longstreet* (1971–72), *Doc Elliott* (1974) and *Hunter* (1977). His movies included *The Valley of Gwangi* (1969), *Beneath the Planet of the Apes* (1970) and he provided the voice of Jonathan in the 1973 film version of *Jonathan Livingston Seagull*. Earlier in Franciscus' career, he was replaced by Paul Burke in the "young cop" role on the reformatted version of *Naked City*.

- Roger Perry (born 1933) proved an affable second lead in such series as *Harrigan and Son* (1960–61), *Arrest and Trial* (1963-64), *Facts of Life* (1981–83) and *Falcon Crest* (1982–85). Perry is perhaps best remembered for his role as an Air Force pilot caught in a time warp in the *Star Trek* episode "Tomorrow Is Yesterday" (OAD 26 January 1967).

- H.M. Wynant (born Haim Weiner on 23 February 1927 in Detroit, Michigan) did an excellent job in roles as a heavy or as an authority figure. He is well-remembered for the chilling *Twilight Zone* episode "The Howling Man" (OAD 4 November 1960). Other guest spots were on *Thriller, Combat!, The Fugitive, The Untouchables, T.H.E. Cat, Garrison's Gorillas* and *The Man from U.N.C.L.E.*

- Ross Elliott (born 1917) co-starred in the syndicated series *The Blue Angels* (1960). Elliot served in the military, then launched his acting career. He became equally adept at drama and comedy on series such as *Combat!, Mr. Ed, SWAT* and *The Andy Griffith Show*. Other series included *General Hospital* (1963–65) and *The Virginian* (1966–70).

PERSONNEL FILE
- Col. Gallagher served at Langley Field, Virginia.

DEBRIEFING
- Gallagher says both the 918th and the 966th have flown missions over

Mainz without destroying the factories there.
- The Eighth Air Force did not bomb Mainz until September 1944.
- Gallagher's call sign is still Ramrod.
- Capt. Enright's ship is referred to as Green X-ray. Then, when Gallagher radios the plane, he uses the call sign Yellow X-ray.

INTELLIGENCE REPORT
- A pilot at the replacement depot tells a desk clerk that he's been mistakenly assigned to the 966th rather than the 918th.
- Capt. Carpenter and Capt. Enright both wear A-2 jackets with 50-star flag emblems.
- Carpenter sneaks aboard Enright's B-17 *So-Wot* to brush up on how to fly the bird.
- When Carpenter does his "homework," we are shown a rarely seen view of the control panel.
- There is a brief transition scene filmed at the makeshift base set.

#60 "DAY OF RECKONING" (8328)

OAD:	28 March 1966
RERUN:	N/R
W:	Halsted Welles
D:	Alan Crosland, Jr.

Wren Sgt. Winifred Broome accompanies a group of new fliers for their orientation at the 918th. Sgt. Broome is in love with the group's chaplain, Capt. Ethan Archer, who conducts the indoctrination. Overshadowing events at the 918th is a Luftwaffe briefing during which Maj. Max Schindler reveals plans to wipe out the American bomber group. After feigning a raid on London, their primary target is the 918th's bomb dump. Maj. Schindler has his plan of attack scheduled according to the time the 918th will be preparing to take off on its own mission. But because bad weather is closing in over the 918th's target, Gallagher orders the mission to start one hour earlier. With the group gone, Chaplain Archer begins the orientation, which is interrupted by a warning siren. Archer concludes the briefing and Komansky comments that the Germans often fly by. But not this time. He 111s bomb the base, spreading fire, destruction and death over the landscape. Chaplain Archer is emotionally damaged. He ignores the other injured soldiers in order to find Winifred Broome, who is critically injured under a pile of debris. Infuriated, Archer runs outside, picks up a rifle and empties its magazine into a parachuting German flier—then reacts in horror as he realizes what he's done. Stovall alerts Wing HQ of the attack, which in turn notifies the group en route to its target. Maj. Schindler, his co-pilot Maj. Bentz and Sgt. Luchen have bailed out. They are captured and confined in what's left of the base. The downed Nazis are intent on escaping and destroying their primary target. Although the runways are still in bad shape, Gallagher is able to commandeer a P-51 and land at home. Stovall briefs him, then gives the colonel a bit of peculiar news: the chaplain wants to quit because he feels he has compromised his calling. Capt. Archer says he is spiritually empty and can't offer counseling to anyone else. Gallagher tosses a Bible at the chaplain and suggests it may help him. Archer clutches his Bible and goes to visit the captive Nazis to confess that he is the one who shot their compatriot. The Nazis take advantage of the situation to overpower Archer and a sentry. They escape and hide in the base chapel, which has been converted to a temporary morgue. From there, they put on American uniforms and begin assembling their makeshift weapons for sabotage. Komansky walks into the chapel and realizes one "soldier" is a phony, but the sergeant is quickly shot by the other Nazi. Luckily, Komansky is able to get off a few warning shots of his own. Gallagher hears the shots, finds Komansky and learns of the two Nazis and their scheme. The colonel races to the bomb dump and finds their homemade bomb. He captures Bentz, who intended to sacrifice himself to allow Schindler to commandeer the P-51 Gallagher used to fly to the base. After Schindler is airborne, Gallagher sends bogus mission orders to the P-51, hoping Luftwaffe fighters are monitoring the transmission. They are and swarm in to send the Mustang down in flames. Col. Gallagher visits the base hospital and finds Chaplain Archer praying over Komansky. Archer admits to the colonel that seeing the Germans' faith in what they were doing gave him the strength to renew his own convictions.

Col. Gallagher, Sgt. Komansky, Maj. Stovall
Capt. Ethan Archer ·················· Charles Aidman
Maj. Gerhardt Bentz ················· Hans Gudegast
Maj. Max Schindler ················· John Van Dreelen
Sgt. Luchen ························· Jan Malmsjo
Capt. Bob Fowler ··················· Robert Dornan
Doc Douglas ······················ Barry Cahill
Winifred Broome ··················· Dinah Anne Rogers
First Soldier ······················ William Cort
GI Workman ······················ Jordan Rhodes
Second Soldier ···················· Gerald Hauser
Guard ··························· Walter Goodrich
Guard ··························· Thurman Brown
Guard ··························· Marty Bolger

TDY

• Charles Aidman (1925–1993) served in the Navy during World War II, and was bitten by the acting bug during naval training. Substantial work on episodic TV, such as *Peter Gunn*, *The Invaders* and *The Twilight Zone*, helped keep him financially solvent while he pursued projects in the theatre. Aidman made four appearances as Jim West's temporary partner Jeremy Pike on *The Wild, Wild West* (1968–69) during co-star Ross Martin's recovery from a broken leg. He also had a successful career as voiceover artist in commercials and movie trailers. Aidman was narrator of the 1985 *Twilight Zone* revival.

· *12 O'Clock High* veteran John Van Dreelen cancelled an eight-city promotional tour for his movie *Madame X* (1966) so that he could have time to appear in this episode.

PERSONNEL FILE
· Doc Douglas speaks German.

DEBRIEFING
· In the mission during the teaser, Fowler pilots Gallagher's plane.

Edward Mulhare

#61 "SIREN VOICES" (8329)

OAD: 4 April 1966
RERUN: 1 August 1966
TP: Carey Wilber
Story: Ed Kelso
D: Robert Douglas

At the very moment that the 918th is on its way to bomb the Focke-Wulf factories at Marienburg, a propaganda broadcast from the Danzig Lady identifies the group, its commander, their target and forecasts that the Americans are finished. Gallagher pulls through, but his group suffered heavy losses and hit the target with just a handful of B-17s. Because Marienburg produces such large quantities of FW fighters, Gen. Britt is under orders to destroy the complex. At Wing HQ, Gallagher explains that he needs to get past the fighters stationed at Drebzing. Then the colonel has a brainstorm: if the Americans can interfere with the Luftwaffe's radio communications, Gallagher can throw off the fighters with bogus information. Meanwhile, Komansky's latest girlfriend, Helen Graham, is jealous of his fascination with the Danzig Lady's program, which features live piano music interspersed with propaganda messages. After

Komansky sees Helen back to her flat, the sergeant watches as she sneaks out and meets up with Mayhew, apparently an Archbury local. Komansky follows them to a cottage, where Mayhew roughs him up and takes him inside. There, the sergeant meets Helen's overprotective father, who reveals that the family name is really Conboy and that his other daughter is Patricia Conboy—the Danzig Lady. Compelled to do his duty, Komansky reports this revelation to Gallagher, who in turn reports the finding to Counterintelligence. It turns out that G-2 has had the Conboys under surveillance and they have been cleared of any potentially traitorous activities. At a local café, Patricia meets a waiter—her contact—who passes a box of matches to her. Their rendezvous is broken up by a Gestapo agent, who shoots the man, while Patricia flees. Back at her flat, Patricia is consoled by her lover, Luftwaffe Col. Kurt Halland, when the Gestapo comes calling. Because of Patricia's status and Col. Halland's influence, the Gestapo men leave. Later, Patricia prepares for her next broadcast by using a message inside a matchbox to encode the score of her piano recital. The unusual music largely puzzles her audience—except for Allied intelligence, which is able to decode Patricia's "message": full details on Luftwaffe fighter strengths, locations, codes and radio frequencies. With that vital information in hand, Gallagher takes up the 918th with Sgt. Froelich aboard to voice the false transmissions. The ruse is a success, but Gallagher is still only able to destroy 50 percent of the target. The Gestapo catches on to Patricia's coded music and warns Halland that further contact with her may damage his career. Col. Halland is not convinced of Patricia's treachery—until he leaves her alone with revised codes and spies her reading them. Although Patricia is able to broadcast the new codes, Halland confronts her. The codes he left with her were fakes. Still, the colonel has arranged for his aide to make sure Patricia gets safely out of Germany. Realizing her life is in danger, Patricia produces a gun and makes her way to the flight control radio. She contacts the 918th to tell them they have the wrong codes, then provides the right information until she's shot by the Gestapo. The data Patricia was able to provide helps the 918th get close to the target before a lone Luftwaffe squadron, commanded by Col. Halland, attacks. Gallagher's group fends them off, sending Halland's plane down in flames, and then successfully takes out the factory complex. That night, Komansky and Gallagher visit the Conboys to fully explain the truth about Patricia and her heroism as a double agent.

Col. Gallagher, Sgt. Komansky, Maj. Stovall, Maj. Gen. Britt
Col. Kurt Halland ···················· Edward Mulhare
Patricia "Pati" Conboy ············· Victoria Shaw
Helen Conboy ····························· Juliet Mills
Ian Conboy ································· Rhys Williams
Mayhew ······································· Michael St. Claire
Capt. Ludvig Hofstein ············· Curt Lowens

Muller	Sasha Harden
Col. Cameron	Byron Keith
Capt. Bob Fowler	Robert Dornan
Waiter	Peter Brocco
Gestapo Officer	Peter Hellmann
Sgt. Froelich	Hank Brandt
Sue	Lynn Peters
German Radioman	Michael Hausserman
Sgt. Ellers	William Wellman, Jr.
German WAAF	Rena Horten

TDY

- Edward Mulhare (1923–1997) began appearing on stage in his native Ireland. That led to movie roles and a three-year stint in the Broadway production of *My Fair Lady*. A contract with Fox led to his appearances in films such as *Caprice* (1967), *Our Man Flint* (1966) and *Von Ryan's Express* (1965), and the TV series *The Ghost and Mrs. Muir* (1968–70). He also co-starred in *Knight Rider* (1982-86). Other TV appearances included *The FBI*, *Hart to Hart* and *Battlestar Galactica*. Mulhare provided the narration for the 1987 documentary *B-17: The Flying Fortress*.

DEBRIEFING

- Danzig Lady's broadcast recaps that Gen. Britt lost the 966th the day before.
- Actual raids on Marienburg and Danzig by the Eighth Air Force were carried out 8-10 October 1943.

INTELLIGENCE REPORT

- The premise of this script was suggested by real propaganda mongers like Axis Sally, Lord Haw-Haw and Tokyo Rose.
- The Conboy family's photo of Patricia was actually a picture of Victoria Shaw during her days as a model.
- The Conboy cottage is the same building used as the Macrae house in #10 "Interlude" and the tavern in #71 "To Seek and Destroy."
- Interim director of photography Ken Peach brings back some of that film noir sensibility, especially in the night scenes featuring intrigue along Archbury Street.
- In Act I, Gallagher and Britt meet in front the makeshift base set. Subsequently, stock footage is used to establish the Chino location.
- The radio studio set was used previously in #49 "The Slaughter Pen" as the manor house library and conference room.

Third Season

Broadcast schedule
Friday 10:00 pm EST, 9 September 1966–13 January 1967

Production run: 17 60-minute episodes filmed in color (De Luxe)

Continuing Cast
Col. Joseph Anson Gallagher	Paul Burke
Maj. Harvey B. Stovall	Frank Overton
T/Sgt. Alexander "Sandy" Komansky	Chris Robinson
Maj. Donald "Doc" Kaiser	Barney Phillips
Brig. Gen. Edward Britt	Andrew Duggan
Lt. Gen. Bill Pritchard	Paul Newlan
Capt. Bob Fowler	Robert Dornan
Brig. Gen. Philip Doud	Richard Anderson
Brig. Gen. Kenneth Chandler	Joe Maross

Key Production Credits
Executive Producer	Quinn Martin
Producer	William D. Gordon
Assistant to the Executive Producer	John Conwell
Associate Producer	Don Ingalls
Story Consultant	Jack Hawn
Director of Photography	Robert Moreno
Music	Dominic Frontiere
Production Supervisor	Jack Sonntag
Unit Production Manager	Robert Huddleston
Assistant Directors	Robert Daley
	Al Westen
Art Directors	Jack Martin Smith
	George B. Chan
Set Decorators	Walter M. Scott
	Glen Daniels
Film Editors	Richard H. Cahoon, ACE
	Jodie Copelan, ACE
	Lee Gilbert
	Jerry Young
Post Production Supervisor	John Elizalde
Sound Effects Editors	Eddie Campbell
	Werner Kirsch
Music Editor	Dan Carlin
Production Mixer	Bill Edmondson

CASTING	Patricia Rose Mock
CHIEF ELECTRICIANS	John Baron
	Robert Woodside
POST PRODUCTION COORDINATORS	Carl Barth, Robert Mintz
COLOR BY	De Luxe
IN CHARGE OF PRODUCTION	Arthur Fellows and Adrian
	Samish for QM Productions
IN ASSOCIATION WITH	William Self for Twentieth
	Century-Fox Television, Inc.

THE THIRD SEASON (OVERVIEW)

#62	9 September 1966	"Gauntlet of Fire"
#63	16 September 1966	"Massacre"
#64	23 September 1966	"Face of a Shadow"
#65	30 September 1966	"Fortress Wiesbaden"
#66	7 October 1966	"A Distant Cry"
#67	14 October 1966	"Practice to Deceive"
#68	28 October 1966	"The All-American"
#69	4 November 1966	"The Pariah"
#70	11 November 1966	"The Fighter Pilot"
#71	18 November 1966	"To Seek and Destroy"
#72	2 December 1966	"Burden of Guilt"
#73	9 December 1966	"The Ace"
#74	16 December 1966	"Six Feet Under"
#75	23 December 1966	"Duel at Mont Sainte Marie"
#76	30 December 1966	"Graveyard"
#77	6 January 1967	"A Long Time Dead"
#78	13 January 1967	"The Hunters and the Killers"

THE EPISODES (IN ORIGINAL BROADCAST ORDER):

#62 "GAUNTLET OF FIRE" (9303)

OAD:	9 September 1966
RERUN:	N/R
W:	John T. Dugan
D:	Joseph Pevney

After flying a punishing schedule of 21 missions during the month of May 1944, the 918th celebrates Gen. Britt's special orders to stand down for 10 days of R&R. No sooner have the men started lining up for their passes than Britt is called into a meeting at Wing HQ with Gen. Pritchard and Air Marshal Kingsford. Every flyable ship in Bomber Command is ordered to take part in the final phase of Operation Point Blank, an all-out bomber offensive to weaken the Channel coast. To achieve this, Britt needs a new G-3 officer and he asks Gallagher to take the job, which would require the colonel to give up flying. Complicating Gallagher's choice: the 918th is ordered back to work and assigned to drop propaganda leaflets over Northern France, a continuous cycle of missions over a four-day

Paul Burke and a prisoner

period. Not only do the men of the 918th show signs of mental and physical exhaustion, but Gallagher begins to fray at the ends as well. Things reach a low point when a brawl breaks out over a shortage of spark plugs—right in front of Gen. Britt. The general confronts Gallagher about the colonel's insistence on flying in addition to running the 918th and, as a result, grounds him. Gallagher sends his executive officer, Lt. Col. Bill Christy, to lead the next day's missions, and both Christy and his co-pilot are killed over the target. With just one more leaflet drop to go, Gallagher musters his worn-out pilots and requests a volunteer. When no one comes forward, Gallagher disobeys Britt's order and heads out to fly the mission himself. After the pilots see that Gallagher is going up, everyone who can rallies around the colonel and joins him. Even Maj. Stovall suits up and flies right seat with the colonel in the *Piccadilly Lily*. Flak and fighters rip up the *Lily*. Gallagher orders a bailout and brings the plane in for a crash landing east of Cherbourg near the coast of France. Gallagher, Stovall and Komansky watch their plane explode, then seek shelter in a nearby abandoned house. Later, a German patrol enters the house but the Americans overcome them and take two prisoners. Just then, American troops approach and are shocked to find the fliers and their captives—and are even more surprised when Gallagher welcomes them to Normandy on 6 June 1944, D-Day. Gallagher comes home to learn that Britt has come to a decision about the G-3 position. Even though the colonel is perfectly qualified for the job, Gallagher is content being a flier and a group commander.

Col. Gallagher, Maj. Stovall, Sgt. Komansky, Doc Kaiser, Maj. Gen Britt,
Lt. Gen Pritchard

Lt. Col. Bill Christy	William Windom
Capt. Bluitt	Linden Chiles
Lt. Wallach	Tim McIntire
Capt. Don Borega	Ron Foster
Sergeant	Richard O'Brien
Air Marshal Kingsford	Ivor Barry
Brig. Gen. Sam Adcock	Byron Morrow
Wounded German	Walter Friedel
Duty Sergeant	Michael Harris
M/Sgt. Fraser	Roy Jenson
German Officer	Eric Forst
Mechanic	Chuck Hicks
Second German	Chris Anders
Right Waist Gunner	Ron Doyle [UNCREDITED]

TDY

- William Windom (born 28 September 1923 in New York City) won an Emmy for his starring role in the James Thurber-inspired series *My World and Welcome to It* (1969–70). Windom first gained wide visibility as co-star of the sitcom *The Farmer's Daughter* (1963–66) with Inger Stevens. Other recurring roles were on *The Girl with Something Extra* (1973–74), *Brothers and Sisters* (1979) and *Murder, She Wrote* (1985–96).

  William Windom on "Gauntlet of Fire": "I used to get a lot of those weak roles. They called me 'Willy the Weeper.'"

- Linden Chiles (born 22 March 1933 in St. Louis, Missouri) specialized in patrician characters on series such as *The Green Hornet, Hawaii Five-O* and *Buck Rogers in the 25th Century*. His roles as a series regular were on *East Side, West Side* (1963–64), *Convoy* (1965), *The Secret Storm* (1970), *Banacek* (1973–74), *James at 15* (1977–78) and *Santa Barbara* (1989–90).

- Tim McIntire (1944–1986) won high praise for his performance as rock 'n' roll pioneer Alan Freed in the biopic *American Hot Wax* (1978). The son of actors John McIntire and Jeanette Nolan, McIntire built a career of his own on shows such as *Kung Fu, Longstreet* and *Then Came Bronson*.

- Byron Morrow (born 8 September 1920 in Chicago, Illinois) specialized in playing respectable characters such as judges, lawyers and clergy. His continuing roles included *The New Breed* (1961–62) and *Executive Suite* (1976–77) and the miniseries *The Winds of War* (1983).

- Roy Jenson (born 1935 in Calgary, Canada) began as a stuntman but branched out into acting in films such as *Harper* (1966), *Will Penney* (1968) and *Chinatown* (1974), and on episodic TV series including *Star Trek, Honey West* and *The Man from U.N.C.L.E.*

PERSONNEL FILE

- The character of Lt. Col. Bill Christy (William Windom) appeared earlier in #42 "Grant Me No Favor," but was played by Frank Aletter. The script for this episode calls Christy "a courageous, sensitive guy."
- The script for this episode gives Gen. Pritchard's first name as Bill.

DEBRIEFING

- Gallagher flies *Piccadilly Lily.*
- On the first leaflet drop, Col. Christy's call sign is Green Leader.
- During the second leaflet drop, the 918th loses Red Able.
- Brig. Gen. Adcock says the 82nd has been used to fill out the 966th.
- For the final leaflet drop, Capt. Bluitt flies *Hundred Proof.* He uses the call sign Red Able.

INTELLIGENCE REPORT

- Working title of this episode was "Gotterdammerung," an allusion to the opera *Götterdämmerung* by Richard Wagner. The literal translation is "Twilight of the Gods," but in common usage refers to a turbulent ending.
- Earlier versions of the script include the character Lady Margaret Mackenzie. The character was written out at the last minute; actor Pamela Light had already been signed for the part. Also axed was the part of a courier, to have been played by *12 O'Clock High* veteran Seymour Cassel.
- Maj. Stovall's A-2 jacket still does not have the flag emblem.
- A newly-filmed sequence depicts airmen at Chino carrying boxes of leaflets from a truck and hoisting them into the *Lily's* bomb bay.
- When a fight breaks out between two mechanics, it was filmed at the ops building at Chino.
- Additional new footage at Chino was filmed around the Archbury tower set.
- As the 918th drops leaflets in Act II, German soldiers shoot back from a brick wall outdoor set at Chino also used in episodes #22 "The Ticket," #46 "Between the Lines" and #60 "Day of Reckoning."
- During the last leaflet drop, Gallagher's plane is shot down. When the plane lands, it has serial number 863 with the *Piccadilly Lily* nose art. As Gallagher and Stovall watch from a distance, it blows up.
- During the invasion, a clip from #69 "The Pariah" is thrown in, showing a line of weary German soldiers walking alongside the command post, with an explosion going off behind them.

• The leaflet drops are a prelude to the D-Day landings at Normandy on 6 June 1944.

TOBY SIGHTING
• In the teaser, the Toby is barely visible in the background of a crowd scene.
• Later, although the Toby is out of frame, Col. Christy goes into the officers' club and says, "Somebody better turn that Toby mug around four times. Tomorrow is a big day."

Kevin McCarthy

#63 "MASSACRE" (9304)

OAD:	16 September 1966
RERUN:	N/R
W:	Carey Wilber
D:	Robert Douglas

Cancelled leaves, no outgoing phone calls allowed and the appearance of Russian Maj. Baladin generate curiosity and speculation throughout the 918th. Gallagher escorts Baladin to a high-level meeting at Wing HQ, where Lt. Gen. Archie Old discloses plans for the first Eighth Air Force shuttle raid to Russia. The combined effort will bomb a key target in Germany, then land at Poltava in the Ukraine to refuel and then strike the primary objective: the Ruhen oil depot and refineries in Berlin. The first leg of the mission goes well until a Russian fighter pulls alongside the group. Maj. Baladin tries to establish radio contact with the plane but receives no reply. Group leader Gallagher orders the group to hold its fire. Convinced the fighter is a Nazi scout, Baladin grabs a .50-caliber gun and shoots down the Russian plane. When the *Lily* touches down in Poltava, Col. Grulov rushes Gallagher to a meeting with his superior, Gen. Vorodenko. At Vorodenko's palatial headquarters, the general tells Gallagher that the plane was piloted by an acclaimed Russian war hero. Being the American commander, Gallagher accepts responsibility, but Vorodenko wants justice. Gen. Vorodenko and Col. Grulov both believe that Maj. Baladin knows who is accountable, but the major is reluctant to speak, even to Lt. Irina Zavanoff, his love interest. Lt. Zavanoff is assigned as an aide to Gallagher and overhears Komansky tell the colonel that Baladin is the shooter. Bad news keeps coming when Stovall informs Gallagher that there are no bombs, fuel or ammunition on the base because

Vorodenko has not ordered any. In private, Gallagher asks Gen. Vorodenko why he's withholding their supplies. Vorodenko counters by questioning Gallagher about the identity of the shooter. When Gallagher reveals that it was Maj. Baladin, the general is understandably outraged. Meanwhile, Baladin covertly strikes a bargain with Doc Kaiser: in exchange for safe passage out of Russia, Baladin discloses the location of the supplies. In turn, Kaiser shows Gallagher the warehouse, and the colonel orders his men to load the fuel and munitions on the American planes. As the American planes prepare to take off, Lt. Zavanoff pleads with Gallagher to turn Baladin over to her because she may be the only one able to save his life. Just then, Luftwaffe planes attack, devastating the Russian base and crippling half of the American planes. Gallagher rushes Lt. Zavanoff into his plane, along with Stovall and Komansky. The airmen man the .50-caliber guns while Lt. Zavanoff goes to the radio compartment to reunite with Baladin. The reunion is bittersweet. Baladin doesn't want to be killed or taken prisoner by Zavanoff, so he walks out of the B-17 and is cut down by gunfire from a Nazi fighter. Gen. Vorodenko is impressed by Gallagher's leadership, so he decides to buck his own system and give the Americans all their supplies and armaments. As Vorodenko reports his transgression to his superior, the American planes take off for Berlin. The mission is a success from all perspectives, as Wing gets a message from Gen. Vorodenko requesting that Gallagher come back for a banquet.

Col. Gallagher, Sgt. Komansky, Maj. Stovall, Doc Kaiser
Maj. Risha Baladin ···················· Kevin McCarthy
Lt. Irina Zavanoff ······················ Kathleen Widdoes
Gen. Nikolai Vorodenko ·········· Michael Constantine
Lt. Gen. Archie Old ················· Himself
Col. Grulov ······························· Jan Merlin
Maj. Simpson ···························· Paul Comi
Capt. Doane ······························ Byron Keith
Aide ··· William Wellman, Jr.
Lt. Gen. William Owen ·········· John Zaremba
Woman Officer ························· Sacha Berger
Archibald ································· Glenn Sipes
Gunner ···································· Thad Williams

TDY

• Michael Constantine (born Constantine Joanides on 22 May 1927 in Reading, Pennsylvania) earned an Emmy in 1970 as Best Supporting Actor for his work as principal Seymour Kaufman in Fox's fondly remembered *Room 222* (1969–1974). He continues to be a working actor, scoring big with the surprise hit movie *My Big, Fat Greek Wedding* (2002) as well as its short-lived TV adaptation.

- Kevin McCarthy (born 15 February 1914 in Seattle, Washington) brought stage experience to his powerful film and television performances. McCarthy earned an Oscar nomination for his first film, *Death of a Salesman* (1951). He is well remembered for the lead in *Invasion of the Body Snatchers* (1956) as well as a cameo in its 1978 remake. Continuing series roles were on *The Survivors* (1969–70), *Flamingo Road* (1981–81) and *Amanda's* (1983).

- Lt. General Archie J. Old (USAF-Ret.) portrayed himself in this episode. As a colonel, Old led the first shuttle raid to Russia on 21 June 1944. The mission package consisted of two fighter escort groups and six bombardment groups that hit their target at Ruhland, Germany and then flew on to Russia. "The plan for using the shuttle was to keep the Germans guessing as to which direction we would be coming from next," noted Gen. Old. "We worked it successfully after that, for the duration." Much of the tension between the Americans and the Russians in "Massacre" was based on fact. During the filming of the show, Old reminisced about the shuttle raid, noting that when he asked the Russians for permission to move his B-17s to a different Russian base to avoid being attacked by the Luftwaffe, the Russian base commander "claimed there wasn't any place to move them. That night the Germans hit. I wanted to put my fighters up, but the Russians had to clear anything like that with Moscow first. We were stuck. And promised to cooperate." Old was promoted to wing commander during the war and later commanded the Fifteenth Air Force until his retirement in September 1965. Regarding his Hollywood experience, Old said, "I was amazed at how real they can make things. I kept expecting the Russians to use interpreters."

- William Wellman, Jr. (born 20 January 1937 in Los Angeles) appeared in the World War I aviation feature *Lafayette Escadrille* (1958), directed by his father. This was his second appearance on *12 O'Clock High*.

DEBRIEFING
- Gallagher uses his Ramrod call sign.
- Maj. Simpson uses the call sign Blue Item. Simpson refers to Maj. Baladin as Friendly Bear.

INTELLIGENCE REPORT
- The teaser opens with a stock shot of activity around ops center at Chino, then cuts to the makeshift base set.
- The set used as Gen. Vorodenko's office was used earlier in #48 "Falling Star," and later in episode #64 "Face of a Shadow" as the main room of the Italian villa.
- The stock footage of the Russian fighter shot down by Baladin actually depicts a U.S. Navy PB4Y Privateer.

- During season one, John Zaremba (Lt. Gen. Owen) appeared in four episodes as Lt. Gen. Homer Stoneman.
- Stovall's A-2 jacket finally has a flag emblem.

FLIGHT LINE
- Gen. Archie Old led the actual shuttle raid on 21 June 1944.

#64 "FACE OF A SHADOW" (9306)

OAD:	23 September 1966
RERUN:	N/R
W:	Dave Lewis & Andy Lewis
D:	Richard Benedict

Luciana Paluzzi

Daily bombing by the Eighth Air Force has driven Nazi war production into Southern Germany, nearly out of range of England-based bombers. To effectively stop the Nazi war machine, a fresh strategy will tag-team the Eighth, attacking from the north, with the 15th Air Force, flying out of their Mediterranean bases to bomb from the south. Col Gallagher, charged with putting the new plan into effect, must work with Col. Arnold Yates, commander of a captured Luftwaffe base in Bellaggio, Italy. Gallagher's job may not be that easy: Col. Yates was the original commander of the 918th but was bounced after fouling up a costly mission. Once the *Piccadilly Lily* is on the ground in Italy, Gallagher is met by Maj. Shull, Yates' executive officer. Gallagher is surprised by the lax discipline with which Bellaggio is run. The lack of security proves a perfect breach for Elmer, an Italian Fascist, and his network of civilian spies. Finally, Yates deigns to meet Gallagher—while sipping scotch, wearing a bathrobe and flaunting Carla, a beautiful Italian baroness, at his side. As the two men verbally spar over their divergent attitudes, Carla is able to signal Elmer. That night, the Germans launch an artillery attack on the base. Gallagher realizes that the villas overlooking the base provide a perfect line of sight for spies and orders the area evacuated. While Komansky and the others go house to house, Gallagher inspects Carla's villa. She is proud of her family's heritage of survival, despite the series of conquerors that have swept through the land, including the Americans. Yates, thinking more clearly, brings an intercepted radio transmission to Gallagher's attention: the Germans have obtained specific details that could jeopardize the mission from a local contact named Luigi. Although Yates wants to win back his self-respect by flying combat again, Gallagher won't include him in the next mission. Meanwhile, Maj. Holtzer, a Nazi officer, comes out of hiding and contacts Carla. Holtzer demands that she stay with him in her villa and, with the Nazi's gun in her back, Carla turns away Yates when he calls for her. That night, Carla's villa becomes a rendezvous point where Elmer's saboteurs join Holtzer to destroy the 918th. After Holtzer leads his men on their mission, Carla shoots the straggling Elmer and, in turn, is beaten by Elmer's man Luigi. At the airfield, Holtzer's raiders take out the American perimeter guards, plant bombs on Gallagher's planes and then are joined by German infantry. Back at the American command post, Luigi is brought in for questioning. Luigi's confession gives the Americans just enough warning to sound an alarm before the bombs go off and the combined Nazi-Italian assault begins. Yates hits on a stroke of defensive genius: he drives a B-17 like a tank across the airfield while Komansky and Gallagher man the ship's .50-caliber guns. Together they are able to wipe out the attackers. The next day, as the mission gets under way successfully, Yates swears off his dependence on booze and Carla.

Col. Gallagher, Sgt. Komansky, Maj. Stovall
Col. Arnold Yates ·························· Jack Lord
Maj. Harry Shull ······················· Phillip E. Pine
Baroness Carla Montaglia ·········· Luciana Paluzzi
Maj. Ernst Holtzer ····················· Alan Bergmann
Elmer DelVecchio ····················· Joe De Santis
Luigi ··································· Daniel Ades
Boy ···································· Kit De Santis
Gruber ································· Michael Mikler
Paolo ·································· Josef Gazal
German Officer ························· Peter Hellmann
Dolan ································· Don Spruance
German Soldier ························· Nickolaus Kopp

TDY
- Phillip Pine (born 16 July 1920 in Hanford, California) was a busy character actor on series such as *Mannix*, *The Untouchables*, *The Outer Limits*, *The Twilight Zone* and *The Adventures of Superman*. He was a regular on *Golden Windows* (1954–55), *The Blue Knight* (1975–76) and *Days of Our Lives* (1976).

- Luciana Paluzzi (born 10 June 1937 in Rome, Italy) was a regular in the Fox series *Five Fingers* (1959–60), which co-starred Paul Burke. At the time of this episode, she was a leading femme fatale in the spy genre. She appeared in the fourth Bond flick *Thunderball* (1965), *The Venetian Affair* (1967) and

TV's *The Man from U.N.C.L.E.* and *The Girl from U.N.C.L.E.*

· Alan Bergmann began his acting career on the New York stage. He won rave reviews for his title role in *Luther*, and when the production hit Los Angeles he was noticed by Hollywood casting directors. Guest shots followed, typically as a malevolent character on series such as *Star Trek, Wonder Woman, Hogan's Heroes* and *The Wild, Wild West*. In addition to performing voiceovers, Bergmann turned to directing episodic TV series such as *Barney Miller, Family Ties* and *Night Court*.

Alan Bergmann on "Face of a Shadow": "That was one of the first television shows I did. Although I did have some small parts in some small movies in New York, I had very little awareness of film. I was still getting the hang of how to work in front of the camera.

"I didn't know Jack Lord at all but he, as best as I could tell, felt a sense of rivalry with me. I couldn't understand why because it was one of my first appearances and he was an established Hollywood star. Luciana and I were preparing to do the scene where I came back from being in hiding and go to her fancy home. It was sort of a semi-romantic, delicate scene. Jack Lord took a chair, picked it up and carried it right to the edge of the playing area and sat down to watch directly in my eye line. He made me very uncomfortable. It was unsporting. But I didn't know that I could go to the director or the assistant director and say, 'Would you please ask him to move out of my line of vision? It's making me uncomfortable.' And I'm sure they would have asked him to leave. I just didn't know that I had the wherewithal to make that kind of request. So I had to do the scene under fire. And I blame myself as much as him for not doing something about it."

PERSONNEL FILE
· Carla calls Gallagher "an American with a German sense of duty."
· Not once does Gallagher say to Yates, "Hey, you look just like my brother, Preston." Jack Lord played Pres Gallagher in #37 "Big Brother."

DEBRIEFING
· Gallagher flies the *Piccadilly Lily*; Stovall is his co-pilot.
· In the Epilog, the Eighth Air Force strikes Stuttgart; the 918th and Fifteenth Air Force attack the Zeppelin works at Friedrichshafen.
· The Eighth Air Force bombed Stuttgart on 6 September 1943, 25 February 1944, 14 August 1944, 5 September 1944, 9 December 1944 and 16 December 1944.
· The Eighth Air Force bombed Friedrichshafen on 16 March 1944, 18 March 1944, 24 April 1944, 20 July 1944, 3 August 1944 and 25 February 1945.

- The title of this episode might have been suggested by associate producer Don Ingalls, who also used it for a script he wrote during his stint on *Have Gun, Will Travel* (1962–63).
- While waiting at Carla's villa for Yates to put in an appearance, Komansky sits at the piano and plays a couple of bars from the *12 O'Clock High* theme song.
- The scene where Maj. Holtzer (Alan Bergmann) is smuggled into town was filmed in an area of the Fox Hills lot called French Alley. Located between existing soundstages, the façade was used in Fox's *Our Man Flint* (1966) and episodes of *The Time Tunnel* (1966–67). The site was also used for the location where scientist Jan Benes (Jean Del Val) is critically wounded in an assassination attempt, kicking off the plot of Fox's *Fantastic Voyage* (1966).
- The set used as the villa's main room was used earlier in episodes #48 "Falling Star" and #63 "Massacre."
- Maj. Stovall's A-2 jacket has a flag emblem.

FLIGHT LINE
- The teaser opens with the superimposed title, "Bellaggio, Italy, July 1944."

(Clockwise from top) Bernard Fox, Paul Burke, Lloyd Bochner and Chris Robinson

#65 "FORTRESS WIESBADEN" (9301)

OAD: 30 September 1966
RERUN: N/R
TP: Carey Wilber
STORY: Michael Lalor Brown
D: Joseph Pevney

Flak over Wiesbaden has prevented both the RAF and the Eighth Air Force from knocking out an important manufacturing center. Before the latest mission takes off, Gen. Britt tells Gallagher that he is catching heat because the 918th has failed to take out the complex. So Britt lays it on the line: either Gallagher destroys the factories at Wiesbaden or he loses command of the 918th. Regrettably, the 918th misses its target once again and sustains 50 percent losses. When Gallagher is ordered to report to Britt at Wing HQ, he takes the proactive approach and submits a request for reassignment to another unit. However, Britt has other plans. He tears up Gallagher's application and explains that British intelligence just reported that the Nazis' ability to put up such devastating flak barrages is due to a cutting-edge, radar-guided, anti-aircraft fire control. Then the general introduces Gallagher to Maj. Michael Mallory, a British commando. Britt's new strategy is to drop Mallory and his demolition team into Wiesbaden, have them destroy the control center, and then launch a maximum-effort bombing raid on the target. Gallagher pilots a single B-17 over Wiesbaden to drop Mallory's team. After the commandos make their jump, flak rips into Gallagher's plane, forcing the colonel to order a bailout. On the ground, a Nazi patrol finds a parachute, and the commandos are forced to kill them. Now on the alert, Mallory's men find Gallagher and Komansky, much to the major's annoyance. The colonel wants to team up with Mallory, then go back with them on their scheduled plane ride home. Battle-hardened Mallory has no use for flyboys but grudgingly takes on the two airmen. When the team reaches the farm of Kurt von Heurtzel, their intelligence contact, they find a woman who says she is von Heurtzel's daughter Frieda, who explains her father was picked up by the Gestapo. Since Mallory calls the shots, he forces Frieda to lead his squad to the radar center, leaving Gallagher and Komansky back at the farmhouse to man the radio. As the commandos lie in wait at the site Frieda leads them to, two trucks full of Nazi soldiers pour out and a firefight ignites. Hopelessly outgunned, the Brits are captured and taken to interrogation. Meanwhile, Germans rush the farmhouse, forcing Gallagher and Komansky to take flight. The airmen run into Frieda, who is clearly a Nazi sympathizer, and take her prisoner. Gallagher and Komansky work up an ambush which effectively surprises the Nazi convoy and enables them to free the commandos—all except for Maj. Mallory, who is fatally wounded. Under Gallagher's command, the team dons Nazi uniforms, uses the trucks to swoop into the compound and then blows it up. The ensuing firefight results in severe injuries, including Komansky. Despite the Brits' urging to leave the sergeant, Gallagher insists on rescuing him. Back at Wing HQ, Britt receives a radio message that the bombers are on target and have encountered no flak. Commando Sgt. Maj. Higgins congratulates Gallagher for having the makings of a good commando. Gallagher points to the bombers overhead and says he relies on the teamwork of an entire crew to do the job. With that, the pickup plane lands to whisk the survivors back to England.

Col. Gallagher, Sgt. Komansky, Maj. Gen. Britt
Frieda von Heurtzel ·················· Christiane Schmidtmer
Maj. Michael Mallory ·············· Lloyd Bochner
Sgt. Maj. Higgins ························ Bernard Fox
Hank ··· Keith McConnell
Spievers ···································· Peter Church
Wing Commander ···················· John Levingston

British Co-Pilot ···························· John Winston
German Guard ······························ Frank Oberschall
Cane ··· Steve Shenton
German Corporal ························· Alex Reichel
German Sergeant ························· Norbert Siegfried
German Soldier ··························· Rick West

TDY
- Christiane Schmidtmer (1939–2003) was born in Switzerland but grew up in Germany, where she pursued a career in modeling and on the stage. Schmidtmer began appearing in films such as *Ship of Fools* (1965) and *Boeing, Boeing* (1965), and on TV series such as *Blue Light, Hogan's Heroes* and co-starring with Robert Drivas in the *Wild, Wild West* episode "The Night of the Burning Diamond" (OAD 8 April 1966).

DEBRIEFING
- The industrial area at Wiesbaden was targeted by the Eighth Air Force on numerous occasions including 4–5 October 1943, 4 February 1944, 28 July 1944, 15 August 1944, 13 September 1944, 19 September 1944 and 10 November 1944.

PERSONNEL FILE
- Gen. Britt says he sat through the night in a meeting with Pritchard and Air Vice Marshal Kingsford; later, Britt takes a phone call from Kingsford. The character appeared earlier in episode #62 "Gauntlet of Fire" portrayed by Ivor Barry.

INTELLIGENCE REPORT
- The standard B-17 flight deck set is redressed with a metallic curtain hiding the top turret to transform it into a British bomber.
- The set used as the anti-aircraft control center was later re-used as the German observation bunker in #71 "To Seek and Destroy" and as a research center in #73 "The Ace."

#66 "A DISTANT CRY" (9308)

OAD: 7 October 1966
RERUN: N/R
W: Jack Curtis
D: Robert Douglas

Pilots of the 918th are less than thrilled with Capt. P.J. Pridie, the group's new instructor pilot. Pridie comes off as arrogant, detached and all business—even with old friend Lt. John Little Eagle. An instrument evaluation flight that goes bad forces Pridie and Little Eagle to make an unexpected landing in France. There they find Lt. Pete Morton, whose ship crashed and is burning with two men badly injured. In an unexpected display of emotion, Pridie orders Little Eagle and Morton to load the two injured men into the B-17 and flies back toward the base. Despite heavy fog, Pridie defies orders to divert his approach and lands safely. Gallagher writes a commendation for Pridie's act, but questions the captain's brutal evaluation of Lt. Little Eagle's performance. To Gallagher, the review is unfair and could ruin a good combat pilot's chances to continue flying—something which Gallagher doesn't think Pridie understands

Roy Thinnes

because the captain has never flown in combat. Pridie isn't fazed, even when Little Eagle slugs Pridie for not confronting him about the review first. Next morning, with Little Eagle drunk, Pridie volunteers to take his place on the mission. At the briefing, Gallagher reveals that the reason his pilots have been reviewed so critically on instrument flying is because of a new tactic: a "bad weather" technique using heavy overcast and radar-equipped pathfinders to penetrate deeper into Germany with minimal opposition. After a few more missions, Little Eagle realizes that he really is bad with instruments—but not soon enough. On a mission, he falls behind and his plane is shot down, much to Pridie's horror. Unable to cope, Pridie goes AWOL, gets drunk and is confined to barracks. Gallagher wants Pridie to face his fears, the way his blood brother, John Little Eagle, would have wanted. Gallagher gives Pridie a choice to fly combat one more time and he accepts. When his plane is ripped apart by flak, his co-pilot is killed and Pridie is blinded. Gallagher flies alongside the battle damaged B-17 and talks Pridie into a successful landing.

Col. Gallagher, Maj. Stovall, Sgt. Komansky
Capt. Paul J. Pridie ···················· Roy Thinnes
Lt. John Little Eagle ···················· Robert Blake
Lt. Fredericks ···························· Wayne Rogers
Lt. Pete Morton ·························· James McMullan
Sheila ···································· Susan Seaforth

Surgeon	Don Ross
S/Sgt. Ludlow	Richard Niles
Capt. Fowler	Robert Dornan

TDY

- Robert Blake (born 18 September 1933 in Nutley, New Jersey) made a rocky transition from juvenile parts in the *Our Gang* shorts and as Little Beaver in the *Red Ryder* movies to adult roles such as his acclaimed performance in *In Cold Blood* (1967). Blake is most recognized for his role as the titular detective in *Baretta* (1975–78).

- Wayne Rogers (born 7 April 1933 in Birmingham, Alabama) had kicked around in the acting game for more than a decade before he found fame as Trapper John McIntyre on *M*A*S*H* (1972–75). The Princeton graduate resigned his naval commission to pursue acting. His other continuing roles on TV included *Search for Tomorrow* (1959), *Stagecoach West* (1960–61), *City of Angels* (1976) and *House Calls* (1979–82).

- Jim McMullan (born 13 October 1936 in Long Beach, New York) was a busy leading man on TV with more than 150 appearances including recurring roles on *Ben Casey* (1965), *Chopper One* (1974) and *Beyond Westworld* (1980).

PERSONNEL FILE

- The script for this episode describes Lt. John Little Eagle as a "tough, instinctual, South Dakota Sioux, full of fun and fury." Robert Blake turns in an energetic performance, but the result is a Hollywood-style caricature of a Native American.
- Although Doc Kaiser does not appear, he is mentioned.

DEBRIEFING

- On the instrument check ride with Lt. Little Eagle and Capt. Pridie, they use the call sign Orchid One.
- The target is Eisenhaven. However, Eisenhaven was not a target of the Eighth Air Force.
- On the mission, Pridie uses the call sign White Leader; Little Eagle is Red Eight.
- In the second raid, Gallagher flies the P-51.

INTELLIGENCE REPORT

- Flag patches on A-2 and shearling jackets have 48 stars.
- B-17 863 is shown on fire.
- The makeshift base set is used for the early-morning encounter between Pridie and a drunken Little Eagle.

• Stovall's A-2 jacket has a flag emblem.

Toby Sighting
• Toby mug is on the mantle of the Officers' Club. Stovall turns it around before the big mission.

#67 "Practice to Deceive" (9307)

OAD:	14 October 1966
Rerun:	N/R
W:	William D. Gordon
D:	Robert Douglas

Eduard Franz

On a return flight from a secret mission to Russia, a Luftwaffe patrol shoots down Gallagher's P-51. He hits the silk and lands in Eastern Germany. Gallagher quickly tries to burn some documents he carried with him, but he's grabbed by some locals and a wounded German soldier who takes the scorched papers. The colonel is turned over to the Germans and undergoes brutal interrogation at the hands of Col. von Datz and Maj. Strasser. After Strasser decks Gallagher, von Datz demands Gallagher be taken to a doctor. Transport by ambulance is arranged, but en route the ambulance is ambushed by anti-Nazi Germans, led by Heidi Voss, who rescue Gallagher. Heidi then escorts Gallagher into town where she leads him to an enclave of anti-Nazi sympathizers which includes Maj. Strasser and Heidi's father, decorated war hero Adm. Sigfried von Kreuter. The admiral pleads for Gallagher's assistance with their plan to end the war. Then, von Kreuter calls a meeting and other members of the group show up. Their plan: kill Hitler and then offer an unconditional surrender. To set the plan in motion, von Kreuter wants Gallagher to fly him to London to meet with the Allied high command. Suddenly, the meeting is broken up when the group is alerted to an impending raid by a squad led by Col. von Datz. Tipped off by a double agent, von Datz vows to break up the plot and sends in his men, guns blazing. One member of the group acts as decoy, allowing the others to escape through the rear entrance. However, Adm. Von Kreuter is shot in the arm and needs medical attention. Col. von Datz knows that Heidi is part of the group but is supremely confident that her father is unimpeachable. So von Datz visits the von Kreuter home and manipulates Heidi into "confessing" to her father. Keeping up the charade, the admiral orders Col. von Datz to take Heidi away. Gallagher and the admiral are now free to make their way to an airfield where a Heinkel is waiting for them. Once in flight, a fighter patrol spots the plane and radios it for identification. The admiral gives a cover story which the lead fighter pilot accepts halfheartedly. The fighter pilot then calls von Datz to relate the suspicious incident and the colonel orders him to turn the plane back or shoot it down. At the sight of a squadron of P-51s, the pursuers veer off—leaving the Mustangs to shoot down the Heinkel. Gallagher struggles to bring in the battered plane and lands on an estate near the 918th base. As Gallagher and the badly wounded admiral make their way from the plane, they're met by troops from the 918th. Maj. Stovall tells Gallagher that a radio broadcast just announced that Hitler was killed by a bomb blast. A follow-up broadcast announces that Hitler is still alive just when Stovall brings the news that the admiral has died.

Col. Gallagher, Maj. Stovall, Sgt. Komansky
Adm. Sigfried von Kreuter ········· Eduard Franz
Col. von Datz ······························· John van Dreelen
Heidi Voss ··································· Diana Hyland
Major Paul Strasser ···················· Jan Merlin
Father Berthold Kreitzer ············· Curt Lowens
Gestapo Officer ························· Sasha Harden
Gunther Ralls ···························· Walter Friedel
Corp. Schmidt ··························· Robert Boon
Capt. Koch ······························· Horst Ebersberg
Col. Chris Gibbons ···················· Barry Russo
Gen. Eric Strohm ······················ Ted Dudomaine
German Woman ························ Maria Schroeder
Doctor ·································· Peter Markus
Count Klaus von Shullendorf ···· Gil Stuart

TDY

- Eduard Franz (1902–1983) gave a distinguished quality to the characters he played in movies, such as *The Desert Fox* (1951), *The Ten Commandments* (1956) and *The President's Analyst* (1967). On TV he appeared on *Stoney Burke*, *The FBI* and *It Takes a Thief,* and was a regular on *Zorro* (1958) and *The Breaking Point* (1963–64).

- Diana Hyland (1936–1977) brought sophistication to guest appearances on *I Spy*, *The Green Hornet*, *SWAT* and *The Twilight Zone*. She had recurring roles on *Young Doctor Malone* (1961–62) and *Peyton Place* (1968–69). Hyland had just begun work on the series *Eight is Enough* when she succumbed to cancer.

- In Gallagher's absence, Col. Gibbons is ordered to take command of the 918th.
- Adm. von Kreuter is an old friend of Gallagher's father.

INTELLIGENCE REPORT
- New footage of the P-51 is used.
- The meeting room set was used earlier as a pub in #35 "Then Came the Mighty Hunter" and reappeared as a tavern interior in #71 "To Seek and Destroy."
- The cellar steps set is used briefly. That set, with modifications, would reappear in #74 "Six Feet Under" and #75 "Duel at Mont Sainte Marie."
- Gallagher and Adm. von Kreuter fly back to England in a Heinkel He 111, a German bomber.
- When Stovall rallies the troops to pick up survivors of the downed Heinkel, they muster at the makeshift base set. The subsequent scene begins with stock footage of the operations building at Chino.

#68 "THE ALL-AMERICAN" (9309)

OAD:	28 October 1966
RERUN:	N/R
W:	Jack Hawn
D:	Joseph Pevney

A top-level directive throws All-American Ted Masters into a public relations frenzy. Masters has been designated as a poster boy for building morale back in the States. Although Lt. Masters is certified to fly, he is not a very good pilot so he is assigned a desk job with the 918th, commanded by his boyhood hero Joe Gallagher. Masters' mentor, press agent Maj. George Praeger, creates a façade of mock heroics around the star athlete that goes well with Masters' sincere idealism. The lieutenant really wants to fly combat and contribute to the war effort. Praeger's zeal turns off Masters' fellow airmen, particularly Capt. Glen King, whose courageous landing of a battle-damaged B-17 is attributed to Masters. Lt. Masters goes over Gallagher's head and calls Gen. Owen to be put on combat status. Instead, Masters is assigned to play in an inter-Air Corps baseball game for publicity purposes. Tired of being put on display, Masters ducks the game, hits the local pubs and runs into Capt. King and correspondent Shirl Pinkerton. By this time, Masters is loose enough so that the sincerity of his gung-ho attitude comes across to King and Ms. Pinkerton. Unfortunately, Masters has had just enough alcohol to wind up in a potentially embarrassing barroom brawl—with photographers eagerly capturing his battered, fallen body. Gallagher has been ahead of the game and knows about Masters' shortcomings as a pilot. Still, the colonel caves in and personally gives Masters flight instruction. Finally, Masters is assigned as Capt. King's alternate co-pilot on a mission. At first, Masters is humiliated by his trivial job, but then King tells Masters outright that he's just not good enough to fly. Praeger finally admits to Masters that he joined the military only to stay close to the young man who's been like a son to him. With that, Masters boards King's plane as it takes off and joins the group. Before hitting the target, German fighters knock out the waist gunners. Then flak over the target takes out the co-pilot, bombardier and navigator, and eventually even King loses consciousness. Masters assumes the controls as Gallagher talks him in for a landing. Uncertain whether his gear is down, Masters does a belly landing at the 918th. When King's plane ignites on landing, Masters works to get the survivors out of the ship. Komansky runs in to help and finally drags Masters to safety just before King's B-17 blows up. King and Masters wind up sharing the same hospital room, where they suffer from severe burns. Masters learns from Gallagher that the colonel has recommended him for the highest possible medal, which means he has proven himself as a hero of substance.

Col. Gallagher, Sgt. Komansky, Maj. Stovall	
Lt. Ted Masters	Mart Hulswit
Maj. George Praeger	Norman Fell
Capt. Glen King	Robert Doyle
Shirl Pinkerton	Susan Brown
Capt. Bob Fowler	Robert Dornan
S/Sgt. Lou Mintz	Peter Marko
English Reporter	Richard Peel
Lt. Wayne Rogers	Steve Harris
British Tommy	Peter Church
GI Reporter	Ron Doyle

TDY

- Mart Hulswit (born 23 May 1940 in Maracaibo, Venezuela) had a relatively brief career in primetime TV but worked on the daytime soap *The Guiding Light* (1969–81). Other TV shows included *Mannix, Combat!* and *Coronet Blue.*

- Jack Hawn based his script on stories told by broadcaster and football star Tom Harmon. Hawn wrote for the *Hollywood Citizen-News* and moonlighted at a number of radio and TV studios, where he wrote news shows for sportscasters. Among his clients was Tom Harmon, who had a nightly show on CBS Radio. "After we would get off the air," Hawn related, "Tom sometimes would tell us a few war stories. He had some harrowing experiences flying in the Pacific Theater, but I got the impression he wasn't a great pilot." Harmon's misadventures provided the basis for Hawn's script. Hawn even made his title character, Lt. Ted Masters, a Heisman Trophy winner, just as Harmon had been in 1940.

PERSONNEL FILE
- Although Doc Kaiser does not appear in this episode, he is mentioned.

DEBRIEFING
- Gallagher flies mission control in his P-51; he uses his Ramrod call sign.
- Fowler gets to pilot Gallagher's B-17 on the mission.

INTELLIGENCE REPORT
- The B-17 that Capt. King belly lands in the teaser sports a triangle A and tail number 1863 but no fuselage designations, only the national emblem. The plane reappeared in the explosive climax of Act IV. It had been used earlier in #46 "Between the Lines" as the plane Gallagher belly landed, which then exploded.
- During Act III, King's plane has tail number 863, but no fuselage designations. Its nose art is not shown. On the mission, Gallagher radios the plane, calling it 863.
- Dominic Frontiere is back with his suspense-building music cues just as he provided in earlier episodes and on *The Outer Limits*.

TOBY SIGHTING
- Toby mug is on the mantle of the Officers' Club. Shirl Pinkerton asks Gallagher what it's all about and he explains the tradition. Later, we get a great close-up of the Toby as Stovall turns it around. The camera holds on the back of the mug.

#69 "THE PARIAH" (9302)

OAD:	4 November 1966
RERUN:	N/R
W:	Robert C. Dennis
D:	Josef Leytes

The assignment to take out the Reiniger engine works becomes a little easier when MSgt. Herman Schultz offers his help. Sgt. Schultz was born in the city of Stettin, site of the Reiniger complex in Eastern Germany, and knows the area very well. In private, Schultz reveals to Gallagher that his real name is Heinz Reiniger, estranged scion of the industrial family. The next day, Gallagher flies the *Piccadilly Lily* to lead a strike on the Reiniger factories, with "Sgt. Schultz" guiding Lt. Lawson, the navigator. Schultz uses his talent for navigation to steer the group away from a new flak bed in Meulendorf that could have

(Left to right) Robert Walker, Paul Burke, Sasha Harden and Albert Salmi

jeopardized the mission. Over the target, Schultz is again able to direct bombardier Lt. Phelan to hit the correct site. The *Lily* is hit by flak which causes its number-two engine to catch fire. The colonel puts his plane into a power dive, which extinguishes the flames but also leaves the B-17 all alone. Without adequate fuel to make it back home, Gallagher orders Lawson to chart a course for the Russian lines. Gallagher brings the *Lily* in for a landing in the middle of a Russian offensive. The *Piccadilly Lily* is met by a Nazi patrol commanded by SS Maj. Brunner, who takes the Americans to a temporary post run by Col. Gerlach. The commandant's men are hurriedly preparing to evacuate ahead of the advancing Russians. Gallagher's crew, including Schultz, is held in a shed and questioned one by one by Brunner. First up is Gallagher, who is told by Brunner and Gerlach that the 918th effectively wiped out the Reiniger works. When Brunner discovers that there is a German among the crew, he brings Schultz in for questioning. After an hour, Gallagher asks a guard to take him to Brunner so he can check on Schultz's well-being. The argument resulting from Gallagher's confrontation with Brunner compels Gerlach to investigate—and Gerlach is flabbergasted to see "Schultz," whom he immediately recognizes as Heinz Reiniger. Brunner wants to shoot Reiniger as a deserter but Gerlach orders the SS officer to treat him as an American soldier because Reiniger emigrated to the States. Just then, a Russian artillery shell explodes in the command post and kills Gerlach, leaving Brunner in charge. A guard takes Gallagher back to the shanty, but en route another artillery shell flattens the guard. Gallagher grabs his rifle, knocks out the sentry and takes cover. Meanwhile, inside the shed, "Schultz" admits to the rest of the captives that he is actually Heinz Reiniger and explains that he has not yet learned to trust people as an American would. Brunner packs up the last of the essential documents and orders the *Lily's* crew to be shot—all except for Reiniger. As the Nazis prepare to shoot, Gallagher opens fire, giving his men the element of surprise and a chance to overpower the enemy. Some of Gallagher's men are wounded or killed, including Reiniger who at last believes he is a Yankee just before he dies. Maj. Brunner walks out of the command post and right into the approaching Russian tanks, causing him to run for his life. Back at the airfield, Gallagher and his crew bury their dead with honors and take off in the repaired *Piccadilly Lily*.

Col. Gallagher, Sgt. Komansky, Capt. Fowler
M/Sgt. Schultz/Heinz Reiniger ···· Robert Walker
Maj. Brunner ················· Albert Salmi
Col. Gerlach ················· Kurt Kreuger
Lt. Jack Phelan ··············· Les Brown, Jr.
S/Sgt. Hunter ················ Peter Duryea
S/Sgt. Arthur Bellingham ········· Steve Bell
German Aide ················· Sasha Harden
Sgt. Hornig ················· Peter Hellmann
Russian Colonel ··············· Peter Coe
Lt. Dan Lawson ··············· Michael Barrier
Melva ····················· Keva Page
German Officer ··············· Walter Friedel
SS Noncom ················· Walter Alzmann

TDY

- Albert Salmi (1928–1990) was a versatile actor, equally effective in roles as a bad guy or the hero's sidekick. He turned in a memorable performance in *The Twilight Zone* episode "Execution" (OAD 1 April 1960) as a 19th century gunslinger who suddenly found himself in the 20th century. Other guest spots included *Route 66*, *T.H.E. Cat* and two appearances as comic pirate Alonzo P. Tucker on *Lost in Space*. Salmi was a regular on *Daniel Boone* (1964–65) and *Petrocelli* (1974–76).

DEBRIEFING

- The Eighth Air Force bombed Stettin on 11 April 1944, 13 May 1944 and 6 October 1944.

INTELLIGENCE REPORT

- This episode featured three second-generation performers: Robert Walker, Jr., son of actors Jennifer Jones and Robert Walker; Les Brown, Jr., son of bandleader and actor Les Brown; and Peter Duryea, son of actor Dan Duryea.

- The teaser uses a night shot of Komansky driving a jeep to the makeshift base set.
- The Russian landing field is actually Chino Airport.

Marlyn Mason

#70 "THE FIGHTER PILOT" (9311)

OAD:	11 November 1966
RERUN:	N/R
W:	E.B. Anderson
D:	Robert Douglas

Replacement planes with green crews are landing at Archbury, when three P-51s sweep out of the sky and buzz the 918th's base. Arriving with the new B-17s is attractive SSgt. Margo Demarest, a spoiled Army brat and old friend of Gallagher's. She stops in to greet the colonel, who is not at all happy with the Mustang pilots' performance. Margo admits she met them on her way to Archbury: Lt. Dominic Dejohn, Capt. Jerry Clinton and Capt. Franz Rausch, each man an ace. The three have been together since enlisting and have just finished a distinguished tour of duty in the Pacific. To stay together, the trio volunteered to ferry the P-51s to the 511th Fighter Group at the adjacent field. Dejohn, Clinton and Rausch try to talk commander Maj. John Davidson into letting them transfer to the 511th. In turn, Maj. Davidson explains the situation to Gallagher, then introduces the three new arrivals to the colonel. Gallagher recognizes that the three demonstrate the kind of record he can use but before they see combat in the ETO, the trio must first learn discipline. Dejohn, a born rebel, breaks Gallagher's first order and goes AWOL to meet Margo at The Star and Bottle. He explains how he, Clinton and Rausch are all AWOL and lied to stay together to get to Europe. Going even further, Dejohn turns on the charm to get Margo to forge new orders for him and his pals. The next day, Gallagher assigns the freshman crews to a training mission during which they will have to deal with simulated fighter attacks. When Dejohn, Clinton and Rausch hear about it, they jump at the chance to fly the assignment. Gallagher reads their intentions and goes up in his P-51, then throws down an open challenge to anyone who wants to fly with him. Naturally, Dejohn goes up but Gallagher flies the pants off the hothead. At a private meeting with the trio, Gallagher explains that he flies a specially configured Mustang that is four hundred pounds lighter than the typical P-51 and generates an extra 100 horsepower. The colonel stresses that teamwork is essential for survival against the Luftwaffe. When a mission is called for the next day, Clinton asks if they can fly it. Since their "orders" have not yet shown up, neither Maj. Davidson nor Col. Gallagher can assign them. Gallagher offers the trio the opportunity to act as observers in his B-17s. They reluctantly accept his invitation but quickly see that air war in the ETO is much different from what they're used to. The B-17 in which Rausch flies is hit by flak, which kills the pilot. Rausch jumps into the left seat and, with a fighter pilot's sensibilities, breaks formation to take evasive action. This maneuver leaves him a sitting duck for Luftwaffe fighters, which rip into the faltering ship. Dejohn, already resentful of Gallagher, is bitter about the death of his long-time wingman and swears vengeance. Lt. Dejohn once more goes AWOL from the base to meet Margo, who has intercepted a notice that he is wanted back in the States for a civilian crime. In turn, Dejohn tells Margo to keep quiet about the notice or else he'll make trouble for her by exposing her for forging government documents. Crushed over being used by Dejohn, Margo turns to her old friend Gallagher and confesses everything to him. Gallagher and Maj. Davidson confront Clinton, who tells how Dejohn punched out a taxi driver, stole the man's cab and wrecked it. Clinton is confined to quarters and Gallagher sends out the MPs to find Dejohn. The next day, the entire wing goes up and Gallagher flies mission control from his Mustang. Dejohn commandeers a P-51 and takes off with the rest of the group. After the wing has successfully bombed the target, Gallagher heads for home—right into Dejohn's sights. The AWOL pilot plans a game of cat and mouse with Gallagher, but instead he's drawn into a duel with the Luftwaffe. Dejohn adds five more kills to his record before his plane is ripped apart and goes down in flames. In his office, Gallagher meets with Sgt. Demarest and Capt. Clinton to make sure that things are cleared up, then closes the book on the exploits of 1st Lt. Dominic Dejohn, fighter pilot.

Col. Gallagher, Maj. Stovall, Sgt. Komansky
1st Lt. Dominic Dejohn ············· Don Gordon
S/Sgt. Margo Demarest ············· Marlyn Mason
Capt. Jerry Clinton ····················· Stephen Young
Maj. Burt Davidson ···················· Mark Roberts
Capt. Franz Rausch ···················· Jonathan Lippe
Lieutenant ································· Ron Husmann
Jimmy Storm ···························· James Divine
Capt. Bob Fowler ······················ Robert Dornan
Mechanic ································ Seymour Cassel
Lieutenant Black ······················· Martin West

TDY
· Marlyn Mason (born 7 August 1940 in San Fernando, California) played

comedy and drama equally well, from *My Three Sons* to *The Mod Squad* to *Dynasty*. She co-starred with Elvis in *The Trouble with Girls* (1969) and was a regular on *Longstreet* (1971–72).

- Stephen Young (born 19 May 1931) had signed to be a pro baseball player but a knee injury forced him to change careers. So Young got into producing TV series in his native Canada and in England. He started acting in bit parts, then won the starring role in the Canadian-produced series *Seaway* (1965). From there, he co-starred in the Fox series *Judd for the Defense* (1967–69), and guested on series such as *Airwolf, The Bionic Woman* and *Hart to Hart*.

PERSONNEL FILE
- Gallagher tries to teach the newcomers the value of teamwork.
- The script for this episode gives Maj. Davidson the first name John. The end titles also credit the role as John Davidson. But, during the episode, on several occasions he is called Burt.
- Maj. Davidson is commander of the 511th Fighter Group.
- On the mission in Acts III and IV, Fowler pilots the *Piccadilly Lily* with Brown as co-pilot.
- Although Gen. Britt does not appear, he is mentioned.

DEBRIEFING
- The B-17 that Jimmy Storm pilots uses the call sign Blue Baker.
- Maj. Davidson's call sign is Meatball Leader.
- Fowler's call sign on the mission is Sycamore Leader.
- Gallagher explains to Clinton and Rausch that he flies a specially configured Mustang that is four hundred pounds lighter than the typical P-51 and generates an extra 100 horsepower.
- Gallagher again uses his Ramrod call sign while flying mission control in the P-51.

INTELLIGENCE REPORT
- Working title of this episode was "The Unholy Four." In that version, Dejohn, Clinton and Rausch were actually a foursome that included a Lt. Black.
- Lt. Dejohn (Don Gordon) sneaks into the P-51 *Spam Can*.

TOBY SIGHTING
- Toby mug is on the mantle of the Officers' Club. Stovall turns the mug, and then Capt. Clinton repeats the legend and asks Gallagher if the three fighter pilots can join the mission.

#71 "To Seek and Destroy" (9310)

OAD: 18 November 1966
RERUN: N/R
W: Glen A. Larson
D: Donald McDougall

Col. Ulrich accompanies Dr. Tanzman, inventor of a rocket guidance system, to a test launching of a "robot bomb." Much to their dismay, the V-1 rocket goes off course and heads northeast toward Sweden. Realizing the robot bomb's potential for destruction, the Allies must disrupt its development one way or another. But without knowing the location of the factories that make the rockets, Bomber Command has no way to effectively halt production. Group Capt. Anthony Carmichael, a rocket expert and former RAF fighter ace, is tapped for a secret mission. In tandem with the 918th and the underground, Carmichael will parachute into Sweden, dismantle the controls and secure the timer. G-2 can then determine where the parts were made and bombers can be sent to destroy the factories. What neither Gallagher nor temporary wing commander Gen. Doud realize is that Carmichael has it in for the Yanks because American friendly fire shot down his plane and ended his flying career. Further complicating matters, Carmichael can only face life when he's drunk, so he carries with him a flask emblazoned with the RAF logo. Knowing they're in a race with the Nazis to recover the V-1, Gallagher, Komansky and Carmichael take off in an unmarked C-47 to meet with the Swedish underground. Landing just ahead of the C-47 are Ulrich and Dr. Tanzman, who make contact with Svensen, their agent in Sweden and begin to scour the countryside. Meanwhile, Gallagher and company rendezvous with Gunnar Karlsen, their underground contact, at a tavern that doubles as a safe house. The others leave Carmichael alone for a few moments, long enough for him to have a few ales. Svensen walks in. Svensen tells a drunken Carmichael that he speaks English and joins him for a brew. Trying to be social, Carmichael offers to fortify Svensen's ale and pulls out his flask, the one with the RAF logo. Svensen feigns an emergency and leaves, only to pick up reinforcements and follow Gallagher and Komansky back to the airstrip. At the same time, Karlsen takes Carmichael to a warehouse where the V-1 is stored. Following a firefight with Svensen and his gang, Gallagher and Komansky head for the warehouse—just ahead of Ulrich, Dr. Tanzman and a Nazi patrol. While Carmichael holds off the Nazis, Gallagher, Komansky, Karlsen and his men move the essential guidance pieces to the airfield. Carmichael sets off the V-1's explosive charge, blowing the warehouse to smithereens. Back at wing headquarters, Gallagher is shown the components, which intelligence has identified by their source of manufacture. With that knowledge, Gen. Doud authorizes a raid at the first opportunity.

Col. Gallagher, Sgt. Komansky

Gp. Capt. Anthony Carmichael	David Frankham
Brig. Gen. Doud	Richard Anderson
Katy Henshaw	Ellen Willard
Gunnar Karlsen	Karl Swenson
Col. Otto Ulrich	Martin Kosleck
Wing Cmdr. McBride	Patrick Horgan
Lindstrom	Paul Sorensen
Svensen	Peter Bourne
Dr. Franz Tanzman	Ivan Triesault
American Airman	Martin Braddock
German Lieutenant	Eric Forst
Swedish Official	Steve Lander
Waiter	Ashley Cowan
Inge	Ulla Stromstedt [UNCREDITED]
WAC Sergeant	Jane Langley [UNCREDITED]
Capt. Brugmann	John Ragin [UNCREDITED]

TDY

- Richard Anderson (born 8 August 1926, in Long Branch, New Jersey) made his screen debut in a bit part in the feature version of *12 O'Clock High*. As an MGM contract player, Anderson appeared in *Forbidden Planet* (1956). Parts in films such as *Paths of Glory* (1957) and *A Gathering of Eagles* (1963) gave him a sense of the military. But it was on TV that Anderson built a reputation for portraying shrewd, intelligent characters in a long series of guest starring roles. His continuing TV series included the Fox series *Bus Stop* (1961–62), *The Lieutenant* (1963–64), *Perry Mason* (1965–66), QM's *Dan August* (1970–71), *Cover Up* (1984–85) and *Dynasty* (1986–87). Anderson portrayed OSI chief Oscar Goldman on both *The Six Million Dollar Man* (1973–78) and *The Bionic Woman* (1976–78). He would return as Gen. Doud in episodes #72 "Burden of Guilt," #74 "Six Feet Under" and #75 "Duel at Mont Sainte Marie."

- Karl Swenson (1908–1978) created a series of frank, but compassionate, characters. He frequently used a Scandinavian dialect in guest star appearances on series such as *Lassie, Gunsmoke, Longstreet* and *Hogan's Heroes*. He also provided the voice for Merlin in Disney's *The Sword in the Stone* (1963). His continuing roles included the early soap *Portia Faces Life* (1954–55) and *Little House on the Prairie* (1974–78).

- The name Glen A. Larson (born in 1937) was ubiquitous on TV screens throughout the 1970s and '80s. Larson's first script was for QM's *The Fugitive*, followed closely by this one. From there, he moved on to writing

and producing a string of hits for Universal including *It Takes a Thief,*
McCloud, Alias Smith and Jones, Quincy, Battlestar Galactica, Buck Rogers in the
25th Century, Magnum PI and *Knight Rider.* He moved over to Fox TV and
launched more series including *The Fall Guy, Manimal* and *Automan.* All that
success sprang from a thriving career in music that earned him three gold
records for songs he wrote and sang as a member of The Four Preps.

PERSONNEL FILE
  • Gen. Doud tells Gallagher that Gen Britt sends his greetings.

INTELLIGENCE REPORT
  • Working title of this episode was "The Midnighters."
  • The set used for the German observation bunker was previously used as the
    anti-aircraft control center in #65 "Fortress Wiesbaden" and would be reused
    as a research center in #73 "The Ace."
  • The tavern interior is the same set as the meeting room in #67 "Practice to
    Deceive."
  • The C-47 cockpit set was used earlier in #67 "Practice to Deceive" as the
    flight deck of a German Heinkel.

#72 "BURDEN OF GUILT" (9312)

OAD:	2 December 1966
RERUN:	N/R
W:	Robert Longsdorf, Jr.
D:	Laslo Benedek

Col. Ray Hollenbeck believes the
surest way to a promotion to brigadier
general is by taking a combat command.
After Hollenbeck leads the 52nd on three
unsuccessful raids on the Nordensholm
submarine pens—his only three combat
assignments—Gen. Doud must relieve the
colonel of his command. In addition,
Doud gives the Nordensholm project to
the 918th. But Doud also gives his acting
G-3, Col. Hollenbeck, an opportunity by
sending him to the 918th as his operations   **James Broderick**
officer to provide the group with the benefit of his familiarity with the target. But
from the start, Hollenbeck schemes to depose Gallagher and use the 918th as his
ticket to promotion. When Hollenbeck arrives on the base, he tells Stovall that
the mission to Nordensholm is imminent. Hollenbeck is also pleased to know

that Gallagher is off-site visiting his brother Preston, and orders Stovall and Komansky not to notify Gallagher of the mission. Streetwise Sgt. Komansky sees the purpose behind Hollenbeck's orders. Gallagher arrives back at the base just minutes before the group takes off for Nordensholm, only to have Doud order him to stand down and let Hollenbeck lead. Following orders, Gallagher does not fly with the group but instead takes up his P-51. The group approaches the sub pens and Hollenbeck's bombardier toggles his bombs where the colonel indicates. Photos of the drop are being taken by a B-17 flown by Maj. Werth and Maj. Stovall. Flak rips into the photo recon plane, killing Werth. Stovall takes over, drops down and sees a sub gliding across the water. Hollenbeck orders Stovall not to break formation, but the major's plane has had its radio disabled. Because of extensive battle damage, Stovall is forced to ditch his plane—along with the strike photos. Back at Wing HQ, Doud grounds Gallagher for not following orders. Making matters worse, two more freighters are reported sunk by Nazi subs. Hollenbeck swears he hit the target and reasons that the subs must have come from another base. Hollenbeck presses a charge of insubordination against Maj. Stovall which results in an inquest. At the hearing, Hollenbeck nearly loses control while pointing out the lax way Gallagher has run the 918th and is adamant about making an example of Maj. Stovall. Meanwhile, Gallagher disobeys orders to attend the hearing and instead ducks the proceedings. He uses his Mustang to photograph the strike zone. Gen. Doud confines Gallagher to quarters for insubordination. Doud explains that he is in a spot, under political pressure, because he is suspected of playing friendship over command with Hollenbeck and Gallagher. Moreover, Doud recognizes Hollenbeck's scheme and tells Gallagher that he's playing right into it. Komansky finally tells Gallagher about Hollenbeck's order not to phone him the night before the mission, and Stovall verifies the story. Once more, Gallagher disobeys orders, leaves his quarters and angrily confronts Hollenbeck in a quarrel that almost leads to blows. Hollenbeck admits he's been wrong but contends that his career hinges on successfully wiping out the sub pens once and for all. The conniving Hollenbeck gets Gallagher to reveal his take on the Nordensholm situation. He believes the sub bases are somewhere in the coastal islands of Krager or Risor. This time, Hollenbeck goes up in a P-51 to scout the area. Although Hollenbeck's plane is chased away by flak and Luftwaffe fighters he radios in that he's found something big. Gallagher and Hollenbeck meet with Doud at Wing HQ, Hollenbeck tells Doud that the base is in either Krager or Risor—passing off Gallagher's theory as his own. Gen. Doud orders a maximum effort combining the 918th, the 966th and the 52nd Bomb Groups commanded by Hollenbeck with Gallagher as lead pilot. When ferocious flak takes its toll on the bombers, Hollenbeck discovers he is incapable of improvising during combat and wants to abort. Gallagher refuses, orders the remaining planes to regroup and takes the bombers over the islands. They wipe out the subs, fuel supplies and all support facilities. In a press conference at Wing HQ, Hollenbeck announces that the sub pens at

Nordensholm have been destroyed. Gen. Doud presents Hollenbeck with the form to sign accepting his promotion to general. In a perplexing move, Hollenbeck refuses and admits that he's discovered his own capacity for failure. He knows he is not a combat leader.

Col. Gallagher, Maj. Stovall, Sgt. Komansky
Col. Ray Hollenbeck ···················· James Broderick
Brig. Gen. Philip Doud ············· Richard Anderson
Maj. Gen. Fox ······························ Wesley Addy
Maj. Harry Werth ······················· Edward Knight
Flight Engineer ··························· John Ward
WAC Sergeant ···························· Diane Strom
Guard ·· Dave Armstrong
Capt. Bob Fowler ······················ Robert Dornan [UNCREDITED]

TDY

- James Broderick (1930–1982) was a young, stage-trained actor when he broke into live TV dramas in the 1950s. Broderick worked a string of New York City-based soaps such as *The Secret Storm* (1960), *As the World Turns* (1962), and *The Edge of Night* (1964). He had continuing roles on *Brenner* (1959, 1964) and the critically acclaimed *Family* (1976–80). Movie roles included *The Group* (1966), *Alice's Restaurant* (1969) and *The Taking of Pelham One Two Three* (1974). He was the father of actor Matthew Broderick.

PERSONNEL FILE

- Gallagher was a star quarterback at West Point.

DEBRIEFING

- Col. Hollenbeck uses the call sign Seagull Leader.
- Capt. Fowler is Hollenbeck's co-pilot.
- In his P-51, Gallagher uses the call sign Ramrod.
- Gallagher encounters a flight of photo recon P-38s over the target area.
- On Hollenbeck's solo flight, he uses the call sign Horseback.
- When Hollenbeck's P-51 is surrounded by German fighters, Gallagher calls in reinforcements from the 511th Fighter Group.
- Nordensholm was not a target of the Eighth Air Force.

INTELLIGENCE REPORT

- Although stock shots of Chino are used, when Gallagher comes out of a building, he is on the makeshift base set. When Hollenbeck drives up to the base for the first time, he is also on the makeshift set.

#73 "THE ACE" (9313)

OAD:	9 December 1966
RERUN:	N/R
W:	Oscar Millard
D:	Robert Douglas

James Whitmore

Intelligence sources have uncovered that the Nazis are very close to completing an atomic weapon. The research is being conducted in Adelsberg, a small German hamlet that must be destroyed. During a meeting at Wing, Gallagher tells Britt he can bomb the research facility and confine the impact to 20 acres. But that's nowhere near good enough. Complicating the mission: high-ranking Allied prisoners of war have been billeted around the facility as insurance against bombing or sabotage. Gallagher suggests Col. Harry Connelly, a highly decorated pilot who can "drop a one-ton bomb in a thimble." In fact, a recent "skip bombing" mission earned Connelly the Congressional Medal of Honor. Since Connelly is Gallagher's good friend and the man who taught him to fly, Gallagher brings him into the planning for the Adelberg strike. Even though Connelly has transferred out of combat flying, he can't pass up the challenge. Connelly insists on flying the mission alone and requests a modified B-25 so that he can drop the bomb by himself at treetop level. Despite keeping up a brash exterior, Connelly has doubts about his ability to do the job. The group takes off with Connelly in his B-25, but when he reaches the target area Connelly must weave around the site to find the target before he drops the bomb. That night, Axis Sally broadcasts the names of POWs the Nazis claim were killed during the raid on Adelberg. A phone call from Gen. Britt confirms it: Connelly hit the wrong building. Britt calls in Connelly for an explanation and a solution to how they can take out the actual target. Connelly is angry because he blames Gallagher for the situation he's in and spouts off to Britt about it. The general believes Connelly is suffering from combat fatigue and orders Gallagher to hit Adelberg with a maximum effort—even if it means leaving 20 acres of dead bodies behind. Meanwhile, Connelly returns to base and greets Gallagher with a sucker punch as payment for Gallagher suckering him into the mission. Gallagher watches his hero collapse, succumbing to combat fatigue. The new plan is for Gallagher to fly the modified B-25. If he is not successful, the group will follow with a saturation bombing. As the group prepares for the mission, Connelly sneaks onto the B-25 and when Gallagher boards they slug it out and Gallagher puts Connelly off the plane. The group takes off and is later met with one addition: Connelly, flying a P-51. The Mustang catches up with Gallagher and Connelly helps guide him to the target and draws off some of the flak. Their combined effort puts teacher and pupil together as Gallagher makes a perfect drop on the installation and heads for home while Connelly draws off the attacking Luftwaffe fighters. Back at Wing, Britt announces that the target has been successfully destroyed. Britt, Gallagher and the other officers involved pay tribute to Connelly's heroic, if irreverent spirit, just as Komansky arrives to announce that Connelly has been picked up in the Channel.

Col. Gallagher, Sgt. Komansky, Maj. Stovall, Maj Gen. Britt
Col. Harry Connelly ················ James Whitmore
Brig. Gen. Kenneth Chandler ···· Joe Maross
Col. Curry ······························ Ben Wright
Reporter ······························· Robert Ivers
Radio Operator ····················· Ron Stokes
Airman ································· Jerry Ayres
Mechanic ······························ Robert Bolger
Barkeep ······························· Mark Harris
British Officer ························ John Levingston
German Lieutenant ················· Eric Forst
Voice of Axis Sally ················· June Foray [UNCREDITED]

TDY

• One of America's most recognizable actors, James Whitmore (born 1 October 1921 in White Plains, New York) has graced stage and screen for more than half a century. He appeared in the 1947 stage version of *Command Decision,* a cousin to *12 O'Clock High.*

• Joe Maross (born in 1923) brought credibility to roles ranging from working class guys to bureaucratic figures on series such as *T.H.E. Cat, The Magician, The Twilight Zone* and *The Rockford Files.* His recurring roles included *As the World Turns* (1966), *Peyton Place* (1968–69) and *Code Red* (1981–82). Maross returned as Gen. Chandler in #76 "Graveyard."

Personnel File

• The first draft of this script included Gen. Doud. Corrections of 20 September 1966 change all references of Doud to Brig. Gen. Kenneth Chandler.
• Gen. Britt refers to the base surgeon but Doc Kaiser is never mentioned by name.
• The script gives Col. Curry the first name Andrew. In the episode, Gen. Britt

calls him Ted, signaling a last-minute change.

DEBRIEFING

- On the mission over Adelsberg, Stovall is Gallagher's co-pilot. Gallagher uses the call sign Ramrod.
- The Eighth Air Force did not strike Adelsberg until 25 February 1945.
- The previous strike was over Marienburg.
- On the second mission, Chandler's call sign is Fox Hound Leader.

INTELLIGENCE REPORT

- A stock sequence of the Chino command center is used, but when Gallagher comes out of the building to watch Connelly practice, it's the makeshift set.
- No new footage of boarding the planes at Chino is shot; instead, vintage stock sequences are used.
- The aerial photo of Adelberg is the same one used to depict Target 802 in #47 "Target 802."
- The research lab set was used earlier in #65 "Fortress Wiesbaden" and #71 "To Seek and Destroy."

#74 "SIX FEET UNDER" (9315)

OAD: 16 December 1966
RERUN: N/R
W: James Doherty
D: Murray Golden

Maj. Tony Dimscek's American 52nd Division overtakes German forces occupying the Belgian village of Argagnol. In a catacomb used by the Nazis as a command post, Maj. Dimscek finds a gold mine of Luftwaffe documents. Meanwhile, Gallagher and Komansky—who have been setting up forward bases in France—are ordered to Argagnol to analyze the documents. When they arrive they are met by SSgt. Nick Battalana, who leads them to the cellar. All three are surprised by Emile, a Belgian teenager, and his younger brother Jacques. Sgt. Battalana chases away the boys. Meanwhile, no one sees a wounded German corporal hiding behind some crates. Maj. Dimscek shows Gallagher the files but reasons that since the documents are written in German no one there can translate them. Dimscek also tells Gallagher that he's fighting off a major counteroffensive, supported by tanks and aerial bombing, which means they may have to evacuate the command post at any second. Unexpectedly, Emile returns pleading for help for his brother, who has been pinned under rubble. The Americans free Jacques and bring him back to the cellar for treatment by a medic. Just then, the wounded German appears, using a grenade as leverage to get help from the medic. After the doctor bandages the German's wounds, the patient edges away to escape, throws his grenade at his hostages and leaves. Komansky dives and is able to toss the live grenade away where it can explode out of harm's way. Emile sees how Gallagher protected him and, in gratitude, agrees to translate the captured Luftwaffe documents. Meanwhile, Stovall and the CIC team are airborne and approaching the drop point. Gallagher radios Stovall to tell him that the Germans would butcher the parachuting agents before they hit the ground, then orders the major to go home and launch a maximum effort air strike as soon as possible. With the Germans closing in, Dimscek orders the stronghold evacuated. Emile has been helping Gallagher determine which documents are most vital and Dimscek's men carry boxes upstairs and load them into a jeep. A shell burst hits the jeep, killing Maj. Dimscek. As boxes of files are removed, a safe—probably containing the most top-secret documents—is revealed, but not even explosives will blow it open. Emile goes back to rejoin his brother when a bomb seals up their only way out. Gallagher and Komansky go to another part of the catacomb and set off hand grenades to blow a hole in the wall so Emile and Jacques can escape. The four are surprised by Germans, but Gallagher shoots them. With no other choice, Gallagher, Komansky, Emile and Jacques seek shelter in the catacomb, which is roughly six feet under ground...also the average location of a grave. The bomber raid led by Gen. Doud strikes, paving the way for the American troops to move back in and retake what's left of the village. The documents are confiscated and shipped to Wing HQ where Doud is ecstatic over their significance to the war effort. Gallagher is preoccupied with two of the smallest victims of the war: Emile and Jacques, who are alive but homeless.

Col. Gallagher, Sgt. Komansky, Maj. Stovall, Brig. Gen. Phil Doud

Maj. Tony Dimscek	Martin Milner
S/Sgt. Nick Battalana	Rudy Solari
Emile	Barry Robins
Commanding Officer	Richard O'Brien
Wounded German Corporal	Lawrence Montaigne
Doctor	Jason Wingreen
Radioman	Jimmy Hayes
Rand	James Sikking
German Corporal	Walter Alzmann
German Orderly	Horst Ebersberg
Jacques	Gerald Michenaud

TDY

- Martin Milner (born 28 December 1927 in Detroit, Michigan), one of TV's most familiar faces, was between series at this time. He had just spent four years on the hit *Route 66* (1960–64). In the mid-1960s, Milner also appeared in Fox's hit *Valley of the Dolls* (1967), then signed on with the long-running

Adam-12 (1968–75). He would return to Fox for the 1975 series *Swiss Family Robinson*.

• This was Rudy Solari's second appearance on *12 O'Clock High*. He would appear in uniform again during the following season as one of *Garrison's Gorillas* (1967–68).

• James Sikking (born 5 March 1934 in Los Angeles) worked minor character parts for nearly two decades before finding the right fit with gung ho Lt. Howard Hunter on *Hill Street Blues* (1981–87). Sikking's other recurring TV roles were on *General Hospital* (1973–76), *Turnabout* (1979) and *Doogie Howser, MD* (1989–93).

PERSONNEL FILE
• Gen. Doud orders an aide to tell Gen. Britt that he'll lead the mission.

DEBRIEFING
• Doud uses the call sign Eagle Leader.

INTELLIGENCE REPORT
• The cellar steps set is the same one used earlier in #67 "Practice to Deceive" and later in #75 "Duel at Mont Sainte Marie."
• Another episode based primarily on the ground.

#75 "DUEL AT MONT SAINTE MARIE" (9305)

OAD:	23 December 1966
RERUN:	N/R
W:	R. Wright Campbell
D:	Josef Leytes

Deadly accurate Nazi artillery fire is holding back the Allied Second Front in Southern France. The German guns are located behind Mont Sainte Marie, site of a mountaintop abbey that houses a venerable shrine. The guns are guided by observers on the steep slopes below the retreat. Gen. Doud orders Col. Gallagher to make a tactical strike on Mont Sainte Marie, then tells the colonel that the shrine is home to nuns and is also a shelter for refugees from the village below. An impassioned Gallagher talks Doud into giving him 24 hours to try to talk the prioress Sister Martha into abandoning the retreat and avoiding an atrocity. Gallagher and Komansky parachute into the area and rendezvous with infantry commander Col. Farnum, who demands bombing, and Chaplain Roman, who desperately wants to facilitate an evacuation. While Komansky and a squad of Farnum's men remain below on watch, Gallagher, Father Roman, SSgt. Jamieson and Francois, a French Resistance fighter, make their way to the convent. When they meet Sister Martha, the prioress adamantly refuses to be driven out. During their conversation, it comes out that Sr. Martha is German, although she has no allegiance to the Nazis. Unknown to anyone else, a frightened Sr. Anne ran to alert Col.

(Foreground, left to right) Lilia Skala and Edward Mulhare

Gehrt Schotten, commander of the Nazi garrison at Mont Sainte Marie. Col. Schotten, who has been currying the favor of Sr. Martha, returns with a squad of his men and faces a standoff with the headstrong prioress, who orders everyone to disarm. A moral tug-of-war ensues between Gallagher and Schotten with the prize being Sr. Martha's sanction. The prioress maintains that the nunnery is her home but will allow anyone else to leave. Father Roman speaks to Sr. Martha in private and tries to make her understand that she is blind to the war around her and that Schotten has used her. The refugees are allowed to leave unharmed. However, when Francois tries to exit he is gunned down by Nazi machine gun fire. Sr. Martha is horrified and finally admits to herself that she is afraid of living outside the security of her sanctuary. With the advantage of outlying troops, Schotten holds the nuns and the Americans as prisoners, waiting for the inevitable bombing. Gallagher refuses to divulge the time of the bombing because Schotten could then order his troops to withdraw to safety. Just then, Komansky bursts in, guns blazing, and provides enough firepower to tip the balance in the Americans' favor. The sergeant's radio has been shot up but Gallagher still uses it to signal the approaching bombers and call for a five-minute delay in the scheduled drop. Sr. Martha acknowledges that God has protected them until now and He will continue to do so. She leads the other nuns out of the convent, over Schotten's objections. Gallagher decks the Nazi and repeats his message to delay the drop. Gen. Doud, leading the 918th, picks up the signal and turns, giving Gallagher, Komansky and Jamieson time to leave. After the bombing, Gallagher revisits the abbey and finds Sr. Martha tending the basement shrine, which has miraculously survived the bombing.

Col. Gallagher, Sgt. Komansky, Maj. Stovall, Brig. Gen. Philip Doud
Sister Martha ···················· Lilia Skala
Father Roman ···················· Joseph Campanella
Col. Gehrt Schotten ·············· Edward Mulhare

S/Sgt. Jamieson	John Milford
Col. Peter Farnum	William Bramley
Francois	Emile Genest
Sister Anne	Adrienne Hayes
Capt. Jay Rice	Paul Mantee
Sister Chlotilde	Eva Soreny
Capt. Hiller	Horst Ebersberg
German Soldier	Pieter Bergema
Woman Refugee	Karen Verne
German Sergeant	Phil Adams

TDY

· Lilia Skala (1896–1994) revisited the role of a nun in this episode after having earned an Oscar nomination for her performance as Mother Superior Maria in *Lilies of the Field* (1963). A few months later, Skala again guest starred as a Mother Superior in the *I Spy* episode "Get Thee to a Nunnery" (OAD 1 March 1967). She also portrayed a nun in the pilot for *Ironside* (1967). Skala's other guest roles featured turns on *Green Acres, McCloud,* and *Trapper John, M.D.*

· Joseph Campanella (born 21 November 1933 in New York City) served in the Navy during World War II, then studied acting under Lee Strasberg. At the time of this episode, Campanella had been working on Broadway, living on the East Coast, and was testing the waters for job prospects in Hollywood. His continuing TV roles were on *The Guiding Light* (1959), *The Doctors* (1963), *The Doctors and the Nurses* (1964–65), *Mannix* (1967–68), *The Bold Ones: The Lawyers* (1969–72), *The Colbys* (1985-86) and *Days of Our Lives* (1988–90). He continues to be a working actor with roles on TV series such as *Cold Case*.

Joseph Campanella on "Duel at Mont Sainte Marie": "Pleasant memories. The regular cast and the guest cast of that show were all top actors. They were all the busiest actors of those days. Ed Mulhare and I were on Broadway. We used to double date occasionally. He was quite a guy.

"Everyone came prepared to work. Most all of us had been in the service at one time or another. Playing a chaplain, well, I'm a Catholic and some of those things we talked about I could actually say. I knew the last rites. It didn't add to the plot but it was a nice, little colorful scene.

"I wish we could do that over again. But, they just don't make 'em like they used to."

· William Bramley (1928–1985) brought a blue-collar sensibility to roles, typically as a tough guy on *Combat!, Emergency!* and *Gunsmoke*. Bramley also played for laughs on sitcoms such as *The Monkees, I Dream of Jeannie* and

Gomer Pyle, USMC.

DEBRIEFING

- The script for this episode describes its core conflict this way: "In appearance and [military] significance, it is nominally a miniature Monte Cassino." The reaction of political, military and religious factions to destroying the convent at Mont Sainte Marie mirrors the actual conflict over bombing the abbey at Monte Cassino. Strategists perceived the abbey to be an obstacle to Allied advances. Despite heated protests, it was bombed into rubble. Ironically, the bombing did not clear the way but, instead, left craters that further obstructed the movement of men and materiel.
- Gen. Doud's call sign is Castle Leader.
- Maj. Stovall flies the concluding mission as Doud's co-pilot.
- Gallagher flies the P-51 to observe the site and uses the call sign Ramrod.

INTELLIGENCE REPORT

- The exteriors of the abbey were filmed at 40 Acres, an independent backlot of standing sets.
- The cellar stair set was used before in episodes #67 "Practice to Deceive" and #74 "Six Feet Under."

FLIGHT LINE

- Col. Gallagher makes the analogy that the events at Mont Sainte Marie are "like Monte Cassino all over again." That means Monte Cassino had already happened, making the date of this episode sometime after 15 February 1944.

#76 "GRAVEYARD" (9317)

OAD:	30 December 1966
RERUN:	N/R
W:	William D. Gordon
D:	Robert Douglas

A shuttle raid to Italy, led by Gen. Chandler piloting Gallagher's plane, goes awry when German fighters attack. Flak badly damages the plane's controls and kills half the crew. Gallagher realizes that they can't reach the designated airstrip in Italy and suggests they put down at a small American airstrip on Sabena Island. Gallagher makes radio contact with Sabena, but the damage to his ship is so severe that he orders the crew to bail out. Meanwhile, the fierce air action over the area continues with P-51s battling Me 109s. On the ground, Komansky, Chandler, Pargon and Banning meet an American who introduces himself as

Maj. Luke. Komansky says they don't know the whereabouts of Gallagher or the waist gunner. Maj. Luke is puzzled because he counted seven parachutes, not six. The extra chute belongs to Luftwaffe Capt. Holtke, who has also landed on Sabena. Maj. Luke's "command" consists of Sgt. Conklin and a group of downed Luftwaffe pilots, who are ordered to bring the wounded Chandler and radio operator to the base hospital. The more Komansky is around Luke the more he feels he knows Luke from somewhere—and that Luke isn't the man's real name. Conklin, an airman whose life "Luke" saved, talks to his comrade in private. "Luke" is really Pvt. Jim Prince, who is twice AWOL, impersonating an officer and ready to go AWOL again to avoid prosecution. "Luke" walks away from the base and, when Komansky goes after him, Komansky finds a small cemetery and locates a marker for Pvt. Prince. Seeing the name brings the story back to Komansky, the story of a former officer who was stripped of his rank because he couldn't pull a trigger. On another part of the base, the waist gunner finally shows up but before he can make contact he is killed by Capt. Holtke. Prince has a chance to stop Holtke but lets him escape. Komansky catches up with Prince just before Gallagher shows up. By this time, Holtke has made his way to the medical tent, shot Conklin and Pargon, and liberated the German prisoners. Holtke radios for help from the Luftwaffe, then leads the Germans to interfere when an American rescue plane lands. While Prince distracts Holtke and the other Germans, Gallagher and Komansky attack from the rear and secure the base. Prince pursues and corners Holtke. When the German opens fire, Prince shoots the enemy and kills him. The rescue plane is finally able to land and whisks away the survivors with an understanding that charges against Prince will be dropped or minimized.

Col. Gallagher, Sgt. Komansky	
Maj. Luke/Pvt. Prince	Ossie Davis
Brig. Gen. Kenneth Chandler	Joe Maross
Capt. Karl Holtke	Jon Voight
S/Sgt. Earl Conklin	Don Marshall
S/Sgt. Pargon	Paul Lukather
Sgt. Shadrack Ellis	William Arvin
Bruno Zemler	Horst Ebersberg
American Major	Dallas Mitchell
Chase Mayhew	Lloyd Haynes
American Pilot	Geoffrey Deuel
German Pilot	Chris Anders
T/Sgt. Banning	Garrison True

TDY
- Ossie Davis (1917–2005) brought dignity and purpose to a long list of roles dating back to his Broadway debut in 1946. Davis was honored for his

contributions as an actor, writer and director. His TV work was initially on New York City-based programs such as *The Defenders, The Nurses* and *Car 54, Where are You?* He appeared in movies such as *The Scalphunters* (1968), *A Man Called Adam* (1966), *Malcolm X* (1992) and the miniseries *Roots: The Next Generation* (1979). Davis was married to actor Ruby Dee.

- Don Marshall (born 2 May 1936 in San Diego, California) would return to the Fox lot to co-star in the Irwin Allen-produced series *Land of the Giants* (1968–70). Marshall is probably best remembered for his role in the *Star Trek* episode "The Galileo Seven" (OAD 5 January 1967).

- Jon Voight (born 29 December 1938 in Yonkers, New York) was still a couple of years away from his breakthrough role in *Midnight Cowboy* (1969). Voight had been in *The Sound of Music* on Broadway in the early '60s. He did a handful of TV roles on series such as *Naked City, The Defenders* and *Gunsmoke* before turning his attention to the big screen. Voight is the father of actor Angelina Jolie.

PERSONNEL FILE
- Although Frank Overton is credited in both the opening and closing titles, Maj. Stovall does not appear in this episode.

DEBRIEFING
- Leading the strike, Gen. Chandler uses the call sign Sure Thing Leader.
- Leading fighter cover, Chase Mayhew uses the call sign Toro Leader.

INTELLIGENCE REPORT
- Even though the U.S. military was still racially segregated during World War II, by 1966 network television reflected an increasingly multiracial world. Bill Cosby was heralded as TV's Jackie Robinson for his breakthrough co-starring role on *I Spy* (1965–68). *Tarzan* was given an African-American friend (Rockne Tarkington). *Hawk* featured a young African-American detective (Wayne Grice). African-American Greg Morris played an electronics expert on *Mission: Impossible*. *Star Trek* had African-American Nichelle Nichols (portraying Uhura) and Asian-American George Takei (as Sulu).
- This episode was based on an experience that series' technical advisor Jim Doherty had while serving with the Fifteenth Air Force. Doherty was shot down over Yugoslavia and subsequently picked up by a medical unit there.
- The sheer cliff face used as the exterior backdrop for the Sabena base was built at the Fox Ranch in Malibu for the 1965 Fox feature *Von Ryan's Express*. When Komansky climbs into the air vent, he's actually crawling along a miniature trestle bridge.

- A fervent political activist, Ossie Davis worked with the Reverend Martin Luther King, Jr., and Malcolm X. Davis and wife Ruby Dee helped organize the 1963 March On Washington and wrote an autobiography titled *With Ossie and Ruby: In This Life Together.* Davis founded Third World Cinema, a production company, to support African American and Puerto Rican filmmakers.

FLIGHT LINE
- The U.S. armed forces were kept racially segregated until President Harry S. Truman's Executive Order 9981 in 1948 desegregated the military, a major step forward in the civil rights movement.

#77 "A LONG TIME DEAD" (9314)

OAD:	6 January 1967
RERUN:	N/R
W:	James Doherty
D:	Gene Nelson

Capt. Calvin Dula volunteers to fly as Gallagher's navigator on a mission to Regensburg. During the preflight check, Komansky tells the colonel he wishes that a jinx like Dula wasn't with them: on Dula's second combat mission, he lost his plane and crew, which is sending the captain for review before a pilot evaluation board. Not only is Gallagher unhappy with his flight engineer's comments, but Dula calls Komansky down to the navigator's station and threatens to punch him out. After the bomb drop, a burst of flak knocks out Gallagher and badly injures his co-pilot, Maj. Stovall. Komansky tries to help while Dula comes to the flight deck and takes over as pilot. In a panic, Dula orders Komansky back into the top turret. When Komansky refuses and instead tends to Stovall's wounds, Dula orders TSgt. Nick Neely to log charges of mutiny against Komansky. After the group returns, Britt informs Gallagher that the mission was unsuccessful. Sgt. Neely seeks Gallagher's advice on the matter of mutiny. When Gallagher calls Dula into his office to discuss the incident, Gallagher is puzzled by the captain's confusion at recalling what happened. Meanwhile, Komansky's girlfriend, Jeanne Springer, throws him a birthday party in her flat. Afterward, Jeanne—who was in love with the flight engineer in the crew that Dula lost—gives Komansky a letter from the lone survivor of Dula's crew: a gunner who wrote from a POW hospital in Germany, accusing Dula of deserting the ship and the crew. Komansky tries to play fair with Dula and tells the captain about the letter. The sergeant also tells his pal Sgt. Neely about the letter and where it's stashed. Still unable to remember details, Dula sees Gallagher in his office and takes a page from the mission logbook so he can refresh his memory. The group goes after Regensburg once more, again with Dula as navigator and Komansky as flight engineer. German fighters attack and their gunfire rips into the lead plane, hitting Komansky's legs. After he is wounded the sergeant slips out of his turret and into the crawlway. Dula slips Komansky into a parachute and, despite attempts by Neely and the bombardier to stop him, dumps Komansky out of the hatch and into a free fall. Back in Gallagher's office, Dula justifies his action by saying he didn't think Komansky would survive the flight back to England. Sgt. Neely turns over the letter to Gallagher who then approaches Jeanne with it. Jeanne is no fan of Dula's because of her boyfriend's death and Komansky's apparent demise. She insists that Col. Gallagher read the letter, which he does and shows it to Britt. The general calls Dula, Doc Kaiser and, reluctantly, Col. Gallagher to an informal hearing. Dula is confused about the details of where they were and the location of Komansky's wounds when he threw the sergeant out of the plane. Capt. Dula is also vague about the specific orders Komansky disobeyed to deserve the mutiny charge. The captain also cannot recall giving a bail out order on his second disastrous mission. Struggling to put the pieces together, Dula realizes that he loses composure under pressure and simply can't remember details. A report comes in that Komansky is alive and recovering in a French field hospital. With the rest of the 918th on a mission, Gallagher flies a plane with Dula and Doc Kaiser aboard to the pick up the sergeant. It turns out that Dula did the right thing because Komansky would have lost a leg if he hadn't been thrown from the plane. Doc Kaiser speculates that Dula must undergo psychiatric care and may not fly again. Gallagher tells Dula that treatment may uncover the truth and alleviate future blackouts.

Col. Gallagher, Sgt. Komansky, Maj. Stovall, Maj. Gen. Britt, Doc Kaiser
Capt. Calvin Dula ·························· Peter Graves
Jeanne Springer ···························· Anne Helm
T/Sgt. Nick Neely ························· Tom Skerritt
Lt. Ken Velsor ······························· Gil Peterson
Maj. Cross ···································· Hank Brandt

TDY
- Peter Graves (born Peter Aurness on 18 March 1926 in Minneapolis, Minnesota) knew about flying because he piloted *Airplane!* (1980) and was familiar with the military from his series *Court Martial* (1966) and movies such as *Stalag 17* (1953), *The Long Gray Line* (1955) and *The Court Martial of Billy Mitchell* (1955). But Graves' most recognized role is as Jim Phelps on the long running hit *Mission: Impossible* (1967–73 and 1988–90).

  Peter Graves on "A Long Time Dead": "I had just returned from doing a series in England, *Court Martial,* for Universal and was still under contract to Universal. But I was allowed to do things outside the studio. I had gone to Texas to promote a Universal film that was about to be released. I was just about to go to bed when I got a phone call to do *12 O'Clock High*. I took the next flight out of Corpus Christi. They sent a script to the house and I was thumbing through it by the time I got to the studio. Although I didn't know anyone well, I had worked with Barney Philips before. But everyone was very professional. Paul Burke knew he had a good series and he wanted to see it done right. For me, playing a soldier was like playing Cowboys and Indians. You dress in all that military stuff and the medals and the .45 at your side. That was all a great deal of fun. And it was kind of a nice story."

• Anne Helm (born 12 September 1938 in Toronto, Ontario, Canada) had a healthy career during the 1960s, working in primetime TV series, such as *The FBI, Dr. Kildare* and *Adventures in Paradise*. She had a recurring role on *Run for Your Life* (1966–68) and was a regular on *General Hospital* (1971–73).

• Director Gene Nelson (1920–1996) was a dancer in MGM musicals, right up there with Gene Kelly. But after an accident ended his dancing career, Nelson turned to directing. His directorial efforts included *Burke's Law, Starsky and Hutch* and *The Andy Griffith Show.*

PERSONNEL FILE
• Gen. Britt telephones Gen. Pritchard, who does not appear in this episode.

DEBRIEFING
• The mission is to Regensburg.
• The Eighth Air Force struck Regensburg on numerous occasions, including 17 August 1943, 22 February 1944, 25 February 1944, 20 October 1944, 23 October 1944, 4 November 1944, 22 November 1944, 9 December 1944, 20 December 1944 and 28 December 1944.
• Maj. Stovall is Gallagher's co-pilot.

INTELLIGENCE REPORT
• Technical advisor and writer of this episode, Jim Doherty, has an almost poetic style, as indicated in the teaser: "An English dawn has infiltrated the 918th's flight line, making partial silhouettes of the B-17s, row on row, that signal this as one of the busiest bases in Britain."
• Production notes indicate that in 1966 there was a Col. Mason A. Dula who had been in uniform since 1939. He had been a captain during World War II and was promoted to major 5 May 1944.
• The teaser opens with a stock shot of readying for the mission at Chino; later, a stock shot shows a jeep driving around Chino.
• Exterior night sequences were filmed at the makeshift base at Fox.
• An exterior shot of a jeep driving away from the Archbury tower is cut with

new footage of Capt. Dula driving up the road into the makeshift base to meet an ambulance.

#78 "THE HUNTERS AND THE KILLERS" (9316)

OAD: 13 January 1967
RERUN: N/R
W: E.B. Anderson
D: Robert Douglas

Ralph Bellamy

Gen. Britt is put in command of a joint Air Corps-Navy operation to destroy the U-boat Wolfpack Leica. Britt's choice for Air Corps leader is Col. Gallagher. To represent the Navy, the general selects Commodore Leon Crompton. The general's plan nearly goes down in flames before it starts. Gallagher and Crompton are at odds over a two-year-old incident in which the commodore lost out on a promotion when he opposed Gallagher's father at a Senate committee hearing regarding the projected long-range bombing program. Because of Crompton's behavior at the time, his superiors broke him and the commodore has had no love for the Gallagher family since then. Demonstrating his distaste, Crompton walks out of a meeting with Britt and Gallagher. Later, the commodore sheepishly phones Britt to ask forgiveness and explain that his career still hangs by a thread. Crompton needs the assignment and he desperately needs it to succeed. Sgt. Komansky drives Gallagher to The Star and Bottle for a meeting with Crompton. While outside, Komansky runs into a friend, attractive WAC Cpl. Terry Cahill, and they make a dinner date. Crompton's car pulls up and the commodore's aide, Seaman 1st Class Obie Sorenson, gets an eyeful of the corporal and cuts in on Komansky's action. The strategy comes down from Gen. Britt: Gallagher's bombers will be the hunters, flying without bombs for a "minimum load, maximum range" tactic. The group is to patrol the area with nine airplanes, in three relays, three B-17s at a time. Once they spot a sub, the 918th will report their positions to Crompton. The commodore's nearby Task Force 10 carrier aircraft will then serve as the killers. The patrols finally yield a sighting of the Wolfpack Leica. Gallagher alerts Crompton, who orders the B-17s to get out of his way and then calls in every ship and Navy attack plane he has at his disposal. Before the B-17s can turn for home, Luftwaffe fighters close in and attack them. Gallagher radios the approaching U.S. Navy fighters for help but Commodore

Crompton orders them to stay with the task force. That night at The Star and Bottle, talk about the day's mission ignites a brawl among the Air Corps fliers, the Navy seamen and everyone else in the pub. Gallagher and Crompton meet in the colonel's office, where Maj. Stovall brings in the only witness, Cpl. Cahill. She explains that Komansky and Sorenson were actually trying to break up the fight. In light of Cahill's explanation, Crompton begins to mellow and by the time Gen. Britt shows up, he and Gallagher have come to an understanding. The program's tactics are modified slightly: Gallagher's B-17s will now carry full bomb loads. The decision comes just in time: the wolfpack attacks Task Force 10 and sinks a carrier. Britt orders Gallagher to move in and hit the wolfpack with everything he's got. Crompton radios Gallagher that he will fire depth charges to bring the wolfpack to the surface, then orders Gallagher to bomb everything— even the commodore's ship. Compounding the action is another wave of Luftwaffe fighters, elevating the conflict to an all-out air-sea battle. Gallagher insists on staying with Crompton's destroyer until help arrives, even though a fire has broken out in his plane. When another sub surfaces, Gallagher drops his bomb load and sinks it. Komansky determines the fuel lines are the source of the shipboard fire and the fire will blow the plane if it reaches the fuel tanks. The colonel orders a bail out before the plane spirals down and smacks into the Channel. Komansky and other crew members are picked up and brought back to base. Crompton and Britt both show up, too. Britt names Stovall temporary commander of the 918th until he finds a suitable replacement. The general implies that Gallagher's injuries won't win him a ticket home but Crompton offers to give the colonel passage back to the States if that's the prescription. Commodore Crompton personally puts in a call to the colonel's father, Lt. Gen. Maxwell Gallagher, to let him know what's happened. In private, Komansky asks if the colonel will return to the 918th. Britt tells the sergeant that he doesn't think a few broken bones will prevent Gallagher from flying again. Leaving Komansky behind, Gen. Britt walks out of the operations building and looks up to see a lone B-17 soaring across the sky.

Col. Gallagher, Sgt. Komansky, Maj. Stovall, Maj. Gen. Britt, Doc Kaiser
Commodore Leon Crompton ····· Ralph Bellamy
Seaman Obie Sorenson ············· Michael Witney
Cpl. Terry Cahill ························ Anna Capri
Capt. Fowler ······························ Robert Dornan
Lt. Cmdr. Collins ······················ Byron Keith
Communications Officer ··········· Ken Drake
Lt. P.L. Gusky ··························· James Secrest
Barkeep ···································· Gil Stuart

TDY
• Ralph Bellamy (1904–1991) at this time was a highly respected elder statesman

of the acting profession. He was a Tony award-winning Broadway actor and was nominated for an Oscar. Bellamy portrayed Franklin Delano Roosevelt on Broadway and in the film version of *Sunrise at Campobello* (1960), and in the TV miniseries *The Winds of War* (1983) and its sequel *War and Remembrance* (1988). Other films included *The Wolf Man* (1941), *The Court Martial of Billy Mitchell* (1955) and *Rosemary's Baby* (1968). Continuing TV roles included *Man Against Crime* (1949–1954), *The Eleventh Hour* (1963–64), *The Survivors* (1969–70), *The Most Deadly Game* (1970–71) and *Hunter* (1977).

• Anna Capri (born in 1944 in Budapest, Hungary) started her career as a juvenile in series such as *Maverick, 77 Sunset Strip* and a regular part on *Room for One More* (1962), which also co-starred Andrew Duggan. She appeared in more adult roles in films such as *The Brotherhood of Satan* (1971) and the martial arts classic *Enter the Dragon* (1973). She is the sister of actor Peter Robbins, who lent his voice to the animated Charlie Brown from 1965–69.

DEBRIEFING
  • During first patrol, Stovall's call sign is Nestlewhite Leader.
  • Fowler pilots a B-17 using call sign Nestleblue Leader.
  • Gallagher uses call sign Nestlered Leader.

INTELLIGENCE REPORT
  • Stock footage of subs, destroyers being sunk and a hand pushing the "fire" button is reused from #72 "Burden of Guilt." Other footage of naval action is lifted from Fox's *The Enemy Below* (1957).
  • The music cue used for the running encounters between Komansky and Obie Sorenson is the lighthearted theme used for Peter Fonda's character in episode #4 "The Sound of Distant Thunder."
  • The destroyer bridge set was used before in #57 "Decoy."
  • Exterior Archbury Street set is used.
  • Stock footage is used showing the tower and command center at Chino. Then the action cuts back to the makeshift set. Later, the Epilog shows Crompton and returning airmen approaching the base hospital, which is the makeshift set.

FOURTH SEASON

Producer William D. Gordon prepared a brochure projecting a fourth season. What he came up with was comparable to the overhaul that took place for the fourth year of *McHale's Navy*. During the hit sitcom's final season, its locale shifted from the South Pacific to Italy.

"In the fourth season," Gordon revealed, "I felt we had run out of stories in the ETO so we would go to the Pacific. There were B-17s and a lot of action in the Pacific. It was easy to lay out or to change our location and make a Pacific Island location of it. There was a lot of footage of air action in the Pacific shot by the Navy. We could use stock footage, and so on and so forth. It seemed to me that that was viable."

THE UNPRODUCED EPISODES

1. "SPY STORY"

W: Dave Lewis and Andy Lewis
Work copy dated 15 December 1965

THE PLOT: Col. Gallagher and Sgt. Komansky trail Cowan, a former officer in the 918th who has turned traitor. The airmen join forces with two British security officers to track down Cowan before he and his Nazi compatriots sabotage a valuable supply depot.

2. UNTITLED

Producer Bill Gordon and technical advisor Jim Doherty wanted to do a story about the "Red Tails"—African-American fliers of the 332nd Fighter Group, also known as the Tuskegee Airmen. The nickname Red Tails originated because the 332nd painted the tails of its P-51s a bright red color. During World War II, Doherty had flown with the Fifteenth Air Force out of Italy. His bomb group was often covered by the Red Tails.

"We were awfully anxious to do something about the contribution of the black American pilots," Gordon explained. "We worked out a plot based on fact. Our Eighth Air Force bombers engaged in a shuttle raid in which they landed in Russia first, refueled, reloaded, and bombed on their way to Italy. They landed in Italy, refueled, reloaded and so on, then came back the same way. While in Italy, they became involved with the Red Tails.

"The Department of Defense, which had to approve every script, flatly said no. There were no blacks in the Eighth Air Force, we knew that. They said we don't want to open that can of worms. So we abandoned the project. We later tried to do something about it in a feature motion picture, but that didn't get off the ground."

Gordon compromised with episode #76 "Graveyard," guest starring Ossie Davis. In "Graveyard," the 918th is given fighter cover over Italy by a P-51 group led by African-American Chase Mayhew (Lloyd Haynes).

AFTERWORD

Throughout their lives, Beirne Lay and Sy Bartlett spun tales of adventure through the media of books, movies, and television. But *12 O'Clock High* is perhaps their greatest achievement, not only for its longevity but also its ability to translate from one medium to the next. From its beginnings as a post-World War II novel, *12 O'Clock High* presented a timeless story of leadership under pressure that over time developed into a motion picture and a television series. It was a story cherished by military veterans and the general public alike, and lent itself well to the training of future leaders in all walks of life. The years have been good to *12 O'Clock High;* it is a popular culture phenomenon that remains a prime example of how truth, when adapted effectively, can make outstanding fiction.

Military themes and *Twelve O'Clock High* were always an important part of Lay's and Bartlett's lives. In 1956, the Air Force recognized Beirne Lay's contributions to military awareness by presenting him with the Distinguished Civilian Service Award, while the Air Force Association honored him with its Arts and Letters Trophy. After serving in the Air Force Reserve for many years, Lay retired in 1963 with the rank of Colonel. Mayor Sam Yorty and the city of Los Angeles honored him by naming 5 October 1963 as "Colonel Beirne Lay, Jr., Day." Meanwhile, Lay worked on the pilot script for the new television version of *12 O'Clock High* and wrote a number of nonfiction books.

In the late 1960s, the 487th Bomb Group, the outfit that Lay had commanded for a short time during World War II, sponsored its first reunion. Lay declined his invitation to attend. He didn't want to discuss the war. "If I had a choice, would I want to relive my wartime experience?" Lay wrote years later. "Definitely not. I couldn't stand the excitement." As he looked over his earlier writings, "the trauma of resurrecting these events . . . released such a freshet of buried memories, an explosion of downright disbelief, that I had to stop writing. My eyes were blinded by tears."

At about the same time, Sy Bartlett was busy introducing *12 O'Clock High* to a new generation of moviegoers. Released by Universal-International in June 1963, *A Gathering of Eagles* was a subtle remake of *12 O'Clock High*. Bartlett produced the film, which starred Rock Hudson and Rod Taylor as officers running a Strategic Air Command wing during a series of high-level inspections. Robert Lansing, future star of the television version of *12 O'Clock High*, played a small but memorable role as a maintenance line chief. *A Gathering of Eagles* was shot on location at Beale AFB in Marysville, California, and at Strategic Air Command headquarters at Offutt AFB, Nebraska. Like its predecessor, *A Gathering of Eagles* featured soaring footage of combat aircraft in flight, this time with state-of-the-art B-52 Stratofortresses instead of B-17s.

Sadly, neither Lay nor Bartlett would see great fortune later in their lives. James Parton, the influential founder of American Heritage Publishing, served as Maj. Gen. Eaker's aide in England during World War II and knew both men well. Parton was very familiar with the firing of group commander Col. Charles "Chip" Overacker, an incident that was fictionalized in the novel *12 O'Clock High*. "I was present at the episode at the 306th Bomb Group which put the idea for the book and film in Bartlett's head," said Parton. "A sad irony of that story is that when the film was made from the book, TV was in such a state of infancy that their agent did not include TV rights in their film contract. Result: Lay died penniless and Bartlett nearly so. TV rights would have made them wealthy."

If it is a noble thing to leave behind a legacy that makes a difference in the lives of those around you, Beirne Lay and Sy Bartlett succeeded beyond their wildest dreams. "I think the air is like the sea," Lay once said. "It's a vast medium into which the writer can probe for a lifetime." By mining their life experiences, Beirne Lay and Sy Bartlett found countless tales to tell.

Appendix I

Twelve O'Clock High Collectibles

First edition of the novel *Twelve O'Clock High.*

Insert poster, measuring 14 inches by 36 inches.

Title lobby card.

A Mexican lobby card.

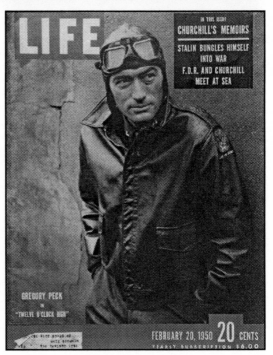

Magazines are always great collectibles, and this issue of *Life* is no exception.

Twelve O'Clock High on laserdisc (left) and the two disc CED version.

Twelve O'Clock High on videotape. The Beta version is second from the left.

The 15 May 1965 issue of *TV Guide* explores Robert Lansing's dismissal from *12 O'Clock High*.

WHY '12 O'CLOCK HIGH' IS GROUNDING ITS STAR
see page 24

LOCAL PROGRAMS • MAY 15-21

TV GUIDE

15¢

Robert Lansing

The Ideal board games are identical except for the cover illustrations depicting Paul Burke and Robert Lansing.

This Milton Bradley game featured flash cards, each card depicting a famous World War II aircraft.

As with the board game, two versions of sheet music for the theme song were produced, one with Robert Lansing and a second with Paul Burke.

Paul Burke on the cover of a TV listings supplement for the Glendale, California *News-Press*.

Milton Bradley produced both boxed and tray format jigsaw puzzles.

A coloring book by
Saalfield Publishing Company
of Akron, Ohio.

A sampling of Aurora's *12 O'Clock High* model kits.

The two issues of *12 O'Clock High* comic books were produced by Dell Publishing, a specialist in TV and movie-based comics.

Talonsoft's *12 O'Clock High: Bombing the Reich* computer game.

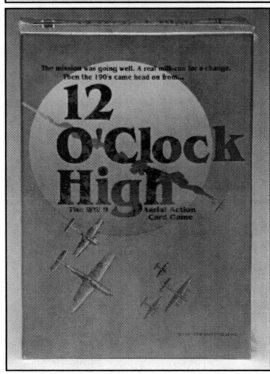

12 O'Clock High, from Wild West Productions, bills itself as "The WWII aerial action card game."

The Toby mug from Air Corps Classics.

APPENDIX II
CONTACT INFORMATION FOR SOURCES
USED IN THIS BOOK

FOR READERS INTERESTED IN CONTACTING THE ORGANIZATIONS MENTIONED IN THE *12 O'CLOCK HIGH* LOGBOOK, FOLLOWING IS A LIST:

AIR CORPS CLASSICS (TOBY JUGS)
Pete Plumb
330 Aviation St
Shafter, CA 93263
(661) 391-9620
(800) 580-3250
www.918thpx.com

918TH BOMB GROUP LIVING MEMORIAL (HISTORIANS AND COLLECTORS)
Michael Faley
12400 Ventura Blvd #113
Studio City, CA 91604
(818) 980-9349
mpfaley@aol.com

306TH BOMB GROUP ASSOCIATION
Russell Strong
5323 Cheval Pl
Charlotte, NC 28205
russell.a.strong306@worldnet.att.net

100TH BOMB GROUP FOUNDATION
Michael Faley, photo archives and historian
10634 N. Evers Park Dr
Houston, TX 77024
www.100thbg.com

487TH BOMB GROUP ASSOCIATION
Arthur Silva
1002 N. Rosalind Dr
Santa Maria, CA 93454
www.geocities.com/CapeCanaveral/1393/

305TH BOMBARDMENT GROUP MEMORIAL ASSOCIATION
Charles W. Wallis, Secretary
26 Woodbury St
Beverly, MA 01915-4744
(978) 922-0365
pilot305th@aol.com
http://www.305thbombgroup.org/

315TH BOMB WING ASSOCIATION
Beverly Green, Executive Director
341 W. Champaign Ave
Rantoul, IL 61866

91ST BOMB GROUP MEMORIAL ASSOCIATION
590 Aloha Dr
Lake Havasu City, AZ 86406
http://www.91stbombgroup.com/

THE MARCH FIELD AIR MUSEUM
Street address: 22550 Van Buren, Riverside, CA 9251
Mailing address: P.O. Box 6463, March ARB, CA 92518
(951) 697-6602
www.marchfield.org

THE EIGHTH AIR FORCE HISTORICAL SOCIETY
P.0. Box 1787
Savannah, GA 31402
(912) 748-8884
www.8thafhs.org

THE EIGHTH AIR FORCE MUSEUM
88 Shreveport Rd
Barksdale AFB, LA 71110
(318) 456-3067 or (318) 725-0055
www.8afmuseum.net

THE MIGHTY EIGHTH AIR FORCE MUSEUM
175 Bourne Ave
Pooler, GA 31322
(912) 748-8888
www.mightyeighth.org

BIBLIOGRAPHY

PART I. THE NOVEL

PRIMARY SOURCES

Armstrong, Frank, Jr., papers, East Carolina Manuscript Collection, J.Y. Joyner Library, East Carolina University, Greenville, NC.

Bevan, Donald, to Albert F. Simpson, Chief, USAF Historical Division, 18 March 1968.

_____, to Allan Duffin, 25 October 1992.

_____, to Allan Duffin, 22 November 1992.

_____. Various interviews by Allan Duffin, May-September 2004.

DeRussy, John H. Interview by Allan Duffin, 14 September 1992.

Faley, Michael, to Allan Duffin, 6-10 December 2004.

Kelley, Bill. "A Thunderstorm in Heaven," eulogy for Frank Armstrong, August 1969. Collection of George Hood.

King, Henry. Interview by Thomas Stemple, 19 January, 9 July, and 15 July 1971. Interview OH 36 v. 3, transcript. Louis B. Mayer Library, American Film Institute, Los Angeles, California.

Lambert, John, to Allan Duffin, 20 February 1993.

Landers, John, to Allan Duffin, 18 December 1992.

Lay, Beirne Jr., and Sy Bartlett. *Twelve O'Clock High* (original draft, 1947). Collection of J. Robert Nolley.

LeMay, Curtis, to Sy Bartlett, 10 May 1948. Records of the Secretary of Defense, National Archives (Record Group 330, Box 677, Stack Area 12W2, Row 14, Compartment 7), Washington, D.C.

Macreading, Howard, to Allan Duffin, 12 November 1992.

McKee, John, to Allan Duffin, December 1992.

Moss, George, to Allan Duffin, 3 March 1991.

Nolley, J. Robert. Interview by Allan Duffin, 6 February 1993.

O'Hara, Richard, to Allan Duffin, 12 February 1993.

Overacker, Charles B, to 306th Bombardment Group Reunion, 1983. Courtesy Jack Ryan.

Pollock, Eugene, to Allan Duffin, 10 February 1993.

Ponte, Eugene, Interview by Susan Stamberg, 26 January 1991. Transcript of *Weekend Edition* on Saturday radio program, National Public Radio.

Public Information Office, Headquarters U.S. Air Forces in Europe. Press Release, 1948. National Archives, Washington, D.C.

Regan, John, to Allan Duffin, 7 February 1993.

Riordan, Robert, to Allan Duffin, 22 February 1993.

Shuller, Dr. Thurman, to Allan Duffin, 12 January 1993 and 5 November 2004.

_____, to Allan Duffin, 26 January 1993.

Shuller, Major Thurman, to Colonel Claude Putnam (Commander, 306th BG), 12 March 1943. Collection of Dr. Thurman Shuller.

_____, to Colonel Claude Putnam (Commander, 306th BG), 21 April 1943. Collection of Dr. Thurman Shuller.

Silva, Arthur, to Allan Duffin, 26 May 2004.

Simpson, Albert F., Chief, USAF Historical Division, to Donald Bevan, 27 March 1968.

Tallichet, David. Interview by Allan Duffin, 2 December 2004.

United States Air Force. Official biography of Frank A. Armstrong, Jr. U.S. Air Force Museum, Dayton, Ohio.

Vangalis, Andrew, to Allan Duffin, 12 February 1993.

Walker, Dorothy (Lt. Gen Armstrong's secretary, 1950s-1961) to Allan Duffin, 1 December 1992.

Wilson, Delmar E., to Russell A. Strong, June 1986. Courtesy Russell Strong.

SECONDARY SOURCES

306th Bombardment Wing. 306th Bombardment Wing McCoy AFB-Reunions. 5 November 2002. 306th Bombardment Wing Association. April-November 2004. <http://www.306thbw.org>.

Air Force Historical Research Agency. Unit histories of the 20th Bombardment Squadron. <http://www.maxwell.af.mil/au/afhra/>.

"Airpower in the News," *Air Force Magazine,* November 1975, 18.

Alexander, Jack. "The Clay Pigeon Squadron." *The Saturday Evening Post,* 24 April 1943, 14-15, 70-75.

AMPAS and the Writers Guild of America West. *Who Wrote the Movie & What Else Did He Write? An Index of Screen Writers & Their Film Works, 1936-1969.* Los Angeles: AMPAS and WGA West, 1970.

Bergan, Ronald. "Obituary, Ellen Drew: A 1940s Hollywood Regular." *The Guardian,* 13 December 2003, 27.

Bevan, Donald. "The Story of Stalag 17: From Utah to Flight Crew; POW Camp to Broadway." *306th Echoes,* October 1993, 3.

Book Review Digest. 1937. Bronx, NY: H.W. Wilson, 1938.

Bowman, Martin W. *Castles in the Air: The Story of the B-17 Flying Fortress Crews of the US 8th Air Force.* Wellingborough, England: Patrick Stephens, 1984.

Carter, Kit C., and Robert Mueller. *The Army Air Forces in World War II: Combat Chronology, 1941-1945.* Washington, D.C.: Center for Air Force History, 1991.

Copp, DeWitt S. *Forged in Fire: Strategy and Decisions in the Air War Over Europe, 1940-45.* Garden City, NY: Doubleday, 1982.

De la Vina, Mark. "Mission Accomplished: Pilot Realizes Dream to Film Their Story (Tuskegee Airmen)." *Philadelphia Daily News,* 25 August 1995, 80.

Dupre, Flint O. *Hap Arnold: Architect of American Air Power.* New York: MacMillan, 1972.

Erskine, Tim. The 487th Bombardment Group Home Page. 8 July 1996. 487th Bombardment Group. August-November 2004. <http://www.geocities.com/CapeCanaveral/1393>.

Faley, Michael, and the 100th Bomb Group Foundation. 100th Bomb Group: The Bloody Hundredth Official Home Page. 5 December 2004. 100th Bomb Group Foundation. April-December 2004. < http://www.100thbg.com>.

Franks, Richard. "Search for girl he loved 50 years ago." *Examiner* (reprinted in *8th Air Force News*), February 1993, 43.

Freeman, Roger. *The Mighty Eighth.* New York: Orion Books, 1970.

_____. *Mighty Eighth War Diary.* New York: Orion Books, 1970.

Frisbee, John L. "AACMO—Fiasco or Victory?" *Air Force Magazine,* March 1995.

_____. "Crisis in the Cockpit" (John C. Morgan). *Air Force Magazine,* January 1984.

_____. *Makers of the United States Air Force.* Washington, D.C.: Air Force History and Museums Program, U.S. Government Printing Office, 1996.

Gravatt, Brent L., and Francis H. Ayers, Jr. *The Fireman: 12 O'Clock High Revisited.* May 1986. Courtesy Jack Ryan.

Hammel, Eric. *Air War Europa: America's Air War Against Germany in Europe and North Africa, 1942-1945.* Pacifica, CA: Pacifica Military Press, 1997.

Hastings, Maj. Donald W., Capt. David G. Wright, and Capt. Bernard C. Glueck. *Psychiatric Experiences of the Eighth Air Force, First Year of Combat, July*

4, 1942 - July 4, 1943. Army Air Forces, August 1944.

"Headlines of May 1945: Lord Haw Haw Captured." *Dayton Daily News* (Ohio), 28 May 1995, 9A.

Jackson, Robert. *Bomber! Famous Bomber Missions of World War II*. New York: St. Martin's Press, 1980.

Kilcoyne, Martin J. "Why Did Armstrong Come to the 306th?" *306th Echoes*, Vol. 5, No. 4, October 1980. Courtesy Jack Ryan.

Kohn, Richard H., and Joseph P. Harahan, Editors. *Strategic Air Warfare: An Interview with Generals Curtis E. LeMay, Leon W. Johnson, David A. Burchinal, and Jack J. Catton*. Washington, D.C.: USAF Warrior Studies, Office of Air Force History, 1988.

Lay, Lt. Col. Beirne, Jr. "I Saw Regensburg Destroyed." *The Saturday Evening Post*, 6 November 1943, 9-11, 85-88.

Lay, Beirne Jr. *I Wanted Wings*. New York: Harper, 1937.

_____. *I've Had It: The Survival of a Bomb Group Commander*. New York: Harper & Brothers, 1945.

_____. *Presumed Dead* (reissue of *I've Had It*). New York: Dodd, Mead, 1980.

_____, and Sy Bartlett. *Twelve O'Clock High*. New York: Harper, 1948.

Leasure, William C. "Frank Armstrong Story," Letters to the Editor, *8th Air Force News*, February 1992, p. 42. Courtesy Mary K. Wiley.

_____. Letter to the Editor, *8th Air Force News*, February 1992, 42.

MacDonald, James. "Bag on Rouen Raid Rises to 23 Nazis." *New York Times*, 14 December 1942, 3.

Martz, Ron. "Memories Soaring at 8th Reunion." *The Atlanta Journal and Constitution*, 24 April 1992, C5.

Maurer, Maurer. *Air Force Combat Units of World War II*. Washington, D.C.: Office of Air Force History, 1983.

May, Hal, ed. *Contemporary Authors, Vol. 107*. Detroit, MI: Gale Research

Company, 1983.

McAllister, Elisabeth. "Beirne Lay Jr. Dies; Pilot, Author." *Washington Post,* 2 June 1982, C8.

McDowell, Edwin. "Publishing: Kosinski's Sales Tactics" (information on reissue of *12 O'Clock High*). *The New York Times,* 3 July 1981, C9.

McCrary, John R. (Tex) and David E. Scherman. *First of the Many: A Journal of Action with the Men of the Eighth Air Force.* London: Robson, 1981.

Miller, Ron. "Overlooked Heroes, Black Pilots Fought Bigotry, Germans in World War II" (Tuskegee Airmen). *San Jose Mercury News,* 20 August 1995, TV-6.

Moody, Walton S. *Building a Strategic Air Force.* Washington, D.C.: Air Force History and Museums Program, U.S. Government Printing Office, 1995.

Murdock, Scott D. Scott's USAF Installations Page. 27 November 2004. Scott D. Murdock. August-November 2004. <http://www.airforcebase.net>.

306th Bombardment Wing. 306th Bombardment Wing McCoy AFB-Reunions. 5 November 2002. 306th Bombardment Wing Association. August-November 2004. <http://www.306thbw.org>.

Obituary (Frank A. Armstrong, Jr.). *Air Force Times,* 3 September 1969.

Obituary (Frank A. Armstrong, Jr.). *Anchorage Times,* 23 August 1969.

Obituary (Beirne Lay, Jr.). *New York Times,* 3 June 1982, B16.

Obituary (Beirne Lay, Jr.). *Newsweek,* 14 June 1982, 84.

Obituary (Beirne Lay, Jr.). *Time,* 14 June 1982, 79.

Obituary (Beirne Lay, Jr.). *Washington Post,* 2 June 1982, C8.

Obituary (John Morgan.) *Chicago Tribune,* 27 January 1991, 6C.

Obituary (John Morgan). *Air Force Magazine,* March 1991, 32.

Obituary (John Morgan). *New York Times,* 21 January 1991, B8.

Obituary (John Morgan). *Sacramento Bee,* 21 January 1991, B7.

Obituary (Sy Bartlett). *Variety,* 7 June 1978.

Owens, Darryl E. "It Was Life, Not a Movie: Scenes of American POWs in Iraq Remind a Former Prisoner of Stalag 17B, a Camp Depicted on Film." *Orlando Sentinel* (Florida), 2 April 2003, E1.

Parks, Steve. "He's in Their Camp: Director of *Stalag 17* Wants to do Right by POW Survivors." *Newsday* (New York), 8 January 2002, B09.

Price, Alfred. "Against Regensburg and Schweinfurt." *Air Force Magazine,* Vol. 76, No. 9, September 1993.

Rubin, Steven Jay. *Combat Films: American Realism, 1945-1970.* Jefferson, NC: McFarland, 1981.

Rust, Kenn C. *The Eighth Air Force Story.* Temple City, CA: Historical Aviation Album, 1978.

Ryan, John L. "Recollections of Charles B. Overacker." *306th Echoes,* 1983. Courtesy Jack Ryan.

Strong, Russell. *First Over Germany.* Charlotte, NC: 360th Bomb Group Historical Association.

"Texaco's Flying Pioneers: An American Hero (John C. Morgan)." *Texaco Topics,* 1977.

Thomas, Kevin. "TV Noir Features Rare, Seminal Programs." *Los Angeles Times,* 13 August 1996, F10.

Title unknown, *Popular Mechanics,* January 1985, 129.

U.S. Air Force. *Official Biography for Lt. Gen. Frank Alton Armstrong Jr.,* 1969.

_____. *Official Biography for Gen. Ira C. Eaker,* 1987.

_____. *Official Biography for Gen. Carl A. Spaatz,* 1974.

The Wall Chart of World War II. Greenwich, CT: Brompton Books Corporation/Dorset Press, 1991.

Who Was Who in American History – The Military. Chicago: Marquis, 1975.

Who's Who in America. 38th ed. New York: Marquis, 1974.

PART II. THE MOTION PICTURE

Primary Sources

(All material from the National Archives is from the Records of the Secretary of Defense, Assistant Secretary of Defense, Legislative and Public Affairs, Office of Public Information, News Division, Pictorial Branch, Motion Picture Section, Topical File, 1943-1952. Record Group 330, Box 677, Stack Area 12W2, Row 14, Compartment 7. National Archives, Washington, D.C.)

Abel, Michael, to Darryl Zanuck, 4 April 1949. 20th Century-Fox Collection, USC Cinema-TV Library, Los Angeles, California.

Air Force to Commanding General, Air Proving Ground, Eglin AFB, (not dated, but probably late February 1949). National Archives.

Air Force Supply. Memo for Record, 10 January 1950. National Archives.

Arthaud, Robert, to Allan Duffin, 17 July 2004.

Bartlett, Sy, and Beirne Lay, Jr. *Twelve O'Clock High* story treatment, 1948. 20th Century-Fox Collection 010 (Box FX-PRS-481, Folder 1010), UCLA Theater Arts Library, Los Angeles, California.

_____. *Twelve O'Clock High* first draft script, 17 September 1948. 20th Century-Fox Collection, USC Cinema-TV Library, Los Angeles, California.

Baruch, Donald E. Memo for Record, 1 October 1948. National Archives.

_____. Memo for Record, 4 October 1948. National Archives.

_____. Memo for Record, 14 February 1949. National Archives.

_____. Memo for Record, 18 February 1949. National Archives.

_____. Memo for Record, 28 February 1949. National Archives.

_____. Memo for Record, 4 March 1949. National Archives.

_____. Memo for Record, 14-15 March 1949. National Archives.

_____. Memo for Record, 17 March 1949. National Archives.

_____, to Army Public Information Division, 13 April 1949. National Archives.

_____, to Public Information Office, Wright Field, 18 November 1947. National Archives.

_____, to Wright-Patterson AFB, 21 September 1948. National Archives.

_____, to Wright-Patterson AFB, 18 March 1949. National Archives.

Breen, Joseph I., to Colonel Jason S. Joy, 25 October 1948. MPAA Production Code File for *Twelve O'Clock High*, Margaret Herrick Library, Academy of Motion Picture Arts & Sciences, Beverly Hills, California.

_____, to Colonel Jason S. Joy, 3 May 1949. MPAA Production Code File for *12 O'Clock High*, Margaret Herrick Library, Academy of Motion Picture Arts & Sciences, Beverly Hills, California.

DeRussy, John H. Interview by Allan Duffin, 14 September 1992.

DeRussy, John H., to Allan Duffin, 10 February 1993.

_____, to Col. Sory Smith, April 1949. Transcript of telephone conversation, National Archives.

Eighth Air Force to Chief of Staff. Telegram, 26 October 1948. National Archives.

Halbisen, Neil W., to Allan Duffin, 22 April 1991.

Holmes, Eric, to Allan Duffin, 8 November 1992.

Horton, Major. Memo for Record, 17 November 1949. National Archives.

Joy, Colonel Jason S., to Joseph I. Breen, 2 May 1949. National Archives.

King, Henry. Interview by Thomas Stemple, 19 January, 9 July, and 15 July 1971. Interview OH 36 v. 3, transcript. Louis B. Mayer Library, American Film Institute, Los Angeles, California.

Leo, Stephen, to Darryl Zanuck, 13 October 1948. National Archives.

Lindley, Lt. Col. William C., to Stephen Leo, 30 September 1948. National Archives.
_____. Memo for Record, 30 September 1948. National Archives.

McCarthy, Frank, to Air Force, no date given (probably mid-November 1949). National Archives.

_____, to General Hoyt S. Vandenberg, 22 April 1949. National Archives.

_____, Memo for Record, 10 February 1949. National Archives.

Muto, Anthony, to Donald E. Baruch, 3 November 1947. National Archives.

_____, to Donald E. Baruch, 27 January 1949. National Archives.

_____, to J.A. Yovin, 18 October 1948. National Archives.

Newlon, Lt. Col. F. Clarke, to Master Positive Stock Footage, Wright Field, 5 December 1947. National Archives.

Nuckols, Colonel William P., to Anthony Muto, 17 November 1947. National Archives.

_____, to Anthony Muto, 17 November 1948. National Archives.

_____, to General O'Donnell, 29 September 1947. National Archives.

Office of the Secretary of the Air Force to Colonel John H. DeRussy, 21 April 1949. National Archives.

Request to the Air Force for Cooperation on *12 O'Clock High,* undated (probably February 1949). National Archives.

Requests for Air Force Personnel and Materiel, 12 January 1949. National Archives.

Robinson, E.H., to Brigadier General George F. Schulden, 22 October 1948. National Archives.

Smith, Colonel Sory. Memo for Record, 21 March 1949. National Archives.

Storie, James H., to Allan Duffin, October 2004.

Temporary Duty Orders for Lt Colonel John H. DeRussy, 15 February 1949. National Archives.

Trent, Captain E.B., to Army Public Information Division, Washington, D.C.,

14 April 1949. National Archives.

Twelve O'Clock High, produced by Darryl F. Zanuck, directed by Henry King, 132 min., Twentieth Century-Fox, 1949, videocassette.

Vandenberg, Hoyt S., to Darryl Zanuck, September 1948 (no day listed). National Archives.

_____, to Darryl Zanuck, 20 April 1949. National Archives.

Wright-Patterson AFB to Deputy Chief of Staff, Material HQ, HQ USAF, Washington, D.C., 28 March 1949. National Archives.

Wurtzel, Paul. Interview by Allan Duffin, 1 February 1993.

Yovin, J.A. Memo for Record, 15 March 1949. National Archives.

Zanuck, Darryl F., to Henry King, 28 February 1949. 20th Century-Fox Collection, USC Cinema-TV Library, Los Angeles, California.

_____, to Henry King, Confidential Report on 1st Preview, October 1949. Henry King Collection, Margaret Herrick Library, Academy of Motion Picture Arts and Sciences, Beverly Hills, California.

_____, to Louis D. Lighton, 28 September 1948. 20th Century-Fox Collection 010 (Box FX-PRS-481, Folder 1010), UCLA Theater Arts Library, Los Angeles, California.

_____, to General Hoyt S. Vandenberg, 17 September 1948. National Archives.

SECONDARY SOURCES

"Ad Lib: Gregory Peck." *Modern Maturity,* November-December 1998, 18.

"The Air Force is Hailed in New War Epic." *Time,* 28 January 1950. Billy Rose Theatre Collection, New York Public Library for the Performing Arts.

Bowman, Martin. "Return to Archbury." *Air Classics,* March 2000, 55, 66.

Bryant, Lt. Col. Clarence J., and Major Paul S. Olchvary. *The Initial Commissioning Kit of Essential Truths (TICKET).* Maxwell AFB, AL: Headquarters Air Force ROTC, 1990.

Coursodon, Jean-Pierre, ed. *American Directors. Vol. I.* New York: McGraw-Hill, 1983.

Crowther, Bosley. "*Twelve O'Clock High,* realistic saga of the Eighth Air Force, arrives at Roxy Theatre." *New York Times,* 28 January 1950, 10.

Dolan, Edward F. *Hollywood Goes to War.* New York: Gallery Books, 1985.

Dorian, Bob, with Dorothy Curley. *Bob Dorian's Classic Movies.* Holbrook, MA: Bob Adams Inc., 1990.

Dunning, Chuck. "*Twelve O'Clock High:* Fact to Fiction." *Aviation History,* September 1999, 42-48, 80.

"An Eighth Air Force Base Comes to Life in Florida." *New York Herald Tribune,* 22 January 1950, page unavailable. Billy Rose Theatre Collection, New York Library for the Performing Arts.

Farmer, James H. "The Making of *12 O'Clock High.*" *Journal of the American Aviation Historical Society,* Winter 1974, 252-253.

_____. "On Location! Santa Maria Airport." *Air Classics,* October 1991, 35.

Foran, Chris. "We'll Miss Them." *Milwaukee Journal Sentinel,* 30 December 2003, 1E.

Garland, Brock. *War Movies.* New York: Facts on File Publications, 1987.

Greenwood, Jim and Maxine. *Stunt Flying in the Movies.* Blue Ridge Summit, PA: Tab. Books, 1982.

Griggs, John. *The Films of Gregory Peck.* Secaucus, NJ: Citadel Press, 1984.

Katz, Ephraim. *The Film Encyclopedia.* New York: Thomas E. Crowell, 1979.

King, Susan. "Mission Accomplished: A Tuskegee Airman Recalls the Rejections Along the Way to the Reality: An HBO Film About an Ignored Chapter of History." *Los Angeles Times,* 20 August 1995, TV-4.

Martin, Mildred. "*Twelve O'Clock High* at Fox is drama of war days." *Philadelphia Inquirer,* 28 January 1950.

"Movie of the Week: *Twelve O'Clock High.*" *Time,* 20 February 1950, 55.

Mueller, Robert. *Air Force Bases, Volume I: Active Air Force Bases Within the United States of America on 17 September 1982.* Washington, D.C.: Office of Air Force History, 1989.

Nash, Jay Robert, and Stanley Ralph Ross. *The Motion Picture Guide Supplement 2.* Chicago: Cinebooks, 1987.

Obituary (Gregory Peck). *The Ottawa Citizen,* 28 December 2003, C6.

Orriss, Bruce W. *When Hollywood Ruled the Skies: The Aviation Film Classics of World War II.* Hawthorne, CA: Aero Associates, 1984.

Parish, James Robert. *The Great Combat Pictures: Twentieth-Century Warfare on the Screen.* Metuchen, NJ: Scarecrow, 1990.

Quinlan, David. *The Illustrated Guide to Film Directors.* Totowa, NJ: Barnes & Noble, 1983.

Review, *Look,* 14 February 1950, 104.

Review, *Movie Story,* March 1959, 31.

Review, source unknown (probably *Variety*). Billy Rose Theatre Collection, New York Public Library for the Performing Arts.

Review, *Variety,* 30 January 1950.

Rubin, Steven Jay. *Combat Films: American Realism, 1945-1970.* Jefferson, NC: McFarland, 1981.

Schnepf, Ed. "An Enduring Legacy of Cinematic Adventure." *The Making of the Great Aviation Films,* 1989, 6.

"Spaatz Sees Film Debut." Newspaper unknown, January 1950. Billy Rose Theatre Collection, New York Public Library for the Performing Arts.

Stanbrook, Alan. "Stiffness Made Him a Star." *Sunday Telegraph* (London), 29 February 2004, 11.

Thomas, Nicholas, ed. *The International Directory of Films & Filmmakers, Vol. 2.* Chicago: St. James Press, 1991.

Thompson, Frank, Editor. *Henry King, Director: From Silents to 'Scope.* Directors

Guild of America, Inc.

Thompson, Scott. *Final Cut: The Post-War B-17 Flying Fortress—The Survivors.* Missoula, MT: Pictorial Histories Publishing Company, 1990.

Twentieth Century Fox. Pressbook for *12 O'Clock High,* 1949.

"25 Years Ago: 1965." *Memories: The Magazine of Then and Now,* June/July 1990, 83.

Vern. Ike. "Out of His Mind—and Back" (Photo essay on Gregory Peck). *Modern Screen,* month unknown, 1949, 61-62, 84. Courtesy John DeRussy.

PART III. THE TELEVISION SERIES

PRIMARY SOURCES

Aletter, Frank, to Paul Matheis, September 2004.

Alston, Howard. Interview by Allan Duffin, January 1993.

Armer, Alan A. Interview by Paul Matheis. 1991.

Bergmann, Alan. Interview by Paul Matheis, September 2004.

Blacker, Robert. Interview by Allan Duffin, June 1992.

Bloom, Harold Jack. Interview by Allan Duffin, September 1992.

Callan, Michael. Interview by Paul Matheis, October 2004.

Campanella, Joseph. Interview by Paul Matheis, September 2004.

Chan, George B., to Allan Duffin, February 1993.

Gallo, Lew. Interview by Paul Matheis, 1993.

Gordon, Maurine, to Allan Duffin, December 1992.

Gordon, William D. Interview by Paul Matheis, 1991.

Graves, Peter. Interview by Paul Matheis, October 2004.

Harvey, Constance. Interview by Allan Duffin, June 1992.

Hawn, Jack, to Paul Matheis, September 2004.

Hayes, Susan Seaforth, to Paul Matheis, September 2004.

Holliman, Earl. Interview by Paul Matheis, October 2004.

Ingalls, Don. Interview by Paul Matheis, 1993.

Korth, Sam. Interview by Allan Duffin, September 1992.

Larson, Charles, to Allan Duffin, February 1993.

Medford, Don. Interview by Allan Duffin, August 1992.

Meriwether, Lee. Interview with Paul Matheis, November 2004.

Moreno, Robert. Interview by Allan Duffin, September 1992.

Mormillo, Frank. Interview by Allan Duffin, July 1992.

Monash, Paul, to Allan Duffin, September 1992.

O'Connor, Tim. Interview by Paul Matheis, September 2004.

Phillips, Frank V. Interview by Allan Duffin, September 1992.

Robinson, Chris. Interview by Allan Duffin, September 1992.

Roley, Sutton. Interview by Allan Duffin, September 1992.

Spencer, William A. Interview by Allan Duffin, September 1992.

Thomas, Greg. Interview by Allan Duffin, June 1992.

Turley, Jack. Interview by Allan Duffin, September 1992.

Ward, Al C. Interview by Allan Duffin, October 1992.

Wurtzel, Paul. Interview by Allan Duffin, February 1993.

SECONDARY SOURCES

"ABC and 20th 'Going Steady,'" *Variety,* 23 October 1963.

ABC Biography. 1965-66. USC Cinema-TV Library, Los Angeles, California.

ABC News: "12 O'Clock High," fall 1964. Billy Rose Theatre Collection, New York Public Library for the Performing Arts.

ABC News press release, fall 1965. USC Cinema-TV Library, Los Angeles, California.

"ABC Television Network Presents an 'Interview Special' with John Larkin," 1964.

"ABC-TV Affiliates Meet Here in June," *The Hollywood Reporter,* 9 May 1966.

"ABC-TV, Air Force Push TV Series," *Broadcasting,* 24 August 1964.

"ABC-TV Spotlights New Program Plans," *Broadcasting,* 15 November 1965.

"ABC's Jan. Reshuffle Most Drastic as Webs Move to Overhaul Skeds," *Variety,* Oct. 19, 1966.

"ABC's Retreat on TV Tint Front," *Variety,* 29 April 1964.

"Actor General Remembers." *ABC Feature* press release, 25 August 1966. Museum of Television and Radio, New York.

Adams, Val. "ABC to Add Movie Night." *New York Times,* 3 November 1966.

Amory, Cleveland. Review of *12 O'Clock High. TV Guide,* 28 January 1965.

Barnouw, Eric. *Tube of Plenty: The Evolution of American Television.* New York: Oxford University Press, 1975.

Brooks, Tim. *The Complete Directory to Prime Time TV Stars, 1946-Present.* New York: Ballantine, 1987.

Broughton, Irv, ed. *Producers on Producing: The Making of Film and Television.* Jefferson, North Carolina: McFarland, 1986.

Brown, Les. *Les Brown's Encyclopedia of Television.* New York: Zoetrope, 1982.

Burke, Paul. Interview by Steve and Diane Albert. *The TV Collector,* March-April 1992.

Castleman, Harry, and Walter Podrazik. *Harry and Wally's Favorite TV Shows.* New York: Prentice Hall, 1989.

Copp, DeWitt S. *Forged in Fire: Strategies and Decisions in the Airwar over Europe 1940-1945.* Garden City, NY: Doubleday and Co., Inc., 1982.

Cupido, Joe. *Chino: Warbird Treasures Past and Present.* Riverside, CA: Fox-2 Productions, 2000.

David, Saul. *The Industry: Life in the Hollywood Fast Lane.* New York: Times Books, 1981.

"Detailed Wrapup of Fall TV Schedules," *Broadcasting,* 7 September 1964.

Dunne, John Gregory. *The Studio.* New York: Vintage Books, 1998.

Eames, John Douglas. *The MGM Story: The Complete History of Fifty Roaring Years,* Octopus Books Ltd., 1975.

Edelstein, Andrew J. *The Pop Sixties: A Personal and Irreverent Guide.* New York: World Almanac Publications, 1985.

"Entertainment: Goal and Glory of William Self," *Broadcasting,* 28 December 1964.

"Fall Line-Ups Keep Changing," *Broadcasting,* 7 March 1966.

"Film Backbone of TV Programs," *Broadcasting,* 5 April 1965.

Finnigan, Joseph. "Bob Knows He Could Be Shot Down by Vets," *The Cleveland Press,* 8 October 1964.

"Fox Hits Peak Earning," *Broadcasting,* 29 March 1965.

Frank G. Tallman to Brig. Gen. Maurice Casey, 20 January 1965. Margaret Herrick Library, Department of Special Collections, Academy of Television Arts and Sciences, Beverly Hills, CA.

Freeman, Roger A., *Mighty Eighth: Warpaint & Heraldry.* London: Arms and Armour Press, 1997.

Freeman, Roger A. *The Mighty Eighth: A History of the US 8th Army Air Force.* Garden City, NY: Doubleday and Co., Inc., 1972.

Freeman, Roger A. *The Mighty Eighth War Manual.* London: Cassell, 2001.

Freeman, Roger A. with Alan Crouchman and Vic Maslen. *The Mighty Eighth War Diary.* London: Arms and Armour Press, 1993.

Garland, J.W. Letter to the editor. *TV Guide,* 29 May 1965.

"Gordon Re-signed to Helm 'High,'" *The Hollywood Reporter,* 2 May 1966.

"Gordon Sets May 23 Date for '12 O'Clock' Start, *The Hollywood Reporter,* 11 May 1966.

Gould, Jack. "TV: Four New Programs—Two Are Good." *New York Times,* 19 September 1964.

Graham, Thomas. *Aurora Model Kits.* Atglen, Pennsylvania: Schiffer Publishing, Ltd., 2004.

"'Green Hornet' Tees Off with Full-Hour Segment," *The Hollywood Reporter,* 9 May 1966.

Hammel, Eric. *Air War Europa Chronology.* Pacifica, CA: Pacifica Press, 1994.

Harding, Henry. "For the Record." *TV Guide,* 15 May 1965.

Hause, Richard F. Letter to the editor. *TV Guide,* 17 October 1964.

Heller, Richard H. *Who's Who in TV.* New York: Dell Publishing Co., Inc., 1967.

Hickey, Neil, and Joseph Finnigan. "You Gotta Have Heart! And Gall and Guts-to Sell a New Television Series (part 1 of 2)." *TV Guide,* 21 August 1965.

"Here's How the Network Programs Shape Up for Next Fall," *Broadcasting,* 28 February 1966.

Hopper, Hedda. "Actor Was Born in Florida Log Cabin," *The Cleveland Press,* 7 February 1964.

Horowitz, Murray. "ABC's Quick Kickoff Clicks," *Variety,* 14 September 1966.

Horowitz, Murray. "Clearance Follies of '66-'67," *Variety,* 7 September 1966.

Horowitz, Murray. *TV 68.* New York: Media Books, 1967.

"How to Bestow a Title," *TV Guide,* 21 July 1962.

Humphrey, Hal. "Burke Shoots Back in Air War." *Los Angeles Times,* 12 October 1965.

Humphrey, Hal. "Lansing Avoids Own 'Funeral'." *Los Angeles Times,* 16 July 1965. USC Cinema-TV Library, Los Angeles, California.

"Ingalls in Policy Row With ABC-TV; Quits 'McPheeters,'" *Variety,* 8 October 1963.

Inman, David. *The TV Encyclopedia.* New York: Perigee, 1991.

"Industry News: Hollywood in High Gear," *American Cinematographer,* May 1964.

Javna, John and Gordon. *60s!* New York: St. Martin's Press, 1983.

Kaufman, Dave. *TV 69.* New York: Signet Books, 1968.

Kaufman, Dave. *TV 70.* New York: Signet Books, 1969.

King, Susan. "Military Transfers." *Los Angeles Times,* 28 May 1995.

Kleber, M. Letter to the editor. *TV Guide,* 29 May 1965.

Kleiner, Dick. "*Naked City* Star Glad and Sad as Series Ends," *The Cleveland Press,* 8 July 1963.

"'Kraft Theatre's Trio of Spinoffs," *Variety,* 23 December 1964.

Lansing, Robert Interview by Steve and Diane Albert. *The TV Collector.* January-February 1992.

"Larkin's role to end." *New York Herald Tribune.* 2 February 1965. Billy Rose Theatre Collection, New York Public Library.

"Levathes Out at 20th; Bill Self In," *Variety,* 31 October 1962.

Leigh, Robert P. Letter to the editor. *TV Guide,* 8 May 1965.

Lewis, Jerry D. "The General Died at Dusk." *TV Guide,* 15 May 1965.

McNeil, Alex. *Total Television: A Comprehensive Guide to Programming from 1948 to the Present, third edition.* New York: Penguin Books, 1991.

Marc, David, and Robert J. Thompson. *Prime Time, Prime Movers.* Boston: Little, Brown, 1992.

McMillan, Penelope. "Quinn Martin, 65, Producer of Hit Television Series, Dies." *Los Angeles Times,* 7 September 1987.

Messina, Matt. "*12 O'Clock High* Series in Bumpy Takeoff on ABC." *New York Daily News,* 19 September 1964. Billy Rose Theatre Collection, New York Public Library.

"More War-Toy Ads for X'mas," *Broadcasting,* 6 September 1965.

Nash, Jay Robert, and Stanley Ralph Ross. *The Motion Picture Guide.* Chicago: Cinebooks, 1987.

"NBC Says Over 18% of U.S. Homes Have Color," *Broadcasting,* 8 May 1967.

"New Season's TV Ratings: Round 2," *Broadcasting,* 28 September 1964.

"No Tint for 20th's 'Bottom of the Sea,'" *Variety,* 15 April 1964.

Obituary (John Larkin). *New York Times,* 31 January 1965.

Obituary (Frank Overton). *New York Times,* 25 April 1967.

Obituary (Adrian Samish) *Variety,* 27 October 1976.

Obituary (Barney Phillips). *New York Times,* 25 January 1984.

Obituary (Jim Doherty) *Variety,* 9 October 1985.

Obituary notes (William D. Gordon). Collection of Mrs. William D. Gordon.

"On Reviews." *Variety,* 23 September 1964.

"The Overnight Scores," *Variety,* 14 September 1966.

Peters, Harriet. "Messerschmitts or TV Script Won't Shoot Down Bob Lansing,"

The Cleveland Press, 14 July 1965.

Peters, Harriet. "New TV Series Pleases Lansing," *The Cleveland Press,* 10 March 1966.

Pilot's Manual for Boeing B-17 Flying Fortress. Appleton, WI: Aviation Publications, 1989.

"Quinn Martin at Production Peak with 4 Vidseries," *Variety,* 12 October 1966.

"Properties Still in High Gear Despite Poor Track Record; Flock on Tap," *Variety,* 14 November 1962.

"'Rat Patrol' Only New TV Series in Nielsen's Top 20," *The Hollywood Reporter,* Tuesday, Oct. 25, 1966.

Review, *New York Herald Tribune,* 19 September 1964. Billy Rose Theatre Collection, New York Public Library.

Review, *Newsweek,* 28 September 1964.

Review, *Newsweek,* 25 September 1964.

Review, *Variety,* 22 September 1965.

Review, *Variety,* 14 September 1966.

Rigdon, Walter, ed. *The Biographical Encyclopedia and Who's Who of the American Theatre.* New York: James H. Heineman, 1965.

"Robert Lansing Plans 'Dirty Heavy' Roles," *The Hollywood Reporter,* 31 March 1965.

Rosen, George. "Unpredictable Mr. Moore," *Variety,* 19 February 1964.

Saxon, Wolfgang. "Quinn Martin is Dead at 65; Produced Popular TV Series." *New York Times,* 7 September 1987.

Schow, David J. "The Outer Limits: And Now a Word form Our Censor." *Rod Serling's The Twilight Zone Magazine,* August 1984.

"Search for Missing Luftwaffe Color Film Continues." *ABC Feature* press release, 24 October 1966. Museum of Television and Radio, New York.

"'64-'65 TV: 48% New, 52% Old," *Variety,* 29 January 1964.

"Six Days to Fateful Showdown," *Broadcasting,* 6 September 1965.

Slide, Anthony. *The Television Industry: A Historical Dictionary.* New York: Greenwood Press, 1991.

Smith, Sam D. Letter to the editor, *TV Guide,* 2 January 1965.

Solomon, Aubrey. *Twentieth Century-Fox: A Corporate and Financial History.* Metuchen, NJ: The Scarecrow Press, Inc., 1988.

Spencer, William. "Emmy Award Photography of *12 O'Clock High,*" by *American Cinematographer,* October, 1965.

"Studios Gandering Feature Backlogs as Telepix Series," *Variety,* 4 July 1962.

"The Big Switch to Color Television," *Broadcasting,* 9 August 1965.

"The Losers: R.I.P," *Variety,* 16 November 1966.

"The Magic Combination for Successful TV Programs," *Broadcasting,* 28 December 1964.

"Their Names are on the Dotted Line," *TV Guide,* 13 April 1965.

Thomas, Bob. "Old Film Sets Make Heart Grow Fonda," *TV Week,* 16 September, 1961.

Thomas, Tony and Aubrey Solomon. *The Films of 20th Century-Fox.* Secaucus, NJ: The Citadel Press, 1985.

Thompson, *Scott. Final Cut: The Post-War B-17 Flying Fortress—The Survivors.* Missoula, MT: Pictorial Histories Publishing Co., 1990.

"Those Cool War Heroes." *Newsweek,* 19 December 1966.

Truitt, Evelyn Mack. *Who Was Who on Screen.* New York: R.R. Bowker, 1974.

TV Guide, 25 September 1964.

"TV's Coming Attractions," *TV Guide,* 23 January 1964.

"*12 O'Clock High*," ABC Press Book 1966-67 Season, ABC Television Network.

"*12 O'Clock High* on Television," *Air Classics, Vol. 2, Issue 1,* March-April 1965.

"*12 O'Clock High* Soars into Third ABC Season." ABC Premiere press release, 24 August 1966. Museum of Television and Radio, New York.

"'12 O'Clock' Syndie Sales," *Variety,* 16 November 1966.

"20th Century-Fox Rides Comeback Trail," *Broadcasting,* 25 May 1964.

"20th Century-Fox Up 58% in Nine Months," *Broadcasting,* 8 December 1965.

"20th Reactivates Its Western Lot," *American Cinematographer,* July, 1964.

"20th-TV Big Push for '63-'64 Season; Self Eyes a Dozen," *Variety,* 12 September 1962.

Walker, P. Letter to the editor. *TV Guide,* 13 November 1965.

"Week's Profile: Quinn Martin," *Broadcasting,* 21 March 1966.

Youman, Roger J. "...But Nothing Sticks to the Ribs." *TV Guide,* 9 January 1965.

Zicree, Marc Scott. *The Twilight Zone Companion.* New York: Bantam Books, 1982.

INDEX

LaVergne, TN USA
25 August 2010
194644LV00005B/18/A